Existential Medicine

New Heidegger Research

Series Editors:

Gregory Fried, professor of philosophy, Suffolk University, USA

Richard Polt, professor of philosophy, Xavier University, USA

The *New Heidegger Research* series promotes informed and critical dialogue that breaks new philosophical ground by taking into account the full range of Heidegger's thought, as well as the enduring questions raised by his work.

Titles in the Series:

After Heidegger?
Edited by Gregory Fried and Richard Polt

After the Greeks (forthcoming)
Laurence Paul Hemming

Correspondence 1919–1973 (forthcoming)
Martin Heidegger and Karl Löwith; Translated by Julia Goesser Assaiante and Shane Montgomery Ewegen

Correspondence 1949–1975
Martin Heidegger; and Ernst Jünger; Translated by Timothy Quinn

Existential Medicine
Edited by Kevin Aho

Heidegger and Jewish Thought
Edited by Micha Brumlik and Elad Lapidot

Heidegger and the Environment
Casey Rentmeester

Heidegger and the Global Age
Edited by Antonio Cerella and Louiza Odysseos

Heidegger in Russia and Eastern Europe
Edited by Jeff Love

Heidegger in the Islamicate World (forthcoming)
Edited by Kata Moser and Urs Gosken

Heidegger's Gods: An Ecofeminist Perspective
Susanne Claxton

Making Sense of Heidegger
Thomas Sheehan

Proto-Phenomenology and the Nature of Language
Lawrence J. Hatab

The Question Concerning the Thing: On Kant's Doctrine of the Transcendental Principles (forthcoming)
Martin Heidegger; Translated by Benjamin D. Crowe and James D. Reid

Existential Medicine

Essays on Health and Illness

Edited by Kevin Aho

London • New York

Published by Rowman & Littlefield International Ltd
Unit A, Whitacre Mews, 26–34 Stannary Street, London SE11 4AB
www.rowmaninternational.com

Rowman & Littlefield International Ltd. is an affiliate of Rowman & Littlefield
4501 Forbes Boulevard, Suite 200, Lanham, Maryland 20706, USA
With additional offices in Boulder, New York, Toronto (Canada), and Plymouth (UK)
www.rowman.com

Copyright © 2018 Kevin Aho

Copyright in individual chapters is held by the respective chapter authors.

All rights reserved. No part of this book may be reproduced in any form or by any electronic or mechanical means, including information storage and retrieval systems, without written permission from the publisher, except by a reviewer who may quote passages in a review.

British Library Cataloguing in Publication Data
A catalogue record for this book is available from the British Library

ISBN: HB 978-1-7866-0482-8
        PB 978-1-7866-0483-5

Library of Congress Cataloging-in-Publication Data
Names: Aho, James A., editor.
Title: *Existential medicine : essays on health and illness* / edited by Kevin Aho.
Description: Lanham: Rowman & Littlefield International, 2018. | Series: New Heidegger research | Includes bibliographical references and index.
Identifiers: LCCN 2017059631 (print) | LCCN 2018011766 (ebook) | ISBN 9781786604842 (electronic) | ISBN 9781786604828 (cloth : alk. paper) | ISBN 9781786604835 (pbk. : alk. paper)
Subjects: LCSH: Medicine—Philosophy. | Existential phenomenology. | Heidegger, Martin, 1889-1976.
Classification: LCC R723 (ebook) | LCC R723 .E95 2018 (print) | DDC 610.1—dc23
LC record available at https://lccn.loc.gov/2017059631

∞™ The paper used in this publication meets the minimum requirements of American National Standard for Information Sciences—Permanence of Paper for Printed Library Materials, ANSI/NISO Z39.48–1992.

Printed in the United States of America

Contents

Acknowledgments ... ix

Editor's Introduction
Existential Medicine: Heidegger and the Lessons from Zollikon ... xi
Kevin Aho

PART I
NEW CURRENTS IN EXISTENTIAL PSYCHIATRY ... 1

1. The Cure for Existential Inauthenticity ... 3
   Shaun Gallagher

2. Emotional Disturbance, Trauma, and Authenticity:
   A Phenomenological-Contextualist Psychoanalytic
   Perspective ... 17
   Robert D. Stolorow

3. Beyond the Ontological Difference: Heidegger, Binswanger,
   and the Future of Existential Analysis ... 27
   Anthony Vincent Fernandez

4. From Anxiety to Nostalgia: A Heideggerian Analysis ... 43
   Dylan Trigg

PART II
PHENOMENOLOGIES OF ANXIETY, PAIN, AND DEATH ... 59

5. The World of Chronic Pain: A Dialog ... 61
   Martin Kusch and Matthew Ratcliffe

6	On the *Autós* of Autonomous Decision Making: Intercorporeality, Temporality, and Enacted Normativities in Transplantation Medicine Kristin Zeiler	81
7	Reclaiming Embodiment in Medically Unexplained Physical Symptoms (MUPS) Jenny Slatman	101
8	Heidegger, Curing Aging, and the Desirability of Immortality Adam Buben	115

PART III
ETHICS, MEDICALIZATION, AND TECHNOLOGY — 129

9	Heidegger's Philosophy of Technology and the Perils of Medicalization Fredrik Svenaeus	131
10	Breathlessness: From Bodily Symptom to Existential Experience Tina Williams and Havi Carel	145
11	Heideggerian Ethics and the Permissibility of Bio- and Nano-Medicine Tara Kennedy	161

PART IV
EXISTENTIAL HEALTH — 177

12	Losing the Measure of Health: Phenomenological Reflections on the Role of *Techne* in Health Care Today Carolyn Culbertson	179
13	Existential Medicine and the Intersubjective Body John Russon and Kirsten Jacobson	191
14	Health Like a Broken Hammer or the Strange Wish to Make Health Disappear Nicole Piemonte and Ramsey Eric Ramsey	205
15	What is it to "Age Well"? Re-visioning Later Life Drew Leder	223

References	235
Index	255
About the Contributors	265

Acknowledgments

Existential Medicine was inspired in large part by the group of scholars who have contributed to this volume and whose work I have been reading and citing for many years. They have all opened me up to the different ways in which existentialism and phenomenology can deepen and broaden our understanding of health and illness and offer more sensitive and humane approaches to health care. I am grateful for their passion and commitment to this kind of work. I also want to thank Gregory Fried and Richard Polt, editors of the New Heidegger Research Series, for their enthusiasm and encouragement when I initially proposed the idea for this volume. The editorial and production team at Rowman & Littlefield International, especially Sarah Campbell and Rebecca Anastasi, have been helpful and supportive throughout the process. And my former student Logan Schulz reviewed each chapter and served as an excellent editorial assistant. I am also, as always, indebted to my colleagues at Florida Gulf Coast University for their friendship and generosity, including Mo Al-Hakim, Carolyn Culbertson, Tom Demarchi, Bob Gregerson, Miles Hentrup, Jo Muller, Rebecca Totaro, and Glenn Whitehouse. And my parents, Jim and Margaret Aho, and teacher, Charles Guignon, have been thoughtful interlocutors on all things existential and phenomenological. Finally, I want to thank my partner Jane Kayser who was with me when I first thought this book might be an enjoyable and worthwhile project. Her emotional support, trust, and encouragement kept me steady through the inevitable upheavals. This book is dedicated to her.

Editor's Introduction

Existential Medicine: Heidegger and the Lessons from Zollikon

Kevin Aho

One of the more remarkable chapters in Martin Heidegger's career was a decade-long series of seminars in Zollikon, Switzerland, toward the end of his life, not with philosophers but with physicians, psychiatrists, and medical students. The seminars initially took place at the University of Zurich's psychiatric clinic known as the "Burghölzli" and later moved to the home of the Swiss psychiatrist Medard Boss during weeklong trips Heidegger took to Zurich every semester. Inspired by *Being and Time* (1927), Boss had reached out to Heidegger in 1947 shortly after the war. Distressed by what he saw as an overly objectifying and mechanistic paradigm in scientific medicine, he believed Heidegger's thought could have a profound impact on the theory and practice of health care. Despite the dark cloud swirling around Heidegger's association with Nazism, Boss nonetheless arranged to meet in the summer of 1949 at Heidegger's mountain hut in Todtnauberg where a deep and lasting friendship was formed. A decade later, the *Zollikon Seminars* began and continued from 1959 to 1969. The seminars were arranged with two stipulations. First, philosophers were not invited; the meetings were open only to medical professionals. And second, attendees were forbidden from asking Heidegger about his Nazi past. Boss maintained, not without controversy, that Heidegger's political commitments in the 1930s were unrelated to his philosophical contributions and that if he had "been forced to live in environmental conditions such as Heidegger at the time, [he] could not swear to avoid falling victim to similar errors" (2001, xvi).

What makes the *Zollikon Seminars* so compelling is the way in which they expose uncritical assumptions in scientific medicine while at the same time acknowledging the importance of medical science. Unlike critics such as Ivan

Illich (1974), there is no attempt in the seminars to discard the enormous contributions of modern medicine. "[It] is not a matter of hostility toward science as such," says Heidegger, "but a matter of critique regarding the prevailing lack of reflection of itself by science" (2001, 95). What takes place in the seminars is a recognition of how the naturalistic standpoint in medicine invariably overlooks more fundamental questions about what it means "to be" human. By interpreting the human being as a physical organism determined by causal laws, Heidegger suggests that a peculiar dogma emerges in medical science, where "only what is measurable is real" (80). But the seminars make it clear that human existence (or Dasein) cannot be reduced to measurements from blood tests, cardiographs, and stethoscopes. Existence, rather, is a *way of being*, an affective, situated, and embodied activity. Heidegger's conception of Dasein, then, is best understood not in terms of "*what* we are" as if the human being was an objectivity present substance, but in terms of "*how* we are." This is why he says:

> Whether [Dasein] "is composed of" the physical, psychic, and spiritual and how these realities are to be determined is here left completely unquestioned. . . . What is to be determined is not an outward appearance of this entity but from the outset and throughout *its way to be*, not the what of that of which it is composed but *the how of its being and the characters of this how*. (1985, 154, emphasis added)

Boss recognized the implications that Heidegger's insight had for healthcare practitioners. Cancer, from the perspective of existence, cannot be reduced to abnormal cell growth in the body. This is because cancer is first and foremost a significant experience that the sufferer feels and lives through. And it is made intelligible only by means of the socio-cultural resources into which one is thrown. This is why two people diagnosed with the same "disease" can undergo two very different experiences of "illness." Following Heidegger's lead, Boss saw that the ways in which one is situated in the world, the discursive resources available to interpret one's condition, and the meaning and value that one ultimately gives to it all shape how we experience our own bodily ailments. The methodologies of natural science are unable to address the experience of illness and the ways in which the experience disrupts and modifies how we interpret ourselves. Indeed, the affective experience and personal meanings of illness are deemed to be largely irrelevant to the objective and technical concerns of medical science. This is why, in speaking to the doctors in Zollikon, Heidegger explains:

> [Science] is dogmatic to an almost unbelievable degree everywhere, i.e., it operates with preconceptions and prejudices [which have] not been reflected upon.

There is the highest need for doctors who *think* and who do not wish to leave the field entirely to scientific technicians. (2001, 103)

For Heidegger, doctors who "think" are more than technicians. They question the assumptions of the natural sciences, make a concerted effort to situate the sufferer within his or her life-world, and attend to their unique experiences and self-interpretations.

By the time the *Zollikon Seminars* were under way in the 1960s, Heidegger's thought had already had a significant impact on the healing professions, particularly in the fields of psychiatry and psychotherapy. His discussions in *Being and Time* of ways in which humans are affectively involved and embedded in the world and structured by "care" (*Sorge*), as well as his penetrating analyses of "being-toward-death" and affective states like "anxiety" (*Angst*) and "fear" (*Furcht*) had influenced the work of leading figures such as Ludwig Binswanger (who developed the approach of "Daseinsanalyse" in the 1920s), Erwin Straus, Kurt Goldstein, and Rollo May. For Boss, Heidegger's influence was apparent in a number of works, including his 1963 volume *Psychoanalysis and Daseinsanalysis*. Although he was a student of psychoanalysis, sat as one of Sigmund Freud's analysands, and appreciated the "talking cure's" ability to help clients open up to their inner conflicts, Boss followed Heidegger in rejecting the metapsychology of psychoanalysis and its naturalistic assumptions (Spiegelberg 1972). When Freud, for instance, claims, "[Psychoanalysis] must accept the scientific *Weltanschauung* . . . [that] the intellect and the mind are objects of scientific research in exactly the same way as non-human things," Boss counters by arguing that such a mechanistic and objectifying attitude overlooks the situated and embodied experience of the sufferer (1964, 171, cited in Askey 2001, 309). Moreover, Boss recognized how this insight applies not only to psychiatry and psychotherapy but to somatic medicine as well. It is just as valuable to internists, neurologists, cardiologists, and surgeons who deal only with the physical body. This is because how one experiences, interprets, and gives meaning to one's physical distress is just as important to health and healing as cutting out diseased tissue or measuring functional abnormalities.

In this way, Heidegger's thought laid the theoretical foundation for Boss's 1971 masterwork *Grundriss der Medizin* (translated in 1974 as *Existential Foundations of Medicine and Psychology*). This book broke new ground by dissolving the traditional dualism between somatic and psychiatric illness, illuminating how the experience of illness, whether mental or physical, is always already shaped and mediated by existence, by "being-in-the-world." The book also made manifest what Heidegger saw as the broader impact of his analysis of Dasein. His existential analytic was certainly valuable for philosophers for, among other things, challenging uncritical assumptions embedded in Cartesian and empiricist epistemologies, dismantling the standpoint that privileges theoretical detachment over everyday practices, and clarifying foundational issues in ontology. But to a wider audience, the book helped to illuminate the unique pain of being human and the extent to which this pain, in spite of all the advances of scientific medicine, is invariably bound up in the human condition itself. As Boss puts it, "[Heidegger] saw the possibility that his philosophical insights would not be confined merely to the philosopher's quarters but also might be of benefit to wider circles, in particular to a large number of suffering human beings" (2001, xvii). These insights provided the groundwork for a radically new approach to issues of health and illness, an approach that can be called "existential medicine." We can now turn to an account of some core themes in the *Zollikon Seminars* and the phenomenological tradition more broadly that inform this emerging field of study.

PHENOMENOLOGY

Against the detached third-person perspective of the physician or medical professional that focuses on causal explanations of the diseased body, an existential approach to health and illness generally begins from the first-person perspective, from the concrete experience of the suffering individual. To this end, the methodological roots of existential medicine are "phenomenological." What distinguishes phenomenology from other philosophical and scientific endeavors is its rejection of the so-called "natural attitude," that is, the philosophical, scientific, and common sense assumptions that we ordinarily impose on our experiences in an effort to explain them. The phenomenologist is not concerned with providing a causal "explanation" (*Erklärung*) of experience. The aim, rather, is to come to an "understanding" (*Verstehen*) of experience from within by returning to "the things themselves," that is, to the structures of experience as they are lived by the individual. By employing the *epoché*, the bracketing out or suspending of traditional and commonsense assumptions, the phenomenologist is able to access and interpret the structures of meaning that constitute our subjectivity.

When applying the methods of phenomenology to the theory and practice of medicine, it is the assumptions of natural science that need to be bracketed out or suspended. The paradigm of natural science generally involves two overlapping presuppositions. First, everything that exists, including mental phenomena, is reducible to physical substances that can be measured. And second, the characteristics of these substances can be explained by appealing to the fixed causal laws of nature. In the *Zollikon Seminars*, Heidegger critiques this paradigm because it implies an objectifying and mechanistic picture of human existence that is blind to the situated activity of being-in-the-world. In his words, the natural sciences "remain bound to the principle of causality, and thus they go along with the objectification of everything that is. In this way they have already blocked forever the view of the human being's proper being-in-the-world" (2001, 233).

The natural sciences are, in many ways, the *bête noir* of the *Zollikon Seminars*. For Heidegger, not only do they decontextualize existence by regarding human beings as objects, but they also reinforce a persistent dualism in modern science between "facts" and "values." Facts, on this view, refer to truths of the physical universe that are objective and measurable, whereas values generally refer to the subjective meanings we impose on things as a result of our socio-cultural background and personal desires and tastes. For medical professionals, then, it is largely absurd to conceive of a value-laden fact. Thus, there is a tendency to dismiss the patient's own account of his or her experience because such accounts are not factual, that is, not objective and value-free. This dismissal is evident in the standard procedure in the clinical encounter, where the physician draws on the patient's medical history and physical exams to gather facts about his or her condition; these facts are then assembled to create an index of potential causes; tests are given which narrows the list of causes; and finally, labs, X-rays, or CT scans are administered to confirm the cause (Mukherjee 2017). In this way, the patient's lived-experience and personal expressions of meaning are dismissed, reduced to impersonal data that is testable, measurable and, therefore, "real."

For Heidegger, human existence cannot be viewed naturalistically as if it were a causally determined entity in the physical world. This is because the physical world and the standpoint of natural science itself are initially revealed and made intelligible against the backdrop of our own lived-experience and everyday ways of "being-in-the-world." The impartial and detached standpoint of natural science, on this account, is derivative and parasitic on the more basic cares and concerns of living our lives. This means the human being "is never just an object which is present-at-hand, [and] it is certainly not a self-contained object" (2001, 3). For Heidegger, humans are *ec-static* in the literal sense of "standing" (*stasis*) "outside" (*ex*) of ourselves insofar as we are already embedded, open, and receptive to the shared values, purposes, and meanings of the world. It is not enough, then, for the healthcare professional to identify a physical cause for a condition or ailment. He or she also needs to be attentive to what that diagnosis means to the patients and how it feels and affects them in the context of their life-world. Thus, what emerges from Heidegger's analysis of human existence is that subjective values and scientific facts are always intertwined.

EMBODIMENT

In the *Zollikon Seminars*, Heidegger introduces an account of the body that clashes with the view of scientific medicine and fills out an account of Dasein's embodiment that is largely absent in *Being and Time*. When it comes to human existence, he makes the puzzling claim that "we *are not* physically present (*körperhaft*)" (2001, 84, my emphasis). Here, Heidegger is employing the German term *Körper* as a reference to the naturalistic view of the body as a bounded, quantifiable, and causally determined entity. This is the decontextualized body the physician examines in the clinic, where the human is reduced to numerical data derived from various diagnostic instruments. But this objectifying standpoint overlooks the phenomenon of embodiment itself, that is, the affective experience and meaning of *my own* body. Again, what scientific medicine often fails to acknowledge are the feelings and perceptions of the sufferer as they are expressed, lived, and made intelligible within the context his or her world. Thus, for Heidegger, a distinction needs to be made "between the different limits of the corporeal body (*Körper*) and . . . the lived-body (*Leib*)." Related to the words for "life" (*Leben*) and "experience" (*Erlebnis*), the "lived-body" is not a discrete, causally determined substance subject to objectification and measurement; it is, rather, "the body [that] is in each case *mine*" (86). Understood this way, the body is not something "I *have*"; it is who "I *am*." It refers to my own existence, to my experiences, perceptions, and feelings as they are lived. However, as Maurice Merleau-Ponty's phenomenology makes clear, it also refers to the mediating, sensory-motor functions of my physiology and the postural and perceptual systems that pre-reflectively situate and orient me in the world. It is for this reason that Heidegger says, "everything we call bodiliness, down to the last muscle fiber and down to the most hidden molecule of hormones belongs essentially to existing." And this is what physicians often fail to recognize, because they reduce "our existeniell bodily being [*existenzielles Leiblichsein*] [to] the corporeality [*Körperhaftigkeit*] of an inanimate, merely present-at-hand object" (232–233). As a result, scientific medicine tends to misinterpret the body by viewing it mechanistically from the perspective of detachment rather than from the situated and affective complexity of individual existence.

When it comes to the distinction between health and illness, there is an enigmatic quality to the body. When we are healthy and absorbed in the acts and practices of daily life, our body tends to withdraw from our awareness. In an analogous way that Heidegger, in *Being and Time*, says the hammer as an object disappears in the pre-reflective act of hammering, our bodies, when they are healthy, tend to disappear in the rhythmic flow of our existence.

When stricken with illness, however, the physiological and perceptual functions that were formerly mediating our experience in the background are disturbed and the body emerges out of its hiddenness. When this occurs, we become aware of our bodies as objects. Heidegger's pupil Hans-Georg Gadamer develops this idea in his account of health and illness. "[We] know only too well," he writes, "how illness can make us insistently aware of our bodily nature by creating a disturbance in something which normally, in its very freedom, almost completely escapes our attention" (1996, 73). The claim here is that when we are ill, the taken-for-granted functions of breathing, digestion, motility, and posture are disrupted and our bodies become objects of our attention as lungs tighten, hearts race, stomachs churn, knees swell, and backs ache. Moreover, because we are always already engaged and situated in the world, the embodied experience of health and illness is fundamentally relational or intercorporeal.

Heidegger illuminates the intercorporeality of our existence by making it clear that Dasein is not an encapsulated or self-contained entity. It is, rather, an intersubjective or relational way of being that is already open and receptive to the bodies, expressions, and concerns of others. This helps explain why Heidegger rarely refers to *a* Dasein in *Being and Time*. Dasein is more akin to a plural or mass term that conveys how human existence is invariably a joint project; thus "'being-in-the-world' is always 'being-there-with-others' (*Mit-dasein*)" (1962, 152). Indeed, it is due to our intercorporeality, our *Mit-dasein*, that I can understand the world and make sense of who I am as a person. My identity as a husband or a father, for example, makes sense to me because of the ways in which I seamlessly embody and enact the shared habits and practices that belong to these roles. When I am healthy, then, I am a "they-self" (*Man-selbst*) who disappears into the relational flow of social practices that constitute my identity. In this way, as Heidegger writes, being-with-others "dissolves one's own Dasein completely into the kind of being of 'the others' in such a way, indeed that the others, as distinguishable and explicit, vanish more and more" (164). Illness disturbs this relational flow. With physical and mental impairments leading to slow or clumsy movements, difficulty handling equipment, and a diminished ability to engage in ordinary social situations, the ill person becomes an object that is judged by others for breaking with the synchronized and fluid patterns of *Mit-dasein*. He or she is often transformed into, what Jean-Paul Sartre calls, a "body-for-others" (*corps pour autrui*) that is stigmatized, embarrassed, and ashamed for failing to "vanish" into the shared practices of the public world. And the internalization of this judgment often results in a feedback loop of isolating behavior and associated feelings of shame and guilt that further exacerbates the suffering (Fuchs 2003).

SPACE AND TIME

A significant portion of the *Zollikon Seminars* is devoted to exploring the ways in which the natural sciences misinterpret the phenomena of space and time. From the perspective of human existence, space is not understood in the ordinary sense as a three-dimensional coordinate system or a container that holds physical objects. In this regard, Heidegger's account of being-in-the-world is not a reference to spatial inclusion or of being "inside" something. "Being-in" refers, rather, to our situated familiarity and involvement with worldly things. As a situated way of being, we do not occupy space like a corporeal thing. "The corporeal thing stops at the skin," says Heidegger, whereas human existence stretches beyond itself by "bodying forth" (*Leiben*), constituting space as an experiential field or horizon (2001, 86). Heidegger explains:

> I walk by occupying space. The table does not occupy space in the same way. The human being makes space for himself. He allows space to be. An example: When I move, the horizon recedes. The human being moves with a horizon. (16)

This means "the limit of bodying forth is the horizon of being within which I dwell" (86–87). When healthy, this experiential horizon is open and expansive and my orientation is geared by a tacit and spontaneous sense of, what Merleau-Ponty calls, "I can" (2012, 139). But when stricken with illness, the mediating activity that constitutes the sense of "I can" breaks down and the boundaries of my horizon begin to contract and close in. With chronic illness, pain, and aging, the spatially constituting activities that I normally take for granted such as going up the stairs, opening doors, or engaging in social situations become difficult, if not impossible. When this occurs, the space of my concerns collapses back onto my corporeality, where I increasingly see myself as a helpless and dependent object, no longer "making space" but simply occupying it as a corporeal thing. And this aspect of spatial collapse has its temporal correlate.

Against the traditional view that regards time as a linear sequence of now-points that can be measured, Heidegger contends that such an account is derived from and made possible by a more primordial form of temporality. Indeed, it is "the human being's richness that consists precisely [in the fact] that he *is not* dependent upon the mere presence of a sequence of 'nows'" (2001, 179–180). For Heidegger, it is not so much a question of "What is time?" that is important. The real question is, "Who is time?" This latter question illuminates the temporal structure of human existence, what Heidegger refers to as "thrown projection" (*geworfen Entwurf*). We are, in his words, "thrown into the kind of being which we call projecting" (1962, 185). To be human is to be "thrown" into a past, into a shared socio-historical situation that we cannot get behind, and it is on the basis of this situation that we press forward or "project" ourselves toward future possibilities. This means human existence stretches into the future but always against the limitations and constraints of the past. For Heidegger, "thrown projection" moves forward and backward, constituting a horizon of meaning that illuminates what matters and is worthwhile in our lives. When healthy, this horizon is seamless and expansive, holding open a wide range of possibilities that one can press into. But when stricken with chronic pain, illness, or the infirmities of age, the temporal horizon begins to contract and narrow, reminding us of our inescapable finitude. In this state of temporal contraction, the future no longer opens an expanse of anticipated and worthwhile projects, and memories of bygone independence and strength appear foreign and strange, as if they belonged to someone else. Future and past collapse, and sufferers often feel trapped in the present, reduced to the moment-to-moment management of pain, weakness, and distress. In the *Zollikon Seminars*, Heidegger refers to the contraction of space and time in terms of diminished freedom, receptivity, and openness to the world; thus "each illness is a loss of freedom, [and] a constriction of the possibility for living" (2001, 157–158).

AFFECTIVITY

One of the enduring contributions of Heidegger's account of "bodying forth" in the *Zollikon Seminars* is the way that it undermines the mind/body impasse that continues to haunt the medical professions. He is cagey when he asks the doctors: "Is bodying forth something somatic or psychical or [is it] neither of the two?" (2001, 101). The question, of course, is misleading because it uncritically assumes the human being is a substance of some sort—an immaterial mind, a causally determined body, or some combination of the two. Again, Heidegger dissolves this problem by positing the idea that Dasein is not a substance at all but a self-interpreting activity or way of being that is always embodied and affectively bound up in the world. This means human existence is structurally affective or "mooded," and he refers to this structure with the neologism *Befindlichkeit*, a notoriously difficult word to translate that is perhaps best rendered as "situatedness" (as the verb *sich befinden* means both "to be situated" and "to feel"). Situatedness, then, is meant to capture the way we invariably "find" (*finden*) ourselves thrown into situations where things affectively count and matter to us. A condition of being human, then, is that one "always finds [oneself] in the mood that [one] has" (1962, 176). In this sense, moods orient and attune us to the world, providing a background sense of how things are going for us and disclosing what is significant and worthwhile in our lives. Thus, unlike emotions, moods are not directed at particular objects in the world. They are more like global affects that color our involvement in the world *as a whole*; they are, in Heidegger's words, "like an atmosphere in which we immerse ourselves in each case and which then attunes us through and through" (1995, 67). This is why it is a mistake to attribute a mood's cause, as a physician or psychiatrist might, to some inner mental state or neurochemical imbalance. The inner/outer distinction does not apply to the situated activity of being-in-the-world. "A mood comes neither from the 'outside' nor from 'inside,'" says Heidegger, "but arises out of being-in-the-world. . . . Having a mood is not related to the psychical . . . and is not itself an inner condition which then reaches forth in an enigmatic way and puts its mark on things and persons" (1962, 176).

When we are healthy and absorbed in the activities of everyday life, we find ourselves pre-reflectively attuned and oriented in the world. Moods, in this regard, are "prior to all cognition and volition, and beyond their range of disclosure" (136). They are seamless and inconspicuous, working behind our backs to create a sense of familiarity with and connection to the world. This is why Gadamer claims, "Health is not a condition that one introspectively feels in oneself. Rather, it is a condition of being involved, of being-in-the-world, of being together with one's fellow human beings, of active and rewarding engagement in one's everyday tasks" (1996, 113). The experience of illness creates an atmosphere that disrupts this tacit sense of familiarity and connectedness, revealing a world that now appears threatening and strange. Activities that we ordinarily took for granted when healthy become difficult, if not impossible, and the affective meaning and significance of these activities is often drained away. In this way, the pain, weakness, and anxiety of illness can fundamentally transform the structure of *Befindlichkeit*, where we now find ourselves in a mooded situation that is "uncanny" or quite literally "unhomelike" (*unheimlich*) (Svenaeus 2011).

EXISTENCE AS HERMENEUTIC

Although he rejected the label, Heidegger's thought has often been associated with the movement of "existentialism" that took hold of the French intellectual scene in the 1940s and 1950s. The association arose largely out of the idea in *Being and Time* that humans exist in a way that is fundamentally different from other animals, a difference captured in Heidegger's claim that *"the 'essence' of Dasein lies in its existence"* (1962, 67). The idea here is that there is no pregiven nature or "essence" that determines who we are. Unlike animals, our actions are not driven solely by necessity (i.e., by physiological or instinctual needs). We have the capacity to rise above or "transcend" our physiological givenness, to create our own being (or identity) by interpreting and giving meaning to our needs and choosing whether or not to act on them. For Heidegger, this means human existence is fundamentally "hermeneutic," that is, we are *self-interpreting* or *self-making* beings that exist in the interpretations and meanings that we create for ourselves. On this view, the story of health and illness does not begin and end when a physician offers a diagnosis and treatment plan based on facts about our physiological ailments. The patient still has to understand and make sense of the diagnosis and perhaps even choose a new self-interpretation in the wake of it. In this regard, illness can be understood in terms of a breakdown of meaning, a loss of the discursive resources required in sustaining a particular identity. My self-interpretation as an active and productive college professor, for example, is vulnerable to breakdown in illness because it undermines my ability "to be" the kind of person I see myself as.

What is required of the healthcare professional, in these situations, is to listen to the patient, not only to his or her own unique experience of suffering but also to broader implications regarding his or her identity and the skein of meanings required in holding that identity together. This may involve introducing new meanings and possibilities that can assist the patient in creating a new self-interpretation in the midst of the breakdown. In his later writings, Heidegger (1993) calls this "poetizing" or "projective saying," referring to a kind of language that opens up a future that was previously concealed. If illness involves a darkening or closing down of worldly possibilities, then returning to health involves a form of poetizing that reveals new discursive resources that can open or light up the world with renewed meaning and significance, making it possible to understand oneself again (Aho and Guignon 2011). For Heidegger, without this aspect of self-understanding, a human being does not exist. This is why he says, "to *exist* is . . . essentially to *understand*" (1982, 276, my emphasis). Healing, on this view, involves more than reading data off diagnostic instruments or adjusting the machine-body to restore physiological functioning. When Heidegger refers to the "physician's will-to-help [the patient]" in the *Zollikon Seminars*, he is not referring to the doctor's mastery of medical technologies, but to his or her capacity to listen to patients and to help them make sense of and give meaning to their suffering (2001, 157). The goal is to provide them with an intelligible and coherent response to the existential constrictions of illness in an attempt to open up new possibilities for living and self-understanding.

Having laid out some of the core ideas of the *Zollikon Seminars* and of the phenomenological tradition more broadly that have shaped the emergence and development of existential medicine, we can now turn to a brief overview of the chapters in this volume that bring these insights up to date and illuminate some of their practical applications in health care today. The chapters will engage areas in psychiatry and psychotherapy; the phenomenology of embodiment, pain, aging, and death; biomedical ethics and the use of medical technologies; and different interpretations of existential health.

CHAPTER OVERVIEW

This volume was conceived in four parts that address important areas of existential medicine. The first part, "New Currents in Existential Psychiatry," examines contemporary issues in the interpretation, diagnosis, and treatment of mental illness; the relationship between mental illness and authenticity; and the importance of understanding the experience of psychopathology from within the context of a life-world. In chapter 1, Shaun Gallagher addresses changes to the most recent edition of the *Diagnostic and Statistical Manual of Mental Disorders* (*DSM-5*) that now treats "grief" as a medical condition. Drawing on the character of Mersault in Camus's novella, *The Stranger*, as well as current research in deep brain simulation (DBS), Gallagher offers an original interpretation of alienation and grief and develops a relational account of authenticity that serves as a powerful alternative to Heidegger's overly individualistic account. In chapter 2, Robert Stolorow continues his pioneering work on the phenomenology of trauma with an essay that expands on Gallagher's critique of the *DSM* by exposing its reductive and atomistic assumptions and argues for the need to contextualize the experience of psychopathology by forwarding a relational account of emotional health. In chapter 3, Anthony Fernandez addresses Heidegger's critique of Binswanger's conception of Daseinsanalysis for failing to distinguish between ontic and ontological features of Dasein. He goes on to show how this failure continues to plague phenomenology's understanding of psychopathology today, resulting in ambiguous and inaccurate portrayals of the experience, especially in severe cases that disrupt the ontological structures of existence itself. In the final chapter of this part, Dylan Trigg turns to Heidegger to explore a possible relationship between anxiety and nostalgia. By identifying the temporal aspects of the two moods and drawing on examples from literature and cinema, Trigg suggests nostalgia might be understood therapeutically in terms of recovering or reimagining, albeit incompletely, a lost sense of familiarity and belongingness, a sense of home that has been destroyed by the "unhomelikeness" of anxiety.

The second part of the book, "Phenomenologies of Anxiety, Pain, and Death," explores existential, diagnostic, and relational issues associated with experiences of chronic pain, live organ donation, medically unexplained physical syndromes (MUPS), and the meaning of death. The first chapter, by Matthew Ratcliffe and Martin Kusch, draws on a first-person account to provide a phenomenology of chronic pain and explores the vital role interpersonal trust plays in medical diagnosis and treatment and how trust shapes the way the patient interprets and experiences pain. The second chapter, by Kristin Zeiler, draws on Merleau-Ponty's phenomenology of embodiment to critically engage the medical ethics literature of decision making with the aim of problematizing the possibility of autonomy for parents who decide to donate live organs to their children. In the next chapter, Jenny Slatman examines the recent upsurge of medically unexplained syndromes, where physical symptoms are present with no somatic cause. Slatman forwards a nuanced phenomenology of the body to undercut the usual medical explanation, which, because of the mind/body impasse, uncritically assumes the syndromes as having mental (psychological) causes. In the part's last chapter, Adam Buben draws on Heidegger's conception of "being-toward-death" to examine whether scientific medicine's effort to "cure" us of aging and death is a worthwhile project. Buben offers a heterodox reading of Heidegger in proposing the possibility that life, radically extended by medical technology, can be meaningful and rewarding.

The third part of the volume, entitled "Ethics, Medicalization, and Technology," consists of chapters devoted to the intersection of themes in biomedical ethics, phenomenology, and technology studies. Fredrik Svenaeus begins with a chapter that draws on Heidegger's *Zollikon Seminars* to critique modern techno-science and explore the risks of "medicalization" and the rise of enhancement medicine. He goes on to identify ways in which these technological trends have ethical implications insofar as they have the power to radically transform our identities and interpretations of health. In the next chapter, Havi Carel and Tina Williams employ the methods of phenomenology to expose limitations in reductive and atomistic treatment models for respiratory disorders. By focusing on how the experience of breathlessness and panic anxiety associated with these disorders can fundamentally alter a patient's being-in the-world, Carel and Williams forward a contextualized treatment model that attends to the life-world of the patient to regain a measure of responsibility and ownership over his or her illness. In the final chapter of this part, Tara Kennedy draws on Heidegger's interpretation of the history of Western metaphysics to describe the phenomenological ethics implicit in his work on technology and the ontological role played by Dasein. She aims to provide an account of how his normative views might inform our use of bio- and nanotechnologies in the practice of medicine.

The volume's final part, "Existential Health," turns to ways in which the methods of phenomenology can be employed to critique an overly instrumental and technical approach to health care and to reframe our current understanding of what it means "to be" healthy. Carolyn Culbertson begins with an analysis of the dehumanizing aspects of technologically mediated health care. She turns to Gadamer to show how this instrumental approach neglects the original meaning of "health," understood in terms of an enigmatic sense of equilibrium and connection that we ordinarily have with the world and that is invariably disrupted in illness. In the second chapter of this part, Kirsten Jacobson and John Russon offer a phenomenological account of the body and intersubjectivity to deepen our understanding of the experience of illnesses such as inflammatory bowel disease (IBD) and HIV-AIDS. In critiquing the impersonal, reductive, and instrumental framework of institutionalized health care, they show how existential phenomenology can open up new ways to re-conceptualize health and illness. In the penultimate chapter, Nicole Piemonte and Ramsey Eric Ramsey draw on Heidegger's famous tool-analysis in *Being and Time* to explore the relationship between health and illness. They broaden the analysis to show how it applies to our "being-with-others" and how the familiar and value-laden sense of "being-with" can be painfully disrupted by illness. In the volume's last chapter, Drew Leder approaches the problem of aging and death from a comparative perspective. He provides a broad social critique of the pervasive death-denial and ageism in modern Western culture and turns to the insights of indigenous and Eastern thought to re-envision different ways to "age well" in our own youth and health obsessed society.

The chapters in this volume show how existential medicine has little to do with applying medical science to fix the malfunctioning body. It is, rather, concerned with unearthing the meaning-structures of human existence itself and exploring the ways in which these structures are modified and disrupted by illness. This kind of phenomenological analysis enables the reader to get a sense of *"what it means"* and *"what it feels like"* to be ill with the aim of "understanding" the experience rather than "explaining" its causes. This not only involves critiques of scientific medicine, but of technological existence itself and the socio-historical forces of modernity that continue to objectify human existence and diminish and constrict possibilities for living. Although an existential approach to issues of health and illness is a relatively recent phenomenon in academic circles, there is already an impressive amount of scholarship in the field. In addition to Boss's pioneering work and the writings of existential psychiatrists and psychotherapists informed by Heidegger's thought, the field now includes an entire generation of philosophers, phenomenologists, biomedical ethicists, and medical humanists. This generation of emerging scholars is following the lead of well-established figures such as Havi Carel, Shaun Gallagher, Kirsten Jacobson, Drew Leder, Matthew Ratcliffe, John Russon, Robert Stolorow, Jenny Slatman, Fredrik Svenaeus, and Kristin Zeiler—all of whom have contributed to the current volume.

Kevin Aho

Part I

NEW CURRENTS IN EXISTENTIAL PSYCHIATRY

Chapter 1

The Cure for Existential Inauthenticity[1]

Shaun Gallagher

The experience of grief is not uncommon following the death of a loved one. One could ask whether this experience is in some sense a good experience to have. There are cases in which one expects a person to experience grief but there is no such reaction, and one could equally ask whether this is something good. For example, Meursault, the central character in Camus's existential novel, *The Stranger*, shows no grief when his mother dies; no grief for the man he murders; no love for his girlfriend:

> He [Meursault's lawyer] asked if I had felt any sadness that day [the day of Meursault's mother's funeral]. The question caught me by surprise and it seemed to me that I would have been very embarrassed if I'd had to ask it. Nevertheless I answered that I had pretty much lost the habit of analyzing myself and that it was hard for me to tell him what he wanted to know. I probably did love Maman, but that didn't mean anything. At one time or another all normal people have wished their loved ones were dead. I explained to him, however, that my nature was such that my physical needs often got in the way of my feelings. The day I buried Maman, I was very tired and sleepy, so much so that I wasn't really aware of what was going on. What I can say for certain is that I would rather Maman hadn't died. But my lawyer didn't seem satisfied. He said, "That's not enough." (1989, 65)

Is Meursault an existential hero, anguished about his isolated existence, and struggling with authenticity? Or is he pathological—manifesting the kind of flat affect associated with major depressive disorder (MDD), or autistic or sociopathic behavior? Deutsch (1937), whom Camus could have read on this topic, documents four clinical cases where reaction to the loss of a beloved one was completely absent. She suggests that the omission "of such reactive responses is to be considered . . . a variation from the normal. . . . [And that] unmanifested grief will be found expressed to the full in some other fashion and constitutes a reaction which must be carried to completion" (12).

Today, in contrast, psychiatry, represented by the *DSM-5* (APA 2013a), seemingly is going in the opposite direction—if someone does manifest grief, he or she should be considered for a diagnosis of depression. In contrast to the *DSM-4* (APA 1994), which specified a "bereavement exclusion" that advised clinicians not to diagnose depression in recently bereaved individuals, the revised *DSM-5* removes the bereavement exclusion in order to "facilitate the possibility of appropriate treatment." This, as some suggest, "medicalizes" grief and encourages over-prescription of antidepressants (Pies 2014).

After reviewing this recent debate about how to treat grief, I examine the classic existential account of authenticity as a kind of anxiety in the face of one's own possibilities toward death (Heidegger) or toward one's freedom (Sartre). A confused response to existential anxiety might be to regard it as something that requires medical treatment, and I'll consider the implications of such a treatment. I'll further suggest, however, that a better strategy is to pursue a philosophical treatment that shifts the account of authenticity toward a relational phenomenon. Here our consideration of grief can be of help. I'll conclude by revisiting the grief *versus* depression distinction.

IS GRIEF OR THE ABSENCE OF GRIEF A DISORDER?

Should we think of the lack of grief (as in Meursault's case) a disorder, and the presence of grief something good, as Deutsch (1937) suggests? What's clear is that by the 1960s we get a reversal of this view. G. L. Engel (1961), for example, suggested that grief is actually a disease syndrome: "It fulfills all the criteria of a discrete syndrome, with relatively predictable symptomatology and course" (18). James Averill (1968, 723) follows Engel and considers the presence of grief a psychological disorder involving individual biological disruptions: "Certain features of bereavement behavior are sufficiently uniform to represent a highly reliable syndrome. It is suggested that the concept of grief . . . be limited to this syndrome."

Consistent with this view, most recently the *DSM-5* maintains that rather than the lack of grief, the presence of grief, in such circumstances of loss, is (or is close to) a disorder. This contrasts to the position of the *DSM-4* which, in a "bereavement exclusion" clause, advised clinicians not to diagnose depression in recently bereaved individuals—that is, within the first two months following the death of a loved one. *DSM-5* removed the bereavement exclusion in order to "facilitate the possibility of appropriate treatment."

Ronald Pies (2014) provides a summary of the debate between proponents and opponents of the bereavement exclusion.

> Critics have argued that removal of the bereavement exclusion will "medicalize" ordinary grief and encourage over-prescription of antidepressants. Supporters of the *DSM-5*'s decision argue that there is no clinical or scientific basis for "excluding" patients from a diagnosis of major depression simply because the condition occurs shortly after the death of a loved one (bereavement). (19)

The *DSM-4* distinguishes bereavement from depression but also provides an "override" to the bereavement exclusion—"if the depressed, bereaved patient were psychotic, suicidal, psychomotorically slowed, preoccupied with feelings of worthlessness, or functioning very poorly in daily life" (20).

The American Psychiatric Association (2013b) continues to differentiate grief from MDD: in grief, painful feelings come in waves, often intermixed with positive memories of the deceased; in depression, mood and ideation are almost constantly negative. In grief, self-esteem is usually preserved; in MDD, corrosive feelings of worthlessness and self-loathing are common. In this published statement of the difference between grief and depression, however, the APA fails to mention one of the important differences. Perper (2013, 6) provides the following comparative chart of clinical indicators.

Clinical Indications of Typical Grief	*Clinical Indicators of Major Depression*
• May have tendency to isolate, but generally maintains emotional connection with others.	• Extremely "self-focused"; feels like an outcast or alienated from friends and loved ones.
• Hope and belief that the grief will end (or get better) someday.	• Sense of hopelessness, believes that the depression will never end.
• Maintains overall feelings of self-worth.	• Experiences low self-esteem and self-loathing.
• Experiences positive feelings and memories along with painful ones.	• Experiences few if any positive feelings or memories.
• Guilt, if present, is focused on "letting down" the deceased person in some way.	• Guilt surrounds feelings of being worthless or useless to others (not related to the loss).
• Loss of pleasure is related to longing for the deceased loved one.	• Pervasive anhedonia.
• Suicidal feelings are more related to longing for reunion with the deceased.	• Chronic thoughts of not deserving, or not wanting to live.
• May be capable of being consoled by friends, family, music, literature, etc.	• Often inconsolable.

The very first contrast is not mentioned by the APA statement, namely, that grief generally involves a maintained emotional connection with others and the capacity to be consoled by friends, family, and others, whereas, someone who is depressed is extremely "self-focused" and feels like an outcast or alienated from friends and loved ones. There seems to be a real difference in regard to social interactions with others. This is an important point to which I will return.

THE CLASSIC EXISTENTIALIST CONCEPTION OF AUTHENTICITY

For now I set aside this debate about the *DSM-5*, grief, depression, and so on. Instead, I turn to the issue of existential authenticity in order to set the stage for some further thinking about grief in the final section of this chapter. I'll focus first on Heidegger's analysis of anxiety and authenticity; and then turn to Sartre's analysis.

For Heidegger authenticity is nonrelational; a phenomenon of being-unto-(one's-very-own-individual)-death revealed primarily in experiences of anxiety. "Anxiety individualizes Dasein and thus discloses it as 'solus ipse'. . . . Dasein is authentically itself in [its] primordial individualization" (1962, 188, 322). *Eigentlichkeit* literally signifies something about one's own, or being one's own (*eigen*). As Werner Marx (1987) has indicated, there is no room in Heidegger's account for the possibility of recognizing that being-toward-death is a condition that we share with others. Indeed, even as the possibility of authenticity seems to be tied to a being-towards a possibility that is said to involve no intersubjectivity at all, that is, being-towards-death, Heidegger characterizes social relations as occasions of inauthenticity. Authenticity consists of being able to withdraw from being lost in the inauthentic crowd and to confront one's ownmost possibilities.

The question of authenticity clearly involves our being-with-others. Heidegger is clear that *Mitsein* (being-with) is part of the very existential structure of human existence. Yet the details of Heidegger's analysis actually make *Mitsein* a secondary phenomenon. Despite his claims that being-with has equal primordial status with being-in-the-world, his analysis tends to privilege the individuality of action by making our encounters with others contingent on our already-established concernful involvement with ready-to-hand instruments and worldly projects. One's encounter with others is "by way of the world" (1985, 239, 242). Thus, we encounter others primarily within the context of the pragmatic affairs of everyday life. Heidegger writes: "Here it should be noted that the closest kind of encounter with another lies in the direction of the very world in which concern is absorbed" (1985, 241).

One comes upon others as unavoidably involved in the same way that one is involved in pragmatic contexts. Heidegger offers what one might take to be a very strong statement of the essential nature of *Mitsein,* namely, that even if we did not encounter others, *Mitsein* still has to be considered part of the very nature of the individual's human existence. At the same time, however, one could take this to indicate that others are actually not essential or necessary for *Mitsein*. Being-with as such does not depend on there being others; Dasein "is far from becoming being-with because an other turns up in fact" (1985, 239). Alternatively, *Mitsein* seems to mean that Dasein is so taken up by the social dimension, and by the dominance of others, by the *Das Man* (the they) that it gets lost in a social inauthenticity in which it understands itself as being the same as everyone else—leading to an interchangeability that we find in our everyday relations with others (1962, §47). "We are inauthentic because our self-relations are mediated by others" (Varga 2012, 92).

Dasein, as inauthentic is "not itself," it loses itself (*Selbstverlorenheit*); it becomes self-alienated (Heidegger 1962, 109, 166). There is a primacy given to Dasein's own existence *per se*, even as being-with, over the actual or possible relations that Dasein could have with others. A number of commentators have seen this as a problem. Karl Löwith (1928), for example, a year after the publication of *Sein und Zeit*, suggested that Heidegger ignored the role of direct interpersonal contact in his account. Ludwig Binswanger (1962), the existential psychiatrist, made similar criticisms and claimed that the idea that Dasein as being-with left him with "a knot of unresolved questions" (1962, 6). Hans-Georg Gadamer remarks: "*Mitsein*, for Heidegger, was a concession that he had to make, but one that he never really got behind. . . . [It] is, in truth, a very weak idea of the other" (2004, 23; also see Gallagher and Jacobson 2012; Pöggeler 1989; Theunissen 1984; Tugendhat 1986; Frie 1997).

Although Heidegger emphasizes the "deficient modes of solicitude" in regard to our relations with others, he does not rule out the possibility of authentic relations with others. At the same time, however, he provides no extensive analysis of authentic relations with others. At best, he characterizes such an authentic relation as a "leaping ahead" (*vorausspringen*), in contrast to "leaping in" (*einspringen*) where we take over for another that with which he or she should be concerned, and make the other dependent on us. To leap ahead "pertains essentially to authentic care—that is, to the existence of the Other, not to a 'what' with which he is concerned; it helps the other become transparent to himself in his care and to become free for it" (158/122). Authentic relations require that I free the other "in his freedom for himself" (1962, 159/122); and likewise that I maintain my own freedom (see also 1962, 344/298). The idea that becoming authentic (understood as a modification of inauthenticity) involves an authentic being-with remains, however, an undeveloped thought in Heidegger, and the major emphasis we find is on the kind of inauthenticity characterized as being lost in the crowd.

Sartre's analysis of authenticity/inauthenticity resonates with the loneliest aspects of Heidegger's account. "For human reality to be is to choose oneself, *without any help whatsoever*, it is entirely abandoned to the intolerable necessity of making itself be—down to the slightest detail" (Sartre 1956, 440–441). For Sartre, authenticity goes hand in hand with autonomy. To whatever extent autonomy, as a realization of one's freedom, disappears, so too does existential authenticity. Thus Sartre's (1956) inauthentic waiter has given himself up as an individual in taking up his professional role. To the extent that one considers oneself or treats oneself as a thing, one is "a being of the world, like the ego of another" (1956, 31). Authenticity means not to get lost in the world, or defined by the world (the system, or a project as defined by others), but to act on the radical freedom of choosing ourselves, which involves a lonely "forlornness" (Varga 2012, 86).

The authentic individual is on his or her own. "I emerge alone and in anguish confronting the unique and original project which constitutes my being" (Sartre 1956, 39). For Sartre, as for Heidegger, our relations with others tend to lead us astray from our fundamental project—our unique projection of possibilities upon which we need to act. That is, relations with others tend to be in bad faith. The early existentialist Sartre (similar to Heidegger) does not rule out good faith relations; but neither does he develop an analysis of such possibilities. At best, in *Being and Nothingness,* we get disclaimers and ambiguous promissory notes.

Even when Sartre finds in Hegel an important realization—that "in my essential being I depend on the essential being of the Other, and instead of holding that my being-for-myself is opposed to my being-for-others, I find that being-for-others appears as a necessary condition for my being-for-myself" (1956, 238)—he immediately gives it up as a model of self-other relations, because the attempt to work out what it means leads directly to the realization that social relations are always inauthentic.

> [M]y consciousness becomes as object for the Other at the same time as the Other becomes an object for my consciousness. Thus when idealism asks, "How can the Other be an object for me?" Hegel while remaining on the same ground as idealism replies: if there is in truth a Me for whom the Other is an object, this is because there is an Other for whom the Me is object. Knowledge here is still the measure of being, and Hegel does not even conceive of the possibility of a being-for-others which is not finally reducible to a "being-as-object." (238)

To be an object is precisely not to be authentic. Sartre then turns to Heidegger to find a better model. But here he seems to miss the direction of Heidegger's analysis. As Sartre interprets Heidegger, "[t]he Other is not originally bound to me as an ontic reality appearing in the midst of the world among 'instruments' as a type of particular object; in that case he would be already degraded, and the relation uniting him to me could never take on reciprocity" (1956, 245). Yet this is precisely where Heidegger does find the other—ontically. Even if *Mitsein* is an ontological dimension of Dasein, this is not in the same framework of our everyday interactions with others, whom we find out there in the world, precisely among the instruments and pragmatic contexts; even if we treat them as different kinds of objects, they are objects nonetheless. Indeed, Sartre is pulled into Heidegger's analysis of inauthenticity just at this point:

> If I am asked how my "being-with" can exist for-myself, I must reply that through the world I make known to myself what I am. In particular when I am in the unauthentic mode of the "they," the world refers to me a sort of impersonal reflection of my unauthentic possibilities in the form of instruments and complexes of instruments which belong to "everybody" and which belong to me in so far as I am "everybody" . . . I shall be my own authenticity only if under the influence of the call of conscience (*Ruf des Gewissens*) I launch out toward death with a resolute-decision (*Entschlossenheit*) as toward my own most peculiar possibility. (Sartre 1956, 246)

In following Heidegger, authenticity leads to solitude once again. "I emerge alone and in anguish confronting the unique and original project which constitutes my being" (Sartre 1956, 39).

The paradigmatic picture of the existentialist analysis of authenticity, then, is summarized in three points.

1 Authenticity is essentially linked with one's self, understood as one's own individuality—one's lonely anxiety in the face of the possibility of death or self-demise; or more positively, one's facing up to the possibilities that open from one's freedom.
2 Inauthenticity involves a denial or running away from one's ownmost possibilities, one's freedom.
3 Being-with-others, or being in relations with others, is the common and perhaps unavoidable occasion for inauthenticity. If authenticity is possible, it is not clear how an intersubjective authenticity is possible. Even if Heidegger and Sartre suggest that it is, the suggestion remains undeveloped, and they provide very few details about it.

A FAINT CLUE FROM NEUROSCIENCE

It's not often that one turns to neuroscience to clarify or update existentialist themes. Indeed, it's not clear that neuroscience actually addresses (or can address) the question of authenticity. Nonetheless, neuroscience has studied a number of related phenomena, such as self, freedom, anxiety, and even "mortality salience"—concepts that seemingly underpin the notion of authenticity. Here I'll mention just one study by Quirin et al. (2011), "Existential Neuroscience: A Functional Magnetic Resonance Imaging Investigation of Neural Responses to Reminders of One's Mortality." Quirin et al. (2011) conducted an fMRI study of patterns of neural activation elicited by mortality threat. Their project was an attempt to identify areas of the brain activated in circumstances where the brain is primed with information related to death. They show increased activation in right amygdala, left rostral anterior cingulate cortex, and right caudate nucleus. To be sure, the priming stimuli were not actual existential threats, but simply priming questions pertaining to death in a "fear of death scale" (Boyar 1964).

Quirin et al. (2011, 196) suggest that such activation is the neural correlate of "existential fear" or anxiety. They suggest that on Heidegger's account anxiety leads to a "cultural worldview defense"—that is, to identifying with values of the larger social group (*Das Man*) to relieve mortality threat. They speculate that activation of the caudate nucleus (CN) suggests this type of response since the CN is associated with stereotypical (social), habitual behavior (e.g., Packard and McGaugh 1992), as well as the experience of love (Fisher et al. 2005)—a kind of existential security. The experimenters are careful to say that this is a tenuous connection and highly speculative.

On the Quirin et al. reading, anxiety leads to seeking consolation in *Das Man*? This view is inverse to the idea that *Das Man* prevents the individual from thinking of death or experiencing anxiety, which is surely one possible reading of Heidegger. For Quirin et al. anxiety activates CN; Heidegger might lead us to believe that anxiety would prevent the activation of CN, thereby leading to less habitual social behavior, experiences of love, and so on. Setting aside this inversion, more generally, the methodological individualism employed by neuroscience, that is, the idea that whatever the case may be, the explanation is something to be found within the individual, fits nicely with Heidegger's conception of *Mitsein*—specifically that it is part of the very structure of Dasein, if not Dasein's brain. If Heidegger were a neuroscientist, he might say that *Mitsein* is hard-wired into the brain—it does not depend on whether there are in fact others in the world.

My motivation for citing this neuroscientific study is threefold. First, it vaguely suggests the possibility of a cure, involving the CN, for whatever the diagnosis may be—anxiety and authenticity or existential social security and inauthenticity. Second, it allows me to suggest that we should reject the methodological individualism of neuroscience as much as the existential individualism of Heidegger and Sartre. And finally, fully admitting that this study provides a faint (and perhaps ambiguous) hint, I want to pursue the interpretation of these experimental results, which goes in the opposite direction to

Heidegger—namely, that death (or death-related information), and possibly an accompanying anxiety, motivates us to turn to others. This turning toward others is not necessarily turning away from death, but confronting it with others.

GRIEF AND THE CONCEPT OF RELATIONAL AUTHENTICITY

In this section I'll argue that grief gives us an alternative way to think of existential authenticity—and to think of it not as a normatively neutral state, but as something that has a positive valence. One can develop this alternative conception of existential authenticity by taking *existence* (not just cognition) to be embodied and socially embedded—leading to a conception of being-in-the-world that is closer to Merleau-Ponty than to Heidegger. In this framework, and on this alternative conception of authenticity, grief replaces anxiety as the most fundamental authentic attitude.

If humans are (ontologically and existentially) embodied and embedded (physically and socially),[2] if this in fact describes their facticity and the way they are, and if being-with is not just hard wired, but entirely dependent on interaction with others, so that we understand self as relational or socially situated, it would be strange to suggest that the authentic life is nonrelational, or in any way non-intersubjective. A concept of authenticity that is informed by this analysis and that emphasizes relationality will differ precisely on the three points that summarize the paradigmatic view of existential authenticity (Gallagher, Morgan, and Rokotnitz 2018).

1. Rather than taking authenticity as essentially linked with one's self, understood as one's own individuality characterized by a lonely anxiety in the face of the possibility of death or self-demise, authenticity should be understood as relational, since human existence is relational. The individual self, as being-with-others, is an intersubjective accomplishment, dynamically intertwined with the existence of others from the beginning of life. Autonomy is itself relational. In the paradigmatic conception of existential authenticity, the notion of autonomy is akin to traditional conceptions that focus on self-sufficiency, self-legislation, or self-determination, ignoring the importance of embodiment and socially embedded action. If autonomy and the self are relational, so must authenticity be.
2. It may still be right to think of inauthenticity as a denial or running away from one's ownmost possibilities, but it would be a mistake to think that one's ownmost possibilities were strictly "ownmost." Authenticity is not facing-up to the nothingness of one's individual existence (as Sartre would

have it), but facing up to the richness and complexity of our situated existence that comes from being in-the-world-with-others.
3 Thus, being with others, or being in relations with others, rather than the common and perhaps unavoidable occasion for inauthenticity, should be seen as the unavoidable occasion for authenticity. It seems much more existential to think of an engaged authenticity, open to possibilities, risking failures as well as successes. Indeed, it is not clear how a non-intersubjective authenticity is possible. Would that not be a running away from what makes our existence existential in the most intense way?

Heidegger fails to see any existential significance in grief or mourning—grief reflects a mode of *Mitsein*, but not one that grasps our own death. For him, encountering the death of the other becomes "a substitute theme for the ontological analysis of Dasein"—related to the interchangeability that we find in our everyday relations with others (Heidegger 1962, §47). What Heidegger misses in his concept of being-with, however, is the notion of *primary intersubjectivity* (Gallagher and Jacobson 2012). Primary intersubjectivity is characterized in development psychology as a form of being engaged with others from the time of infancy (Trevarthen 1979). Primary intersubjective face-to-face relations are relations that involve embodied interactions even before we engage in secondary intersubjective, pragmatic, and interchangeable relations. They have, from the start, and throughout our lifetime affective and attachment dimensions, and in these relations, where individuals are not interchangeable or characterized by their pragmatic role, the death or loss of the other elicits grief. Grief thus reveals our relational nature and allows us to face up to the possibilities of our existence together—possibilities that are removed by the death of the other. Grief reveals the fragility of those relations—and reveals them to be precisely not interchangeable.

As Heidegger's student, Werner Marx (1987) pointed out that shared mortality is precisely the thing that calls for a responsibility toward one another, and moves us toward a very different conception of authenticity—in the form of authentic relations with others. On this view, even facing up to the possibility of one's own death, which Heidegger takes to be the most isolated and individuating phenomenon, can be something intensely intersubjective since we all share mortality—we are all in the same boat in this regard. Grief brings this to the fore; it makes us confront what living together means (or has meant) and perhaps makes us confront our failures in those relations, or appreciate our successes.

Does grief take the place of anxiety in the analysis of authenticity? I am not suggesting a one-for-one substitution. Anxiety seemingly puts us face-to-face with the possibility of our own death. But that could also lead us to a kind of anticipatory grief for the potential loss of our relations with others that can come from our death, or theirs. That is, without anyone dying we can think about the other's death—what would life be like without them?—or we can think of our own death in terms of the grief that it would cause others. This, in turn, can motivate more careful (authentic) relations with the people we love or the people with whom we live and work. In this respect, grief is a good thing—good in an ethical sense in that it allows us to realize the value of others and to motivate a responsibility toward them.

A MEDICALLY INCURABLE CONDITION: REVISITING THE GRIEF/DEPRESSION DISTINCTION

Just as, on the classic account of existential authenticity, according to which anxiety leads in one of two directions—toward authenticity, or away from it if it becomes too difficult to bear—so grief could lead us to a relational authenticity and bring us closer to others in order to share our grief,[3] or it could lead to isolation and depression in various contexts. This takes us back to the debate surrounding the *DSM-5*'s removal of the bereavement exclusion. Should we treat grief as a prequel to depression and seek a cure, and what would a cure look like?

As Quirin et al. and other studies suggest, the activation of the CN is associated with positive social affect in connection with others; it is also the case that deactivation or damage to CN results in loss of drive, and possibly depression or obsessive compulsive disorder (OCD) (see Villablanca 2010). Whether death-related thoughts and associated anxiety activate CN and strengthen our connections with others, leading to a Heideggerian form of inauthenticity (as Quirin et al. suggest), or grief deactivates CN, leading to depression, a withdrawal from social interaction and a failure of relational authenticity, one might think that some kind of treatment is in order.

One treatment that might work for those like Meursault who lack the capacity for grief, as well as for those who are driven to depression by grief, is the establishment of a more balanced activation of CN. In fact, deep brain stimulation (DBS) that specifically targets CN has been used, experimentally, to treat depression and anxiety associated with OCD (Aouizerate et al. 2004; see Kim et al. 2016; Ryder and Holtzheimer 2016). The downside to this treatment involves negative side effects of DBS leading to changes in some patients' self-experience, including feelings of self-estrangement. Schüpbach et al. (2006), for example, list the following side effects: *Feelings of estrangement*—patients could no longer "find themselves"; they were "not feeling like themselves anymore"; *Feelings of helplessness*—patients felt "mentally unable to resume a more normal life style"; *Loss of meaning in life*—feelings of emptiness or meaninglessness. Reflecting the already strong ambiguity associated with such treatment, and the phenomenon of inauthenticity it would seek to treat, Kraemer (2013) suggests that the experience of alienation from one's previous self disrupts the sense of authenticity—a feeling of being who one is.

To state my view more clearly, I think that "existential neuroscience" (Quirin et al. 2011), and the latest medical advice from the *DSM-5*, as well as the paradigmatic existential analysis of authenticity found in thinkers like Heidegger, Sartre and Camus, all suffer from the same problem—an overly individualized conception of human existence. In this regard, the cure for existential inauthenticity is not DBS, but a strong dose of primary intersubjectivity, leading to *relational* authenticity. By considering grief rather than anxiety, I think we can get a more developed concept of relational authenticity, which focuses on our embodied, primary-intersubjective relations with others. The notion of relational authenticity would also provide the basis for a fuller conception of *Mitsein*, which Heidegger may have intended, but failed to deliver.

Moreover, I think a better delineation between grief and depression can be found in Merleau-Ponty. He describes a pre-personal level of bodily existence that "plays the role of an innate complex" below the level of personal experience, and that maintains an autonomous continuity of being-in-the-world. Depression affects the pre-personal aspect of existence in a way that brings personal-level activities to a standstill. Grief may do something similar, but only for a short time.

> When I am overcome with grief and wholly absorbed in my sorrow, my gaze already wanders out before me, it quietly takes interest in some bright object, it resumes its autonomous existence. . . . [With this] time (or at least pre-personal time) again begins to flow, and it carries with it if not our resolution, then at least the heartfelt emotions that sustained it. (Merleau-Ponty 2012, 86)

Returning to the debate about grief and depression, then, we should say that grief is relational, and this distinguishes it from major depressive disorder. Grief allows for relational authenticity, and even during grief, we remain (or are soon re-) connected in the mode of embodied primary intersubjectivity with life and with others.

NOTES

1. I thank the Humboldt Foundation's Anneliese Maier Research Award for its support of my research. I also want to thank audiences at the following conferences for helpful comments on earlier versions of this chapter: Conference on Neglected Emotions, University of Louisville (April 13–14, 2017); *Workshop on Mood and*

Bodily-Affective Disorders. University College, Dublin (November 4, 2016); and Conference on *The Nature of Grief: Philosophical and Interdisciplinary Perspectives*. University of Vienna (March 2016, 17–19).

2. Ricoeur (1992) criticizes Heidegger for suppressing embodiment and failing to develop the notion of *Leib* "as a distinct existentiale." For Ricoeur the lived body is the "primary otherness" required for our openness to other people. "If the theme of embodiment appears to be stifled, if not repressed, in *Being and Time*, this is doubtless because it must have appeared too dependent on the inauthentic forms of care" (Ricoeur 1992, 328). An impoverished conception of the body leads to an impoverished conception of being-with (1992, 341ff). This suggests that inauthenticity is more properly a denial or a running away from one's embodied intersubjective relations.

3. This is consistent with Peter Goldie's (2011) idea that grief is a process or complex pattern best captured in a narrative account—grief might actually take the form of a narrative told to or shared by others. This doesn't mean (as Goldie suggests) that grief is not a feeling, however.

Chapter 2

Emotional Disturbance, Trauma, and Authenticity: A Phenomenological-Contextualist Psychoanalytic Perspective

Robert D. Stolorow

PHENOMENOLOGICAL PSYCHOPATHOLOGY

Beginning with its origins in the work of Karl Jaspers (1913), phenomenological psychopathology has traditionally been an investigation of the experiential worlds associated with particular mental disorders or psychiatric entities. The subtitle of a recently published anthology on the subject (Stanghellini and Aragona 2016) makes this focus explicit: *What Is It Like to Suffer from Mental Disorders?* Of the eighteen chapters between the introductory and concluding ones, twelve explicitly name a psychiatric diagnosis in their title. As is typical of such studies, the validity of this diagnosing is left unchallenged.

A particularly good example of this tradition in phenomenological psychopathology is provided by a recent book by Matthew Ratcliffe (2015), and I will be referring to it throughout this chapter. Central to his perspective is a conception of the experiential world as a space of possibilities and a distinction between intentional feelings—those that are about a particular intentional object—and pre-intentional feelings—those that indicate the kinds of intentional states that are possible within an experiential world. The latter, what Ratcliffe calls *existential feelings* (see also Ratcliffe 2008), disclose the existential structure of experience, one's pre-intentional ways of finding oneself in the world. Ratcliffe's book—and here is its highly valuable contribution—is a study of changes in existential feeling—shifts and disturbances in the kinds of possibility that experience incorporates. His particular focus is on the loss or diminution of kinds of possibility. One such loss that figures prominently in Ratcliffe's analysis is the loss of existential hope—the loss of a sense of the future as a domain of possible meaningful change for the better. Such pre-intentional existential hopelessness entails loss of the very basis for particular intentional hopes. Particular hopes and aspirations themselves become unintelligible, as the world is emptied of significance. Existential hopelessness emerges in Ratcliffe's analysis as a richly variegated, multidimensional unity. It can include a sense of eternal incarceration and irrevocable guilt. The sense of freedom of will and personal agency is often diminished or lost, and there is an accompanying alteration in the felt bodily "I can." Perhaps most important, existential hopelessness entails a profound alteration of temporality, the lived experience of time. Instead of being a linear unfolding toward an open future marked by possibility, time is felt to be circular, with a closed future characterized by endless repetition. Lastly, there is a feeling of profound alienation from others deriving from a sense of living in a reality different from that inhabited by everyone else.

Ratcliffe's analysis of the unity of existential hopelessness is quite elegant and very valuable. Would that he had stopped with that, rather than linking it with traditional psychiatric diagnosing! But he presents it to us as a phenomenological account of "experiences of depression," the unfortunate title of his book. But what is this "depression," the phenomenology of whose experiences he gives us? At several points he acknowledges that the word refers to something that is very heterogeneous and of questionable empirical validity. Correspondingly, he cautions against associating specific forms of experience with specific diagnostic categories. It does not help to claim that depression is an "ideal type," as Ratcliffe does, because he continues to refer to it as if it were a psychiatric entity or illness (he does the same with schizophrenia), a condition with particular symptoms from which it can be diagnosed. After commenting on the inadequacy and questionable validity of psychiatry's *Diagnostic and Statistical Manual of Mental Disorders (DSM)* (American Psychiatric Association 2013a), Ratcliffe proceeds to use two of its categories—"major depressive episode" and "major depressive disorder"—as the organizing psychiatric framework for his studies.

Recent research has called into question the most recent *DSM*'s creation of new diagnostic entities and categories that are scientifically unsubstantiated and that over-pathologize vulnerable populations such as young children, the elderly, and the traumatically bereaved (Frances 2013). More fundamentally, the *DSM* is a direct descendent of Descartes's (1989) metaphysical dualism, which divided the finite world into two distinct basic substances—*res cogitans* and *res extensa*, thinking substances (minds) with no extension in space, and extended substances (bodies and other material things) that do not think. This metaphysical dualism concretized the idea of a complete separation between mind and world, between subject and object. What, after all, could be more separate than two realms of being constituted by two completely different substances? Descartes's vision can be characterized as a radical decontextualization of both mind and world. Mind, the "thinking thing," is isolated from the world in which it dwells, just as the world is purged of all human significance. Both mind and world are stripped of all contextuality with respect to one another, as they are beheld in their bare thinghood, their pure presence-at-hand, as Heidegger (1962) would say. The ontological gap between mind and world, between subject and object, is bridged only in a relationship of thinking, in which the "worldless subject" somehow forms ideas that more or less accurately represent or correspond to transcendent (i.e., mind-independent) objects in an "unworlded world."

The *DSM* partakes of what might be called *the illusion of perceptible essences* (Stolorow and Atwood 2017). Wittgenstein (1953) explained how such an illusion is constituted by the use of a single word to denote an array of items that bear a "family resemblance" to one another—that is, items that share some qualities but not others. When such items are grouped together under one word, a reified picture is created of an essence that each of them instantiates. The *DSM* will present several symptoms that are claimed to be characteristic of a diagnostic entity, say depression, and a patient—or better, the patient's mind—is said to be afflicted with this disorder if a certain proportion of those symptoms are manifest. That is, people whose sufferings bear a family resemblance to one another become, through the reified picture that has been named, instantiations of a metaphysical diagnostic essence, a disordered Cartesian mind.

In his existential analytic, Heidegger (1962) seeks interpretively to re-find the unity of our being, split asunder in the Cartesian bifurcation. Thus, what he calls the "destruction" of traditional ontology is a clearing away of its concealments and disguises, in order to unveil the primordial contextual whole that it has been covering up. His contextualism is formally indicated early on, in his designation of the human being as *Dasein*, to-be-there or to-be-situated, a term that already points to the unity of the human kind of being and its context. This initially indicated contextualization is to be further fleshed out as Heidegger focuses his hermeneutic-phenomenological inquiry, with its contextualist interpretive perspective, on our average everyday understanding of our kind of being. His aim is to "lay bare a fundamental structure in Dasein: Being-in-the-world" (Heidegger 1962, 65), also described as Dasein's "basic state" (constitution) or "constitutive state" (78). In introducing the idea of Being-in-the-world, Heidegger makes clear both that he has arrived at it through hermeneutic inquiry and that his interpretive perspective is a contextualist or holistic one:

> In the ***interpretation of Dasein***, this structure is something *"a priori"*; it is not pieced together, but is ***primordially and constantly a whole***. (65, bold emphasis added)

With the hyphens unifying the expression *Being-in-the-world* (*In-der-Welt-sein*), Heidegger indicates that in his interpretation of Dasein the traditional ontological gap between our being and our world is to be definitively closed and that, in their indissoluble unity, our being and our world "primordially and constantly" always contextualize one another. Heidegger's ontological contextualism, in which human being is saturated with the world in which we dwell and the world we inhabit is drenched in human meanings and purposes, provides a solid philosophical grounding for a *psychoanalytic phenomenological contextualism* (Atwood and Stolorow 2014), replacing the Cartesian isolated mind that underpins both traditional diagnostic psychiatry and classical Freudian psychoanalysis.

The *DSM* is a pseudo-scientific manual for diagnosing disordered Cartesian isolated minds. As such, it completely overlooks the exquisite context-sensitivity and radical context-dependence of human emotional life and of all forms of emotional disturbance. Against the *DSM*, Atwood and I (Atwood and Stolorow 2014) have contended that all emotional disturbances are constituted in a context of human interrelatedness—specifically, contexts of emotional trauma. One such traumatizing context is characterized by relentless invalidation of emotional experience, coupled with an objectification of the child as being intrinsically defective—a trauma that is readily repeated in the experience of being psychiatrically diagnosed. This retraumatization, in turn, can actually co-constitute the manifest clinical picture.[1] Ratcliffe elaborates a phenomenological account of existential hopelessness that invites exploration and appreciation of its context-embeddedness, but he encases it in an objectifying psychiatric diagnostic language that negates this very embeddedness! I contend that this criticism holds for the field of phenomenological psychopathology in general.

EXISTENTIAL ANXIETY AND EMOTIONAL TRAUMA

Ratcliffe notes an important similarity between his characterization of existential hopelessness and Heidegger's phenomenological description of existential anxiety (*Angst*), in which the everyday world becomes devoid of practical significance. In Heidegger's ontological *account* of anxiety, which Ratcliffe does not discuss, the central features of its phenomenology—the collapse of everyday significance and the resulting feeling of uncanniness, of not being at home in the everyday world—are claimed to be grounded in what Heidegger called authentic (nonevasively owned) *Being-toward-death*. Death, in this account, is a distinctive possibility that is constitutive of our existence—of our intelligibility to ourselves in our futurity and our finitude.

In my own work (Stolorow 2007, 2011), I have contended that emotional trauma produces an affective state whose features bear a close similarity to the central elements in Heidegger's existential interpretation of anxiety and that it accomplishes this by plunging the traumatized person into a form of authentic Being-toward-death. Trauma shatters the illusions of everyday life that evade and cover up the finitude, contingency, and embeddedness of our existence and the indefiniteness of its certain extinction. Such shattering exposes what had been heretofore concealed, thereby plunging the traumatized person into a form of authentic Being-toward-death and into the anxiety—the loss of significance, the uncanniness—through which authentic Being-toward-death is disclosed. My description of trauma's impact in disrupting our experience of time and our connectedness with others is remarkably similar to the corresponding features that Ratcliffe attributes to existential hopelessness. Trauma, I contended, devastatingly disrupts the ordinary, average-everyday linearity of temporality, the sense of stretching-along from the past to an open future. Experiences of emotional trauma become freeze-framed into an eternal present in which one remains forever trapped or to which one is condemned to be perpetually returned. In the region of trauma, all duration or stretching along collapses, the traumatic past becomes present, and future loses all meaning other than endless repetition. Because trauma so profoundly modifies the universal or shared structure of temporality, I claimed, the traumatized person quite literally lives in another kind of reality, an experiential world felt to be incommensurable with those of others. This felt incommensurability, in turn, contributes to the sense of alienation and estrangement from other human beings that typically haunts the traumatized person. Experiences of severe emotional trauma are the contexts, concealed by Ratcliffe's devotion to a decontextualizing psychiatric language, in which the existential feelings that he so beautifully elucidates take form. And not accidentally, these same contexts of severe trauma are those in which the emotional disturbances that are objectified by the *DSM* also take form (Atwood 2011). There are no diagnostic entities, only devastating contexts.

What enables us to exist authentically—that is, to own our Being-toward-death and to bear the existential anxiety that such owning entails? Heidegger does not tell us, but the phenomenology of trauma and the relational contexts that facilitate its transformation contain clues as to what makes authenticity possible.

I have contended that emotional trauma can be borne to the extent that it finds a context of emotional understanding—what I call a *relational home*—in which it can be held. In a sense, in the context of a receptive and understanding relational home, traumatized states can cease to be traumatic, or at least cease to be enduringly so. Within such a relational home, traumatized states are in a process of becoming less severely traumatic—that is, of becoming less overwhelming and more bearable—thus making evasive defenses less necessary. Thus, within a holding relational home, the traumatized person may become able to move toward more authentic (nonevasive) existing. Authenticity as a possibility in the wake of trauma, I am proposing, is embedded in a broader contextual whole within which traumatized states can evolve into painful emotional experiences that can be more fully felt and articulated, better tolerated, and eventually integrated. Authentic existing presupposes a capacity to live in the emotional pain (e.g., the existential anxiety) that accompanies a nonevasive experience of finitude, and this capacity, in turn, requires that such pain find a relational context in which it can be held.[2]

The counterpart of inauthenticity in the phenomenology of trauma is called *dissociation*, a defensive process discussed by most authors on trauma. I think of defensive dissociation phenomenologically as a kind of *tunnel vision*—a narrowing of one's experiential horizons so as to exclude and evade the terrifying, the prohibited, and the emotionally unbearable. Such narrowing of one's horizons entails the keeping apart of incommensurable emotional worlds, a process that contributes to the devastating impact of emotional trauma on our experience of temporality. I use the term *portkey*, which I borrowed from *Harry Potter* (Rowling 2000), to capture the profound impact of emotional trauma on our experience of time. Harry was a severely traumatized little boy, nearly killed by his parents' murderer and left in the care of a family that mistreated him cruelly. He arose from the ashes of devastating trauma as a wizard in possession of wondrous magical powers, and yet never free from the original trauma, always under threat by his parents' murderer. As a wizard, he encountered portkeys—objects that transported him instantly to other places, obliterating the duration ordinarily required for travel from one location to another.[3] Portkeys to trauma return one again and again to an experience of traumatization. The experience of such portkeys fractures, and can even obliterate, one's sense of unitary selfhood, of being-in-time.

The endless recurrence of emotional trauma is ensured by the finitude of our existence and the finitude of all those we love.[4] Authentic temporality, insofar as it owns up to human finitude, is traumatic temporality. *Trauma recovery* is an oxymoron—human finitude with its traumatizing impact is not an illness from which one can recover, and innocence lost cannot be regained. "Recovery" is a misnomer for the constitution of an expanded emotional world that coexists alongside the absence of the one that has been shattered by trauma. The expanded world and the absent shattered world may be more or less integrated or dissociated, depending on the degree to which the unbearable emotional pain evoked by the traumatic shattering has become integrated or remains dissociated defensively, which depends in turn on the extent to which such pain found a relational home in which it could be held. This is the essential fracturing at the heart of traumatic temporality. From this perspective, authenticity may be understood as a relative ease of passage between the expanded world and the shattered world of trauma.

Authentic existing that seizes and affirms its own nullity must bear the dark foreboding that accompanies it as the signature affect of traumatic temporality. I have contended (Stolorow 2007, 2011) that the darkness can be enduringly borne only in relational contexts of deep emotional attunement and understanding. This contention has crucial implications for the therapeutic approach to emotional trauma.

THERAPEUTIC IMPLICATIONS

I have been moving toward a more active, relationally engaged form of therapeutic comportment that I call *emotional dwelling*. In dwelling, one does not merely seek empathically to understand the other's emotional pain from the other's perspective. One does that, but much more. In dwelling, one leans into the other's emotional pain and participates in it, perhaps with aid of one's own analogous experiences of pain. I have found that this active, engaged, participatory comportment is especially important in the therapeutic approach to emotional trauma. The language that one uses to address another's experience of emotional trauma meets the trauma head-on, articulating the unbearable and the unendurable, saying the unsayable, unmitigated by any efforts to soothe, comfort, encourage, or reassure—such efforts invariably being experienced by the other as a shunning or turning away from his or her traumatized state.

If we are to be an understanding relational home for a traumatized person, we must tolerate, even draw upon, our own existential vulnerabilities so that we can dwell unflinchingly with his or her unbearable and recurring emotional pain. When we dwell with others' unendurable pain, their shattered emotional worlds are enabled to shine with a kind of sacredness that calls forth an understanding and caring engagement within which traumatized states can be gradually transformed into bearable and nameable painful feelings.

What is it in our existential structure that makes the offering and the finding of a relational home for emotional trauma possible? I have contended (Stolorow 2007, 2011) that just as finitude and vulnerability to death and loss are fundamental to our existential constitution, so too is it constitutive of our existence that we meet each other as "brothers and sisters in the same dark night" (Vogel 1994, 97), deeply connected with one another in virtue of our *common* finitude. Thus, although the possibility of emotional trauma is ever present, so too is the possibility of forming bonds of deep emotional attunement within which devastating emotional pain can be held, rendered more tolerable, and, hopefully, eventually integrated. Our existential kinship-in-the-same-darkness is the condition for the possibility both of the profound contextually of emotional trauma and of the mutative power of human understanding. I suggest, as does Vogel (1994), that owning up to our existential kinship-in-finitude has significant implications for what might be called an *ethics of finitude*, insofar as it motivates us, or even obligates us, to care about and for our brothers' and sisters' existential vulnerability and emotional pain.

CONCLUSION

I have presented a critique of traditional phenomenological psychopathology for failing to challenge and move beyond traditional diagnostic psychiatry and its Cartesian isolated-mind thinking. Such objectifying thinking obscures the embeddedness of emotional disturbances in constitutive contexts of emotional trauma. There are no psychiatric entities, I have contended, only traumatic contexts. And I have shown that Heidegger's existential analytic provides not only a philosophical grounding for a psychoanalytic phenomenological contextualism but also a pathway for grasping the existential meanings of emotional trauma.

What would phenomenological psychopathology look like if it were to incorporate my criticisms and claims? On one hand, it would illuminate the dimensions of emotional worlds that are disrupted and altered in particular forms of emotional disturbance. Ratcliffe (2015), as I have said, has provided an excellent example of such phenomenological description in his analysis of existential hopelessness. On the other hand, it would seek to identify the particular contexts of emotional trauma—not psychiatric diagnoses!—that are implicated in the formation of these disturbed emotional worlds. Without reified psychiatric entities and with a focus on contexts of emotional trauma, phenomenological psychopathology could become more relevant to psychoanalytic therapy and more truly phenomenological!

NOTES

1. See Atwood (2011, chapter 2).
2. I have suggested (Stolorow 2011, chapter 9) that during the period when he was working on the ideas in *Being and Time*, Heidegger found such a relational home in his close bond with Hannah Arendt. When he looked into the abyss of nothingness, he had his sustaining muse at his side.
3. My wife, Dr. Julia Schwartz, first brought this imagery of portkeys to my attention, as a metaphor that captures the impact of trauma on the experience of temporality.

4. I have claimed (Stolorow 2011) that authentic Being-toward-death entails owning up not only to one's own finitude but also to the finitude of those we love. Hence, authentic Being-toward-death always includes Being-toward-loss as a central constituent. Just as, existentially, we are "always dying already" (Heidegger 1962, 298), so too are we always already grieving. Death and loss are existentially equiprimordial. Existential anxiety anticipates both death and loss.

Chapter 3

Beyond the Ontological Difference: Heidegger, Binswanger, and the Future of Existential Analysis

Anthony Vincent Fernandez

The "ontological difference"—that is, the difference between being and beings—is a central theme in Martin Heidegger's philosophy. The proper interpretation of this difference is, however, contentious. One of the most famous misinterpretations is found in the work of Ludwig Binswanger, the founder of existential analysis—a fusion of psychoanalysis and phenomenology. Binswanger adapted Heidegger's philosophy of human existence for his own studies of mental disorder and, in the course of this adaptation, critiqued Heidegger's philosophy. Heidegger, initially supportive of Binswanger's application, later accused him of grossly misunderstanding the ontological difference. According to Heidegger, Binswanger's studies of particular psychopathological cases should be taken as *ontic* (i.e., as a study of concrete beings—in this case, the concrete human being) rather than as *ontological* (i.e., as a study of the meaning of being—in this case, what it means to be human). Binswanger readily admitted his error but claimed that it was, in the end, a "productive misunderstanding"—a characterization that did little to satisfy Heidegger.

In many tellings, this is where the story ends: Binswanger initially misunderstood Heidegger's ontological difference but later admitted his error, corrected his interpretation, and properly characterized the nature of his own psychiatric project. This story, however, presents the disagreement as a quibble between two thinkers. It neglects the broader influence of Binswanger's misinterpretation—specifically, how this misinterpretation produced the philosophical foundations of phenomenological psychopathology, or the phenomenological study of mental disorders.

In this chapter, I revisit this dispute and explain how Binswanger inspired the philosophical foundations of phenomenological psychopathology. In following this thread, I do not deny that Binswanger misunderstood Heidegger's ontological difference. I suggest, instead, that Binswanger's misunderstanding of Heidegger points us toward the correct understanding of human existence. However, to achieve this new understanding, we will have to clarify the nature of the ontological difference and resolve the ambiguities in Binswanger's approach.

This chapter proceeds in four parts: First, I provide an interpretation of the ontological difference, laying the foundation for subsequent sections. Second, I use this interpretation to justify Heidegger's critique, and to highlight the ambiguities in Binswanger's approach. Third, I show how Binswanger's application of Heideggerian phenomenology, despite his misunderstanding of the ontological difference, inspired Michel Foucault's and Maurice Merleau-Ponty's approaches to psychopathology.[1] Fourth, I develop a new account of what it means to overcome the ontological difference, and I argue that this manner of overcoming the difference provides the metaphysical foundations that phenomenological psychopathologists require.

THE ONTOLOGICAL DIFFERENCE

What is the ontological difference? The nature of this difference is not entirely clear in Heidegger's own work and, as a result, has been interpreted in a variety of ways. Before articulating the nature of Heidegger's critique, and Binswanger's apparent error, it will be helpful to make my own interpretation of the ontological difference explicit.

Ontology is the study of being, or of what it means for something to be what it is. Heidegger contrasts ontology with ontic investigations, which are studies of particular beings, rather than their *being*. For instance, I might consider my coffee mug ontically: It's white, made of ceramic, four inches high, holds eight ounces of liquid, and so on. These are ontic facts about my coffee mug. But, if I wanted to get philosophical (or ontological), I could ask what it means to *be* a coffee mug: What makes a coffee mug what it is? Which features or qualities must something have in order to be considered a coffee mug at all? Is a coffee mug with a hole in the bottom still a coffee mug? Is a painting of a coffee mug a coffee mug? What about a sculpture of a coffee mug? Rather than asking about ontic facts that pertain to my particular coffee mug, or even ontic facts that pertain to all coffee mugs, these questions aim at determining the being—or, we might say, the essence—of coffee mugs.

Of course, Heidegger's concern wasn't to clarify the being of coffee mugs. It was to understand the meaning of being in general, or what it means to be at all. But, in order to properly ask this question, he first had to answer another: What does it mean to be human? According to Heidegger, we need to articulate the essence of human existence before we can properly inquire into the meaning of being as such. This is because human beings are the ones who ask ontological questions in the first place. Human beings are "pre-ontological," because they already have some vague understanding of what it means to *be* (Heidegger 1962, 36–37). For our purposes, we can focus exclusively on this ontological question of what it means to be human; how this question differs from ontic questions about human *beings* gets us to the heart of Binswanger's apparent misunderstanding.

How does Heidegger approach the distinctive ontology of the human being? In *Being and Time*, he aims to discover and describe the basic "structures" of human existence. These are "not just any accidental structures, but essential ones which, in every kind of Being that factical Dasein may possess, persist as determinative for the character of its Being" (Heidegger 1962, 38). By "factical Dasein," he refers to a particular human existence, a human being with a concrete history, situation, and so on. In other words, Heidegger's goal is to discover those structures of human existence that hold across all particular human beings. And these structures must be "determinative"—they must play a central role in what it means to be human. For Heidegger, to be human is to be world-disclosive: Human existence is being-in-the-world.

What, then, are these essential structures? They are what Heidegger calls "existentials"—structures that play a role in our existentiality, or transcendence and openness toward the world. For example, the existential that Heidegger calls "situatedness" (*Befindlichkeit*) refers to the fact that we are always situated in the world through some mood or affective attunement. Perhaps you are situated through a mood of joy, while I am situated through a mood of boredom. Neither joy nor boredom is an essential structure, or existential, because they are just one way that a particular subject might be attuned to the world. But no matter which mood we are attuned through, we are always situated and attuned through some mood, so it is the basic structure of situatedness that is essential (Fernandez 2017; Heidegger 1962).

The particular affective attunement that we are situated in, our mood, is what Heidegger calls a "mode" (Heidegger 1962, 179–182). Modes are the phenomena that belong to some existential, or category, of human existence.[2] Moods are the modes of affective situatedness, but each existential has its own set of modes, such as modes of understanding, modes of spatiality, and modes of temporality. In the case of temporality, for instance, I might find myself in the temporal mode of eager anticipation, or the temporal mode of whiling away the time. But the world is always presented to me through *some* temporal mode, which means that temporality is an essential structure of human existence—that is, an existential. Each existential therefore encompasses a set of phenomena that share the same basic features, and the total set of existentials is the structure of human existence in general—what Heidegger sometimes calls our "categorial structure" (Heidegger 1962, 37).

What does this all have to do with the ontological difference? Existentials are, on Heidegger's account, ontological features of human existence; modes, in contrast, are ontic features of human existence. To provide a complete ontology of what it means to be human, I will need to articulate all of the existentials, all of those structures that are essential to and determinative of human existence in general. But I won't need to provide an account of any particular modes of human existence. Particular modes are accidental, or non-essential, and are therefore not in the purview of ontology.

But what if I wanted to understand the experience of a particular individual, say, a person living with severe depression? According to Heidegger, this investigation would be ontic, rather than ontological, because it concerns a particular human being—not the structures that hold across all human beings. Instead of studying the essential structure of affective situatedness, I might investigate the particular mode of affective situatedness that the depressed person finds himself in—that is, his depressed mood. This doesn't mean that existential, or ontological, features of human existence play no role in my ontic investigation. They provide a useful framework for my particular inquiry. If I know that all human beings are affectively situated, and have some spatial and temporal orientation, then I might decide to study the modes of situatedness, spatiality, and temporality in this particular human being. Nevertheless, the ontological and ontic approaches to human existence are fundamentally different projects, with different aims and subject matter—even if they can reciprocally guide and inform each other. With this clarification of the ontological difference in hand, we can turn to Binswanger's misunderstanding of this difference, and Heidegger's critique.

BINSWANGER'S MISINTERPRETATION

Binswanger was one of the first psychiatrists to draw upon twentieth-century phenomenology. He found in Heidegger's work a new way of conceiving the nature of human existence and, thus, a new way of conceiving the nature of *disordered* or *pathological* forms of human existence. He developed his own phenomenological approach to psychiatric research and practice, which he called "existential analysis." Heidegger initially supported Binswanger's project, and the two engaged in a long—if not too frequent—correspondence. However, Binswanger's work was not merely an application. He also argued that there were important aspects of human existence that Heidegger neglected. While Heidegger was initially open to these criticisms, he eventually turned on Binswanger with a damning criticism of his own: Binswanger's attempt to supplement and modify Heidegger's project was based on a fundamental misunderstanding of the nature and aims of Heidegger's work, and especially of the ontological difference.

For the sake of clarity, we can focus on one example that received considerable attention from Heidegger and illustrates Binswanger's general misunderstanding. One of the central existentials that Heidegger discusses in *Being and Time* is care (*Sorge*).[3] According to Heidegger, when we take human existence in its totality, or as a whole, we find that it is first and foremost care. This means that the world, and everything within it, is always given to us as meaningful. Even when I say "I don't care," this is a way of caring. Whatever it is that I don't care about is meaningful to me, or makes sense to me, precisely *as* that which is not worth my time, my consideration, my attention, and so on. Furthermore, Heidegger stresses that care should be understood in an "ontologico-existential manner" (1962, 237). This means that care, as an existential, should be taken as an ontological category that includes an array of ontic modes. As Heidegger says,

> Care, as a primordial structural totality, lies "before" ["vor"] every factical "attitude" and "situation" of Dasein, and it does so existentially *a priori*; this means that it always lies *in* them. So this phenomenon by no means expresses a priority of the "practical" attitude over the theoretical. When we ascertain something present-at-hand by merely beholding it, this activity has the character of care just as much as does a "political action" or taking a rest and enjoying oneself. "Theory" and "practice" are possibilities of Being for an entity whose Being must be defined as "care." (Heidegger 1962, 238)

In other words, any particular way of taking one's world or environment as meaningful is already grounded in this existential. No matter which attitude or concrete situation we might find ourselves in, that situation is always meaningfully available to us through care.

Binswanger was intrigued by Heidegger's notion of care as the human being's openness toward a meaningful world. But, he believed that Heidegger's notion was incapable of accounting for certain kinds of interpersonal relationships because it neglected the importance of love. He argued that Heidegger provided an account of how we can be *with* other human beings, mutually directed toward our world, but failed to provide a robust account of what Martin Buber called the "I and thou" relation—that is, a relation in which we are directed *toward* the other, rather than directed toward our world *with* the other (Buber 1972). Central to this form of interpersonal directedness is love. Binswanger "believed that true psychotherapy was dependent upon the emergence of a loving relationship between the patient and therapist—a relationship that was always attuned to the affective complexities of interaction" (Frie 1999, 249).

As I noted earlier, Heidegger's criticism centered on Binswanger's apparent misunderstanding of the ontological difference.[4] But what does love have to do with the ontological difference? Heidegger explained his concern with Binswanger's work when he lectured to a group of Swiss psychiatrists at the home of Medard Boss.[5] In these lectures, Heidegger disparaged Binswanger's existential analysis:

> Binswanger's misunderstanding consists not so much of the fact that he wants to supplement "care" with love, but that he does not see that *care* has an existential, that is, *ontological* sense. Therefore, the analytic of Da-sein asks for Dasein's basic *ontological* (*existential*) constitution [*Verfassung*] and does not wish to give a mere description of the ontic phenomena of Dasein. (Heidegger 2001a, 116)

As Heidegger argues here, Binswanger's account of love is not problematic in itself. Rather, it reveals a deeper misunderstanding that Heidegger wants to correct. Binswanger thought he needed to supplement care with love because he misunderstood care from the start. Moreover, he misunderstood care because he misunderstood the difference between the ontological and the ontic. He took care as one particular way that human beings can be oriented toward their world, and wanted to show that there is another way we are oriented toward our world (and especially toward others) that Heidegger neglected. Heidegger admitted that he didn't develop a robust account of love, but he argued that nothing in his account of care conflicts with an adequate account of love. Care, taken ontologically, refers to the fact that we are always open to a meaningfully articulated world. Our particular *mode* of meaningful articulation—love included—can change over time, and differ between subjects. But that the world is meaningfully articulated through the existential of care is never in doubt.

If Binswanger understood this, then he might have gone forward with his account of love anyway, but he would not have portrayed it as a critique of Heidegger's ontological account of care. Rather, he would have portrayed love as an ontic *mode* of care—one that Heidegger did not adequately articulate in his own work. Despite Heidegger's negative response, Binswanger took the criticism well and ultimately admitted his "productive misunderstanding." However, Binswanger's misunderstanding was not as clear-cut as Heidegger makes it out to be. Binswanger did not simply mistake an ontological phenomenon for an ontic one. Rather, his entire approach is grounded in an ambiguous relationship between the ontological and the ontic—even if Binswanger himself did not bring this ambiguity to the fore.

In some cases, Binswanger seems to present the relationship between his own project and Heidegger's with the utmost clarity. For example, in his essay "The Existential Analysis School of Thought," he characterizes Heidegger's philosophy of being-in-the-world as an "ontological thesis" about the "essential condition that determines existence in general" (Binswanger 1958b, 191). Binswanger's existential analysis, in contrast,

> does not propose an ontological thesis about an essential determining existence, but makes *ontic statements*—that is, statements of factual findings about actually appearing forms and configurations of existence. In this sense, existential analysis is an empirical science, with its own method and particular ideal of exactness, namely with the method and the ideal of exactness of the *phenomenological* empirical sciences. (192)

Here, Binswanger suggests that his ontic, or empirical, project in no way challenges Heidegger's ontological project.

But some of his other comments are more ambiguous. For example, he later says that Heidegger's account of the structure of existence provides him with a "norm" from which to study deviations. These deviations are, in turn, understood as new "forms," or even new "norms," of being-in-the-world (Binswanger 1958b, 201). This might suggest that he relies on Heidegger's ontological account of human existence as a basic starting point, a framework that guides his studies of individual subjects living in concrete situations with particular psychopathological conditions. But it could also mean that the ontological structure itself can deviate or alter in pathological cases. This position would clearly pit his philosophical underpinnings against Heidegger's, insofar as Heidegger believes that the ontological structure itself cannot change or alter.

This ambiguity is reinforced, rather than resolved, in his case studies and analyses. For example, when studying pathologies of temporality in his famous analysis of Ellen West, he says, "temporality . . . has for us an ontological meaning. This must always be kept in mind, even when, in the analysis of a specific human existence, we must limit ourselves to showing what anthropological metamorphoses this ontological meaning goes through" (Binswanger 1958a, 302). We might interpret this in a way that respects the boundaries of the ontological difference. When Binswanger says that the "ontological meaning" of temporality undergoes "anthropological metamorphoses," he might simply mean that at the anthropological level, the structure of temporality manifests through a variety of ontic modes. However, his concrete analyses undermine this charitable reading. Providing another example of temporal alterations in the case of Ellen West, he says,

> the temporalization shows the character of a shortening or shrinking of existence, that is, of the sinking of its rich and flexibly articulated ontological structure to a less articulated level: the unity of the structure falls apart into

its different ex-stasies; the ontological relation of the ex-stasies to each other dissolves; the ex-stasy "future" recedes more and more, the ex-stasy "past" predominates, and coinciding with this the present becomes the mere Now or, at best, a mere time-span. (Binswanger 1958a, 310)

Here, he clearly suggests that the ontological structure of temporality has itself undergone some dramatic alteration. In spite of his attempts to draw a line between his ontic investigations of particular psychopathological cases and Heidegger's ontological investigations of human existence as such, this distinction does not hold up in his concrete investigations. This ambiguity is doubtless frustrating to readers seeking a clear and coherent program for the phenomenological study of mental disorders. But, as I show in the following section, this ambiguity is precisely where later French philosophers find the promise of a new way of understanding human existence.

EXISTENTIAL ANALYSIS AND THE FOUNDATIONS OF FRENCH PHENOMENOLOGY

Foucault and Merleau-Ponty found in Binswanger's existential analysis the seeds of a new philosophical outlook—one that actively challenges the distinction between the ontological and the ontic, or the transcendental and the empirical. Neither fully articulated the nature or implications of this challenge, but I here outline what they took to be the promise of Binswanger's existential analysis.

Foucault finds in Binswanger's early work the key to a new way of conceiving human existence—a way that takes us beyond the ontological difference. When Foucault was a doctoral student, he was invited to write an introduction to the French translation of Binswanger's 1930 essay, "Dream and Existence." In his introduction, he praises Binswanger's approach:

> In contemporary anthropology, the approach of Binswanger seems to us to take the royal road. He outflanks the problem of ontology and anthropology by going straight to concrete existence, to its development and its historical content. Thence, by way of an analysis of the structures of existence (*Existenz*)—of this very existence which bears such and such a name and has traversed such and such a history—he moves continually back and forth between the anthropological forms and the ontological conditions of existence. (1984, 32)

Traditionally, ontology and anthropology are distinguished in the following way: Ontology is the study of being; anthropology is the study of human life. However, when we ask what it means to be human, the boundary between the disciplines blurs. On Foucault's reading, Binswanger overcomes this traditional distinction by moving between the "anthropological forms" (i.e., the factical modes of human existence) and the "ontological conditions" (i.e., the existentials, or the essential structures of human existence that make experience possible).

Foucault says that Binswanger "continually crosses a dividing line that seems so difficult to draw, or rather, he sees it ceaselessly crossed by a concrete existence in which the real limit of *Menschsein* and *Dasein* is manifested" (1984, 32). Therefore,

> nothing could be more mistaken than to see in Binswanger's analyses an "application" of the concept and methods of the philosophy of existence to the "data" of clinical experience. It is a matter, for him, of bringing to light, by returning to the concrete individual, the place where the forms and conditions of existence articulate. Just as anthropology resists any attempt to divide it into philosophy and psychology, so the existential analysis of Binswanger avoids any a priori distinction between ontology and anthropology. One avoids the distinction without eliminating it or rendering it impossible: it is relocated at the terminus of an inquiry whose point of departure is characterized not by a line of division, but by an encounter with concrete existence. (32–33)

Importantly, Foucault does not claim that Binswanger misunderstands or eliminates the ontological difference—characterized here as the difference between ontology and the ontic science of anthropology. Rather, he claims that Binswanger "avoids the distinction" by placing it at the end of his study rather than at its beginning. But how does a study that begins from concrete existence avoid the distinction between ontology and anthropology? Traditionally, concrete existence stands in the domain of anthropology. The necessary conditions for human experience and existence, by contrast, stand in the more abstract domain of ontology. But Foucault believes that Binswanger's distinctive approach merges these disciplines by starting from "the place where the forms and conditions of existence articulate."[6] This "place" can be nothing other than the concrete human being. Foucault seems to suggest that the ontological structures of human existence always inhere in a concrete subject. And if these ontological structures—these "conditions of existence"— are made concrete, it follows that our ontological structures are susceptible to disturbance and disorder.

But Foucault never spells this out for us. Following his praise for Binswanger's approach, he says, "[t]o be sure, this encounter [with concrete existence], and no less surely, the status that is finally to be assigned to the ontological conditions, pose problems. *But we leave that issue to another time*" (Foucault 1984, 33). Regrettably, this time never came. Foucault soon became disillusioned with existential analysis and turned to the poststructuralism that we associate with him today. However, Foucault was not the only philosopher to find the promise of a new philosophical program in Binswanger's existential analysis.

In *Phenomenology of Perception*, Merleau-Ponty examines a number of psychopathological cases with the intent of revealing the shortcomings of traditional approaches to the study of consciousness, and he defends existential analysis as a viable alternative. He believes that the two dominant approaches—"empiricism" and "intellectualism"—fail to adequately account for the nature of psychopathological experience. According to Merleau-Ponty, an empiricist approach assumes that consciousness is made up of a number of distinct parts: "If consciousness were a sum of psychic facts, then each disturbance should be elective"; that is, each disorder should be capable of altering a single structure of consciousness without disturbing the others (Merleau-Ponty 2012, 138). This approach fails to acknowledge how an alteration in one aspect of consciousness has ramifications throughout the entirety of consciousness.

The intellectualist approach, on the other hand, assumes that consciousness is complete and unchanging: "If consciousness were a 'representation function' or a pure power of signifying, then it could exist or not exist (and everything else along with), but it could not cease to exist after having existed, nor could it become ill, that is, it could not be altered" (138).[7] According to Merleau-Ponty, if one presumes the necessity and invariance of the structures of human existence, then "[t]he empirical variety of consciousness—morbid consciousness, primitive consciousness, infantile consciousness, the consciousness of others—cannot be known or comprehended. One thing alone is comprehensible, namely, the pure essence of consciousness. None of these other consciousnesses could fail to actualize the *Cogito*" (126–127). If one presumes necessity and invariance, then one sets strict constraints on how a disorder can be described and explained. Changes in consciousness can only occur at a relatively superficial level; they cannot involve alterations in our fundamental structures. Historically, Merleau-Ponty suggests that this has forced the philosopher or psychologist to devise absurd accounts of the disorder in question, such as the following: "*Behind* his delusions, obsessions, and lies, the madman *knows that he is* delirious, that he makes himself obsessive, that he lies, and ultimately that he is *not* mad, *he just thinks he is*" (127). According to Merleau-Ponty, the very idea of genuine madness is made incoherent by the metaphysical presumption of essential structures.

Merleau-Ponty embraces existential analysis as a way to coherently understand psychopathological existence: "The study of a pathological case has thus allowed us to catch sight of a new mode of analysis—existential analysis—that goes beyond the classical alternatives between empiricism and intellectualism, or between explanation and reflection" (138).

What Merleau-Ponty finds in Binswanger's existential analysis is an approach that acknowledges both the holistic nature of consciousness and its deep contingency. For him, it acknowledges that the human being constitutes her lived, meaningful world. But it also admits that the world itself—our life events, or personal experiences, our history and circumstances—reshapes us at a fundamental level. However, just how fundamental this level is is left ambiguous in Merleau-Ponty's writings. Like Binswanger, Merleau-Ponty sometimes makes strong claims that seem to undermine the necessity and invariance of our ontological or transcendental structures. But, in his case studies, he often fails to distinguish between those disorders that do not involve alterations in our basic existential structures, and those that can be made sense of only if these basic structures are contingent and variable.

BEYOND THE ONTOLOGICAL DIFFERENCE

In light of its challenge to the ontological difference, Foucault and Merleau-Ponty found immense promise in Binswanger's existential analysis. But they did not adequately articulate what it means to overcome this difference and thereby failed to adequately articulate the philosophical foundations for the study of human existence. In light of this, I here develop an account of what it means to overcome the ontological difference and show how this account opens up a space for phenomenologists to study psychopathological existence.

Remember that Heidegger makes a distinction between the essential structures of human existence, which he calls existentials, and the non-essential ways that these existentials manifest, which he calls modes. Each existential is an ontological category, and this category encompasses a diverse array of ontic modes. It is the category, or categorial structure of human existence, that is essential—not the diverse modes that it encompasses.[8]

This helps us understand the ontological difference. But how does it help us understand what it means to go *beyond* the ontological difference? If anything, it seems that this way of drawing the distinction makes the difference abundantly clear: Ontological categories are different from the ontic phenomena that they encompass. What could it mean to overcome this difference—to complicate or blur this boundary?

To overcome the ontological difference, we would have to show that the features of ontological existentials and the features of ontic modes do not differ as much as Heidegger believed. But what are these distinguishing features? Existentials are necessary and categorial; modes, on the other hand, are contingent and particular. Now, we're hardly going to show that existentials aren't categorial, but we might show that they are contingent—rather than necessary and invariant—features of human existence.

I'll begin with an example of a contingent existential in a psychopathological condition, and then articulate its implications for overcoming the ontological difference. Depression is often characterized as a distinctive mood, or feeling. The depressed person may feel sad, hopeless, or guilty, and this feeling shapes how he experiences and understands his world. On a Heideggerian reading, then, depression is a modal disorder—it consists in a particular mode of human existence that discloses the world in a distressing or pathological way. In this case, the basic structure of human existence remains unchanged. The depressed person is still affectively situated in the world, which means that he or she retains the existential of situatedness.

A phenomenologist who holds Heideggerian commitments to the ontological difference would argue that all psychopathological conditions should be understood in this way. Through our ontological investigations, we discover "essential structures" that hold for all factical subjects. Therefore, any alterations in human experience and existence can involve only changes in nonessential features, such as the ontic modes of human existence. This outlook clearly accommodates the cases of depression mentioned earlier and might accommodate a wide range of other psychopathological conditions, such as attention deficit hyperactivity disorder (ADHD) and personality disorders. But let's consider some more severe disorders, such as melancholic depression and schizophrenia, to see how well they mesh with these philosophical assumptions.

In severe forms of depression, including cases diagnosed as melancholic depression, many people report a general loss of feeling, rather than a kind of feeling. In fact, despite a general association of depression with feelings of sadness, despair, and grief, many people diagnosed with depression report an inability to have these feelings—at least to any significant degree. Chase Twichell, for example, recounts one of her childhood experiences of depression:

> I'm about eight, reading in bed when my mother comes in to tell me that my dog, hit by a car the day before, had died at the vet's. I put my face in my hands, a self-conscious and exaggerated expression of sorrow. My first impulse is to act the part of a grieving child. I am a grieving child, of course, but the real grief is inaccessible to me at that moment. In its place is a calm, numb kind of consciousness, out of which I can fake the expected responses. (2001, 22)

Andrew Solomon reports a similar experience:

> The first thing that goes is happiness. You cannot gain pleasure from anything. That's famously the cardinal symptom of major depression. But soon other emotions follow happiness into oblivion: sadness as you know it, the sadness that seemed to have led you here; your sense of humor; your belief in and capacity

for love. Your mind is leached until you seem dim-witted even to yourself. . . . You lose the ability to trust anyone, to be touched, to grieve. Eventually, you are simply absent from yourself. (2001, 19)

How would a Heideggerian phenomenologist account for such experiences? Which changes in subjectivity would she appeal to in order to make sense of an inability to grieve, to feel, to be affectively touched by the world? If she remains committed to Heidegger's belief that situatedness is an essential structure for human existence, then she would have to redescribe the loss of feeling as a *feeling of not feeling*. That is, rather than taking reports of not feeling at face value, the Heideggerian phenomenologists would explain these reports away by saying that when someone reports a loss of feeling, he is actually reporting a peculiar *feeling* of things not mattering, or not having value. Such a feeling might be possible, but the phenomenological psychopathologist should not confine herself to such an account in advance.

If we put our essentialist assumptions aside, and allow for alterations in the ontological structures themselves, then what kind of account would we be able to offer? How would a phenomenologist make sense of a genuine loss of feeling, without redescribing it as a feeling of not feeling? Some phenomenologists already provide these alternative accounts of depression, although they don't necessarily characterize their accounts as overcoming or challenging the metaphysical presuppositions of the ontological difference. Thomas Fuchs, for instance, argues that melancholic depression involves a loss of bodily resonance—one's lived body loses its affective attunement to others and the world (Fuchs 2013). I, on the other hand, argue that some people diagnosed with severe depression are de-situated—that is, the depressed person loses the capacity to be affectivity situated in and attuned to her world (Fernandez 2014a, 2014b). For our purposes, we don't need to distinguish these views. Both appeal to a general degradation in our ability to be affectively situated in and attuned to our world. And, therefore, both suggest an ontological change in human existence. If one is not affectively situated at all, then we might argue that the ontological category—the existential of situatedness—is lost. An entire category of experiential phenomena has been annihilated from the subject's world. Alternatively, if we allow only for partially diminished affective situatedness, then we might argue that the category itself has been constrained, or altered. The entire category of affective phenomena is less intense.

Alfred Kraus also characterizes melancholic depression as a loss of moods and feelings: "At its core, the melancholic mood alteration is—paradoxically formulated—rather a lack of mood" (Kraus 2003, 208). However, he also points out that this lack of mood can involve a loss of ipseity, or selfhood. Typically, moods situate us in a world. As Heidegger says, we always *find* ourselves through a mood, or affective attunement. But, in a melancholic episode, moods are lost, and melancholic depersonalization sets in. The subject feels strangely distinct from himself, as if he cannot be himself. This is different from feeling that he hasn't lived up to his own expectations, or that his character or values have changed over time. The sense of selfhood that is lost in cases of depersonalization is, rather, a condition for having these kinds of experiences.

In both the loss of mood and the loss of ipseity we find an ontological alteration—a change in the existential itself—rather than a change from one ontic mode to another. This kind of deep ontological alteration likely occurs in other conditions as well, such as bipolar disorder (Fernandez 2014b), schizophrenia, and some neurological disorders. The phenomenological literature on schizophrenia, for instance, focuses on another disturbance of ipseity. As Louis Sass and Josef Parnas explain, positive symptoms of schizophrenia are "*defined* by a kind of diminished self-affection—that is, by a loss of the sense of inhabiting one's own actions, thoughts, feelings, impulses, bodily sensations, or perceptions, often to the point of feeling that these are actually in the possession or under the control of some alien force. Along with this diminishment, the very distinction between self and other may disappear" (Sass and Parnas 2003, 431). We might characterize this as a crisis of identity, but it's of a fundamentally different sort from the kind of crisis one might undergo when leaving behind a career, immigrating to a new country, or revealing one's sexual orientation. In these cases, one can only have a crisis of identity because there is a distinct sense of self and other—*I* left my career, *I* immigrated, *I* revealed my sexual orientation. In the case of schizophrenia, by contrast, this distinction between self and other breaks down, producing bizarre experiences of alien control.

What we find in these cases are alterations in the ontological structures themselves. In some cases, an entire ontological category of phenomena might be lost. In other cases, the ontological category remains, but all of its ontic modes are altered. All of one's moods, for instance, might have diminished intensity. Or one's ability to distinguish one's own identity and agency from those of others might be compromised. Notably, these alterations can show up to us as distinctly *ontological* only if we have already distinguished ontological existentials from their ontic modes. Without this distinction, we wouldn't be able to know when an alteration is truly ontological, or simply ontic. When we fail to draw this distinction, we end up with the ambiguities that we find in Binswanger's existential analysis, as well as Foucault's and Merleau-Ponty's adoptions of this program. These philosophers offer provocative, but ultimately ambiguous, characterizations of psychopathological conditions.

In order to establish a sound foundation for phenomenological psychopathology, we first have to determine what kind of alteration has occurred in the condition in question. And we can determine this only by (a) distinguishing the ontological from the ontic and (b) admitting a deep contingency in the ontological structures themselves. If we haven't distinguished the ontological from the ontic, then we can't determine at what level an alteration has occurred. And, if we haven't admitted contingency in the ontological structures, then we will look for alterations only at the ontic level. To admit contingency in the ontological structures is, in a sense, to particularize them—to admit that they are always instantiated in a concrete human existence and are therefore susceptible to disturbance and disorder. This admission moves us beyond the ontological difference, beyond the distinction between the ontic human being and the ontological structure of human existence in general. To properly understand psychopathological existence, we have to admit that our questions about the particular human being might, at the same time, be questions about what it means to be human.

ACKNOWLEDGMENTS

I would like to thank Kevin Aho, Francisco Gallegos, and Robin Muller for helpful comments on earlier drafts of this chapter. I would also like to thank the Killam Trusts for providing the time to complete my research on this project.

NOTES

1. Foucault is typically characterized as a post-structuralist, rather than as a phenomenologist. However, as I discuss later, Foucault's early work owes much to Binswanger's existential analysis, which is broadly phenomenological in scope and orientation. For more on the relation between Binswanger and Foucault, see Smyth (2011).

2. In Heidegger scholarship, it is common to stress the distinction between "existentials" and "categories." On Heidegger's account, existentials apply to human existence, and categories apply to nonhuman entities, whether they be physical objects, social events, or even ideas. However, the refusal to refer to existentials as "categories," or "categorial structures," is based on a misunderstanding of Heidegger's distinction. Heidegger doesn't want to confuse existentials with Aristotelian categories, but this doesn't mean that existentials aren't ontological categories or don't function as categories. In fact, throughout his early lectures, Heidegger often referred to the "categorial structures" and "categorial determinants" of human existence (Fernandez 2017; Heidegger 2005, 2008).

3. This existential is unique, insofar as it includes three existentials within it: situatedness (*Befindlichkeit*), understanding (*Verstehen*), and discourse (*Rede*). However, for our purposes, we can set this feature of care aside.

4. Richard Askay's afterword (2001) to the *Zollikon Seminars* provides a detailed analysis of Heidegger's criticisms. According to Askay, Heidegger leveled five critiques against Binswanger's project. However, I take it that all of these critiques stem from Binswanger's failure to fully understand and acknowledge the ontological difference, so I do not distinguish among these critiques here.

5. For a work that addresses Heidegger's, Binswanger's, and Boss's approaches to the study of mental disorders, see Kouba (2015).

6. The wording in this sentence is unclear, but I take it that Foucault means that the "forms" and "conditions" of human existence are only ever articulated in a concrete human being.

7. It is important to note that Heidegger's philosophy does not fit neatly under the label of "intellectualism." Some of Merleau-Ponty's critiques of intellectualism are even Heideggerian in character. However, one aspect of this critique—the critique of essentialism, or the belief in necessary and invariant structures of human existence—can be leveled against the philosophical presuppositions of Heidegger's *Being and Time*.

8. It might be tempting to argue that at least some modes are essential. Take, for example, the centrality of the mode of anxiety (*Angst*) in Heidegger's philosophy. Maybe all human beings are open to the possibility of anxiety. Maybe all human beings even experience anxiety at some point in their lives. This still doesn't make anxiety "essential" in Heidegger's sense. Heidegger says that he aims to uncover essential structures that persist "in every kind of Being that factical Dasein may possess" (Heidegger 1962, 38). Therefore, when Heidegger calls something "essential," he means that it holds in all cases. Affective situatedness is essential because we are *always* affectively situated. Temporality is essential because we are *always* temporally open to the world. But, we are not always in the mode of anxiety, in the same way that we are not always in the temporal mode of eager anticipation. Modes, on Heidegger's account, are not essential.

Chapter 4

From Anxiety to Nostalgia: A Heideggerian Analysis

Dylan Trigg

As we grow older we feel an increasing nostalgia for our own deaths, through which we have already passed.

—J. G. Ballard, "News from the Sun"

The preceding epigraph from J.G. Ballard's story "News from the Sun" suggests a relationship between anxiety and nostalgia. In this chapter, this relationship is explored through the lens of Heidegger. Anxiety and nostalgia, an uneven and strange pair it might seem. If anxiety has tended to be regarded as the philosophical mood *par excellence*, venerated in equal measure by Kierkegaard, Sartre, and Heidegger, then nostalgia on the other hand has fallen by the wayside, at best as an impoverished concept and at worse a sentimental indulgence. In the canonical works of twentieth-century philosophy—much less twenty-first century—, very little attention is given to the issue of nostalgia. Part of this neglect perhaps stems in part from nostalgia's apparently regressive characteristics. Unlike anxiety, which engenders a critical awareness of the gaps and discontinuities in existence—and thus carries with it the promise of engineering new insights—nostalgia presents itself as a mood that seeks to conceal those gaps, grounding itself in an idealized image of the past as fixated in time.

Despite their apparent differences, however, anxiety and nostalgia are joined in at least one key respect: They are each governed by an affective concern with time. Anxiety's temporality is in large futurally oriented and concerned in part with an anticipation of uncertainty. Indeed, anxiety's force is rooted in an anticipatory awareness of the future as a source of irredeemable alterity. As Sartre would have it, "*Anything, anything* could happen"

(Sartre 1998, 77). This hyper-vigilance over the future as a source of threat is a feature that appears time and again in both the conceptual and clinical literature on anxiety, and is best registered in experiential terms by the repetition of the phrase *what if* (Trigg 2016). What if my heart suddenly decides to give up? What if the metro stops between stations? What if the sun no longer rises in the morning? Questions such as this prey on anxious subjects though the same questions are often present, though in a less forceful way, for non-anxious subjects. In each case, the question of *what if* points toward the contingency in our knowledge of the world. An imperceptible limit cloaks our understanding of how things work, and confrontation with this limit tends to induce anxiety. We are, in a word, subjected to processes outside of ourselves and which lie ahead of us, and these processes nevertheless continue to constitute who we are.

Both moods operate according to a certain efficacious pathology, in which an overproduction of meaning is imposed on the future in the case of anxiety and, in an inverse way, conferred upon the past in the case of nostalgia. In each direction, the spontaneity of the future and the indeterminacy of the past are augmented with an appeal to a fixed axis termed *the I*. Through this efficacious power, pastness and futurity gain the distinction of being subordinated to the sovereignty of selfhood. For the anxious subject, the future unfolds, not as an unmapped horizon shaped by the contingencies of history and the pathos of intersubjective relations—a future in which hope lives alongside failure, in which uncertainty accompanies certainty—but through a singular and unflinching lens, driven by an unceasing egology and shaped above all by one character alone: apprehension.

In contradistinction to anxiety, nostalgia's temporality is *prima facie* rooted firmly in the inexhaustible richness of the already lived past. As it is commonly thought, nostalgia involves less a turning toward the unmapped future and more a retreat from such uncertainty in favor of a landscape already wrought by experience. Such a terrain is charged with the pathos of a familiarity that is at once strange and intimate. This movement of turning back surrounds nostalgia's divisive character, framed as it by a resistance to change and an inclination toward stasis. Yet nostalgia's time is not simply an uncritical affirmation of the past in its generality and homogeneity. Nostalgia's phenomenology is selective. Throughout, the mood gravitates in and around a time that impresses itself actively upon the construction of the self, and which continues to exert a presence upon the present (Trigg 2012). As with anxiety, nostalgia's time is a living and dynamic one, haunting the present in both an ambiguous and uneasy way. If it reaches out from the past, then such a past is not one that is affixed to an objective date, but—again like anxiety—stems from a general atmosphere. For this reason, nostalgia's objects do not gain their power through the objective ordering of temporal data. Over a slow duration, phenomenal objects—buildings, streets, the faces of people we once knew but have since lost contact with, totems of a life once lived but no longer immediately accessible—assume a vital halo of meaning. Those same objects are not dormant in the background of the past, as representations of a history that now stands ready to be archived. Rather, through playing some elemental role in the crystallization of selfhood, they protrude through the past, announcing their presence as a form of lack, which the nostalgic subject grasps all too acutely as a specific kind of pleasurable longing.

An uneven and strange pair, then. But is their commonality merely a contingent rapport with time in all its adumbrations or is there something more substantial to this relation? In this chapter, I would like to reflect on this pairing of apparent opposites. I propose here that what binds nostalgia and anxiety, alongside their temporal orientation, is a concern with the *home*. By "home," we do not just mean that physical site implanted into the terrain of the Earth's surface, which we return to after a day's work. More than this, home is better understood less as a fixed noun and more as a dynamic verb, that is, as a sense of *being-at-home*. To be at home is, in one sense, to be integrated in a complex series of ways: spatially, temporally, subjectively, intersubjectively, and so forth. To be ill-at-home—or homesick—is precisely to have these taken-for-granted nodes of familiarity and directionality uprooted. One such way this interplay between homeliness and unhomeliness comes into play is in the dialog between nostalgia and anxiety.

Our plan for studying this liaison is to forge a collaboration with Heidegger. Heidegger belongs to a set of philosophers whose conceptual orientation is to some extent phrased as a recovery project. Indeed, accusations of Heidegger's nostalgia, evidenced in his ontology as well as his aesthetics, are a standard trope in the secondary literature, such that we need only mention it in passing here. In the present reflection, we wish to bypass this subgenre of Heidegger studies and aim, instead, to elicit an *unthought thought* in his philosophy. The thought concerns whether or not we can formulate a theory of nostalgia from Heidegger's phenomenology in order to understand its relation to anxiety and selfhood. Our method for this exploration consists of looking at the function of home in Heidegger's early work. Our claim is that home acts as a pivot, upon which both anxiety and nostalgia gravitates, channeling each affect into the same orbit. We shall defend this thought in the following way.

First, we will consider the function of anxiety in Heidegger, as it figures in *Being and Time*. As we do this, we will give particular attention to the role the home and an adjoining sense of unhomeliness play in motivating Heidegger's analytic of anxiety. In the second movement, we will be led to the phenomenology of nostalgia. This move is predicated on the conviction that nostalgia aims at the *reintegration of familiarity and spatial-temporal continuity*—two aspects that are structurally and thematically undermined during anxiety, and which are central to a sense of being "at home." Through situating anxiety and nostalgia in dialog with one another, then, we will see that far from a strange alliance, each mood in fact works in tandem to safeguard against the destruction of home, anxiety through signaling an incipient threat, nostalgia through working to recover the damage invoked by an already-established threat.

HEIDEGGER'S ANXIETY

Let us, then, begin with Heidegger's anxiety. Heidegger joins both Freud and Lacan (alongside Kierkegaard and Sartre) in phrasing anxiety as a mood that has both an epistemic and transformative function. As is widely known, for Heidegger, anxiety is the philosophical mood *par excellence* insofar as it discloses the manner in which the world as a totality is revealed to us. To understand this, a prior understanding of Heidegger's idea of moods is required. According to Heidegger, we are entities who are in the world insofar as our existence is shaped by the moods (*Stimmungen*) we find ourselves in (Heidegger 2008). Far from an ephemeral or psychological state, mood is the pre-reflective way in which the world is both disclosed and interpreted to us. If our moods are subject to variation and variability, then we are always in a mood, even if that mood is one of indifference. Mood is thus not an interior realm that shades an otherwise neutral world. Rather, things in the world assume a specific meaning according to the mood we find ourselves in. For this reason, different moods shed light on different attributes of the world. The mood of boredom reveals a world that is boring; a jubilant mood aligns with a jubilant world, and an anxious mood coincides with an anxious world. Things portend into my experience as both provoking anxiety and being objects of anxiety.

As Heidegger sees it, certain moods carry with them a philosophical or foundational value. Anxiety is one such mood that carries with it both an experiential and conceptual significance. His justification for turning to anxiety is thus in the first respect a methodological one. The discussion appears in §40 of *Being and Time* and is prefaced by the question of how Dasein can gain understanding of the "totality of the structural whole" that is Being (Heidegger 1962, 229). Such a question is, of course, one that concerns Heidegger from the outset and is manifest in his privileging of Being over beings. How is it, so Heidegger will ask time and again, that Being can become an issue for beings? How, furthermore, can we grasp Being as a whole and not just the being which takes up that existence as a series of parts? So long as we are tied up in the world, as though the world just existed in a habitual and constant sense, then such questions are for the most part lost on us. As Heidegger presents, it is anxiety that "might . . . perform some such function" of disclosing Being as a whole (230).

Heidegger is careful from the outset of his analysis to distinguish anxiety from fear, and the distinction is notable. In contrast to anxiety, fear has a localizable object that is situated as a "detrimental entity within-the-world" (230). An object of fear—be it a precipice, a wolf hiding in the forest, or the smell of old furniture—can be avoided and thus managed. Anxiety assumes a more nebulous force. While there is an ambiguity between fear and anxiety, insofar as one can become anxious about the objects we fear, anxiety is not reducible to those objects; anxiety's object, if we are to speak in paradoxical terms, is not specific things as such, but instead "Being-in-the-world" itself (230). Such an ontological anxiety may well take form in specific things (apparent not least in the production of phobias that seek to delimit and curtail anxiety), but anxiety in Heidegger's sense is faceless in that it does not belong to a given entity. What we are anxious about is our very existence rather than the existence of the things themselves. Anxiety itself does not spring from those things, as though we could turn away from what threatens us. Instead, anxiety comes from "nowhere"—and we do not, as Heidegger has it, ultimately know what we are anxious about (231).

For all that, anxiety's evasive presence does not mean it is experientially absent. Because it is nowhere it is also everywhere, "so close that it is oppressive and stifles one's breath" (231). Entities themselves, as Heidegger has it, fall by the wayside in their insignificance and deprivation of meaning. As things fall away, so the world presents itself to us as that which was there all along but only now figured through anxiety *as* a world. What Heidegger is describing here is a specific kind of nonconceptual groundlessness that is ordinarily masked in our habitual everyday existence. In and through anxiety, existence is revealed as being grounded in nothingness. As understood in this context, nothingness is not a negation of my world but a preclusion of myself as being a discernible *thing*. Heideggerian anxiety, then, is experientially grasped as a confrontation with the contingency of meaning that ordinarily constitutes the existence of things—both objects and relations—in such a way that for a brief moment, the world as a whole in its infinite contingency is revealed as a whole. In this vertiginous anxiety, I as a singular being am individuated from my dependency and complicity with others who might otherwise provide a buffer between myself and the world. As Heidegger will develop in his analysis of being-toward-death, anxiety's "negativity" is thus only transitional. Far from bringing about the dissolution of Dasein, anxiety forges a space in which a confrontation with finitude and contingency brings about the possibility of rendering contingency and finitude one's own.

Up until that resolution, however, anxiety appears for us as signaling the advent of uncanniness. Heidegger uses the term *unheimlich* to describe the state of being uncanny, though he stresses that uncanniness also means "not-being-at-home" (233). Phenomenologically, our taken-for-granted existence consists of several key dimensions that enable us to proceed through the world without having to reflect in abstraction on how things work and assume the meaning they do. Think here of any given moment in the world. For the most part, we are at-home in the world insofar as the world presents itself to us a nexus of familiar pathways and pregiven meanings. When I leave my apartment, and take to the surrounding area, then I do so with an implicit confidence that the world will conform to a pattern that is habitually familiar to me.

The world as a home-world is precisely given to me as a relational whole and is structured at all times in an intersubjective manner. It is a world in which things have their place, and from which I stand ready to make use of things. An atmosphere of familiar consistency thus envelops this world, rarely drawing attention to itself except for when it dissents from my expectations. In all this, home serves as a foundation, without which, not only would I be disoriented and displaced, but I would also be exposed to an unfamiliar and indeed unhomely world.

Through anxiety, we are, so Heidegger suggests, confronted with precisely such a situation, in which our average taken-for-granted attitude is disrupted. The world, as such, no longer performs in the way we expect it to. Anxiety undermines this homely intimacy we have with the world, individuating us from our "absorption" in the world, and dislodging the complicity we have with others who share that world (233). "Everyday familiarity," so Heidegger writes, "collapses" (233). What this means is not that the world suddenly dissolves, as though it were made of liquid; but instead that the roles one assumes and the meaning, action, and purpose one finds in things appear now as contingent constructs. In the face of this loss of familiarity and intrinsic meaning, we flee back into the state of being "at-home" of established patterns within a public sphere, such that "complete assurance" can coexist alongside the "threat" of the uncanniness that haunts Dasein from the outset (234). Heidegger's anxiety, then, is not marked by a paroxysm of panic (he even goes so far as to dismiss "physiological" anxiety as being the same as the rarer "real" anxiety) (234). Rather, it sits there quietly and perhaps even innocuously, forming an atmosphere of subtle disquiet in our everyday existence, which, from time to time, flares up as an ecstatic realization that paralyses us into inaction and on occasion into action.

For the most part, however, Heidegger thinks that we are creatures who flee anxiety through cultivating a series of fears that take the place of anxiety. Fear is not a flight away from the objects that engender fear, but instead a flight precisely *toward* those things (233). What Dasein is in flight from, then, are not those objects of fear that are common to many—and thus shared in a complicit and familiar compact between oneself and others. Such objects merely defer and detain an anxiety greater than that of anxiety itself, as he has it: "Fear is anxiety, fallen into the 'world,' inauthentic, and, as such, hidden from itself" (234). As such, the very motive to flee is a movement that registers what we are fleeing from, that is, the "not-at-home" which "must be conceived as the more primordial phenomenon" (234). As primordial, anxiety is not unfortunate disintegration of an otherwise-unified existence to be redeemed through the cultivation of a "heroic" facade, but instead an encounter with the infrastructure that propels us to construct such a facade in the first place. In this respect, Heidegger radicalizes the primordiality of homelessness as an ontological rather than existential given. Homesickness is, as it were, the beginning point for any genuine creation of being at-home.

FROM ANXIETY TO NOSTALGIA

Heidegger's analysis of anxiety is striking in several respects. But how does this analysis lead to nostalgia? In response to this question, three points are worth bearing in mind. First, in contradistinction to the Freudian model, which posits anxiety as the result of repressed drives, for Heidegger, anxiety is primary in the structure of subjectivity (to use language that is distinctly un-Heideggerian). Anxiety is not reducible to an affective mood, much less one that can be placed within the tradition of a humanism. Rather, the affective—or ontic—dimension of anxiety springs from its ontological status as signaling the indefinite and contingent ground of existence. In the second case, because of its elemental place, for Heidegger, the status at-homeness is not a given of perceptual experience, but an achievement that we secure through fleeing from anxiety. In the final case, then, anxiety engenders a movement of taking flight. Taking flight means proscribing anxiety, drawing a limit on it, and otherwise putting it in a place. Perhaps it is through cultivating a fear or a phobia that can be managed or perhaps it is through fostering complicity with the public world of *the they*; in each case, the motive is to quieten anxiety's capacity to render us ill-at-home in the world.

To move from anxiety to nostalgia, I want to suggest the following hypothesis: The emergence of nostalgia is motivated (but not caused) by the onset of anxiety, such that nostalgia aims toward the reintegration of familiarity and spatial-temporal continuity—that is, the sense of being at-home—without ever realizing that homecoming. Let us say, in a Heideggerian sense, that nostalgia is anxiety in the mode of taking flight. Of course, the phrase *takes flight* sounds like a rapid, indeed flighty, movement. Nostalgia is precisely at odds with such velocity; this is why it is not a "response" in the sense of being provoked by stimuli. Rather, it is analogous to an atmosphere that accumulates over a given timescale. The remainder of the chapter proceeds in three ways to unpack this claim. First, I outline a brief phenomenology of nostalgia; second, I reflect on the function of nostalgia; finally, I situate nostalgia in relation to Heideggerian anxiety.

A BRIEF PHENOMENOLOGY OF NOSTALGIA

The story of nostalgia, to phrase it hyperbolically, is a story of impossible returns (Boym 2001). The term *nostalgia* itself was coined in the seventeenth century by a Swiss medical student, Johannes Hofer, to describe the pain experienced by Swiss mercenaries when separated from their home (Hofer 1934; Trigg 2006). The word, a composite of *nóstos* (homecoming) and *algos* (pain), reflects this tension. The pain of the Swiss mercenaries descending their mountainous home in order to fight was so intense that the soldiers were advised to avoid the sound of cowbells in case of being reminded of the homeland (Illbruck 2012). Through time, nostalgia has been reconceived as less concerning *algos* and more tied up with the sentimentality of *nostos*. Its quality as an ambiguous emotion—pleasurable and painful, familiar and unfamiliar, homely and unhomely—has to some extent been diminished, reflected above all in the appropriation of nostalgia as a consumable entity. Contemporary psychological research on nostalgia reflects this trend and tends to accent its positive function as generating meaning and "well-being" (Routledge et al. 2010; Routledge 2015).

Despite this rich history, the nature of nostalgia has proved elusive, and a series of questions continue to remain critical for ongoing debates in the field. How is nostalgic remembering different from non-nostalgic remembering? Is nostalgia a "positive" affect? What role does nostalgia play in consolidating meaning? And does culture produce the conditions for nostalgia? Such questions are beyond the purview of the current investigation, but any inquiry into nostalgia first has to address what constitutes the mood. To proceed, at least three points need to be remarked on, namely, the intentional (or noetic) structure of nostalgia, the thematic (or noematic) content of nostalgia, and the broader existential function of nostalgia. We begin with the first point.

Nostalgia is often thought of as a variant of remembering. More specifically, a variant of remembering imbued with a particular kind of affective sensation, most typically a sensation of bittersweet yearning. Already this seems problematic, however. To phrase nostalgia as content plus affect seems both misleading and reductive. After all, it is quite possible to recall a given experience at one moment without there being an affective content while on another moment the same content is imbued with deep emotional resonance. Likewise, that a memory has an affective content is by no means a guarantee of it constituting a nostalgic experience. Moreover, there is an additional and compelling sense in which *all* intentionality is affective in varying degrees. Our orientation in the world is not led by a series of abstract calculations but is instead mediated by a set of meanings that govern our existence more generally. In a word, things matter to us. As such, the presently topical phrase *affective intentionality*, *prima facie* a suitable candidate for nostalgia, is thus too vague to capture the specificity of nostalgia's intentionality.

If volitional memory alone does not ensure the affective thickness of nostalgia, then what is the role of memory's counterpart, namely, imagination? Such is the approach phenomenological thinkers such as Gaston Bachelard and Edward Casey have provided when accounting for the intentionality of nostalgia; as Bachelard has it, "Every great image has an unfathomable oneiric depth to which the personal past adds special color" (Bachelard 2014, 53; Casey 1987). For Bachelard, nostalgic intentionality concerns a past that is anterior to personal experience, marked with both a "history and a prehistory" (53). As a result, the significance of the nostalgic object does not reside in its factual and objective status as a thing located in the past. Rather, the object in question is reinvented and augmented with an appeal to the present, a process that seems especially suited to the work of imagination. On a corresponding note, Edward Casey writes: "What recollection cannot accomplish by the mere assembling of particular memories, productive imagination achieves in forging a unity in which their affinity is expressed" (Casey 1987, 367). As Casey makes clear, far from aimless, the work of imagination is productive in scope, bordered at all times by the horizons of the past, which anchors nostalgia in a partly dissolved mixture of past and present. Here, Proust offers us a clue on how to proceed. Of the confusion of temporal poles, he writes how "the past was made to encroach upon the present and I was made to doubt whether I was in the one or the other" (Proust 1970, 133). Neither memory nor imagination, nostalgia's intentional structure, unfolds, to follow Proust, as that of a *reverie*.

The notion of reverie captures nostalgia's peculiar orientation. Rather than unfolding in the manner of a subject correlating with an object, as, for example, in the case of a nightmare, reverie's aim is neither the recollection of data nor an attention on a localized object, which remains fixed. Rather, reverie spreads its intentional force across a series of horizons, which, if beginning in one point, nevertheless is cast afar from its origins, as Bachelard writes:

> Reverie is entirely different from the dream by the very fact that it is always more or less centered upon one object. The dream proceeds on its own way in a linear fashion, forgetting its original path as it hastens along. The reverie works

in a star pattern. It returns to its center to shoot out new beams. (Bachelard 1987, 14)

To think in dialog with Bachelard, nostalgic reverie takes it strength from a point of inception in the past, be it a childhood home or a city at dusk. Yet the reverie is not bound by these objects; rather, the objects appear for us as a beacon, which emits a signal beyond its own materiality. Faraway cities and remote corners of the Earth are all one possible expression of a much broader relation, which is already formed in advance of their expression. Objects such as these can vary in scope and scale, from the microcosmic to the macrocosmic, and they emerge as origins, which, if returning to themselves, also recede into the background in order to propel the nostalgic reverie further afield.

THE ROLE OF HOME

If nostalgia unfolds in the manner of a reverie, does this mean that it lacks a discernible correlating noematic object? In reply to this question, much depends here on what we mean by noematic object, and quite obviously now is not the time or place to assume a Husserlian detour. Nevertheless, if we are to advance in this task of understanding the relation between anxiety and nostalgia we must consider *what is it that we are nostalgic for*. Nostalgic intentionality, even if ambiguous and vague, is registered *as* nostalgia in and through its affective content, and there is, to be sure, a phenomenology peculiar to nostalgia, which I have addressed elsewhere (Trigg 2012). While it is true that nostalgia differs from reproductive memory and outright phantasy, the mood nevertheless has a root in the past, even if the past that nostalgia draws its inspiration and lifeblood from is subject to a series of ongoing transformations. Here, I would propose that the history of nostalgia as once being inseparable from homesickness is both telling and incisive; in a word, its thematic content remains that precisely of *home*.

Home can be understood here in at least two senses. In the first case, home can be thought of as in its historic sense as a physical site or region that serves as a locus of familiarity and orientation. Such a home is manifest as a series of relations be it to a community, to a neighborhood, to a culture, and so forth. Here, the formulation of nostalgia as a mode of homesickness remains intact. Nostalgia is provoked by distance and is registered experientially as a yearning for reunification. As understood in this way, the seventeenth-century "cure" for nostalgia was grounded in the conviction that an actual return to the homeland would cure sufferers—classically, Swiss soldiers—of their longing before rehabilitating them for their next voyage. However, as both history and experience attest, such a mythical return is often met with failure and disappointment. As we know from returning to one's childhood haunts, if we can return to the place of our origin, then we can never return to the time of that origin (cf. Trigg 2012).

In the second case, we can think of the home, less in terms of a set of spatial references, and more in phenomenological terms as a general *atmosphere* that encompasses, embodies, and expresses a specific era. As understood in this way, what we are nostalgic for is not a definite place or time, but more to a certain atmosphere that is characterized by plenitude, integration, unity, and perhaps above all, an innocence marked by the complete absence of nostalgia itself. It is within an atmosphere that specific objects—houses, people, a petite Madeline—gain their importance as indexing and articulating a more global sense of at-homeness.

Critically, these two concepts of home—alongside no doubt a series of other formulations of home—operate and unfold in an ambiguous relation to one another, such that home as a localized thing and home as an atmosphere meld into the same zone. What is at stake in each variation of home is not the individual status of objects themselves, but rather the role these objects serve as magnetic forces that point toward the quality of *at-homeness* more generally (and in this respect, the word *atmosphere* is thus accurate). In effect, objects—be it the home, a neighborhood, or a particular place—become emblems of at-homeness.

THE THREAT OF ANXIETY

With the intentional and thematic orientation of nostalgia provisionally established, let us turn to the critical issue at stake in our present investigation: nostalgia's relation to anxiety. Whether or not nostalgia involves an orientation toward home as a fixed locale or toward a general atmosphere of homeliness, nostalgia is predicated on the idea that at least two different states come into contact with one another. Emblematically, these two states are played out in terms of a tension between the familiar and the unfamiliar; an already-lived past that is familiar in terms of being a locus of unity and, moreover, returnable in the sense of still being reachable, but unfamiliar enough to merit the urge toward nostalgia in the first place. More than this, the relation between these two states must involve a return of sorts, be it actual or otherwise, successful or not. Such a disparity does not concern the temporal difference between different ages—old age wistfully recollecting youth—but instead between the lived duration of temporal distance, such that in principle one could be nostalgic for a time that is objectively speaking still proximate to the present.

One way we can think about these different states is in terms of being-at-home and not-being-at-home. We recall that for Heidegger, being-at-home means several things. In its earlier incarnation—that is, in *Building, Dwelling, Thinking*—he famously makes a distinction between having a shelter and being at home. The truck driver is at home on the highway, but he cannot be said to dwell there. As understood in this way, at home refers to a certain taken-for-granted relationship to our surrounding environment, such that we have an implicit knowledge of how that environment works, be it the interior of a truck or the domesticity of a kitchen. We also know, however, that Heidegger's account of being at home is not a materialist account. Indeed, his principal question in the early works is whether buildings hold any guarantee of dwelling. Dwelling for him marks a particular kind of relation to the world.

It is worth narrowing this focus on at-homeness to the account Heidegger develops in *Being and Time*. In this context, at-home refers to how the world presents itself to us a nexus of familiar pathways and pregiven meanings. We are caught up in the world of being-at-home insofar as the world serves as an expression of our being-in-the-world. As Husserl would have it, the homeworld may in turn become impregnated with an alien quality, but it nevertheless remains alien from the standpoint of an already-established home (cf. Steinbock 1995).

We have also seen how anxiety threatens the sense of being-at-home. How does it do this? One overreaching way anxiety achieves this is through a process of *defamiliarization*. The world ceases to conform to my expectations, and in revealing itself as irreducible to me, it undermines the meaning I invest within it. Ontically speaking, it becomes strange and alien. Fragments of familiarity exist alongside unfamiliar dimensions, establishing a world that is both uncanny and unhomely. Heidegger does not expand upon the implications defamiliarization has upon selfhood—indeed, such language is distinctly un-Heideggerian. In response to this lacuna, however, we propose here that anxiety threatens the sense of being at-home through a breakage in both *spatial-temporal continuity* and *familiarization*. This is evident in at least two respects.

First, the onset of anxiety marks not only two ways in how the world presents itself to us, but it also marks a rupture in the temporal continuity of selfhood. The point can be expressed by considering the temporality of mood. Each mood that we embody is in some way exclusive. The mood of sorrow leaves no space for that of joy, and the sorrowful world is absolute in the sense that each and every aspect of the world is laden with a quality of sorrowfulness. When the mood passes, then it becomes difficult to again adopt the mood of sorrow as if by volition. There is thus a discontinuity here such that sorrow and joy do not neatly segue into one another, but instead form a sharp discord. The same is true of anxious and non-anxious states; there is no consolidation between them, and they each inhabit entirely opposed worlds. Temporally, the implication is that different modalities of the subjective existence fail to reconcile. This is reinforced from a clinical perspective, where many patients of spatial phobias consider their phobic episodes as interruptions in an otherwise-functioning and "normal" existence (Trigg 2016).

In the second case, the breakage in temporal continuity leads to a rupture in our familiar grasp on things. Anxiety's presence is impersonal, and we register it less in terms of its positive attributes and more in terms of what it deprives us of. As we have seen from Heidegger, anxiety deprives us of the implicit meaning we ordinarily take for granted. The world ceases to be a nexus of interrelated meanings and instead becomes a site of anonymity and fragmentation.

REFAMILIARIZATION AND SPATIAL-TEMPORAL CONTINUITY

Together, the breakage in spatial-temporal continuity and the rupture of familiarization invoked by anxiety leads to a more global sense of *defamiliarization*. Given this movement of defamiliarization, it may be countenanced that nostalgia assumes a decisive role in engineering the resumption of spatial-temporal continuity coupled with a process of *refamiliarization*. Refamiliarization and spatial-temporal continuity are two components of being at-home, where we understand "home" in the sense of either a discernible set of relations or an atmosphere of integrated unity. How, then, does nostalgia contribute to the work of home restoration? The clues are in nostalgia's intentional and affective structure.

In the first case, nostalgia engenders *spatial-temporal continuity* through the act of reverie. As we have seen, the intentional structure of nostalgia is different from that of reproductive memory. Its concern is not recollection but *re-invention*. As such, nostalgia's temporal structure does not resemble an arrow pointing backwards. Rather, its intentional structure is, as we have said, that of a reverie. Think here of how the intentionality of a reverie unfolds. When we are in a state of reverie, then we do not aim at one particular source, nor do we confine ourselves to a singular timescale. Rather, our attention is contextualized and framed by the mood we are presently in. The movement between times and places is porous and indivisible, such that there is a confusion of aspects. For this reason, in the mood of nostalgia, it is not strictly accurate to say we inhabit the past, as though the past were a static site; rather, we inhabit a borderline between times. In fact, the borderline we inhabit is that of an atmosphere, which, if taking its inspiration from the past, nevertheless extends itself in and through time.

In this respect, nostalgic intentionality is transformative; it disregards the objective standing of things and subsumes those things within a more opaque atmosphere. The upshot of this intentional structure is evidently the establishment of continuity across time—what James Hart rightly calls in his critical analysis of nostalgia, "aeonic time" (Hart 1973). The past is not an archaic and archived reserve, but instead an active and dynamic presence that continues to exert an influence upon the present. And the present is not the plentiful present of Husserl, but a present laden with the retention of a partly familiar undercurrent. If time is regained, as Proust would have it, then it is not the specificity of *a* time, but rather the felt quality of pastness generally.

The second point concerns the establishment of a *discernible set of relations*. Here, too, we are concerned with spatial-temporal continuity; now our concern is only with continuity in a thematic sense. How does nostalgia achieve its aim on a thematic level? The answer must involve a response to the defamiliarization peculiar to anxiety, that is, to say, through nostalgia's capacity to enact *refamiliarization*. This capacity is best understood in the context of nostalgia's bittersweet tonality, which involves less the whimsy of imagination as a free and spontaneous movement, and more the construction of a past to mimetically resemble the present and likewise a present that resembles the past. Cinematic and literary treatments of nostalgia—to think of Andrei Tarkovsky's *Nostalghia*, or Alfred Hitchcock's *Vertigo*, and indeed many motifs in David Lynch—often involve precisely this interplay of disparate temporal figures entering the same orbit, with a view of morphing the present into the shape of a partly memorized, partly imagined past. Invariably, of course, the attempt fails, and it is on the borderline between an idealized past and an actual present that anxiety appears. Anxiety appears within this movement of home restoration not only through an expression in particular things but rather as an impersonal cloud that is experientially received as a force of defamiliarization. As Heidegger would have it, anxiety's presence is revelatory; it uncoils the anonymous existence that underpins our personal life, drawing attention to the radical contingency structuring the genesis of meaning itself. By contrast, nostalgia enters into a dialog with this movement through the restoration of that which is irreducibly the most personal and the most ineffable of things—namely, our own history, imagined or otherwise, personal or collective, private or political, upon which we ascribe a sense of *homeliness*.

CONCLUSION

Today, perhaps more than ever in recent times, the relation between anxiety and nostalgia has assumed a critical tone. Brexit, Trump, to name but a few recent tokens of our own time marked by the collision of, on the one hand, a nostalgic urge to reclaim a past that was, in a strict sense, never truly present, and, on the other hand, by an anxiety to ensure that the value imbued in this narrative is immunized from further threat, whether that threat is marked by terrorism, the loss of national identity, movements of immigration, or otherwise. Be it personal or political, the story we tell ourselves of who we are and what the world is like is seized through anxiety. Anxiety, in no uncertain terms, undermines the meaning we ascribe to these plotlines, not only dissolving a given narrative but also calling into question the nature of temporal and spatial narrativity more generally.

Against this backdrop, nostalgia appears *prima facie* as an atmospheric "safe space"—to use a current phrase—which insulates the subject from a broader state of peril, which is both uncontainable and impersonal. In this respect, the current psychological treatment of nostalgia is correct; nostalgia serves as a form of "terror management," assuaging the anxieties that emerge when our taken-for-granted relationship to the world is undermined (cf. Routledge et al. 2010). As we have seen, being-at-home not only means invoking the restoration of home as a localized site, but it also means generating a more atmospheric concept of home that is dispersed through the world. Nostalgia, as we have also seen, is able to do this through the confusion of times, led throughout by the act of reverie. In the final act of consolidation, nostalgia aims to restore familiarity and continuity through seizing the world in and through an already-formed lens, which is then mapped over the present.

Yet does this movement of taking flight invoke an actual homecoming? It is notable that much of the current treatment of nostalgia overlooks the radical discordance between the nostalgic vision of the world and the non-nostalgic world that serves as a foundation for that vision. If time is reshaped, slowed down, and wholly augmented, then it is never transformed to the point where homecoming is itself possible. As Kant demonstrated in his lecture on anthropology, to return home would be to see nostalgia for what it is—an affective force that is incapable of seizing time in place. Literature and cinema is also especially rich in drawing attention to the gaps and ruptures that are situated at the heart of nostalgia's movement from familiarity to a temporality that not only offsets the familiar but also destroys it (cf. Trigg 2017). In this respect, nostalgia's "value" does not reside in its capacity to invoke an actual homecoming, but rather in a protracted homelessness that underscores the contingency of home itself. To follow a Heideggerian route, the response to anxiety is not to quieten it much less to remove it, but to live alongside it. The same is true of nostalgia; its purpose resides less in the sanctuary of home, and more in the ambiguity of an impossible homecoming, which amplifies and problematizes rather than subdues and assuages our capacity to call our temporal and spatial existence into question.

Part II

PHENOMENOLOGIES OF ANXIETY, PAIN, AND DEATH

Chapter 5

The World of Chronic Pain: A Dialog

Martin Kusch and Matthew Ratcliffe

This chapter is a dialog in more than one sense. To begin with, it results from several face-to-face discussions between the two coauthors, who are colleagues in the same philosophy department. But what divides them is more important: only Kusch (subsequently "MK") is a chronic-pain patient, and only Ratcliffe has a background in the philosophy of illness. This chapter is the result of our attempt to bring these two forms of "expertise" together. The starting point for our dialog was a document entitled "Pain," which was the basis for a talk given by MK. His experience with chronic pain had become known to the organizers of a conference on "Philosophy and Medicine," held in early 2017 in Vienna, and they invited him there to speak "bluntly" and "directly" about pain. He decided to focus on the year 2014, when chronic pain—and the treatments he received—brought him close to madness and death. The talk came as a shock to the audience of medical professionals, but it has since opened up something of a dialog between MK and some German and Austrian pain therapists. In the interest of authenticity, and in order to anchor our dialog in a firsthand experiential account, we decided to reproduce the whole document here (in English translation).

Our subsequent discussion starts from some key elements of "Pain," rather than attempting to cover all aspects of MK's account. We focus on the *phenomenology* of chronic pain and emphasize two interrelated points: (a) an experience of chronic pain is inextricable from how one relates to other people and, more specifically, what one anticipates from them and (b) certain experiences of pain are both concretely focused and yet, at the same time, all-encompassing, thus challenging commonplace assumptions about the nature of intentionality.

One might question the reliability of our somewhat undisciplined philosophical approach. Can we generalize about the nature of chronic pain by reflecting on one single case? Almost certainly not. Are a philosopher's first-person reflections on the experience of chronic pain, mediated by occasional, informal conversations with another philosopher, likely to be reliable? Possibly not. Nevertheless, such exercises can draw attention to aspects of human experience that are more usually not so conspicuous. What we gain are philosophical possibilities that might otherwise have evaded explicit consideration. Once these possibilities have been brought to light and developed into explicit philosophical claims, they can then be defended on independent grounds, as they are here. Our conclusions do not concern "the experience of pain" or even "the experience of chronic pain." After all, pain experiences are highly diverse. Rather, we reflect upon *an experience of pain* in order to develop and defend claims about human experience and interpersonal relations that have much broader applicability.

PAIN

Patient file: Patient (male, married, three children under twelve years old, professor for philosophy of science at the University of Cambridge); since spring 2008 frequently suffers from pain in the right upper jaw. On the "numerical rating scale" (NRS) for pain intensity (from 1 to 10): 5–6. Dull pain. In early 2008 root-canal treatment of the penultimate tooth (in the right upper jaw). The tooth is capped with a dental crown. Pain returns irregularly. Since 2009 patient lives in Vienna (and works for the University of Vienna). In 2012 dentist A diagnoses malocclusion (bad bite), which she seeks to correct by fitting fixed braces. NRS 7. Dull and stinging pain. The third-to-last tooth is extracted in the summer of 2013. Increased pain in the area of fourth-to-last tooth. Extracted in February 2014. Subsequently increased pain in the fifth-to-last tooth as well as in the areas of previous extractions. Increasing distress.

January 2014: Dentist A presents the case of the patient at an international conference as a success-story of orthodontics. She declares the pain situation to be "beyond the realm of dentistry." Transferral to kinesiologist (practitioner of a form of alternative therapy focused on bodily movement).

March 2014: Patient changes dentist and begins treatment in dental clinic X. Dentist B extracts the fifth-to-last tooth. NRS 8 in the resulting gap and around the sixth-to-last tooth. Patient continues to work. Insomnia, nausea. Patient begins treatment with pain therapist 1. Prescription of antidepressant and neuropathic drugs.

April 2014: Oral surgeon α of dental clinic X diagnoses putrescent nerve material in the jawbone. First jawbone operation.

May–June 2014: Three further jawbone operations to remove putrescent nerve material. NRS 8–9. Patient unable to work. Weight loss from 85 to under 70 kilograms.

July 2014: Dizzy spells and nausea. Admission to the oral surgery division of Vienna's Central Hospital against the will of the head of department, oral surgeon β. Extraction of samples from the jawbone. β wants to cut the facial nerve to reduce pain level. Patient resists.

August 2014: MRI of the head; diagnosis: "unremarkable." Negative side effects of the neuropathic drugs. Frequent spells of dizziness and disorientation. Feelings of loss of control. Depression. Diagnoses based on analysis of the jawbone samples: chronic jawbone infection. Patient is prescribed high doses of antibiotics. Start of an acupuncture treatment. No improvement.

September 2014: Patient put on waiting list for pain therapy in Vienna's Central Hospital. On his way home, patient prevents the suicide of a psychiatric patient who had just been released. The specialist for infectious diseases refers patient back to the oral surgery division. Patient begins private treatment with pain therapist 2. The latter prescribes opiates, neuropathic, and other pain killers. Patient takes about twenty-five different pills per day. Pain therapist 2 prescribes increasing doses of opiates. Depression and suicidal thoughts.

October 2014: Patient begins treatment with dentist C and oral surgeon γ. C wants to do a further jawbone operation. γ is unsure. Pain therapist 2 is opposed.

November 2014: Patient is admitted to the psychiatric ward of Vienna's Central Hospital. Against medical advice he leaves again the next day in order to discuss relativism with the philosopher Paul Boghossian. Patient decides to start afresh. He changes to pain therapist 3, and is helped by a psychiatrist, a psychologist, and a physiotherapist. He stops taking drugs that can cause suicidal thoughts. He attempts to start living positively with pain. NRS recedes slowly to 5–6. Clear improvement of mental balance.

December 2014: Admission to Vienna's Central Hospital with (life-threatening) epiglottitis. No connection with the jawbone problems. Discharge one week later.

Summary: Since that time, a chronic pain patient. NRS 3–8; the type of pain varies. Causes of the pain still unknown. Mentally stable. Since 2015, able to work. Positive attitude. Frequently happy.

IMAGES OF PAIN

The medical taxonomy of pain is crude: On the NRS scale from 1 to 10, what is the intensity of pain? Is the pain drilling, dull, or stabbing? And how often does it occur? Someone who knows the answers to these questions does not yet understand the first thing about strong chronic pains.

In my "annus horribilis," 2014, I experienced my chronic jawbone pains as both extremely concrete and highly abstract. "Extremely concrete" since I could always tell, with great accuracy, where exactly it hurt the most. "Highly abstract" since my whole self-image and *Weltbild* had acquired the modality of pain. I was shackled inside my pain as if it were a straitjacket; and I was unable to relate cognitively or emotionally to anything without at the same time experiencing and thinking of myself as a sufferer. This applied first and foremost to my relationships with others. I categorized them into two groups: those who supported me, and those who weren't interested. (Strangely enough, this dichotomy did not coincide with the distinction between "friends" and "mere acquaintances.") Put differently, the world of the chronic pain patient differs from the world of the person free of pain. Many certainties of the healthy world are suspended. And there are new, terrible, certainties: "I will not be able to stand this for much longer"; "I will never be free of this pain again"; "I am desperate"; "Life continues without me."

Psychologically, pain is most grueling when, in addition to being chronic and strong, it is also *undiagnosed* or perhaps even *undiagnosable*. (The medical euphemism for "undiagnosable" is "atypical." This semantic shift would be worth a separate investigation.) The undiagnosed and atypical pain is an invisible opponent whose next step is unpredictable. And all is possible: perhaps it is a sign of deadly disease, perhaps "merely" psychosomatic. Dentist B thought a cancer diagnosis was a near-certainty; a "life-coach" suspected it was either the pain of parting (from Cambridge) or due to facial tension caused by excessive "wearing of masks" in social interactions; a psychotherapist saw as the cause the love toward my father—in World War II, shrapnel wounded him in the exact same spot. Who knows, maybe all of these causes are relevant. Perhaps the wisest course of action would be to give up all hope of a definitive diagnosis. But hope springs eternal: Even today there is a naïve voice inside me that counts on, one day, getting the liberating truth: "the mother of a diagnoses," the diagnosis that brings the end to the sheer endless diagnostic efforts.

Pain is painful not least because, from childhood onward, we associate it with punishment. In 2014, this association led me to see my pain frequently in the context of guilt and failure. Did I wait too long before I went to the dentist? Did I properly follow the advice of the doctors? Was the pain the punishment for more general wrongdoing? What or who was the punishing authority? Perhaps even a god?—There are no limits to the feelings of guilt of the patient with atypical, chronic, and strong pains.

IMAGES OF MEDICAL DOCTORS

Before the onset of my jawbone pains, I spontaneously perceived medical doctors as specialists whose time one "rents" for them to repair—efficiently and without personal attachment—breakdowns in one's body. I trusted doctors when I had reason to assume that they would be the most suitable "craftsmen" for the given damage.

The distress of strong, chronic pain changed my relationship with, and trust in, doctors completely. This had different causes. To begin with, I spontaneously conceived of the relationship in terms of moral categories. In situations of acute and serious plight, we normally assume that any person who (alone) is able to help will do so immediately and fully. Imagine, for example, that you have medical knowledge and witness a traffic accident with seriously injured people. There would be no question concerning your moral obligation to help. And this obligation would overrule whatever else you had planned to do with your time. In 2014, I initially saw my relationships with dentists, oral surgeons, and pain therapist in analogous fashion.

Compared with the seriously injured in a traffic accident, a further consideration also seemed pressing: to wit, the fact that I had entrusted myself to the doctor and that I had told them about my distress and worries. In everyday life, we do this only with our spouses or partners, with close friends and relatives. Indeed, it is often precisely the entrusting of such plights that constitutes and reconstitutes the intimacy of a relationship. Alas, this too was a problematic analogy. It seduced me into thinking my openness toward the doctors had gained me the entitlement to receive attention beyond the minimum level of medical treatment—two to five minutes in the surgery of the jawbone specialists at Vienna's Central Hospital.

But there was also a third mistake, and it was the worst. The first two were in any case part of the third. I am referring to what one might call "self-infantilization." When the distress peaked, I tended to fall back into infantile forms of feeling and thinking. Demoralizing long-term pain and increasing doses of opiates made it impossible for me to think clearly: my higher—self-reflective and self-corrective—functions became more and more restricted. This created an area for archaic, primitive, infantile cognitive, and emotional patterns. It led me to see the medical doctor as a father figure, and to build up expectations that only a father could possibly have fulfilled. The fear of losing the doctor—what will I do if he refuses to treat me any longer?—also had irrational elements that are best explained on the basis of the equation of the doctor with a parent. (Note in passing that this fear is nourished by the ways in which all too many doctors signal their impatience with patients who suffer from complicated, hard-to-diagnose, and hard-to-treat illnesses.)

I doubt that I alone suffered from the cognitive and emotional patterns relating to these projections. At least I see many parallels in the texts of pain patients on the Internet. At the same time, it has become increasingly clear to me—now that the *annus horribilis* has passed—that no doctor can fulfill the expectations I had built up. Given dozens of distressed patients with similar entitlements to help, the doctor cannot give any one of them the amount of time they demand in their depressive moods. Not to forget that doctors have a life of their own, whatever our chronic pains might happen to be.

The doctor thus needs strategies and tactics in order to block or therapeutically use the mentioned projections. Unfortunately, my experiences of 2014 have led me to suspect that many doctors approach this difficult task no less unreflectively and no less inappropriately than I approached my role as a chronic pain patient. In what follows, I shall propose—*sine ira et studio*—the sketch of an analysis of medical defense tactics. I shall be as direct and blunt as I was when writing about myself.

The first common way in which doctors block patients' projections is by using a strictly ritualized form of communication that leaves no space for suffering and despair. Pain therapist 2 confined the communication to checking the pain table: Where is the pain on the scale from 1 to 10? Is it dull, stabbing, or drilling? And are there variations in these two dimensions? That was it. In order to nevertheless fill the time slot of forty-five minutes, and thus to justify the price of €220, he then needed thirty minutes for issuing the prescription and the bill. He did this with an expensive, thick, and shiny fountain pen. And he wrote so slowly and calligraphically that producing the two documents took forever. During this important work one was not allowed to speak. Whatever time remained was then used for the complex search for a new appointment.

The above already identifies the main motif in all strategies for preventing patient projections: establishing a clear difference in authority between patient and doctor. (It does not make a difference if the patient is a university professor.) The doctor forces the patient into the role of a subordinate or supplicant. This connects with, and re-enforces, the begging attitude of the self-infantilized patient. It is not difficult to establish the claim to authority vis-à-vis a distressed pain patient: Whatever ability to resist the patient might have had, it has been reduced to a minimum by high doses of drugs—opiates, neuro- and psychopathic medications—as well as the fear of losing the doctor.

The methods for establishing the power differential are sometimes rough. For instance, one does not shake hands when the patient comes in; one does not talk *with* the patient, one talks *about* the patient with the nurse; one interrupts the patient or forbids the patient to speak; one shouts at the patient or declares the therapies of other doctors to be useless. In the surgery of the oral surgeons in Vienna's Central Hospital, such methods are the norm. Especially degrading was the order to walk on my own from the oral-surgery ward to the operating theater, dressed only in a much-too-short nightdress. To cover my genitals I had to pull the gown down with both hands and lean forward.

Or, when I arrived at the Central Hospital with epiglottitis, I learnt only from the phone call between the doctor and the ward that my condition was life-threatening. Or, when I told pain therapist 2, despite his unwillingness to listen, that I was suffering from suicidal thoughts, and when I asked him about psychological help, he replied: "Listen man: you have to get over it. Without that psychological nonsense. Don't be a chicken." It was the first and only time since my childhood that I let anyone talk to me in this way.

I don't want to be misunderstood: I do not regard these patterns of behavior as individual, personal, moral failures. We know from the classic social-psychological studies by Milgram and Zimbardo how easy it is for all of us to suppress and humiliate others when the situation invites this behavior, and when there are no controls. And we should not forget that the role of the unrestricted authority makes it easy for the doctors to convince the patient to accept uncomfortable but potentially effective forms of therapy.

The Escape: It is the essence of authority not to tolerate too much competition. This rule also applies to doctors: hence the many negative remarks about their colleagues and other specialities. And yet, since almost all doctors engage in this practice, and since even the pharmacists act likewise, the long-suffering patient sooner or later confronts a massive cognitive, emotional, and social dissonance. Since the patient usually needs more than one doctor—in my case, for instance, a dentist, an oral surgeon, and a pain therapist—and since they offer different, incompatible diagnoses and therapies, the patient eventually no longer knows whom to believe and trust.[1]

This is not a positive development for the patient. The self-infantilization, the transfer of responsibility and decision making to the doctor, also has a calming and consoling side to it. Once one is confronted with more and more competing medical claims to authority, one suddenly has to make one's own decisions again. And this—at least in my case—at a point in time when my thinking had been shackled by many years of strong pains and by opiates; at a point in time when I could not tell whether my attempt to think would result in rational plans or in illusions. I was "condemned to be free"; I had to choose. Even a patient with thirty years of work in the philosophy of science can be overwhelmed by this situation. I can easily imagine patients unable to meet this challenge, and despairing.

I came close to this hell. But at least I still had the inner strength to go voluntarily to the psychiatric ward in the Central Hospital in order to gain control over my depression and suicidal thoughts. And then I got lucky: that sleepless night in the four-bed room on the psychiatric ward, surrounded by loudly snoring, crying, and groaning men, men whom I could still somehow help with consoling words. This night generated in me a feeling of defiance, a last great rearing up of my desire to determine my own fate. All the better that on the next day I had the chance to discuss relativism with Paul Boghossian.

I fired all my doctors and put together a new team according to my own criteria. It helped me to escape the role of the victim and learn how to live with pain. The pain is still there, chronically; but it no longer stands between me and a good life; it is a hurdle that I have to surpass as part of my daily duties. But only a part of my daily duties. And, fortunately, my life consists of a lot more than just duties.

I have here confined myself to speaking about the phenomenology of pain and my interactions with doctors. But, of course, there is so much more to talk about. Especially about my wife and children who were reason enough not to give up, even in greatest despair, and who helped me, over many months, in endless ways. And about the friends and colleagues whose encouragement and support was so important. But they know what they have meant to me and will mean to me in the future. Even without a talk.

THE UNPLEASANTNESS OF PAIN

We now turn from MK's first-person report to our more systematic attempts to make sense of some of its details. We will begin by asking what, exactly, it is about (chronic) pain that makes it so unpleasant.

To understand the nature of chronic pain, one approach is to start by formulating a more general account of pain, which can then be refined. Pain either *is* or at least *includes* a kind of sensory experience: A pain in one's jaw involves a distinctive type of sensation, emanating from a bodily location. Philosophers have offered various conflicting accounts of what this sensation consists of. There is disagreement over whether it is representational and, if so, what it represents; whether its nature is exhausted by representational properties; whether it is partly or wholly perceptual in nature; and which theory of perception might be best placed to accommodate it (e.g., Aydede 2005). Although one could get dragged into these debates, perhaps never to return, they can be avoided for current purposes. While we accept that pain has a sensory component, we will remain agnostic about its specific nature. Of more interest to us are distinctions that have been drawn between the sensory, affective, and motivational constituents of pain. There is compelling evidence that these can come apart in various ways. For instance, a condition called "pain asymbolia" is said to involve pain-sensation but without any sense of unpleasantness or any motivation to avoid or seek relief from pain. Conversely, the characteristic feeling of unpleasantness and associated behavioral tendencies can occur without pain-sensation (Grahek 2007; Corns 2014b).

Note, moreover, that the unpleasantness of pain is not reducible to an inclination to avoid or escape something, and that pain need not have motivational force. As Bain (2013) observes, the unpleasantness of pain "rationalizes" action, whereas behavioral tendencies do not, suggesting that the two are distinct. Complementary empirical evidence seems to show that one can dislike one's pain without seeking avoidance or relief. According to Grahek (2007, 39), only pain asymbolia involves complete retention of pain-sensation with complete loss of affective response and motivational tendencies. Certain other cases that are described in terms of "pain without unpleasantness" actually involve finding the pain disagreeable but not feeling inclined to act upon it in any way.

It is doubtful that any one ingredient is *sufficient* for pain. Grahek refers to sensation without affect/motivation as "pain without painfulness" and to affect/motivation without pain-sensation as "painfulness without pain." Given this terminological choice, one might take it that sensation alone suffices for "pain." However, he also emphasizes that it bears little resemblance to what we would ordinarily call pain: it "becomes a blunt, inert sensation, with no power to galvanize the mind and body for fight or flight" (Grahek 2007, 73). Perhaps pain-sensation is at least *necessary*, but even that much is debatable. Corns (2015) considers what is sometimes referred to as "social pain," where emotional distress arises due to a change of interpersonal circumstances, without any pain-sensation. There are, she suggests, insufficient grounds for maintaining that this really does constitute *pain*. After all, unpleasantness without pain-sensation does not, in other contexts, add up to pain. For instance, a horrible taste in one's mouth is not literally "painful." In contrast, Radden (2009, 111) does allow for "pain and suffering that is nonlocalized and nonsensory." One option is to endorse a pluralistic account, according to which pain can involve various different components, none of which are necessary or sufficient (Corns 2014a). Here, we take it that what is referred to as "pain," in everyday, scientific, and medical contexts, ordinarily encompasses sensory, affective, and motivational aspects of experience, and that this applies equally to chronic pain. Consistent with this, we adopt an inclusive conception of chronic pain.

Of course, chronic pain also has more specific properties. Defined minimally, it is a pain that endures for a prolonged period. In addition to this, it is often taken to have no identifiable biological cause or a biologically inappropriate cause. Chronic pain is also likely to have distinctive affective and motivational properties, given the uncertainty over when or even whether it will end, along with an inability to find long-term relief. In what follows, we seek to show how these properties are inextricable from one's expectations concerning other people.

One interesting feature of MK's experience is that, over time, he learned not to expect that the pain-sensation would ever change. Indeed, the first words of his most recent (extremely helpful) pain therapist were: "Let us start from the premise that you will always have this pain; and now let us see how we can find a way for you to live happily." What the therapist was proposing involved separating the pain-sensation from the affective-motivational dimensions to which it had previously been tightly linked. Consistent with this, MK's coping strategy now is not to "care" too much about the pain-sensation. Learning this strategy meant of course unlearning a web of associations that comes naturally to all of us, which link pain to depressive moods, withdrawal, (self-)pity, and anger.

All of this suggests that the painfulness or distress of pain can be manipulated, at least to some extent, by explicit strategies involving reappraisal and/or by indirect manipulation of emotional feeling (e.g., by listening to music and playing musical instruments, in MK's case). Hence an experience of suffering is not insulated from one's wider cognitive repertoire. That view is consistent with empirical research on pain. As Radden (2009, 115) observes, pain research has increasingly come to recognize that "all pain is less simple, more cognitively mediated, and thus more *like an emotion* than had previously been supposed." Pain experiences, she adds, are thus shaped by "memory, personal and social attitudes, role expectations, and life experience, as well as mental and emotional health and bodily traits." The inclusion of such factors further indicates that experiences of pain are susceptible to *social* and *cultural* influences.[2]

Regardless of how pain might be socially shaped, regulated, and interpreted, some of our readers might still think of its unpleasantness as an experiential quality that is *constitutively* independent of interpersonal and social relations. However, MK's experience suggests otherwise. Recall from "Pain," earlier, how MK ran from dentist to dentist, oral surgeon to oral surgeon, pain therapist to pain therapist, and life coach to psychiatrist in order to get help; and how the level of his suffering grew steadily in parallel to the number of disappointed promises, false diagnoses, and mistaken therapies and interventions.

As this sequence of events illustrates, the distress of chronic pain is tied up with a nonlocalized feeling of helplessness. Central to this feeling is what we might call a *style of anticipation*—one expects more pain; one expects no relief from it; and this impacts on what one expects from the world more generally. The phenomenologist and psychiatrist Eugène Minkowski (1970, 87–89) remarks that, in the realm of human experience, activity is not opposed to mere passivity but to expectation, to waiting. In our goal-directed interactions with the world, we are solicited to act by our surroundings and drawn in by them. When we wait for something to happen, our activities are suspended, something that he associates with a form of "anguish." Instead of actively engaging with the future, moving toward it, "I feel, in an immediate way, the future come toward me in all its impetuousness." Minkowski also observes that this form of expectation is structurally similar to an experience of "sensory pain." Elsewhere, he further suggests that a shift from active engagement toward passive expectation is inseparable from the phenomenology of sensory pain:

> Intrinsically bound up in pain is the feeling of some external force acting upon us to which we are compelled to submit. Seen in this light, pain evidently opposes the expansive tendency of our personal impetus; we can no longer turn ourselves outward, nor do we try to leave our personal stamp on the external world. Instead, we let the world, in all its impetuousness, come to us, making us suffer. Thus, pain is also an attitude toward the environment. (Minkowski 1958, 134)

The interesting point here is not simply that pain is often attributed to a specific physical cause, one that acts upon us. Rather, it is that pain experience includes the predominance of a certain kind of passive expectation. This aspect of pain is not localized—pain alters an overarching orientation toward the future; it tips the balance from activity toward expectation. The unpleasantness of pain is thus constituted, at least in part, by a certain way of anticipating.

Of course, pain's unpleasantness varies considerably (both quantitatively and qualitatively), as does the extent to which it includes feelings of helplessness and anxiety. Nevertheless, as MK's experience suggests, this kind of anticipatory structure is a conspicuous feature of at least some pain experiences. Remember his "certainties": "I will not be able to stand this for much longer"; "I will never be free of this pain again"; "I am desperate"; "Life continues without me."

Consider also the effects of prefrontal lobotomy, when used as a treatment for chronic pain. Although it is sometimes said that the outcome is pain without distress, closer scrutiny suggests that lobotomized patients still find pain stimuli noxious and still seek relief from episodic pain. Their indifference is specific to enduring forms of pain. But, even here, the pain still feels unpleasant. What is lacking is any distress over what is coming next—a kind of anxious anticipation and associated helplessness that more usually characterizes chronic pain. In contrast to the experiences of these patients, the distressing quality of chronic pain more usually includes a sense of "its lasting meaning or significance" (Grahek 2007, 135–137).[3] What MK's coping strategy seeks to achieve is similar in one important respect: It also involves decoupling pain-sensations from a certain kind of anticipatory structure.

Once it is acknowledged that chronic pain can have an anticipatory structure, one that is inseparable from the experience of distress, we can come to see why the phenomenology of chronic pain *must* be bound up to some extent with interpersonal relations and expectations.

TRUST, DOUBT, AND HELPLESSNESS

Havi Carel (2013b) has proposed that experiences of serious illness centrally involve a loss of "bodily certainty," something that is replaced by "bodily doubt." This, we suggest, provides a helpful way of thinking about the interpersonal and social dimensions of chronic pain. Ordinarily, Carel says, people go about their business with a sense of pre-reflective certainty regarding their bodily abilities and the continuation of their bodily functions. It is not a matter of reflectively or pre-reflectively endorsing however many propositions about what one's body does, can do, and will continue to do. Rather, it consists in a habitual, bodily, practical confidence that could equally be described as a kind of *feeling*: a "feeling of possibility, openness, and ability that characterizes routine and familiar actions" (2013b, 181). What Carel calls "bodily doubt" involves losing this habitual certainty, in a way that can vary in degree and scope. With a loss of bodily certainty, one's body becomes conspicuous, problematic, and one's practical performances are monitored carefully, their outcomes no longer taken for granted. Felt doubt of this kind thus involves a pervasive sense of anxious uncertainty and helplessness: "The natural confidence in her bodily abilities is displaced by a feeling of helplessness, alarm, and distrust in her body" (Carel 2013b, 184).[4] Although bodily doubt need not be associated specifically with pain, what we have said so far implies that where there is both bodily doubt and pain, the former can contribute to the latter. Chronic pain, as we have seen, can similarly include a sense of anxiety and helplessness—a style of anticipation that interferes with habitual, practical, bodily immersion in one's surroundings.

The concepts of certainty, doubt, and distrust are helpful to us here because they make salient the affinity between bodily experience and our relations with other people. Indeed, we suggest that the predominance of bodily doubt is dependent, to some degree, on one's trusting relations with other people. The style of anticipation that permeates chronic pain can be characterized in terms of propositions such as "this will never cease"; "nothing can be done to stop this"; "there is nowhere else to turn"; "the world offers nothing else"; "there is even worse to come." While this amounts to an erosion of trust in one's own body, it equally implies an erosion of trust within the interpersonal sphere. More usually, we depend on others to diagnose and treat medical conditions, to manage pain, to sustain a sense that there remain alternative possibilities, that something can be done, that there is something or someone to fall back on. Propositions such as "nothing can be done to stop this" are incompatible with propositions such as "someone can help me." Only when the latter is negated can the former be accepted.

The point applies equally to modes of non-propositional, affective anticipation. Trust in another person need not involve explicitly entertaining various propositions. Interpersonal encounters are also shaped and regulated by more inchoate sets of expectations, embedded in one's various practices, which involve taking for granted that others are well-meaning, capable, qualified, and so forth. When interacting with a given individual, there might be a general feeling of discomfort and suspicion. Alternatively, and more usually, interactions are permeated by a sense of confidence or ease, which might relate to a specific problem/subject matter or apply more generally. This contrast can apply not only to our relations with specific individuals but also to our relations with those in certain professions or roles, to whole institutions, and even to other people in general.

As with bodily trust or "certainty," a sense of what other people have to offer is, in many circumstances, pre-reflective and taken for granted. Thus, when it is lost, there is similarly a kind of bewilderment. What is overturned is not one or more contestable propositions but something presupposed by all of one's experiences, thoughts, and activities, something that one took as given. It is difficult to find a philosophical terminology that allows us to speak about this thick and multifaceted layer of "certainties." One possible source is Ludwig Wittgenstein's posthumously published *On Certainty* (1975), assembled from his last notebooks. Here, Wittgenstein distinguishes between various such certainties: some are propositional; some are "animal" or pre-propositional; some concern other people; some concern oneself and one's body. These certainties are closely connected; sometimes the removal of one of them can bring down the whole structure. Successful communication presupposes that most of the certainties are shared. Accordingly, Kusch (2017) has analyzed the "*Sprachnot*" (linguistic despair) of Holocaust survivors in reporting their horrendous experiences as due to the difficulty of communicating a situation in which so many of our ordinary certainties are destroyed. Although the situation of the chronic-pain patient in no way compares to the horrors these people struggle to describe, communicating one's predicament can sometimes feel difficult for (distantly) similar reasons.

The sudden destruction of "trust in the world" has been captured with unforgettable precision by Jean Améry (1999, 28), in his account of his arrest and torture by the Gestapo. He remarks on how, with the "very first blow," one loses "trust in the world." This loss is attributable, in part, to others failing to respect one's bodily integrity in a way that can never be taken for granted again. More importantly, though, there is a subversion of something more usually assumed. Ordinarily, when we are injured, we cry out to others for help. In so doing, we anticipate that they will help. We do not ordinarily have to think about this; we reach out without thinking, without doubting.

The torture victim is faced with something that runs contrary to an engrained system of anticipation. The other person is herself the agent of harm, and there is nobody else one can call to:

> Even on the battlefield, the Red Cross ambulances find their way to the wounded man. In almost all situations in life where there is bodily injury there is also the expectation of help; the former is compensated by the latter. But with the first blow from a policeman's fist, against which there can be no defence and which no helping hand will ward off, a part of our life ends and it can never be revived. (Améry 1999, 29)

To reiterate, we do not mean to compare the doctor–patient relationship with the torturer–prisoner interaction. Instead, we draw on Améry's example to further illustrate how interpersonal encounters usually involve certain expectations, of a kind that we might call "trusting." Loss of these expectations, in various different contexts, can be disorientating and profoundly challenging. Furthermore, the effects inevitably extend beyond the interpersonal domain. In MK's case, loss of trust in the medical profession was inextricable from loss of bodily trust and thus from the unpleasantness of chronic pain. The relevant process can occur gradually, as when one is faced with conflicting opinions and diagnoses, unhelpful attitudes, and lack of empathy, or it might occur more quickly. But, regardless of the precise trajectory, we maintain that a sense of one's pain as inescapable, a sense of dread and helplessness, and an inability to effectively act upon one's situation are all inseparable from a loss of certain interpersonal possibilities: "They" are not to be trusted; nothing they can do will help; I cannot call on anyone else and so there is nothing to be done.[5]

Loss of interpersonal trust (of a kind that varies in degree and scope) is thus inseparable from the distressing nature of one's pain, from a sense of helplessness and anxiety. This aspect of pain is nonlocalized—it permeates every aspect of the experienced world. To return to Minkowski, we ordinarily experience our surroundings in terms of various kinds of significant possibility, some of which solicit activities and draw us in. This kind of engagement is balanced by expectation, waiting. Chronic pain involves a pervasive disengagement from the social world and, with it, an alteration of the balance between engagement and expectation. Instead of anticipating the practically significant possibilities offered by one's meaningful surroundings, one anticipates more pain and, with this, one's continuing helplessness.

Our reflections on the loss of trust perhaps also help to make sense of MK's onetime strategy of "self-infantilization." After all, this centrally involved a sense of having lost control of his life. One might think that it originated in a loss of trust in his *own* previously taken-for-granted ability to reason clearly and make reasonable decisions, rather than in a loss of interpersonal trust. But such abilities cannot be extricated from their wider, interpersonal context. What MK also lost (at least when it came to understanding and managing his chronic pain) was a way of engaging with and relying on the judgments of others that confident practical decision-making more usually presupposes. However, self-infantilization is not just a *loss* of ordinary certainties. It is also the attempt to fall back on something else, perhaps on the vaguely remembered certainties of one's childhood. The certainty "I am a reasonable person, able to make the right decisions for my own life" is partially overwritten by the child(ish) certainty "I am a helpless creature but there are good people, parents, who will do everything they can to protect me from misfortunes." The transition between them is perhaps not unlike the scenario where someone eventually falls to the floor and begs a tormentor for mercy, having exhausted all other avenues of persuasion and been left with no other resources to draw on. Of course, the attempt is unlikely to succeed, since reality does not readily comply; although doctors might sometimes intentionally or unwittingly encourage the childish attitude (say, by chastising or consoling the patient in parent-like manner), they do not ultimately act like good parents. The failure of self-infantilization then further exacerbates the sense of distrust, helplessness, and abandonment in which it originated—"even now you can't, or won't, help me."

THE TWO-SIDEDNESS OF EMOTIONAL INTENTIONALITY

To conclude, we want to offer a Heideggerian vocabulary to explicate the following passage from "Pain":

> I experienced my chronic jawbone pains as both extremely concrete and highly abstract. "Extremely concrete" since I could always tell, with great accuracy, where exactly it hurt the most. "Highly abstract" since my whole self-image and *Weltbild* had acquired the modality of pain. I was shackled inside my pain as if it were a straitjacket; and I was unable to relate cognitively or emotionally to anything without, at the same time, experiencing and thinking of myself as a sufferer.

The all-enveloping character of certain pain experiences is philosophically puzzling. We have attributed it to the manner in which pain alters the significance of the surrounding world, including the interpersonal domain, something that involves a pervasive sense of disengagement. Pain, or at least the affective-motivational aspect of pain, can thus resemble what Heidegger, in *Being and Time*, refers to as a "mood" (*Stimmung*). According to

Heidegger, we do not first of all find ourselves situated in a world and only afterward impose a superficial, subjective coloring upon it in the guise of a mood. Instead, he claims, it is only through one or another mood that we find ourselves situated in a world at all: *"The mood has already disclosed, in every case, Being-in-the-world as a whole, and makes it possible first of all to direct oneself towards something"* (Heidegger 1962, §29, 176). In other words, a mood—in this sense of the term—is presupposed by intentionally directed experiences and thoughts with one or another content, such as thinking about *p* or seeing *q*. And it is not simply an intentional experience with a very wide-ranging content, such as being in a bad mood about one's life. Rather, moods constitute a sense of the kinds of significant possibilities that the world incorporates, something that intentional states with whatever content take for granted. For instance, in order to find something threatening, one must be open to the possibility of threat and, in order to hope for something, one must be open to the possibility of things changing in a good way. A mood constitutes an openness to certain kinds of possibilities and not others. For instance, a mood of profound despair involves lacking any sense that anything could ever change for the better; the world is bereft of that kind of possibility (Ratcliffe 2013). Heidegger refers to "finding oneself in the world through one or another mood" as *Befindlichkeit*. Following Joan Stambaugh, we translate this as "attunement" (Heidegger 1996).

One could thus say that chronic pain consists of, or is at least integral to, a Heideggerian "mood" or "mode of attunement." However, it is here that we encounter a problem. Heidegger appears to endorse a distinction between intentionally directed experiences and the more enveloping phenomenological role of moods. And many other philosophers assume a similar distinction. Even those who construe moods as intentional states with very general objects endorse a distinction between specifically focused emotions and more encompassing moods. However, chronic pain—it seems—is both at the same time. MK's pain was (and still is) located quite specifically in his jaw. Regardless of which ingredients of pain are admitted as intentional and which are not, the object of distress was clearly an apparent condition *of the jaw*. At the same time, however, this amounted to a way of Being-in-the-world, characterized by helplessness, anxious anticipation, and practical disengagement.[6]

Others have also emphasized how pain can come to engulf a world. In an influential discussion, Elaine Scarry (1985, 35) writes that intense pain "destroys a person's self and world, a destruction experienced spatially as either the contraction of the universe down to the immediate vicinity of the body or as the body swelling to fill the entire universe."[7] Now, it could be that the kind of pain she is addressing is nonlocalized—one does not feel it as arising in a specific part of one's body. However, this does not apply to MK's jaw pain. It seems plausible to us that many other pain experiences (and not just experiences of chronic pain) share this same two-sidedness; they are experienced as located in a particular part of one's body but also permeate the world in which one's body is situated. For instance, Jonathan Cole (2004) offers an intriguing description of what he experienced after being injected in the arm with pepper extract under experimental conditions, having been told (correctly) that the ensuing pain would last for around sixteen minutes:

> I could think of little but the pain . . . my pain was difficult to localize; it was out there and below me, though I was no longer sure quite what that meant. It filled my arm, my body, and my sense of self. Pain destroyed my perspective and even my perception of me. . . . In an existential way, the pain removed my feeling of being embodied; I just had pain. My perception of a shaped arm and hand was absent, overwhelmed and driven from me by the pain. I could think of nothing. (Cole 2004, 7–8)

Although Cole writes that the pain was "difficult to localize," he does not mean by this that it was distributed evenly throughout his body. What he is saying is that the pain in his arm was so intense that it eroded a wider sense of localization, changing—albeit briefly—how he experienced his arm, his body as a whole, and his relationship to the surrounding world. Again, it seems that a pain can have a felt location and yet be diffuse and all-pervasive.

A simple response is to reiterate that pain has different components. While the sensation is localized, the associated affective-motivational tendencies are more diffuse. Now, one cannot infer, on the basis that two physiological processes are dissociable, that an associated experience itself has "components", however an "experiential component" might be conceived of. And, even if one could, it is not merely the pain-sensation that has an apparent location. The associated distress has the jaw as its *object*: the jaw is experienced *as* the source of distress. And this same experience of emotional distress also amounts to an altered way of inhabiting the world. It can be added that the same applies to certain profound and sometimes long-term emotions, thus ruling out an explanation in terms of contingently associated, localized sensations. For instance, the object of profound grief is the loss of something quite specific (a particular person and/or particular relationship). But it also amounts to a profound disturbance of one's wider experiential world (Ratcliffe 2017). Nevertheless, the two-sidedness of affective intentionality is especially salient in the case of pain. The pain is *right there*, in the jaw, but it is also the shape of the world one inhabits, within which one has a jaw.

What might Heidegger say about this? His discussion of the "mood" of fear is of particular interest. Even though Heidegger appears to insist that moods do not have specific objects, he is also adamant that fear is a mood. And he is not just referring to *fear of nothing in particular*. He explicitly distinguishes between "that in the face of which we fear," "fearing," and "that about which we fear" (1962, §30, 179).[8] The first of these is the intentional object—whatever we are afraid of; the second is the attitude of fearing that object; and the third is what we are afraid for (ourselves). So how are we to reconcile the specificity of fear with the all-enveloping role of mood? Consider the following remark:

> Fearing, as a slumbering possibility of attuned Being-in-the-world (we call this possibility "fearfulness" ["Furchtsamkeit"]), has already disclosed the world, in that out of it something like the fearsome may come close. (1962, §30, 180)[9]

One way of interpreting this is to identify fear with a specifically directed intentional state and "fearfulness" with the "mood of fear." So fearfulness is an all-enveloping mood of a kind that incorporates the possibility of being threatened (among other types of possibility) and thus of fearing something. It is therefore a condition of possibility for an intentional attitude of fear (of the kind that arises within a pregiven world). This was the approach adopted by Ratcliffe (2013). However, we now want to consider an alternative interpretation, inspired by the reflections of this chapter. Instead of identifying fearfulness with a particular mood, we can conceive of fearfulness as *having the potential to enter into a mood of fear*. That potential is integral to our attunement, to our *being mooded at all* rather than to our being in a particular mood. And, when we actually *are* in a mood of fear, we do indeed encounter a specific intentional object as threatening. At the same time, however, we encounter it as threatening to ourselves and, by implication, to our world as a whole. Hence fear is at the same time both specifically directed and all-enveloping. This interpretation is consistent with the following:

> Whether privatively or positively, fearing about something, as being-afraid in the face of something, always discloses equiprimordially entities within-the-world and Being-in—the former as threatening and the latter as threatened. (1962, §30, 181)

So perhaps what Heidegger is trying to get at in appealing to "mood" is not something presupposed by intentionally directed emotion but, rather, an aspect of it that is often overlooked or misinterpreted: Encountering something in an emotional way is at the same time an experience of its destabilizing a wider system of salient possibilities—one's world. Similarly, when we suffer from chronic pain, what *pains us* might be a part of the body, but our *pain* is also the shape of our world; we are *in* pain.

It is doubtful, however, that this interpretation serves to accommodate all aspects of Heidegger's discussion. For instance, he writes that even what seems to be a mundane lack of mood is in fact a certain kind of inconspicuous mood (1962, §29, 173). And this is not something that can be ascribed a specific intentional object. There is also the question of what we say about "moods" such as *Angst*, which do not have an object *within* the world, even if we allow that they do have an "object" in the guise of Being-in-the-world itself.

Nevertheless, we suggest that one of the things Heidegger is trying to convey, at certain points in the text, is not something *underlying* emotional intentionality but something *integral* to it, something that passes unnoticed when we interpret intentionally directed emotional experience as arising against the backdrop of a stable world. In so doing, we fail to acknowledge the manner in which these experiences are also episodic or sustained disruptions of world. This, we have argued, applies to some forms of pain as well. It can be added that such experiences can therefore be very difficult to convey to others. The pain is located here, but it is also everywhere. It is a disturbance of the shared world that you continue to obliviously accept as a backdrop to your interpretation of my experience. We encounter here, once more, the "linguistic despair" of the pain patient.

ACKNOWLEDGMENTS

Martin Kusch thanks his doctors and his family. Matthew Ratcliffe thanks Jonathan Cole and Emily Hughes for helpful conversation, correspondence, and comments.

NOTES

1. We should emphasize that, in this chapter, we do not wish to make any claims concerning "how medical doctors in general behave," even if the scope of these generalizations is restricted to a particular cultural or social environment. What we present in this section is an account written by MK in a very different context. The various patterns of behavior he was faced with are likely to reflect wider practice to varying degrees.

2. See also Morris (2013) for a discussion of the cultural anthropology of chronic pain.

3. The claim that chronic pain incorporates a type of affective anticipation is consistent with various other discussions. For instance, Price (2000, 1769) identifies both "pain affect" (defined as the "moment-by-moment unpleasantness of pain, made up of emotional feelings that pertain to the present or short-term future, such as distress or fear") and also "secondary pain affect" (involving "emotional feelings directed toward long-term implications of having pain"). Complementing an emphasis on anticipation, Loeser and Melzack (1999, 1609) remark that "because chronic pain is unrelenting, it is likely that stress, environmental, and affective factors" are integral

to the "intensity and persistence of the pain." And, from a phenomenological perspective, Geniušas (2015) suggests that chronic pain involves a way of experiencing time—an anticipatory structure that offers only *more of the same*. This cuts one off from a meaningful past and a meaningful future, thus amounting to a sense of being stuck in an expansive present.

4. Various others have offered complementary descriptions of bodily conspicuousness. See, for example, Leder (1990). However, it should not be assumed that all experiences of bodily conspicuousness take this form.

5. While we have emphasized diffuse sets of expectations concerning other people, of a kind that could be expressed in terms of various different propositions, we acknowledge that more specific, explicit attitudes of trust and distrust also have an important role to play. In turning to the contents of these attitudes, we face difficult philosophical questions concerning (a) when, where, and why trust, distrust, or neither is appropriate or inappropriate and (b) which criteria should be employed to assess appropriateness (see, e.g., Hawley 2015). As acknowledged in "Pain," some of MK's initial expectations concerning the medical profession were misguided, as was the conduct of some of his doctors. The kind of pervasive, affective distrust that we have emphasized here could thus arise through various kinds of interpersonal and social process, involving—among other things—more localized attitudes of trust and distrust.

6. See Morris (2013) and Svenaeus (2015) for complementary accounts of how chronic pain can reshape what is offered by the surrounding world, in such a way that nothing is left undisturbed. As Svenaeus writes, "Pain is in everything, in the things one does, in the things one sees, hears, thinks, says, and so on. In this way pain, at least intense and chronic pain, is a *total* experience" (117).

7. Scarry's discussion is confused by the fact that she describes the effects of pain while at the same time focusing on the effects of pain inflicted under torture. So it is unclear what should be attributed to the pain and what is specific to torture. If what we have said about interpersonal experience, pain, and anticipation is correct, then it is not possible to separate the experience of pain from an experience of the interpersonal situation in which it arises.

8. The original German terms are *das Wovor der Furcht, das Fürchten*, and *das Worum der Furcht* (Heidegger 1993d, §30, 140).

9. We have altered the Macquarrie and Robinson translation from "Being-in-the-world in a state-of-mind" to "attuned Being-in-the-world," so as to better reflect the original German "schlummernde Möglichkeit des befindlichen In-der-Welt-seins" (1993d, §30, 141).

Chapter 6

On the *Autós* of Autonomous Decision Making: Intercorporeality, Temporality, and Enacted Normativities in Transplantation Medicine

Kristin Zeiler

Eric: It felt unreal, being back at [a previous] stage. It was a horror that one hopes one will never need to experience again.

Ann: It's this, it was so frustrating for us, when he was that damn sick. Eric and I said, "But hello, there are two kidneys here! Take them out! Take them now and put them in." The answer we got was that they [the medical professionals] couldn't do it. I couldn't take that. "No, unfortunately, we cannot do that, because he would not handle transplantation now. That's how ill he is." He would not handle the surgery.

—from "Moral Tales of Parental Living Kidney Donation"

Of course, you want to donate. This is what Eric and Ann, two of the interviewees in a project on parental live kidney donation in Sweden, emphasized (Zeiler et al. 2010, 228). Eric and Ann narrated their frustration when the medical examination procedures that all potential live kidney donors undergo dragged on. Their son Simon was eight years old when diagnosed with end-stage renal disease (ESRD).

For persons living with ESRD in Sweden, dialysis and kidney transplantation are the alternatives for saving or extending life.[1] In Sweden in 2014, 3,859 persons were undergoing dialysis, 437 persons were undergoing kidney transplantation, and 5,361 persons were living with a functioning transplanted kidney (Gabara et al. 2015). During recent years, around 40 percent of all kidney donations in Sweden come from live donors (SOU 2015, 84, 442).[2] For Simon, live kidney donation was the alternative that his parents described as what they wanted. However, while his father Eric started to undergo medical tests, he was eventually deemed medically unacceptable as a donor. At this stage, Simon's mother Ann started her evaluation procedure, but this coincided with their son's state of health deteriorating. The healthcare staff explained that they needed to postpone the transplantation even if Ann were to be accepted as a donor.

Eric's and Ann's narration brings out their thorough dissatisfaction when told that donation wasn't possible at this time. Their narration also offers a first possible angle on what will be called the "no-choice" dimension on the part of parents in studies of parental live kidney donation. This refers to the recurring parental description of this donation as self-evident, natural, and not a matter of choice (e.g., Burnell et al. 2015; Zeiler et al. 2010; Knibbe et al. 2007; Forsberg et al. 2004; Lennerling et al. 2003). Less commonly voiced or addressed in such studies are parental narratives of feeling relieved when not "needing" to donate, because one is not medically accepted as a donor, and being ashamed of this feeling (see, however, Zeiler et al. 2010).

Parental narrations about donation in no-choice terms have evoked concerns within some medical and bioethics literature. While acknowledging that parents may make decisions on the basis of a "volitional necessity," that is, when they act as they do because they feel that they cannot not do so (Frankfurt 1998), medical and bioethics literature discusses why someone doesn't experience or perceive there to be a choice in a particular situation, how to differentiate between situations where this should be a reason for concern and those in which it shouldn't, how to assess whether someone's consent to donate is pressured and, if this is the case, whether this should be an ethical concern (Biller-Andorno 2011; Spital 2005; Fujita et al. 2004; Forsberg et al. 2004).

This chapter brings phenomenological philosophy to these bioethics debates. It clarifies why both discussions of parental live kidney donation in terms of coercion (Kärrfelt et al. 2000) and as indicative of parents' autonomy (if it expresses what they want or who they want to be, see Crouch and Elliot 1999) fail to make sense of the complexity of the situation. Noting that the rich literature that explores relational aspects of subjectivity and conceptualizes autonomous individuals as making decisions situated within and dependent on particular social contexts (see Freeman 2011; Donchin 2001; Mackenzie and Stoljars 2000; Christman 2004; Friedman 1997) *still rarely addresses the role of the body*, the chapter addresses the role of embodiment for perception and choice.[3] It argues for the need to think through what may be labeled as the *autós* of autonomous decision making and, more precisely, the focus on one's *own* reflected choices that have come to characterize much autonomy discussions in bioethics, via phenomenological philosophy.

The chapter is divided into three parts. First, I make use of the phenomenological understanding of the intercorporeal self as being-in-the-world, in a discussion of how pain, fear, or bodily symptoms of ESRD that unfolds in the shared space of child and parent can shape both of them in relation to each other (c.f. Käll 2013; Zeiler 2014a), feed into their *bodily style of being-together*, and help form parents' perception of actions within reach, for them. Second, I shift the focus from the parent–child dyad to the larger semiotic–material context of hemodialysis and kidney transplantation in Sweden. This allows for an examination of embodied and enacted normativities, through an engagement with what Martin Gunnarson (2016, 128) has identified as a "dominant . . . orientation towards transplantation" in Sweden and Latvia. This second part also combines the discussion of an orientation toward transplantation with that of how norms about parenthood may be incorporated and excorporated into parents' lived bodies,[4] thereby making it possible to show why the no-choice theme in previous empirical work is understandable but more disconcerting than may first be assumed. Third, I argue that the acknowledgment of intercorporeal dimensions of bodily existence (argued for in Sections 2–5) and the role of orientation (argued for in Sections 6–7) demonstrates the need for a thinking-through of the *autós* of autonomous decision making, that is, the understanding of the "ownness" of this decision making, in ways other than those argued for in much of the bioethical autonomy and relational autonomy literature.

INTERCORPOREALITY AND THE CASE OF PARENTAL LIVE KIDNEY DONATION

Like many other parents, Eric and Ann described how they had followed the ups and downs of their son's state of health, accompanied him to various clinics, comforted him and tried to help him (Zeiler et al. 2010). Such narrations bring out the sociality of living together with someone with ESRD, in ways that don't start from the assumption that such sociality is primarily troubling. Rather, it situates their frustration. Phenomenological philosophy offers conceptual tools for the explication of such sociality.

Phenomenological accounts of embodiment typically start from a radical departure from mind *versus* body and subject *versus* object dichotomies, often along the lines of Maurice Merleau-Ponty's (1964, 1968, 2006) works. Subjectivity is understood as embodied and embedded in the world, the bodily subject exists neither only as consciousness nor as a thing, and the notion of the lived body is introduced to refer to the "intertwining" of body and world (Merleau-Ponty 1968, 138). My lived body, "to the extent that it is inseparable from a view of the world and is that view itself realized, is the condition of possibility" for me *and* a part of the world, oriented in and conditioned by it (Merleau-Ponty 2006, 388). The lived body is a lived relation to a world immersed in meaning, opened up to me through my bodily senses, and a site of self-becoming, "in which the interface with others—both objects and living beings—constructs a dynamic self in which abstract singularity plays no part" (Shildrick 2002,110).

Formulations such as these bring out an understanding of subjectivity as intersubjectively, and in other ways thoroughly relationally, structured. Rather than being sealed up, inaccessible to the other and remote from the world, subjectivity is "above all a relation to the world" (Zahavi 2001,163), and the world is given to us, by others, through a dynamic sharing of meaning. This "giving-through-sharing" (Zeiler 2014b) renders the semiotic-material world that we live familiar to us, and the familiar is both that which is given to us by others and that "which in being given 'gives' the body the capacity to be oriented in this way or in that," as put by Sarah Ahmed (2006, 7). The notion of intercorporeality has been used to further bring out the non-discreteness and basic openness of bodies, the relational becoming of bodily selves (where singular, i.e., unique and different, lived bodies are continuously shaped and come to be in exchanges between bodies), and the relations between bodily selves as constitutive for selfhood (e.g., Weiss 1999; Marrato 2012; Shildrick 2008; Käll 2014; Zeiler 2014b; Fuchs 2016) that already underpin much such reasoning. Intercorporeality, states Gail Weiss (1999, 105), "defies any attempt to affirm the autonomy of the body apart from other bodies or from the disciplinary, technological practices that are continuously altering or redefining them." My relations with others co-constitute my being who I am: The involvement with others and things constitutes the embodied self as being-in-the-world.

For the first point I want to make—about how pain, fear, or bodily expressed symptoms of ESRD that unfold in the shared space of child and parent can shape both of them, feed into their bodily style of being-together, and help form parents' perception of actions within reach for them—I turn to Lisa Folkmarson Käll's (2013, 34, 36) discussion of how "singular lived bodies emerge in mutual intercorporeal exchange" where "the expression of pain breaks forth and unfolds between self and other in the space that we share, that forms both of us in relation to one another and that we in turn also form."

PAIN AND OTHER BODILY EXPRESSION IN SHARED SPACE

Phenomenologists have offered detailed examinations of experiences of pain and illness (see, as some examples, Slatman 2014; Zeiler 2010; Aho and

Aho 2009; Svenaeus 2009; Carel 2008; Toombs 2001; Leder 1990). Previous such work has explored how intense and moderate pain may result in a "spatiotemporal constriction" where the subject in pain cannot but attend to his or her hurting bodily here and now, and how this transforms the experience of time and space (Leder 1990, 75) while also examining how others' ways of encountering the subject in pain can help shape his or her experience of being-in-pain (Zeiler 2010; Carel 2008). This sociality of pain is captured, from the angle of living with her chronically ill mother and witnessing her mother's pain, when Ahmed (2004, 30) describes how this witnessing "would give her [mother's] pain a life outside the fragile borders of her vulnerable and much loved body," draw them together, and yet remain "shrouded in mystery."

Ahmed is careful to differentiate between the pain involved when witnessing someone else's pain and the other's experience of pain. Acknowledging this, Käll (2013) suggests that we may preferably understand bodily expressions such as those of pain as unfolding in the shared space between self and other. Käll engages with Merleau-Ponty's understanding of the lived body as "our expression in the world, the visible form of our intentions," which explicates how bodily expressions typically aren't neatly kept within the individual's physical boundaries but carry meaning beyond them. Her point, however, is not only that another person's anger can manifest itself through facial, gestural, and interoceptive changes, and that someone else can see and sense that anger with her body and be immediately and pre-reflectively aware of it, through a basic sentience, that is, something that many phenomenologists have explored. The idea is also that the language of bodily expressions that unfolds between self and other allows for a shift in focus as to how self and other, as embodied beings, are dynamically formed in relation to each other (Käll 2009). Käll's discussion invites a focus on how the subject-in-pain may experience his or her pain differently depending on how others encounter and acknowledge him or her as someone in pain—and calls for an exploration of how someone's bodily expressed pain and way of curling up in bed can form others' way of seeing him or her *as* suffering, just as their way of responding to his or her pain will shape the way he or she emerges "as a self in pain, expressive of pain and dealing with pain" (Käll 2013, 36).[5]

Emotions and other bodily expressions that unfold in shared space can help *do* things because they are not confined to the physical boundaries of one's body: Affect can help shape self and other in relation to each other, and not only in supportive ways. Whereas we may feel with the pain of the other in an immediate way through our sentience, desensitization just as receptivity to others' pain varies with situation and person, and both may have far-reaching effects. Havi Carel puts this lucidly when retelling her experience of living with a lung condition: the "pain, disability or fear is exacerbated by the apathy and disgust with which you are sometimes confronted when you are ill. There are many terrible things about illness; the lack of empathy hurts the most" (2008, 45). Carel narrates her experience of being in the respiratory department for her breathing tests, and how she braced herself for a decline in her breathing capacity. When the tests showed the decline, she sobbed quietly, but her physiologist for the day was impatient. Carel (2008, 47) recalls:

> Now I'm crying and can't do the other tests. I'm spoiling her day, getting her behind schedule. I collect myself; ask her for a glass of water. A sulky hand presents me with a dripping paper cup. She doesn't look at me or say anything. I am alone.

The others' affective response may aggravate the experience of pain, disability, fear, or loneliness. Furthermore, the encounter between self and other may be "shaped by longer histories of contact," as Ahmed (2004, 31) writes in her analysis of how the intense emotion of hate in racist encounters and the perception of the other as threatening can be shaped by past "histories of contact which allow the proximity of a racial other to be perceived as threatening" and make bodily subjects move away from each other. Such past histories of contact may also be of a more supportive kind and have just as formative effects.

HABITUATION, TIME, AND BODILY ACQUISITION WHEN LIVING WITH ESRD

Symptoms of advanced chronic kidney failure, that is, a pre-stage of ESRD, include swelling and edema, fatigue, muscle weakness, headaches, bleeding, weight loss, loss of appetite, nausea and vomiting, dry skin and itching, bone pain, and difficulty concentrating. Being given a diagnosis at an early stage of kidney failure can allow for time to process possible implications, but symptoms of this failure can nevertheless be experienced as frightening. Depression, fear, anxiety, emotional distress, and posttraumatic stress disorder have been reported among teenagers living with ESRD (Tong et al. 2009). Few studies focus specifically on children's or teenagers' lived experiences of falling ill with ESRD, but in one of the few that does, young people use descriptors as "*shock, hard, difficult, horrible, nervous, mad, different, upset, disappointed, concerned, depressed, frustrated, guilty, sad, confined,* and *worried*" when narrating the introduction and presence of ESRD in their lives (Nicholas 2011, 165, see also Tong et al. 2009). This is not to say that children and parents do not also develop various strategies for how to live with ESRD, and that some describe how they live a "normal" life *and* how the illness affect them (Snethen et al. 2001, 165).

The everyday parent–child living together when the child develops ESRD can, of course, involve multiple and possibly conflicting emotions. Reaching out to one's child, comforting and in various ways caring, may be expressions of love, fear of what may come if illness aggravates, and other emotions as well, which can forcefully attune parents to, and shape the specific situation of, living together with their child. Watching one's child suffer is hardly a neutral experience, and, as noted by Knibbe and colleagues (2007), in the context of live liver donation, the perception of having choice or having chosen (as a parental potential donor) may well depend on the acceptability of the alternatives. However, phenomenology adds to such reasoning by questioning disembodied understandings of decision making and offering conceptual tools for making sense of the role of embodiment, affect, and temporality for what we perceive as choices for us.

Merleau-Ponty repeatedly establishes that the perception or judgment of a situation presupposes a prior bodily acquisition—a certain hold—of it without which it could not stand out as a situation for us. With his formulation, unless

> there are cycles of behaviour, open situations requiring a certain completion and capable of constituting a background to either a confirmatory or transformatory decision, we never experience freedom. Choice of an intelligible sort is excluded . . . because choice presupposes a prior commitment. (Merleau-Ponty 2006, 509)

Even when we make choices after careful deliberation, we do not make them as if we had no prior commitments, no habituated style of being that makes some options stand out as alternatives more than others in the first place. Stakes "have been 'put down,'" as Maria Talero (2005, 448) frames it, "by my body in a particular orientation *from which* its possibilities are enclosed."

The idea, familiar to readers of Merleau-Ponty's work, is that there are intelligible structures in our behavior that constitute our sedimentation in the world; repeated experiences, ways of acting or interacting, can become part of our habitual mode of being—past interactions can become part of my bodily style of being, form what I "just" do, and help shape perception. Habit, here, is a residue of action, and if present actions are shaped by habits, it is because of how past actions have left traces in one's habitual bodily mode of being-in-the-world. The point is also one of a dynamic development of specific body–world relations, and how such modified or new body–world relations (which are part of the bodily subjects' mode of being-in-the-world) help shape what one can do.

For Merleau-Ponty, repeated action can come to sediment into pre-reflective layers of existence and become part of a basic bodily know-how, and the enactment of this know-how doesn't require reflection. Put differently, there is a temporal thickness to embodiment, whereby my past can feed into my present via my bodily pre-reflective mode of being, anticipate future actions, and structure my perceived field of possibilities so that not all actions stand out as equally within my reach.

This is to bring out how embodiment may enable or constrain actions. It is also to exemplify the development of what Merleau-Ponty coins as a style of being, which gives the subject's bodily existence stability without stagnation. Having a style of being is a matter of "being a body and having a history," as Linda Singer (1981: 161) puts it, and the affective dimensions to the dynamic development of a style of being may become particularly evident in this parent-child case.

MAKING SENSE OF THE NO-CHOICE DIMESNION: TIME, BODILY ACQUISITION, AND SHARED SPACE

When holding one's child's head, when he or she leans over the toilet when vomiting, or when seeing the child's curled up body in bed when he or she suffers from itching, fatigue, or bone pain, it is hardly surprising if bodily expressions that are located in the child's body, but which unfold in the shared space between the child and the parents, do something with the child and with those who are there with him or her. To make use of the previous reasoning: the suffering child and the parent are dynamically formed in relation to each other within shared space, and the child's way of curling up in bed can form others' ways of seeing him or her as suffering, just as their way of responding to his or her pain will shape the way he or she emerges as suffering. Furthermore, if a parent and a child with ESRD have lived together, if bodily expressions have unfolded in the shared space between them and shaped both of them in relation to each other; if the parent has comforted and in other ways tried to support the child, they may have developed what could be called a *bodily style of being-together*, as *this* child and *this* parent. If such a specific bodily style of being-together co-shapes their way of engaging with each other, then this style (which is informed by their specific past histories of contact where they may have developed an habitual mode of sharing suffering) can be difficult to disrupt and the very thought of doing so—by saying no to donation—may simply not be experienced as an option. Past interactions, past commitments, can feed into and help form their being-together in the present, without this implying any determinism.

To put this in the terminology of intercorporeality: intercorporeality, as the dynamic and relational becoming of bodily selves, brings out how bodily expressions that unfold between self and other can help shape both of them. The intercorporeal self comes to be, in relation to the other, and the starting-point for understanding embodiment, in this reasoning, is a "dynamic intercorporeality through which bodies are formed and individualized" (Käll 2013, 38). This is to understand relationality as something primary, yet it allows us to acknowledge the contingent ways in which the dynamic intercorporeal becoming can play out—as in the development of a specific bodily style of being-together. Such a style of being-together doesn't imply that differences between self and other are dissolved, far from it; it does imply that what we perceive as for us is influenced by our intercorporeally shaped bodily grip of the world, where our bodily thickness allows for a "sediment of past activity" to remain "alive in the present," even if present actions can "mutate into new patterns," transform, and, if repeated, give rise to new habits (Crossley 2001, 120, 125). Bodily expressions that unfold in shared space can help shape the parent–child bodily style of being-together, and this shouldn't be seen as remarkable or a reason for concern, but as highlighting both relational and corporeal dimensions of subjectivity.

This is to add the role of embodiment to discussions on donation—not in opposition to reasoning on how love can make someone want to donate—but as a way of acknowledging our rootedness in the world, the way we live in it together with others, and how this rootedness matters for the perception of something *as* choice. It explains why what we perceive as choices for us depends on whether we see their implications as acceptable, and why there is more to it.

For Merleau-Ponty (2006, 514), our "freedom does not destroy our situation, but gears itself to it." Having shared the child's suffering, the parent's freedom may have geared itself to this particular situation in such a way that this is the one alternative that stands out for this parent: It is the one alternative that is within reach, the one alternative that they desire and see as for them given their present situation. And if this is the case, it seems misleading to conceptualize the no-choice dimension in terms of coercion. If parental live kidney donation is what parents perceive as for them under conditions such as those so far discussed, we may agree with Robert Crouch and Carl Elliot (1999, 258): Such donation can express what parents want and/or who they want to be and, in this sense, "give voice to [their] autonomy."

However, a phenomenological analysis concerned with situated selfhood, and with a critical bite, could preferably engage also with (other) sociocultural and material dimensions that help co-shape the perception of dialysis and transplantation as longed for or preferred alternatives, before reaching the preceding conclusion. This is where I turn to what Martin Gunnarson (2016, 349) identifies as a "dominant orientation towards transplantation" and a "pragmatic orientation" in his culturally phenomenological and ethnographic study of hemodialysis and kidney transplantation care in Sweden and Latvia.[6]

ORIENTATION TOWARD TRANSPLATION

Within medical and bioethics literature, organ transplantation has been described as "one of the most remarkable medical inventions" (Ambatgsheer et al. 2013, 2) that gives organ recipients a "second chance at a normal life" (Omar et al. 2010, 21) and as a "great medical miracle of the 20th century" (Monaco 2007, 89). Individuals on dialysis, by contrast, have been described as persons who "desperately" want an organ transplant since dialysis is a "wretched experience" (Radcliff-Richards et al. 1998, 1950, 1951) and since they may "die while waiting" for a transplant (Matas 2004, 2007). Quoting these and related formulations, Gunnarson (2016, 21) notes how they encourage a hierarchical ordering where transplantation gets to be preferable to dialysis. Not only does organ donation get to be positioned as a route to normalcy, but limited organ supply also gets to become *the* problem at the expense of other difficulties with transplantation such as remaining rejection problems (Gunnarson 2016, 324).

Gunnarson is careful to point out that medical studies unequivocally show that kidney transplant increases the quality of life and reduces the risk of dying more so than dialysis, on aggregated levels. His concern is with how the "superior survival rate and quality of life are linked to powerful concepts such as health and normality" (Gunnarson 2016, 130). Through such linkage, promises are made about a return to normalcy after transplantation, and such promises, he shows, may be difficult to keep.

Just as other studies (e.g., Ziegert et al. 2009; Russ et al. 2005), Gunnarson's brings out the radically transformed temporality that dialysis treatment often entails, and the resulting frustration that individuals on dialysis can experience. He also offers a detailed examination of ways of coping with the situation, such as embracing a biomedical understanding of the disease that enables persons with ESRD to think of their kidney only or primarily in terms of functioning, that is, as a filter, acceptance of the situation as one where there is no choice, and "thought-monitoring" in the sense of avoiding "meaningless" or "harmful" thoughts (Gunnarson 2016, 165, 166). Furthermore, without downplaying the complexity that hemodialysis can entail, Gunnarson notes how he himself first took it for granted that individuals on dialysis wanted kidney transplantation. Step by step, however, his analysis brings out kidney transplantation as a normatively charged therapy that helps shape potential recipients' expectations. At stake, he suggests, is a particular orientation toward transplantation—in the phenomenological sense of the term.

Orientation, in phenomenology reasoning, is about familiarity. It is, as Ahmed puts it (2006, 7), an "effect of inhabitance," and it involves work of inhabitance. To formulate it this way is to bring out the efforts that the transformation of something unfamiliar into the familiar implies, and such efforts may be glossed over in formulations in terms of the givenness of being-in-the-world. At the same time, the language of being given brings out relationality: Because others give us the world as meaningful, and we make it meaningful with them, we are not orientated "by ourselves." Rather, how we are orientated and orientate ourselves, which directions we take, need to be understood in light of how others orientate themselves and are orientated.

In contrast to the notion of a dominant discourse, that is, a dominant way of talking about and making sense of a particular phenomenon or practice, the phenomenological notion of orientation explicitly holds together the semiotic, social, and corporeal. As before, focus is on the embodied self as being-in-the-world, but more specifically on what it means for bodies to be situated in space and time. Ahmed (2006) adds the language of "lines," stating that we are "in line" when we face the direction that is already faced by others. Being in line, she holds, allows bodies to extend into spaces that have, as it were, already taken shape and been shaped by how they have been ordered and infused with cultural significance by others, in the past and the present, and to be orientated is to be "in line." Furthermore, lines both depend on the repetition of certain patterns of thinking, of conventions and of norms *and* are created as a result of this repetition, and this has far-reaching effects: Depending on our orientation and on what is "in line" with our orientation, certain things (acts or ways of being or thinking) will be excluded for us, and what is "reachable" for us will depend on how we are orientated.[7] If we follow a line that others in our sociocultural setting also follow, we may not even notice this, since the line, through being repeatedly enacted, can come to function as a taken-for-granted feature of our bodily being-in-the-world with others.

For Gunnarson, this makes orientation an apt concept when making sense of kidney transplantation. The point is not only that organ transplantation is talked about as a desirable route to normalcy, even if this is the case, but that this way of understanding it, through being repeatedly expressed and enacted, can come to shape the perception of what someone wants, and perhaps even should want, when living with ESRD. Kidney transplantation becomes what one "just" assumes that "everyone" wants. It is indicative that Gunnarson himself first shared this assumption.

Gunnarson identifies a pattern where individuals with ESRD who haven't had an organ transplant focus on the possibility of being given a transplant, and expect life to go back to "normal" after transplantation, just as the medical and bioethical literature mentioned earlier suggested. As one of his interviewees put it, when describing how she had been thinking and feeling about the transplant before receiving the first of her transplants: "Well, it was the saviour. It was, oh, it was . . . transplantation was like 'Yes!' then everything would resolve itself" (Gunnarson 2016, 131). Transplantation became self-evidently positive, and candidates for transplantation, Gunnarson shows, orientated their lives accordingly, emotionally and practically, as was the case for one interviewee who struggled to lose weight in order to be eligible for transplantation, since the doctors "promise me fifteen to twenty years of normal life after it" (133).

In Gunnarson's analysis, survival, health, normality, and freedom from the regular medical treatments were among the expectations that patients with ESRD waiting for their first kidney transplant expressed. However, in the posttransplantation stage, and especially for kidney recipients who did not experience the normality and health that they expected, the result was a clash with this dominant "line" toward transplantation. Patients' orientation toward transplantation, Gunnarson notes, "tended to shift quite drastically after they had undergone it" (124). For some of the recipients, having been given a kidney implied a feeling that they *should* be happy now. As one of these recipients put it, others told her that " 'you're off dialysis now,' implying that I should be happy about this. But when I didn't feel well, I couldn't" (136). For others, who had learnt how to be highly aware of toxic food and do everything to avoid it, as part of taking responsibility for their health when on dialysis, the transition to voluntarily feeding their bodies with toxic substances, for example, the immunosuppressive drugs, was thoroughly disturbing, and resulted in a stark shift from the perception of transplantation as a "wonder capable of opening up" life to something more disconcerting or even "inferior" to hemodialysis due to the toxicity (126). Still others, whose experiences did not fit along the dominant "line" where transplantation was understood as a re-entry to normalcy, recalled their frustration with Swedish patients' and support groups' newsletters for organ transplantation, explaining that they didn't recognize themselves in the very positive stories about posttransplant life.

To put this in the language of orientation, if persons living with ESRD previously were orientated along the dominant line toward transplantation, their bodies could no longer smoothly extend themselves along this line. Extension failed. In Ahmed's reasoning, failed extension typically implied disorientation, if only temporarily. In Gunnarson's analysis, some of these persons would still be orientated toward transplantation and perceive it as what they, overall, still appreciated or may want should the present graft fail, but no longer along the very positive dominant line. Instead, Gunnarson explains, they now orientated (or re-orientated) themselves along a pragmatic line: This was a "pragmatic orientation" characterized by lowered expectations about what transplantation may imply, more concerns with the limited duration of (some) grafts, and doubt about whether to opt for being put on the waiting list for yet another transplant (Gunnarson 2016, 126). And at this stage, Gunnarson's interviewees also reflected on their own complicity in describing transplantation as a saving event. Even though information may have been available about the possibility of graft failure, some of them said that it may not be easy to hear and take in that kind of information, in light of one's desire to get back to one's previous pre-ESRD life (135).

ORIENTATION, NORMATIVITY, AND PARENTAL CHOICE

Gunnarson uses the notion of orientation in order to explicate how individuals with ESRD talked about and emotionally and practically orientated themselves toward transplantation as an event that would give them back life as it was experienced before. My focus is instead on parental decision making. However, if a dominant orientation toward transplantation shows how transplantation, for some, comes to be perceived as a desired route to health and normalcy, then this may also inform family members' perception and narrated experiences of non-choice.

I will now turn to examples of parental narrations in my past studies of parental live kidney donation in Sweden (Zeiler et al. 2010; Zeiler and Lennerling 2014), with a conceptual eye on normativities that are expressed in parents' narration of considering whether to donate a kidney to their ailing child. In these studies, parents talked about a "parental responsibility" to donate if someone has "brought a child into this world," and contrasted medical reasons for not undergoing the donation with "egoistic" ones in reasoning where there are no good reasons for not donating, if a parent is medically accepted as a donor and doesn't want to be egoistic (Zeiler et al. 2010, 228). As put by one parent,

> If one hadn't agreed to donate. If we had seen Jimmy [this parent's son] get worse and worse [without taking action], then one just couldn't live with oneself. . . . One wouldn't have any respect for oneself . . . as a human being. (231)

Such narrations, if we follow Gunnarson (2016), take place in a sociocultural context where a dominant orientation toward kidney donation prevails, and in a clinical setting where parents are duly informed that recipients of live kidney transplants have a better survival rate than those on dialysis and postmortem donations (Kärrfelt et al. 2000). However, while the phenomenological notion of orientation is promising to bring out how bodies can align themselves with each other along certain sociocultural shared, and lived, normative patterns, the established phenomenological notion of incorporation and the neologism of excorporation (Malmqvist and Zeiler 2010; Zeiler 2013) are particularly apt if we want to explore how normativities that we live are shaped, expressed, enacted in everyday life, in interactions with others (and typically not simply captured in terms of "what others tell us to do"), can feed into and help shape the embodied singular self, his or her experiences, perception, and choices. And this is my current focus.

The phenomenological concept of incorporation refers to the process where something—be it an object, skill, or bodily expressed or enacted assumptions and norms—through repeated action, or through repeatedly being expressed or enacted, can come to be experienced as of-a-piece with one's experience of one's lived body (Merleau-Ponty 2006 [1962]; Leder 1990; Malmqvist and Zeiler 2010; Zeiler 2013). Drawing on the phenomenon of "focal disappearance," that is, how I cannot at the same time attend *to* something, as an object of attention, and engage with the world *from* or *through* it, Drew Leder (1990, 104) discusses incorporation as being what enables smooth and seamless action via Merleau-Ponty's example of a blind man with a stick. For this man, repeated use of the stick helped modify his bodily know-how, his set of body-world skills that enable action. Through repeated motor activity, the stick can become incorporated into his lived body, enable his walking because he no longer needs to attend, reflectively, to it, and enlarge the radius of the man's "touch." The stick recedes to pre-reflective layers of his bodily existence, and should he attend to the stick in the activity of walking (rather than *through* it *to* his environment), he is likely to stumble, even if the stick is "semitransparent" in the sense that the man is implicitly aware of it as his stick (Ihde 1979; Leder 1990).

This reasoning has also been used to discuss how some assumptions and norms, through repeatedly being enacted, can come to function on habituated, pre-reflective levels of bodily existence (Malmqvist and Zeiler 2010; Zeiler 2013). Arguably, if bodily expressed or enacted assumptions and norms are deeply engrained in our habitual bodily existence, experienced as of-a-piece with our existence, they can—in a related way—help shape the things "we simply do" and intuitively feel that "we *should* do." Furthermore, if assumptions and norms are incorporated into someone's lived body, this can enable seamless interaction as long as others have incorporated similar assumptions and norms—through a tacitly shared bodily know-how. And this helps make sense of the elusiveness of some choices: Incorporation can shed light on the experienced naturalness of something we "just" do or "just" think that we should do.

For Eric, that is, the father quoted at the beginning of this chapter, "the problem with transplantation is not that parents don't want to donate, but that they maybe are not allowed to do so" (Zeiler et al. 2010, 228). At first glance, such a statement may be understood as leaving little room for a discussion in terms of habituation of assumptions and norms about live kidney donation. It may seem indicative of a highly reflective and discursive consideration of this donation. However, this interpretation is not the only one in light of studies that show how quickly many parents say *yes* to donation, before they are informed in detail of what it entails (see Spital 2001). Furthermore, to say that parents have incorporated assumptions and norms about parenthood is not to say that some such assumptions and norms aren't *also* discussed. Even if being a parent involves reflections, at times, on how he or she may best respond to his or her child in a specific situation, there can also be dimensions of parenthood that a parent "just" doesn't think about nor question. In this way, it is no contradiction to say that someone may live a desire to do what he or she can to help his or her child, on pre-reflective levels, even though this person also reflects on what would be a preferable route of action in some specific situations. To put this differently: Even if a parent explicitly reflects on whether to donate, parents may have incorporated certain assumptions and norms about parenthood, which make some actions appear as "within reach," for them, more so than others—and the speed of decision making and the "naturalness" of saying yes to donation can be understood in light of incorporation of assumptions and norms about parenthood.

If parental consideration of whether to donate takes place within a setting which is orientated toward organ transplantation as a route to normalcy, *if* parents are told that recipients of live kidney transplants have a better survival rate than those on dialysis and postmortem donations, *if* parents and children have developed a bodily style of being-together where parents in different ways seek to alleviate suffering, and *if* parents have incorporated assumptions and norms about parental responsibility including a desire to do what is within their power to help their child, then saying no to donation may "just" not be perceived as an option for them. And if they donate under these circumstances, this can also reiterate the orientation toward, in this case, live kidney transplantation.

Parental narrations of wanting to donate, of deep concern and frustration if not allowed to do so, are common in past empirical research. However, there are also other—less often told—narrations and cases, which this phenomenological reasoning also needs to be able to make sense of. One such example is that of a father, who though being explicit about his thorough fear of surgery, nevertheless couldn't make himself say either *yes* or *no* to the donation, when he had been medically accepted for it (Zeiler and Lennerling 2014). In order to shed light on such experiences, the notion of excorporation can be helpful.

Whereas incorporation was a gradual process, the notion of excorporation refers to a reverse incorporation, which is typically abrupt and implies that what someone previously lived on a taken-for-granted level of existence now becomes that which *he or she cannot but attend to* (Malmqvist and Zeiler 2010; Zeiler 2013). The effect, just as in the case of a clash with a dominant line as Ahmed would have it, is temporarily disorientating. Whereas having incorporated assumptions and norms enable our bodies to expand in space, excorporating them implies at least a temporary disruption of my lived body–world relation.

On the one hand, what characterized the father's situation, was a difficulty to express what he was going through, what he felt or thought about donation; the details of the turmoil that he may have experienced were not narrated, and perhaps, non-narratable. On the other hand, if this is the case, such a situation is what the notion of excorporation intends to capture—situations of blockage, where we live disruptive movements that break the lived body apart and where that which one previously lived as integrated dimensions of one's being-in-the-world becomes a hindrance for this very mode of being. If parents previously lived the assumption that they would do all they could for their child, realizing, when explicitly asked about donation, that they cannot make themselves do this, can imply more than cognitive dissonance, that is, more than the frustration involved in situations with conflicting assumptions or behavior, where individuals may seek routes to resolve the dissonance. It may imply a painful excorporation of previously lived normativities.

If parents excorporate norms about how they want to live as parents, this is because something has happened that no longer allows them to "just" live these norms. They cannot but attend to these assumptions and norms; these were previously lived, and perhaps still reflect how parents want to live as parents, but not donating somehow clashes with them. Still, others may continue to live the same incorporated norms as before, which can make it particularly difficult to put the hesitation about donation into words. As put by some interviewed parents who, while stating that they wanted to donate, also described how relieved they felt when they thought that their partner, and not themselves, would be medically accepted for the donation: One shouldn't feel relived if not being medically accepted for donation. Feeling relief, they added, was something they felt "ashamed" of (Zeiler et al. 2010, 230).

In contrast to the situation where some choices "just" appear as self-evident, because they are in line with our bodily style of being and our orientation along dominant lines, the example of not being able to say either *yes* or *no* and feeling relieved, and being ashamed of this, may qualify as a case of "moral breakdown" in Jared Zygon's use of this term, where one "no longer dwells in the comfort of the familiar, unreflective being-in-the-world, but rather stands uncomfortably and uncannily *in* the situation-at-hand" (Zygon

2007, 138). Something has happened that makes it (at least temporarily) difficult to "just" live the previously incorporated assumptions and norms about parenthood.

To sum up: From within this reasoning, there are choices to make, but that which stands out as a choice is formed by our bodily modes of acting and interacting with others and the world, and some alternatives may come to be perceived as "within reach," more so than others, depending on our orientation and what assumptions and norms that we have incorporated into our lived bodily existence and coexistence—without this implying any determinism. This is why the no-choice theme in previous empirical work is understandable, and why it also can be a reason for concern: While there is no reason to see parental live kidney donation as generally coercive, perception is intercorporeally structured, and that which is perceived as an alternative for the singular parent in Sweden needs to be understood in light of analysis of the dominant and the pragmatic lines, as identified by Gunnarson (2016).

CONTRIBUTIONS TO BIOETHICS

The principle of respect for autonomy is commonly understood as a bioethical cornerstone and pivotal ethical qualifier that needs to be protected if bodily exchanges in medicine should be deemed acceptable, and informed consent a way to accomplish, or at least to promote this. Despite variations in formulations, policies that stipulate conditions for such consent typically center on the importance of donors being adequately informed of risks and benefits to the donor and the recipient, and about alternative treatments available to the recipient, having the necessary capacity to comprehend the situation and information given, being able to reflect on alternatives and make decisions, and being willing to donate and free from coercion (for some examples, see Abecassis et al. 2000; Beauchamp and Childress 2001; Del Carmen and Joffe 2005; Spital 2001). Such reasoning values potential donors' own reflected choices, and debates focus on how to safeguard this choice. This chapter contributes to such reasoning, through its examination of the role of embodiment, temporality, and lived normativities for decision making.

Phenomenological reasoning offers conceptual tools for making sense of the complexity of the situation where corporeal self-formation takes place in relations with others, things, discourses, and practices of transplantation and dialysis, and this is needed for a better understanding of decision making in these contexts. The reasoning so far, I hope, has brought out how faulty it is to understand one's own choices as anything but intercorporeally formed.

Three insights can be drawn from this approach. First, the reasoning on the temporal thickness of intercorporeal self as being-in-the-world, on the development of a bodily style of being-together when sharing pain and suffering over time shows how *we omit a great deal if we focus strictly on choice at a specific moment in time* in discussions of decision making, sharply set apart from how our past interaction can help shape what we perceive as possible actions. From within the phenomenological reasoning in this chapter, the choices we make need to be understood in light of our rootedness in the world, the way we live in it together with others, and this rootedness matters for perception of something *as* choice. A parent may have geared his or her freedom in such a way that live kidney donation stands out as the one alternative that is within reach, and this needs to be understood in light of the parent–child bodily being-in-the-world together with others and the larger situational whole.

Second, orientation along dominant lines can help shape choice and action, and this may first be distinguishable in retrospect or when questioned. In everyday life, we often do not *see that which makes us see certain things or choices as for us,* until we start to think about this. As already noted, this is one of the points that the phenomenological notion of incorporation captures. As a notion that brings out how things, skills, or norms can come to function as an integrated and tacit part of our dynamic body–world relation, incorporation explicates how interaction can be enabled because we need not attend *to* things that we use or *to* norms that we may live, express or enact, but *through* these *to* others and the world. That which is incorporated is that which we don't attend to; that which can help enable action, orientate us, without us seeing how or that this takes place. For a discussion of choices, incorporation helps explain how some choices can be tacit. They are what we "just" choose, without really thinking about this in any detail, sometimes because these choices express what we want, and at all times because they are in line with our bodily mode of being, as singular situated subjects.

Third, there is no sharp division between limits on decision making from the "inside" and "outside" in this perspective. While the common distinction between internal (e.g., weakness of the will) and external constraints (e.g., what others tell us to do) on "free" choices may be informative for certain analytic purposes, it is misleading in order to understand many nuances of lived decision making. The possible limits to our choices need to be understood differently: While there are choices to make, that which stands out as a choice is formed by our bodily modes of acting and interacting with others and the world, including bodily styles of being-together.

These points bring out some of the complexities of choice and make it necessary to think through the *autós* of autonomy. While the term *autós* has come to refer to one's own or one's own self in discussions of autonomous choices as choices made by self-governing individuals, the phenomenological reasoning on the embodied self as being-in-the-world and the embodied self as intercorporeally formed allows for an acknowledgment of how someone's "ownness" is intrinsically bound up with various dimensions of otherness. Not only are embodied subjects formed in relations over time, but subjectivity and agency are also thoroughly dependent on the larger situation in which they are articulated. This is part and parcel of the being-*in*-the-world, which also implies that human existence is never autonomous if this means characterized by independence (cf. Slatman et al. 2016; Devisch 2010).

The reasoning in this chapter has sought to acknowledge and discuss the co-formation of corporeal subjectivity, perception, and choice in everyday interactions with others and in ESRD treatments—without dismissing the concern that much of the autonomy and informed consent literature addresses: how some situations limit, or hamper, choice. Whereas choice always is situated, and any independent agency of the bodily subject as being-in-the-world inherently dependent on the situation in which it is articulated, some choices may be more limited, or limited in more troubling ways, than others (see Käll and Zeiler 2014). If someone finds himself or herself in a situation where he or she sees no alternatives than to donate, but doesn't want to do so—then his or her freedom arguably is suppressed—in contrast to that of parents who explain that donation is not a matter of choice but self-evident for them and what they want. However, and in any case, attendance also to temporal, relational, and corporeal dimensions is crucial if we want to understand the conditions for decision making, and this will take us beyond dichotomously formulated foci on either coercion or choice. And phenomenological philosophy is helpful in this regard.

ACKNOWLEDGMENTS

This chapter is part of my work as Pro Futura Scientia Fellow at the Swedish Collegium for Advanced Study, funded by the Swedish Foundation for Humanities and Social Sciences.

NOTES

1. Whereas the outcome for the person with ESRD would be fatal without either dialysis or transplantation, the availability of these alternatives makes transplantation qualify as a possible means of enhancing the recipients' health and well-being rather than as life-saving.

2. In Sweden, health care is a public service funded through taxes, and the tax-funded healthcare and welfare system covers almost all costs related to ESRD treatment (e.g., Wikström et al. 2007), even though there is a small co-payment. In 2017, a patient can only pay a maximum of SEK1,100 (€110) per year for medical care, and a maximum of SEK2,200 (€220) per year for prescription drugs or a maximum of SEK1,980 (€198) per year for travel to hospital. Donors receive no incentives for the donation, but they are financially compensated for loss of income and other verified costs during hospital stay and sick leave. Organ donation is regulated by the transplantation law (SFS 1995: 831 om transplantation m.m.).

3. For an analysis of bodily relational autonomy, see Käll and Zeiler (2014).

4. The notion of incorporation is an established phenomenological term, whereas the phenomenological notion of excorporation is a neologism, coined and discussed in Malmqvist and Zeiler (2010), further elaborated in Zeiler (2013), and used in order to examine norms about sexed embodiment and teenage girls' narrated experiences of having no or a small vagina (Zeiler and Guntram 2014).

5. To this we may add differentiations of how different forms and intensities of pain color, delimit, and shape our encounters with others. Others' responses to my intense acute pain that borders on unconsciousness may arguably have less of an impact on my dealing with it, in that particular moment, than may be the case as regards their responses to my moderate chronic pain. Käll's point, however, would still hold: Bodily expressions—such as those of pain—when unfolding in shared space between self and other—have a "formative force"; that which takes place in this "between" is formed by how we express ourselves in the shared space (Käll 2014, 51).

6. Gunnarson offers a culturally phenomenological and ethnographic study of hemodialysis and kidney transplantation care in Sweden and Latvia, which includes interviews with individuals on dialysis, those on the waiting list for transplantation, and those who have undergone one or more kidney transplantations but who are back on dialysis.

7. For analysis of how expressed and enacted normativities within specific medical practices can help shape perception and action, see Zeiler and Wickström (2009) and Bremer (2011).

Chapter 7

Reclaiming Embodiment in Medically Unexplained Physical Symptoms (MUPS)

Jenny Slatman

"One of the biggest challenges faced by people who have chronic illnesses is that of being believed. Of being listened to by professionals, and finding people who understand that conditions like fibromyalgia, M.E. [myalgic encephalomyelitis] and so on are real, physical illnesses." This heartfelt cry stems from Emsy's Internet blog on medically unexplained physical symptoms (MUPS).[1] If you browse the Internet, you will soon discover that there are many people like Emsy: people who (chronically) suffer from bodily pain or fatigue, while their suffering is not recognized as a "real, physical illness." Since MUPS can imply any kind of physical distress, it rather involves a general "working diagnosis" than a specific diagnosis (Olde Hartman et al. 2013). Examples of MUPS include chronic fatigue, musculoskeletal pain, headache, stomachache, nausea, palpitations, and dizziness.

Figures about estimated prevalence of MUPS are widely divergent, depending on different types of MUPS and different medical disciplines. It is estimated that for about 40 percent of physical complaints that are presented to a general practitioner no specific cause can be found (Steinbrecher, Koerber, Frieser, and Hiller 2011). Even though a large number of unexplained complaints disappear automatically or can be easily treated by some household remedy, chronic MUPS form a major challenge for contemporary health care. Since MUPS are hard to treat, the majority of patients are major "consumers" of medical care, which causes a considerable economic burden for society (Konnopka et al. 2012). On the individual level, MUPS often involve poor communication between therapists and patients, which, on the one hand, causes feelings of misrecognition and stigmatization in patients, and on the other, feelings of being powerless in therapists and physicians. Physicians become frustrated, which has a negative impact on the patient–physician relationship (Salmon 2007; Wileman, May, and Chew-Graham 2002).

Because of this problem of communication and recognition, MUPS patients widely share their experiences on the Internet and through various kinds of social media, like Emsy did. Her call for recognition, not in the consultation room, but in the public space of the Internet, illustrates the limits of what contemporary (conventional) medicine can accomplish. As I will suggest at the end of this chapter, however, the blogosphere should not only be seen as a place where people can dump their (unheard) complaints. It can also be seen as a space that enables possible writing which can "touch the body" (Nancy 2008a, 9). To give voice to the body in MUPS, as I will argue here, we need a kind of talking and writing that does not rigidify the body. The Internet might be an appropriate place for writing that resists fixed meanings because of its transient nature.

The "unexplained" of MUPS, undeniably, lays bare the epistemological deficit of medicine. It is striking, however, that in actual practice this "unexplained" does not refrain professionals from providing explanations. Similar to the usage of various other terms and labels, the usage of MUPS often goes together with the reasoning that if there are no physical causes to be found, the cause of these kinds of symptoms should be looked for in some psychological or emotional disturbance. This kind of reasoning is called psychosomatics: physical, somatic problems are caused by psychological problems.

One could say that the origin of this reasoning goes back to Freud's psychanalysis of hysteria (Wilson 2004). Freud claimed that symptoms such as paralysis or speech loss in cases of hysteria are caused by a conversion of psychological pain or anxiety into neurological symptoms. The term *conversion* or *conversion disorder* is still used nowadays. Other terms that are used to express the (one-way) traffic between the realm of the psyche and the soma include: *somatoform disorders, functional disorders, somatic disorder,* and *somatization*. Besides the fact that these different labels, according to the categorization of the *Diagnostic and Statistical Manual of Mental Disorders* (*DSM*), refer to (slightly) different clinical phenomena, they also have different connotations. For the purpose of my analysis I will not discuss these differences, but will focus on the general reasoning underlying nearly all these different labels, that is, the idea that the unexplained physical symptom is related to some sort of psychological trouble. Whenever this searching for psychological causes is based upon a dualistic ontology—which is often the case in contemporary health care—it looks like a ghost hunt: searching for the "ghost in the machine" (Ryle 1949).

The purpose of this chapter is to explore whether and how it is possible to do justice to MUPS without resorting to psychological explanation. I believe that this is only possible if we start with a redefinition of the concept of the body in medicine. Psychological explanation is always lurking, exactly because of a very limited, narrow concept of the body. Contemporary medicine embraces the idea of the body as an extended and individual thing, as a machine that works in a mechanical way, as an object that as such is ontologically similar to a dead body, a corpse or cadaver (Leder 1992). To provide a richer concept of embodiment, I will first draw on phenomenological ideas on the body and will then discuss a phenomenological explanation of MUPS as provided by Bullington (2013). Even though this explanation implies a rejection of the concept of the body as extended thing, it does not suffice to avoid psychologization. Alluding to Shusterman's (2005) work, we can say that Bullington's analysis suffers from "somatic attention deficit." Yet, as I will show, Shusterman's pragmatist criticism is not sufficient for truly regaining the physical, material body.

To be able to reclaim the body in MUPS, we need to revise phenomenology in such a way that the experience of the lived embodied subject also includes the experience of the subject's physical, material existence. For this materialist switch, I will draw on the work of the French philosopher Jean-Luc Nancy. As we will see, his analysis of embodiment will also imply a reconsideration of Descartes's idea of material extension. Since Nancy's work is highly abstract, aphoristic, and sometimes even impenetrable, it is not obvious to translate his thought to the practical world of health and medicine.[2] I believe, however, that his reflections on the body can help us addressing MUPS in such a way that its physical, material dimension can be recognized.

PHENOMENOLOGY AND MUPS

Whereas medicine, generally speaking, considers patients' bodies as things, objects, or defective machines that can be repaired, phenomenologically oriented studies show that experiences of health, or able-ness, and of illness and disability cannot simply be reduced to physical "normality" or "abnormality." Phenomenology of health and illness therefore claims that we should also take into consideration patients' lived experiences of their bodies (Aho and Aho 2009; Carel 2011, 2012a; Leder 1990; Toombs 1993, 1995). Accordingly, the majority of present phenomenological studies on healthy, ill, able, and disabled bodies fall back on the distinction between the objective body (*Körper*) and the lived body (*Leib*).

Husserl writes in his *Ideas II* (1989, §§36–38) that whereas *Körper* refers to the meaning of one's body in terms of an intentional object, that is, an object perceived and apprehended through an array of adumbrations (*Abschattungen*) and to which one may attribute physical features, *Leib* refers to the meaning of one's own body as a "non-thing" (Waldenfels 1989), a non-intentional experience of one's own body localized in one's body, in one's sense organ. In an earlier section of *Ideas II*, Husserl described the *Leib* as the "organ of perception" (*Wahrnehmungsorgan*), which is the medium (*Mittel*) of all perception, and which is necessarily involved in all perception (*ist bei aller Wahrnemung nowtwendig dabei*) (§18). So, according to Husserl, the *Leib* forms the condition for the possibility of perception. In contrast with Kant, he thus maintains that rather than the so-called pure forms of intuition (the forms of time and space) it is the existence of an organ of perception that conditions the appearance (*Erscheinung*) of spatiotemporal things.

Most typical about the *Leib* is that it is caught in a circle of constitution: It is constitutive for perception in the sense that no perception can take place without it, but it is also itself constituted, which means that it is not pregiven as a non-experienced structure. Rather, the *Leib* is constituted by means of sensorial experience. It is thus a constituting-constituted structure. In phenomenological discourse this means that the *Leib* not only conditions appearance but also appears itself, albeit in a typical way. As Husserl explains in §36, the *Leib* is constituted through localized sensations that he calls "sensings" (*Empfindnisse*). These localized sensations are materialized mainly by the senses of touch, warmth, cold, proprioception, kinesthetic sensations, and pain. On the basis of these "sensings," one's body does not appear as a thing in adumbrations, but merely as an embodied "here" and "now," a zero-point for all movement, orientation, and perception.

It is this idea of *Leib* as the embodied, nonformal, condition of world disclosure that has become a central idea in Merleau-Ponty's *Phenomenology of Perception*, where it is called the subject body (*corps sujet*), the lived body (*corps vécu*), or one's own body (*corps propre*). In his early work, Merleau-Ponty writes that it is especially by means of motor intentionality that the "transcendental" embodied subject discloses its world. Drawing on Merleau-Ponty's distinction between objective body and lived body Bullington (2013) provides an analysis from the "psychosomatic body." According to her, the lived body should be understood as "someone's lived relationship to the world" (30). She thus emphasizes the lived body's potential to disclose the world and its capacity to give meaning to the world. Consequently she considers "psychosomatic pathology" (i.e., MUPS) as a breakdown in the dialog between a person and the lifeworld. And this breakdown goes together with a reduction of experience to "being-in-the-world *as body*" (59). Causes for this breakdown are, according to Bullington, challenging situations in a person's life, such as family and/or marital problems, economic worries, problems at work, and sexual difficulties (63). People produce psychosomatic problems or MUPS when they respond to these challenges through a low level of sense-making. In Merleau-Pontian terms this would mean that these people's "intentional arc" becomes smaller and smaller, which goes together with reducing all situations and experiences to "body and habit" (70). With this, Bullington means that people get fixated with their body as a physical organism, including its acquired habits. In other words, through the psychosomatic breakdown the body loses its capacity of "lived body" and is reduced to an object.

Even though Bullington sheds some new light on the thorny problem of psychosomatics or MUPS, I feel that her account is not entirely convincing, for two reasons. First, her explanation of psychosomatics in terms of a lifeworld breakdown seems to be too general. In fact, from a phenomenological perspective, any illness or disorder—whether it is psychosomatic or not—goes (often) together with the shrinking of the body's meaning: from subjective embodiment to the body as object. Bullington seems to endorse such a general phenomenological view on illness and embodiment, since she explicitly refers to Kay Toomb's description of her life with MS, which is clearly a somatic and not a psychosomatic problem, to explain the decrease of bodily intentionality (62).

There is a second, more profound, problem with her theory. This becomes clear if we look at her suggestions for treating psychosomatic problems. The most important step in the treatment is, according to Bullington, to redefine the problem of the body into a lifeworld problem (72). Patients need to be supported to "get from body expression back to personal, higher order meaning constitution" (70). Elsewhere in the texts she writes that the "patient must let go of the body" (16). It seems to me that this approach to MUPS is in fact very similar to psychological approaches according to which patients are invited to use their cognitive capacities (turning negative thoughts into positive ones; coping strategies) in order to relieve their problems. The only difference here is that Bullington does not use the psychological vocabulary but instead hints at a phenomenological one. But one might wonder what in actual fact the difference is between the development of "higher-order meaning constitution" and "changing one's mindset." What I find even more troubling is that this higher order meaning constitution apparently needs to go together with a rejection of the focus on the physical body. This requirement of "letting go of the body" will certainly not help to de-stigmatize MUPS. More likely it will only reinforce the view that the physical problem is "not real." Bullington's nonpsychological vocabulary has the advantage that one could no longer say that "it is all in the head," but one can wonder whether the judgment "it is all in the lifeworld" is more effective.

HOW EMBODIED IS THE LIVED BODY?

Bullington's analysis teaches us that health—the absence of psychosomatic problems—is predominantly related to the degree in which the lived body is not bothered by experiences in which the objective, physical body is in the foreground. In that sense her analysis is very much in line with phenomenological accounts of health and illness, which stress that the least our body is present for ourselves the better our health. This is nourished by the view that the "lived body" when engaged in actions and not troubled by itself is in the back of our experience, or as Leder (1990) puts it, is "absent." The experience of the lived body, so it seems, does not go together with very distinct experiences of one's own physical body. This is a point of criticism that is, for instance, raised by Shusterman (2005). He claims that Merleau-Ponty's work suffers from a "somatic attention deficit." He writes: "Although surpassing other philosophers in emphasizing the body's expressive role, Merleau-Ponty hardly wants to listen to what the body seems to say about itself in terms of its conscious somatic sensations, such as explicit kinesthetic or proprioceptive feelings" (151). According to him, Merleau-Ponty creates a dualism between representational consciousness of one's body and pre-reflective body awareness, while subsequently criticizing the first form of body experience as if this would not result in genuine knowledge concerning one's own body. Shustermann claims that this focus on pre-reflective awareness ignores the value of specific forms of "somatic attention."

Merleau-Ponty stresses that people become skillful in handling their world through pre-reflective habit formation. Shusterman argues that this might all be true as long as our bodily habits are "good" in the sense that we do not suffer from them. To cure of bad bodily habits—for example, poor bodily posture, insufficient movement of one's entire body while throwing a ball, too tensed shoulder muscles while sitting behind a computer—somatic attention is indispensable according to Shusterman. Various types of body work, including yoga, meditation, and the *Feldenkreis* method, "seek to improve unreflective behavior that hinders our experience and performance" (166).[3] As we all know, many people who suffer from MUPS resort to therapies that include some sort of somatic attention training.

We thus see that Bullington's approach of MUPS, while endorsing the phenomenological account of the body as the zero-point of world-disclosure, involves the request of paying less attention to the physical dimension of the lived body in order to be able to restore a higher level of sense-giving. Shusterman, by contrast, pleas for more somatic attention, while criticizing phenomenology's assumed premise that we should not be explicitly aware of our own lived body. As to the possible treatment of MUPS, Bullington's approach would fit in a psychotherapeutic program, whereas Shusterman's view would fit into a physiotherapeutic one. It is not my intention here to compare which kind of approach is more efficient to actually treat MUPS. If we look at various clinical studies, both kinds of therapies can have their merits.

The unexplained in MUPS refers to not being possible to indicate the underlying pathology in the physical body. This "unexplained" may disappear if the body is considered as different and more than just a physical thing. This is also what Bullington aims at in her analysis. However, the problem in her analysis, as in many phenomenological ones, is that the phenomenological difference between *Leib* and *Körper* easily falls prey to a new form of dualism. It is as if the lived body, the sense-giving body, in fact, becomes a sort of replacement for what previously was named "soul," spirit, and so on. This, for sure, is caused by the fact that Husserl and Merleau-Ponty's philosophies are still transcendentally oriented. The lived body is seen as a transcendental structure; it is the condition of possibility of world-disclosure. Shusterman, however, claims that the lived body need not always imply a transcendental position: "To treat the lived body as subject does not require treating it *only* as a purely transcendental subject that cannot also be observed as an empirical one" (174). According to Shusterman, who draws more on pragmatism than on phenomenology, the distinction, made by Mead, between the perceiving "I" and the perceived "me" "should not be erected into an insurmountable epistemological obstacle to observe the lived body" (175).

To respond to the epistemological question of how to reconcile the radical different ways in which we may have access to our own body and how we can know it, Shusterman suggests the possibility of a constant switching between a transcendental and an empirical position. However, he does not touch upon the more fundamental question of transcendentality as such. It seems to me that the idea of the lived body as a transcendental subject which is not purely transcendental does not simply imply that it can switch from positions, from being transcendental to being empirical. More fundamentally, if we take embodiment of the lived body seriously, impure transcendentality implies a circle of constitution: It implies that the (transcendental) constituting subject is constituted by the empirical. The lived body, as zero-point, discloses the world, but at the same time it is no absolute zero-point, since it is the point that is formed, constituted by empirical sensations of being felt, of sensing oneself. The deeper philosophical problem, which is not further explored by Shusterman, is the question how we must understand the constitution of meaning, *Sinngebung*, without presuming a pure transcendental, sense-giving subject.

To address this thorny question, I will now turn to the work of Jean-Luc Nancy. In fact, Nancy's many different philosophical analyses—whether they address issues of politics, religion, ontology, art, or literature—all circle around the question of sense, meaning (*sens*). Sense-making, for sure, is related to human beings, but as Nancy makes very clear, we should not understand this process starting from individual sense-giving subjects, individual beings-in-the world. By contrast Nancy claims that the origin or beginning of sense-making consists of the worldly, nontranscendental fact of bodies, human and nonhuman ones, that coexist next to one another (Nancy 2008a,

39–41). To understand how the physical, extended body is involved in sense-making, we need to take into account that existence implies coexistence. In the following sections, I will unravel Nancy's complex notion of embodiment while explaining his notions of coexistence, subjectivity, and his interpretation of Descartes. After this theoretical detour, I will assess in what ways Nancy's ideas may help us to find a way to make sense of the body in MUPS.

RETHINKING EXISTENCE

Nancy's philosophy can be seen as an elaboration of Heidegger's existential analysis of human beings although his starting point is entirely different. Whereas Heidegger prioritizes humans' singular existence over humans' being with one another (*Mitsein*), Nancy claims that existence's singularity and *Jemeinigkeit* are conditioned by a fundamental *etre-avec* (being-with) or *être-ensemble* (being-together). Interestingly, Nancy does not simply refer here to the social life of humans. "Being-with" involves the being with bodies, all kinds of bodies. As he writes: "The ontology of being-with is an ontology of bodies, of every body, whether they be inanimate, animate, sentient, speaking, thinking, having weight, and so on. Above all else, 'body' really means what is outside, insofar as it is outside, next to, against, nearby, with a(n) (other) body, from body to body, in the dis-position" (Nancy 2000, 84). What all bodies have in common is that they are material and are extended: They occupy a certain place, which at that very moment cannot be occupied by another body. Bodies that are with one another therefore exist in the mode of what Descartes had called *partes extra partes*. They are next to one another, outside one another. As such they do not fuse or coincide but remain different.

The term *partes extra partes* is abundantly used by Nancy in various texts (e.g., 2000, 2008a). It is interesting to note here that Merleau-Ponty also uses this term in the first part of his *Phenomenology of Perception*. While Nancy uses it to describe the way in which bodies exist next to one another, and thus to define an alternative ontology of bodies, Merleau-Ponty uses it to criticize the Cartesian mechanistic view on the body, that is, the body as a thing. According to Merleau-Ponty, *partes extra partes* implies a mechanical and external relation between bodies, and between body and world, instead of an intentional relation (Merleau-Ponty 2006, 73). Nancy would agree with Merleau-Ponty that the *partes extra partes* implies an external relation, but in contrast with Merleau-Ponty he would claim that the body as subject can only emerge from the "*extra*." Nancy uses the term thus not so much as to focus on the parts as such, but exactly on the fact that they exist outside one another. We have to focus on the "*extra*," which is the principle of differing and spacing.

Since Nancy considers the ontological "being-with" in terms of *partes extra partes*, his ontology entails a materialist view. But it is crucial to underline that he distances himself from mainstream materialism. For him, matter is not the same as substance or mass. Matter as substance or mass involves that which is self-containing and coinciding with itself. By contrast, Nancy writes: "'Matter' is not above all an immanent density that is absolutely closed in itself. On the contrary, it is first the very difference through which *something* is possible, as *thing* and as *some*" (Nancy 1993, 57). In line with this, Nancy differentiates between a body belonging to a crowd (*foule*) and a body belonging to a mass. And then he immediately adds that a body as mass is not worth the name body (Nancy 2008a, 124). The body as mass is the body of a mass grave; it is the body as cadaver; it is the body that does not sense anymore: the body as substance or self-coinciding mass. It is clear then that Nancy, like all phenomenologists, rejects the idea of the body as substance, yet at the same time he claims that the body is material. The body is matter, but not in the sense of substance. It is matter in the sense of non-coincidence.

We could say that the plurality of material bodies which differ from one another forms the condition of possibility of a singular being in the world, even though Nancy would not use the term *condition of possibility*, since he only wants to employ an "empirical logic, without transcendental reason" (Nancy 2008a, 53). In order to understand the singularity of being-in-the-world, we should take seriously the materiality of given bodies. Hence Heidegger's existential analysis gets a materialist underpinning.[4] It is difference (or différ*a*nce) that "constitutes" individual existence or *Dasein*. Difference and non-coincidence are given with the "*extra*" of the *partes extra partes*. It is also through the *extra*, the being distinct of bodies, that world-disclosure and thus sense-making takes place. For Nancy, world-disclosure is like a creation *ex nihilo*; there is no other fundament for this creation than the plurality of bodies, which differ from one another. Therefore he claims: "The world *no longer has* a sense, but it *is* sense" (1993, 8). The world is sense for us, not because we are intentionally related to it, but because we as embodied beings are part of the plurality of bodies. Or as James writes, we are "plugged into" the world of bodies (2006, 145). We are part of the ongoing differing between bodies.

EXTENDED, TOUCHABLE BEINGS

Now that we have seen how sense, world, and body emerge from the ontological structure of "being-with" and *partes extra partes* it is time to explore how this typical body ontology can help us in analyzing people's bodily experiences and how to think of experiences of bodily pain and discomfort when no lesions or pathology can be found in the body. As we have seen, Bullington's phenomenological account of MUPS boils down to an explanation according to which the body as material entity has to let go of in favor of higher-level sense-making. Her analysis thus implies a turn from the material body to nonmaterial sense-making. In that sense, she reinstalls a dualism between the material and the nonmaterial. While intending to escape from the Cartesian legacy of body-mind dualism, Bullington eventually remains stuck in the dualism between the being extended and outside of the body and some alleged interiority of sense-making.

Nancy circumvents this trap, not so much by criticizing Descartes but, conversely, by providing an alternative reading of Descartes's work. According to Nancy, Descartes's error does not so much consist in his description of the body as *res extensa*, as the majority of phenomenologists would claim, but only in the fact that he considered the *extra* of the *partes extra partes* as an empty space, a void, instead of the "place of differentiation" (Nancy 2008a, 97). If we look closely at Descartes's texts, so Nancy argues, we will see that the Cartesian *cogito* is not determined by some interiority, but that it is, from its very outset, determined by extension. Ultimately, Nancy claims that it is an error in reasoning to presume that all kinds of mental activities (thinking, feeling, experiencing, etc.) stem from some interiority.

In his early text *Ego Sum*, published in 1979, and only recently translated into English, Nancy (2016) aims at showing that the soul is extended while reading Descartes's *Meditations*. The turning point from doubt into indubitable truth is marked by the following passage from the second Meditation: "So that, having weighed all these considerations sufficiently and more than sufficiently, I can finally decide that this proposition, 'I am, I exist' [*ego sum, ego existo*], whenever it is uttered by me, or conceived in my mind, is necessarily true" (Descartes 2008, AT VII: 25). Nancy draws our attention to the fact that Descartes in this passage uses the personal pronoun *"ego"* even though this usage is redundant—*sum* and *existo* would have sufficed.[5] Following Beneveniste's idea that the (utterance of the) personal pronoun *"ego"* constitutes the *ego*, Nancy reveals the performativity which is at stake here.

Let me rehearse Nancy interpretation here quickly—elsewhere, I have discussed it in more detail (Slatman 2014, 151–154). The human "I" utters, externalizes itself, by the articulation of *ego*. At the moment I say "I," I am no longer a *cogito* withdrawn into myself, but my thought is extended, and my mind is embodied in the matter of the sounds I emit. Saying and thinking "I" constitutes the unity of body and mind. This unity does not exist as a substance; the *ego* does not coincide with itself, nor has it the permanent mode of being of a substance. The *ego* exists as the "convulsion" of "orality": it exists only when it is uttered, cried out, whispered, or moaned. This is why the first evidence of *cogito ergo sum*, which of course has been cited to death, needs to be revised. In common readings of this statement the "I" (or *ego*) in *cogito* is understood as a thinking substance (*res cogitans*). In contrast, the *ego* that, according to Nancy, surfaces as a spasm of "orality" exists indubitably, but is no substance. The *ego* in *cogito* should be thought of as *"for,"* that is, "I speak" or "I utter": "Hence *cogito*, or from now on, *for* (I say, I fabulate, I discourse, I perform, I am performing) is the performative of performation" (Nancy 2016, 85). The mouth is the "place" where thought is "outside," and where thought externalizes itself. "The incommensurable extension of thought is the opening of the mouth" (111). In sum, the so-called Cartesian subject is not based upon interiority—it is always already outside and extended.

According to Nancy, the subject is opposed to substance. The subject is the "I" or *ego* without a self-enclosed character. Being subject means "being open." In his later work, Nancy develops this idea of subjectivity while using the concepts of touch and exteriority. Touch and touching are the key concepts of his materialism. Only matter can be touched, and only matter can touch other matter. Matter can be touched and touching as a result of its quantitative quality, which is primarily described as *outwardness* or *exteriority* (*extériorité*). Human bodies, or subjects, Nancy claims, exist as a touch (*une touche*). We are material bodies that just like all other matter can be touched, but in addition we can sense or feel being touched: Through our experience of our touchability, we have a relationship with our own materiality. We differ from ourselves because we can sense our own matter. We are matter *and* we sense matter. The difference of the body is given with feeling—*le sentir*. The body that senses its own matter is the *sentant* that simultaneously senses (*sent*) and is sensed (*senti*) (Nancy 2008a, 127). It is through this difference at the heart of any experience that "I am an outside to myself" (128).

It is along these lines that Nancy claims that Husserl's description of the two touching hands, which produce localized sensations and thus a *Leib* experience, should not be read as if this *Leib* involves some subjective interiority. To be able to touch myself, I need to have an exteriority (that can be touched) and I have to be "outside" of myself (128). According to Nancy, the lived body is always material, physical, extended, and therefore he abolishes the distinction between *Körper* and *Leib* (Morin 2016). Of course, we do not just have experiences of something that literally touches our skin. We may be "touched"—*être touché*—in many other ways; for instance, we may be deeply moved when hearing a piece of music. Likewise, we have particular internal physical experiences, such as a sudden stitch in our side. Should we see this as a disqualification of the theory of exteriority as the basis of physical experiences? Don't we always experience a certain intimacy in our internal physical feelings as well?

In this respect Nancy refers to the description of health according to the eighteenth-century biologist and physiologist Marie François Xavier Bichat:

When we do not feel our stomach, heart, and intestines, there is a "silence" of our organs. In his view this may well be called an "intimacy" (129). But this intimacy eventually means nothing but a non-experience. It is a condition in which we do not experience anything, and in such situation there is no body as subject. This intimacy that cannot be experienced merely plays out at the level of mass or substance, not at the level of the subject. We can only speak of a body when it undergoes a certain experience, and experience is only possible when the body is "outside" of itself.

MAKING SENSE OF MUPS

This idea of touch and exteriority can help us to reclaim the body in MUPS. A major problem with MUPS is that experiences of pain, discomfort, and fatigue may seem to be strictly subjective and not objectifiable by means of medical measurements and tests. It is exactly because of the "subjective" character of these symptoms that most theorists and professionals resort to some idea of interiority—the realm of the mind or the psyche—as their possible cause and solution. Nancy does not deny the occurrence of private subjective experiences. Rather he denies that such experiences *emerge* from some private interior. Pain, like joy, emerge from touch, and are therefore experienced "at the outside." Exactly because of the outwardness structure of all bodily experiences they cannot be "all in one's mind." Someone who, for instance, suffers from chronic back pain, while no somatic cause has been identified, is nonetheless touched by something. Instead of restlessly searching for the cause of this pain, it would be better to simply acknowledge that the material, extended body is in pain.

This is the first step in recognizing that MUPS are physically "real." But this, obviously, is not sufficient. Here we touch upon the problem of how to give words to a physical pain or discomfort which cannot be measured by medical tests. It is clear that the medical vocabulary, which is also eagerly used by patients and laypeople, falls short for naming this pain. Nancy would probably claim that this limit in naming is actually a positive thing. This might sound strange, but according to Nancy we must be very careful when we talk about the body. It is very easy to attribute all kinds of meanings to the body, but in such discursive practices we lose sight of the ontological given that the body does not "have" sense, but rather "is sense." The body expresses sense through the fact that it is given as unique and singular, as different from any other body. In that sense, the material body should not be considered as a sign or signifier of something else (e.g., a sign for some hidden psychological problems). The paradox of writing and talking about the body, then, is that this creates a discourse of the body, which reduces it to a sign or signifier.

According to Nancy, the (mainstream) idea that the body functions as a sign or signifier (and thus refers to something else than itself) is anchored in the Christian doctrine of incarnation. Indeed, incarnation implies that the word (*logos*) becomes flesh (*sarx*); that the immaterial God is incarnated in his material son (Nancy 2008b). What thus happens is that something immaterial gets into something material, penetrates it. And subsequently the material entity (the son) becomes the representation of the immaterial entity (God). Following this logic of incarnation, material bodies are often seen as the material and visible sign of some immaterial meaning behind or beyond it. Nancy contradicts this logic of incarnation while, again, referring to the ontological meaning of the *partes extra partes*. If we take seriously that the way of being of bodies is constituted by the fact that they exist "outside" (*extra*) one another, this implies that they do not penetrate one another, and that they do not fuse with one another. Bodies are impenetrable by means of the *partes extra partes*. This also means that a material body cannot be penetrated by something nonmaterial, by some immaterial meaning or sense, or by some immaterial psyche or soul. If, however, a body is penetrated, this implies the destruction of the *extra* and as such the death of the living body: "A body's material. It's dense. It's impenetrable. Penetrate it, and you break it, puncture it, tear it" (2008a, 150).

James (2006) rightly observes that Nancy's rejection of the idea that we should see bodies as signs or signifiers forms a criticism of social-constructivists accounts of embodiment. Nancy's account can therefore do more justice to the actual, material body which is at stake in medicine (115). But still the question remains, if the material body is not a sign or signifier, how, then, can we make sense of it, and how can we talk about it? Nancy claims that this is only possible by means of *excription* (2008a, 9–13). This neologism refers to a process that can be seen as the opposite of signification. Instead of attributing sense to words, *excription* implies "flushing out signification" (21), the detachment of sense from words (71). *Excription* takes place at the limit, the edge of sense. I would translate this idea as follows: Making sense of the body (without reducing it to something else) is possible only if we do not attribute specific meaning or sense to the body. We rather have to free the body from given meanings. To consider sense-making in such a way is totally counter-intuitive, and it seems to be in sharp contrast with what happens in medical practices. Professionals and patients constantly (have to) talk and write about the body and constantly (have to) give it specific meanings, and are therefore constantly in a process of signification. The idea of writing "outside the text" seems to be more suitable for poetry than for accounts of physical illness experiences.

Still I believe that the call for *excription* can be met to a certain extent. *Excription* does not mean the end of writing, but rather the "fragmentation of writing." It is through fragmentation that writing responds to "the ongoing protest of bodies in—against—writing" (2008a, 21). If we want to give voice to the body in MUPS, we need to interrupt, disturb the rigidified meanings of "body" and "mind," such as they are widely used by professionals, patients, and laypeople, and release alternative elusive and fragmented meanings. I believe that such fragmentation can take place through a huge variety of body words, words that resemble or not, synonyms or antonyms, but always differ from one another. This kind of writing could, undoubtedly, take place in the virtual space of the Internet in which digital signs materialize as quickly as they de-materialize. Evidently, the majority of people who use the Internet to write about their bodies in pain and discomfort still rehearse the dominant body-mind vocabulary here, and as such do not yet use the full potential of the Internet as *excription* space. To get unconventional "body words" to circulate, we first have to establish which different meanings different people attribute to bodies in pain and discomfort. This is the aim of my new research project.[6]

NOTES

1. This excerpt stems from a blog that was posted in 2014: https://emsyblog.wordpress.com/2014/03/03/medically-unexplained-symptoms/

2. His philosophy is, to date, only scarcely used to rethink the medical encounter (e.g., Devisch 2012; Devisch and Vanheule 2014).

3. Shusterman also performs and teaches various somatic attention exercises: see the Somaesthetcis YouTube channel: https://www.youtube.com/channel/UCgKznM1s94HVgivuQQROeeA

4. "If Dasein must be characterized by its Jemeinigkeit (the 'being-each-time-my-own' of its event), by the singularity of a someone having or making sense of 'mineness' (or ipseity), this someone would be unthinkable without the material-transcendental (existential) resource of some oneness of the thing in general, without the reality of the res as material difference. Matter means here: the reality of difference—and différance—that is necessary in order for there to be something and some things and not merely the identity of a pure inherence" (Nancy 1993, 57).

5. It is common in Latin to omit the personal pronoun in verbal constructions. As we all know, we say *cogito* and not *ego cogito*.

6. This project, *Mind the Body: Rethinking Embodiment in Healthcare,* is funded by the Netherlands Organization for Science (NWO) in the form of a VICI grant (016.VICI.170.026). In this project, which runs from 2017 until 2022, my research team and I will explore the meaning of embodiment in MUPS, obesity, and depression.

Chapter 8

Heidegger, Curing Aging, and the Desirability of Immortality[1]

Adam Buben

There is growing optimism in certain circles that medical technology will eventually advance to the point of finding a "cure for aging" and putting a stop to death. However, even if such a thing is achievable, we might still wonder if it is something we truly want. This has long been a topic of great interest to philosophers. In *Death and the Afterlife*, Samuel Scheffler joins what John Martin Fischer (2013) has disparagingly called "the Parade of the Immortality Curmudgeons" (350). These curmudgeons believe, for various reasons, that a life without end would be at best undesirable. In Scheffler's case, this is largely because the value or meaning we often attribute to life depends upon its temporal finitude. Without the urgency, order, and risks that come with such finitude, Scheffler doubts that the things we ordinarily value about human life would continue to be meaningful. Although not entirely without precedent, his account is importantly different from the more frequently discussed, and disputed, "boredom argument" made famous by Bernard Williams. Whereas Williams (1973) holds that the life of any individual maintaining the consistency of character necessary to preserve identity over an extended period of time would eventually become tedious, Scheffler (2013) claims that "an eternal life would, in a sense, be no life at all" (95).

Because the debate surrounding the desirability of personal immortality takes place largely within the analytic tradition, thinkers like Martin Heidegger, with his famous notion of human life (or something like it) as essentially "Being-towards-death," are frequently neglected. On its surface this idea appears to line up quite nicely with the account that Scheffler provides, and, in fact, on the rare occasions that Heidegger's name comes up in the surrounding literature, it is usually placed on a list of likely immortality curmudgeons. When properly grasped, however, it turns out that his sense of the importance of death for structuring the meaning of life allows for a rather un-curmudgeonly view of immortality. Since I think Scheffler and those with similar sentiments are unnecessarily pessimistic about the prospects of an unending life, I would like to consider the critical and corrective insights the often-misunderstood Heidegger has to offer. My hope for this chapter is twofold: While I ultimately want to undermine the arguments of curmudgeons like Scheffler, I also want to amend the standard superficial reading of Heidegger so that I might enlist him in my subversive efforts.

THE CURMUDGEONS

There are a number of reasons why philosophers of death have argued that the meaning of human lives depends on those very lives being snuffed out. However, it should not be necessary to rehearse them all here since other thinkers have already provided helpful catalogs (e.g., Fischer 2013). Nonetheless, there are three main arguments that are especially relevant to the present discussion of Heidegger and the significance of temporal limitations. For the sake of convenience, I will call them "the stages argument," "the risk argument," and "the urgency argument."

The stages argument claims that human values are dependent upon and organized by the stage of life in which one finds oneself. As Scheffler (2013) puts it, "Our collective understanding of the range of goals, activities, and pursuits that are available to a person, the challenges he faces, and the satisfactions that he may reasonably hope for are all indexed to these stages" (96). Of course, the specific stages might vary from place to place, or era to era, but, Scheffler emphasizes, they always begin with birth and end in death. While particular activities and goals derive their meaning from the stage they belong to, the particular stage one is in makes sense largely in reference to a complete normal series of stages that ultimately comes to a conclusion. The problem that Scheffler sees in an infinite life is that there can be no notion of a complete series. It is certainly possible that an infinite life might still have stages of some sort, but without such completeness, the significance of these stages, and the values they generate, would be essentially different from what ordinary finite human lives are founded upon (203).

A related idea suggests that the meaning of a human life is essentially narrative in structure. According to this view, given that stories generally require endings in order to make sense (although there may be different ways of telling stories), a human life would not be properly meaningful if it just dragged on forever without arriving at a point (cf. May 2009, 68, 72). Endings shed light after the fact on the plans and activities that came before. In explaining the narrativity thesis, Connie S. Rosati (2013) claims that "whether a person successfully completes a project or fails . . . affects the welfare value of her life by determining whether her earlier efforts were vindicated or wasted" (376). Furthermore, the kind of ending that death provides seems to fix or permanently define the value of a life, insofar as no sequel is possible and nothing more can be added: "If a life is to be good for the person living it, it must play out and conclude a successful narrative arc, thereby resolving in a satisfying way what to think and feel about that life, considered as a whole" (Rosati 2013, 376; cf. Fischer 2013, 347). In a life that has no possible conclusion, it seems that the meaning of our decisions and actions would always remain somewhat indeterminate.[2]

The risk argument holds that human lives derive much of their meaning from the constant danger of premature death. Although we know on some level that death will eventually come for us, we spend our lives weighing risks and taking chances (or not) in the shadow of its ever-present possibility (cf. May 2009, 50). For example, I might go out with friends in the middle of winter even though it is cold outside and I could catch the flu, or I might not take that trip to Egypt due to concerns about civil unrest. Scheffler (2013) claims that "in a life without death, the meaning of" several fundamental concepts "would be called into question"; he mentions "health, gain, safety, security, and benefit," as well as their opposites (97). Martha Nussbaum (1994) says much the same thing about more abstract ideals like courage, moderation, and justice (227–228). Absent ordinary worries about health and safety, to stick with the simpler concepts, the idea is that decisions to go out in the brutal cold or travel to unstable destinations just do not matter as much. This may be true, but as in the case of life stages, Scheffler and company do acknowledge that some kinds of risk might still persist even in an infinite existence—for example, there might be the risk of losing someone's affections, being imprisoned, or catching a nonlife-threatening illness.[3] Nonetheless, given that our current understanding of these risks, and the values associated with them, has been formed against the backdrop of finite life, both Nussbaum (1994, 229) and Scheffler (2013, 204) go on to claim that it is perhaps a mistake to suppose that infinite beings would have similar notions.

The urgency argument relies upon the idea that value and scarcity go hand in hand—it says that human values can exist only if there are limited opportunities for our pursuits. "*Every* human decision is made," according to Scheffler (2013), "against the background of the limits imposed by the ultimate scarce resource, time"; "our assignments of value are a response to the limits of time" (99). In a life that cannot end, in which time is no longer scarce, there would be less need to prioritize certain activities over others, or rule any out altogether. There is nothing that one could not eventually get around to under such circumstances, and so it seems that nothing one might do would matter as much. Todd May (2009) explains that "the urgency we associate with our engagements, and urgency that stems from the fact that sooner or later we will have lost the time to complete or at least to participate in them, goes missing in immortality" (63; cf. Nussbaum 1994, 229; Smuts 2011, 140–141). Now someone might point out that having unlimited time is not the same thing as being absolutely free from all chronological constraints; after all, certain activities have temporal deadlines built right into them. Kolodny (2013) mentions the example of proposing marriage to the object of one's affections before his or her other suitors can do so (168). While Scheffler (2013) grants that this sort of example might add a bit of temporal scarcity, and therefore urgency and value, to an infinite life, he is unconvinced that this much weaker, and merely situational, limitation would lead to the kinds of values that humans have developed in the face of the more profound and all-encompassing scarcity caused by death (99, 206).

Having presented several of the major cases for thinking that immortality would undermine the specific values and general sense of meaning that exist in ordinary finite human life, we are now in a position to consider some rebuttals. In fact, the beginnings of some possible responses by immortality enthusiasts have already been suggested along the way. The problem mentioned at the outset, however, is that other resources available for generating thoughtful responses have been poorly utilized. Making the effort to clarify Heidegger will show immortality enthusiasts that they might find support where at first glance they saw only more opposition.

HEIDEGGER'S VIEW OF DEATH

In support of Williams's curmudgeonly position, A. W. Moore (2006) says that "for Heidegger . . . a life in which life itself was not always at issue, that is to say a life in which death was not always a possibility, would be a standing invitation for meaninglessness to reassert itself" (327). Timothy Chappell (2007), a noted defender of immortality, adds: "Some people—perhaps the Heidegger of *Being and Time* is one—will respond that a life without death at the end of it would be meaningless because it would be shapeless" (35; cf. Fischer 2013, 340). Passing comments like these, from proponents and critics of immortality alike, are really all that has been said about Heidegger in the course of this debate. While it may appear as though he is arguing that death provides the limit or boundary necessary to give life shape and meaning, I believe that the reverse is true of his notion of death as "a way to be" (Heidegger 1962, 289)—it is meant to demonstrate a kind of indefiniteness and thereby liberate individuals, rather than constrict and define them. A life surely has its limitations, but according to Heidegger, these come primarily from other aspects of existence—aspects that would not necessarily be threatened by immortality.

Heidegger's main goal in *Being and Time* is to provide a phenomenological account of what exactly a human is without importing the assumptions or narrow scope of inquiry that the various sciences take for granted. Thus, rather than considering the biological characteristics of a species or the theological implications of God's creation, for example, he is interested in the much broader project of describing the way existence generally shows up for beings like us—especially our own existence. Even the word *human* is too loaded with biological and anthropological baggage for Heidegger's purely phenomenological project, so he adopts the term *Dasein*, which stands for the sort of "entity which understands what it is to be" (Guignon 1983, 68); it is the entity that is capable of having a meaningful existence (Heidegger 1962, 193). Embarking on his quest, then, to provide a thorough characterization of Dasein, problems arise once it appears that "there is in every case something still outstanding" about it (Heidegger 1962, 276). As Dasein shows up to itself (or, in more common terms, as I experience my life), there is never a conclusion, and so, it seems that the task of providing a thorough account of Dasein cannot be completed. Following Epicurus (1994), who famously points out that "when we exist, death is not yet present, and when death is present, then we do not exist" (Section 125), Heidegger adopts the view that death, at least in the ordinary sense of the cessation of life, is not a part of existence (cf. Watts 2011, 103); "Dasein" literally means "being-there," while death actually means not being there.[4]

Heidegger avoids this apparent difficulty by pursuing a complete structural account of the way Dasein is "in-the-world," rather than a description of what transpires between the literal birth and death of this entity. The latter type of inquiry would seem to have the shape of a biology, physiology, anthropology, or some other science that deals with a specific sense of human development, and this is precisely what Heidegger (1962) says he is not interested in seeking (291–292). Instead, he spends much of *Being and Time* making a case that Dasein can be understood in its entirety as "ahead-of-itself-Being-already-in-(the-world) as Being-alongside (entities encountered within-the-world)" (237). This is what he calls Dasein's "care structure," and he says that "the authentic potentiality-for-Being-a-whole becomes visible as a mode of care. . . . In terms of temporality, the articulated structural totality of Dasein's Being as care first becomes existentially intelligible" (277). Dasein is a moving into and relating to its rather indefinite future from its current set of involvements, which has arisen from a fairly defined background or past. It is the moving forward, or "ahead-of-itself," characteristic of Dasein that Heidegger somewhat misleadingly discusses in terms of "Being-towards-death."[5] I say "misleadingly" because this expression might give the impression that Heidegger is especially concerned with Dasein's end point, when his emphasis is in fact on the "Being-towards." Although death in the sense of

"Dasein's own concluding event" is not part of existence, death in the sense of "a way to be towards future possibilities" very much is. Heidegger states, "The 'ending' which we have in view when we speak of death, does not signify Dasein's Being-at-an-end [Zu-Ende-sein], but a *Being-towards-the-end* [*Sein zum Ende*] of this entity. Death is a way to be, which Dasein takes over as soon as it is" (289).

This distinction has been one of the most difficult issues for scholars of Heidegger to grasp, if the disagreement and confusion in the secondary literature is any indication (see Dreyfus 2005). Jean-Paul Sartre is among the first (and perhaps the most notable) in a long line of critics and commentators to struggle with it when he conflates Heidegger's sense of proper Being-towards-death with waiting for biological demise. Against Heidegger, Sartre (1956) argues that "sudden death is undetermined and by definition can not be waited for at any date; it always, in fact, includes the possibility that we shall die in surprise before the awaited date and consequently that our waiting may be, *qua waiting*, a deception or that we shall survive beyond this date; in the latter case since we were only waiting, we shall outlive ourselves" (536). Piotr Hoffman (1983) wonders if Sartre "has missed Heidegger's point" (82, 107–108) given that Heidegger's more technical use of "death" has nothing to do with an event that can be waited for at an uncertain time, but refers instead to a way of being toward available possibilities, however long one exists. The interesting thing about Sartre's mistaken critique of Heidegger is that he ends up relying on something like the Epicurean position that Heidegger has already granted. For example, Sartre (1956) states,

> Thus death haunts me at the very heart of each of my projects as their inevitable reverse side. But precisely because this "reverse" is to be assumed not as *my* possibility but as the possibility that there are for me no longer any possibilities, it does not penetrate me. . . . Death is not an obstacle to my projects . . . and this is not because death does not limit my freedom but because freedom never encounters this limit. . . . Since death escapes my projects because it is unrealizable, I escape death in my very project. Since death is always beyond my subjectivity, there is no place for it in my subjectivity. (547–548)

This passage sounds precisely like something Heidegger would agree to when it comes to the event of physical passing away. What Sartre, and numerous others, seems blind to is the fact that Heidegger has moved on to another way of talking about death in which it does come to mingle with life.

Now, this is not to say that Heidegger is completely uninterested in talking about the more ordinary sense of death. He actually thinks that reflection upon common everyday issues and the often thoughtless ways we respond to them can provide some indication of the structure or form of Dasein. Frank Schalow (1994) describes Heidegger's method of "formal indication" as looking to everyday "factical life as the inroad for developing concepts to bring what is hidden on a pre-philosophical level to an explicit philosophical understanding" (311). The important thing to notice about this method is that while reflecting on common ideas, such as "everyone must die," can highlight aspects of existence that often go unseen, the common ideas themselves are not the deepest and most essential insights about what we are. As suggested earlier, it is not having an end point that essentially defines Dasein, but rather its forward projection as long as it exists. Unsurprisingly, it is through thinking about the often uncritical and disowned everyday attitudes toward death that Heidegger is able to get a handle on the nature and significance of this projection.

For example, he draws attention to the everyday failure to acknowledge that physical demise can come at any moment and that it often disrupts the projects and relationships that one cares so much about (Heidegger 1962, 302). Just to be clear, it is not the fact that we can expire that makes it true that our specific engagements can be dissolved at any moment. This is always true; I can always sever ties and abandon projects. Heidegger simply finds reflection on the cessation of life helpful (perhaps as a sort of reminder) for bringing this truth into the light. Some might wonder about the point of harping on about something so obvious, but as Heidegger's observations of everydayness suggest, we do not always pay attention to the obvious. Instead we tend to get wrapped up in our day-to-day affairs, rarely giving even a moment's thought to our impending doom. When death does occasionally force itself onto our radar, we do our best to remove the bogey as quickly as possible and get back to life as usual. Thinking through this ordinary situation leads Heidegger to the conclusion that it is not any specific projects or relationships that allow Dasein to find itself meaningful, but rather its capacity for engaging in them. Despite various pressures (especially social and cultural) to see certain items, associations, and activities as necessary for living a good and meaningful life, the fact that one's engagements can be dissolved at any moment is an indication that they are perhaps not so compulsory after all. For Dasein, it seems the only thing necessary is that it "at the most basic level is a reaching forward into possibilities" (Guignon 2011, 197); and realizing this has a liberating effect.

Consider the following, admittedly very obscure, passage:

> Death, as possibility, gives Dasein nothing to be "actualized," nothing which Dasein, as actual, could itself *be*. It is the possibility of the impossibility of every way of comporting oneself towards anything. . . . The anticipation of this possibility . . . signifies the possibility of the measureless impossibility of existence. In accordance with its essence, this possibility offers no support for becoming intent on something, "picturing" to oneself the actuality which is possible, and

so forgetting its possibility. Being-towards-death, as anticipation of possibility, is what first *makes* this possibility *possible*, and sets it free as possibility. (Heidegger 1962, 307)

What Heidegger is getting at here is that Dasein, as Being-towards-death, has a sort of freedom in the sense that it is somewhat indeterminate when it comes to its specific engagements in the world. Hubert L. Dreyfus (1991) agrees that Heidegger's point is "that Dasein can have neither a nature nor an identity, that it is the constant impossibility of *being* anything specific" (312; cf. Heidegger 1962, 308, 311). Obviously, we define ourselves, intentionally or not, through all kinds of activities and relationships, but the idea is that no particular involvement or approach to life can ever be definitive for Dasein in the same essential manner as its pure possibility. The benefit of understanding itself in this way is that it allows Dasein to take ownership of itself and the choices it makes in the face of the aforementioned pressures to conform and "do what one does."[6] Realizing that you are not essentially determined to be anything specific means accepting that you are free from necessary determination by thoughtless everyday norms and expectations (even if you end up doing the things that these norms and expectations would have dictated).[7] In accepting this freedom, however, Dasein simultaneously loses the comfort and ease of carelessly going along with the ready-made decisions it previously depended upon. The price of taking on responsibility for attributing meaning to oneself is an anxious awareness of one's independence (Heidegger 1962, 310–311).[8]

Although Heidegger believes that a bit of anxiety is an important aspect of Dasein (especially conscientious Dasein), he is careful not to overstate this independence or suggest that Dasein's freedom makes absolutely anything available. Dasein may well be a somewhat open-ended pursuing of possibilities, but it does not determine which possibilities are available to pursue; it has been thrown into circumstances that leave some options open and others closed. Heidegger (1962) states, "Every Dasein always exists factically. It is not a free-floating self-projection; but its character is determined by thrownness as a Fact of the entity which it is" (321). At any given moment, we have already been delimited by where and when we exist, our various capabilities, and our ever-growing and changing assortment of previous decisions and experiences, just to mention a few key examples. As Dreyfus (1991) sees things, Dasein is especially in debt "to the culture for an understanding of itself" (308). Within a horizon of predetermined possibilities, Dasein is responsible for making something of itself that it can find valuable. In the structural terms introduced earlier, Dasein is "Being-already-in" as much as it is "ahead-of-itself" and "Being-alongside."

To summarize, Heidegger's understanding of the limitations that help to give shape and meaning to existence does not include necessary chronological finitude. In fact, apart from the foundational boundary setting he describes, we experience existence as a rather open-ended projection into the future. Thus, it seems that Heidegger need not see immortality as a threat to meaningfulness. In the one place where he brings up the possibility that "Dasein 'lives on' or even 'outlasts' itself and is 'immortal'" (Heidegger 1962, 292), he actually does not have much to say, for or against;[9] he just does not find it especially relevant to his discussion of Being-towards-death. I do not want to make too much out of this point given that Heidegger seems to be entertaining a more religious or "other-worldly" sense of immortality (transhumanist techno-optimism was even more marginal in his day than it is in our own), but he has a clear opportunity, at this point in the text, to call attention to the axiological perils of immortality of any kind by making common chronological finitude part of his account of the structure of Dasein, and he does not do it (cf. Call 2013, 127–128; Watts 2011, 103–104). If he does not express concern that an afterlife—which at least in most Christian accounts has a sense of continuity with what came before—would jeopardize the possibility of meaning for the recently deceased, then it is not obvious to me that he would be concerned about the prospect of such continuity in the here and now. Just to be clear, I am not suggesting that Heidegger would be an advocate for immortality of any sort (and again, he does not seem to feel that what might be "after death" is a pressing issue in *Being and Time*), but I do not see any reason to think that his views on death and meaning commit him to opposing immortality. Thus, it is not out of the question that he might offer helpful resources to those hopeful that it could be meaningful. Because he never introduces a mandatory ending for Dasein, Heidegger's account could apply to mortal and immortal Dasein alike. However long Dasein exists, it will always be engaged in the process of meaning-making described in this section. On this view, mortal and immortal existence could be relevantly similar, and this is precisely what Scheffler and his sort of immortality curmudgeon doubt.

IMMORTALITY AND INHUMANITY

In response to his account of Dasein, perhaps some naysayers will argue that Heidegger just is not speaking about what humans actually find meaningful in their own lives. His very broad view of what we are appears to allow for specific notions of significance and value that might be too far removed from our own current notions to find worthwhile. Perhaps, but this is a fairly contingent and superficial point. Specific interests, values, and projects are always malleable; I imagine that early humans, and maybe some of our other ancestors in the genus *Homo*, had interests, values, and projects that would be difficult for contemporary humans to relate to. I also find it somewhat difficult to relate to the interests, values, and projects that I had early in my own finite life. Nonetheless, what I have in common with both my ancestors and my younger self, what is most characteristic and interesting about us (what makes us all Dasein), is our capacity to take an interest in our own existence. Given this shared essential ability to find ourselves meaningful, despite the variety of specific ways we might go about it, I have difficulty understanding why thinkers like Scheffler (2013) worry so much about the way humans happen to see things at any particular moment: "If we never died, then we would not live lives structured by the kinds of values that now structure our own lives or by the kinds of values that have structured the lives of other human beings now and in the past" (207). There is no doubt some truth in this statement; things would be different without death. However, few (perhaps, for instance, Williams) would deny that, in both our own particular histories and the general history of beings like us, there is evidence of a capacity to develop and adapt to new values without losing all connection to what came before (cf. Chappell 2007, 34–35; Smuts 2011, 138).[10]

What Heidegger shows us is that our sense of meaning comes not from any particular point of view or set of specific circumstances (including human fragility and deterioration), but from the basic constitution of our encounter with existing. Even though each Dasein has a certain starting point, its thrownness is constantly shifting and expanding as long as it is, and it is this malleability that contributes to the possibility of taking on new values and projects in the future, including those that an earlier version of oneself might have had a hard time imagining. It may be the case that no human has ever had the perspective of an immortal, but this fact does not preclude the possibility that an immortal could find his or her existence deeply meaningful in a way that is not relevantly dissimilar from the way ordinary humans find meaning in their mortal lives. Scheffler's claim that the absence of chronological finitude would necessitate too great a leap in this regard is at best unfounded speculation.

Returning to the various curmudgeonly arguments considered earlier, we have already seen that some comparable conceptions of stages, risk, and urgency, which were all deemed necessary for generating a sense of significance and value, might still persist in an immortal existence. Of course, Scheffler is quick to point out that "comparable" is not "the same" as the conceptions mortal humans currently have, but if we, equipped with a Heideggerian sensibility, can be more flexible than Scheffler in accepting the many ways stages, risk, and urgency manifest themselves, then immortality really does not appear so threatening to many of our current ideas of value and significance.[11] In the cases of risk and urgency, our notions of value obviously depend upon our having limitations. Heidegger's position is that our most important and relevant limitations (e.g., our spatiotemporal location, our various personal capabilities, and our previous choices) have little to do with our current mortal situation, and it would appear that many of our experiences of risk and urgency line up with this idea.[12] Although I am a philosopher of death who gives his own impending doom considerable attention, it is rarely the case that my decision-making process involves concerns about how my actions might lead to my premature demise. In fact, most of the value-generating risk I encounter has to do with things such as the repercussions of landing a new job, my comfort level when teaching unfamiliar material, and what I might be missing when I have to rule out certain activities in order to engage in others. That is, the risk is inherent in the situation I am thrown into and the activities it allows me to choose from. In the same vein, most of the value-generating urgency I experience has to do with my ability to meet the responsibilities I have taken on. That is, I usually worry about things like whether or not I will be able to write a good paper by the submission deadline, while my bucket list only occasionally comes up. Even in a thoughtful and self-aware existence, as Heidegger might see it, for the most part one does not so much fear death as feel anxious in the face of one's limited, but still significant, capacity for choice and action.

Now some might argue that the threat to risk and urgency posed by immortality is more profound than I have acknowledged thus far. Aaron Smuts (2011), for example, claims that even if certain activities have their own sense of risk and urgency built in given "the forward march of time" (140), the prospect of infinite duration would practically guarantee that anything one might want to do or experience would eventually come around again. If so, then failure to succeed or complete a task on time would cease to matter much (143). Smuts supports this claim by pointing out that the sorts of limitations Heidegger attributes to Dasein seem to make one's set of realistic goals, hopes, and projects finite. In his words, "If we could grow no smarter, no more powerful, then we would run out of projects that we would be capable of completing" (144), and end up in a state of perpetual boredom or frustration. Even if we could expand our capacities and be meaningfully occupied for billions of years, given unlimited time and any limitations at all on our capabilities, we would eventually run out of ways to see our lives as unique and valuable.

There are a few things to say in response to this line of argument. First, while it might be true that beings like us are essentially limited, Smuts has not established that the world in which we live holds only finite worthwhile possibilities for beings like us.[13] He seems to believe this to be true, even dismissing the notion that he might simply be "suffering from a dearth of imagination" (Smuts 2011, 144), but without a proper demonstration, it remains unclear why one should deny that there are infinite possibilities to occupy infinite time. I also think that Smuts (135–136) is too quick to dismiss Fischer's (2009) notion of "repeatable pleasures." After all, I have already experienced a variety of pleasures (e.g., ice cream, sex, and my favorite books) that continue to drive me forward, and it is not at all obvious to me that there is some limited number of times I might enjoy them. Nor is it immediately clear that a life consisting of such pleasurable experiences is somehow beneath my human dignity. But perhaps the primary reason why I am unconvinced by the argument that infinite time with only finite capabilities would necessarily spell disaster is that certain existing human projects and activities might be perpetually interesting, despite our basic limitations. I agree with Heidegger that the process of self-cultivation and ownership is not something to be finished with or actualized; it is a project that lasts however long you do. The possibility of continual progress is one issue to consider here, but there is also the constant need to adjust to shifting external circumstances and the danger of backsliding to worry about.

And speaking of never being finished, it will be helpful to say a little more about the alleged significance of the normal stages of a complete human life, and the idea of meaningful life as a concluded story. Heidegger points out that we never really experience such completeness or culmination, and he seems to suggest that it would be misguided to try to base the meaning of one's existence even partially on something that is not really part of one's existence.[14] If a conclusion in the ordinary sense of death is not part of any potentially meaningful mortal existence, it should not matter if it would not be part of an immortal existence. Freed from the sort of dubious completeness stipulation that Scheffler and some narrativists make, it seems possible to embrace a variety of meaningful stages (or chapters), familiar or otherwise, without needing to die. Scheffler himself admits that the specific stages of finite life are already somewhat contingent and variable, so I can see no reason to think that finite life and infinite life are essentially different in this respect. Surely, they would diverge in relatively superficial ways, but they could both still be understood in terms of orienting stages. With a renewed confidence in the value-generating capabilities of mostly ordinary notions of stages, risk, and urgency, and an optimistic attitude about the prospects of a relevantly similar life laden with particular values we may have yet to consider, I remain largely undaunted by the concerns of the immortality curmudgeons.

NOTES

1. This chapter is a revised and abridged version of Buben, A. 2016. Heidegger and the supposed meaninglessness of personal immortality. *Journal of the American Philosophical Association* 2(3): 384–399 © American Philosophical Association, published by Cambridge University Press, reproduced with permission.

2. Although I rely on her account here, Rosati is not the advocate for narrativity, and death's role in completing the life story, that thinkers like Paul Fairfield (2014, especially 26, 131) and Jeff Malpas (1998, especially 127–131) are.

3. As Niko Kolodny (2013) points out, some losses/risks would be much worse in a life that cannot end (167; cf. May 2009, 64; Nussbaum 1994, 228); in the case of losing someone's affections, death might actually serve as sweet relief from crushing regret.

4. Witnessing the death of another will not help here, since "we have no way of access to the loss-of-Being as such which the dying man 'suffers'" (Heidegger 1962, 282).

5. In one prime example of his association of these two concepts, Heidegger (1962) claims that "this item in the structure of care has its most primordial concretion in Being-towards-death" (294).

6. *Eigentlich*, which is the word translated as "authentic" in *Being and Time*, can be more literally translated as the rather awkward "enownment." The suggestion here is that becoming authentic amounts to an owning up to oneself or becoming one's own.

7. Heidegger (1962) puts this sense of freedom in terms of having "*been released from the Illusions of the 'they'*" (311).

8. Note well that anxiety here has to do with Dasein's essential lack of unequivocal guidance and support in making something of itself, which is demonstrated in Being-towards-death. Making an important distinction between anxiety and fear on these very pages, Heidegger points out that Dasein is not anxious because of some coming event, even if some might fear it.

9. For a number of reasons (chapter length among them), I am not addressing potentially relevant ideas in the later Heidegger. For an example, see Malpas (1998, 134), who covertly (and I think mistakenly) attempts to show that *Being and Time* ideas support Williams's anti-immortality sentiments.

10. On the personal level, consider the example of religious conversion in which one takes on values that might conflict dramatically with those previously held while still retaining something of one's former identity (even if metaphors of rebirth suggest otherwise).

11. Incidentally, it is not always clear whether Scheffler (2013) imagines immortal beings with a birthday or has in mind instead perpetual beings that have no origin (e.g., 203–205). Either way, he believes that these beings are unlikely to have values like ours. If he is speaking about beings with an origin, this fact (i.e., having an origin) alone might be sufficient to generate and maintain at least some values like ours. If he is speaking about beings without an origin, Scheffler might have a point, but this

just is not a problem I (and I assume anyone reading this) could personally ever have to worry about.

12. Nussbaum (1994, 232) seems a bit more amenable to Heidegger's view of our limitations than May (2009, 57–59) and Scheffler (2013, 204), who see death as the most significant of human limitations.

13. In fact, depending on one's views about the boundaries of this universe or the possibility of unlimited other universes, there might be reason to believe that this understanding of our world is false.

14. On Heidegger's view of these matters, see Malpas (1998, 129–131, 134n20) and Fairfield (2014, 91), who offer a narrativist reading, and Guignon (2011, 195–196), who argues against such a reading. Also see Tony Fisher (2010) for a helpful (if slightly out of date) orientation in this debate (247–248). Given my account of Heidegger's sense of wholeness, I obviously side with Guignon's recent position.

Part III

ETHICS, MEDICALIZATION, AND TECHNOLOGY

Chapter 9

Heidegger's Philosophy of Technology and the Perils of Medicalization

Fredrik Svenaeus

New medical technologies are increasingly transforming the meaning patterns of everyday life. The new diagnostic and therapeutic possibilities that medicine offers transform and question borders between life and death and normality and abnormality in direct and indirect ways. Technologies of assisted reproduction are reshaping the forms of the beginning of life and the ability to choose what will happen in its course. Organ transplant techniques and life-supporting technologies make it possible to postpone death and being "born again" with new organs or mechanic devices. Genetics and stem cell research play major roles at both ends of life in developing the knowledge and techniques of starting, predicting, and prolonging life in various ways. Neurophysiology and psychiatry offer us ways of understanding and changing persons and their personalities by aid of brain imaging technologies, implants, prostheses, and pharmaceuticals.

This development has only begun, and within the discipline of biomedical ethics philosophers are presently examining the ethical challenges that future medical "enhancement" technologies will bring (Hauskeller 2014; Parens 2015; Savulescu et al. 2011). This is an important work: Our ability to handle new technologies—and not let the technologies handle us—will be decisive for the society to come. However, in these analyses, phenomenology is too rarely brought into play in any substantive way to understand how new medical technologies are changing the patterns of our everyday lives in direct ways, and also reshaping our images of life, health, personality, and the good life in a more indirect manner. In the present chapter I will attempt to do so by exploring how Martin Heidegger's phenomenological critique of modern techno-science is relevant to medical ethics, especially as concerns the issue of medicalization (see also Aho and Aho 2009; Svenaeus 2013).

HEIDEGGER'S PHILOSOPHY OF TECHNOLOGY AND MEDICINE

In the essay "The Question Concerning Technology," published in 1954, Heidegger sets himself the aim of articulating what he calls the "essence" of modern technology (1977). According to Heidegger, modern technology has allied itself with science in such a way that the character of modern technology must be seen as fundamentally different from the character of traditional technologies based on craftsmanship. To implement modern technology is not only a matter of shaping nature in order to satisfy human goals; modern technology also entails an "enframing" worldview (in Heidegger's German: "*Gestell*"), whereby nature is viewed purely as an energy resource in a scientific-economic calculus.

The concept of technological "enframement" is related to what Heidegger in his first major philosophical work *Being and Time*, published in 1927, calls "being-in-the-world" (1996). It is an attempt to name and characterize the basic meaning pattern through which things appear as such-and-such things for us. Heidegger's point is that modern technology has decisively changed the meaning pattern of the world, which traditionally has involved a number of different natural and cultural features constitutive of human practices. His point is also that modern technology has done so in a way that we should find problematic and strive to move beyond because it severely limits what we are able to see, think, and do in the world.

His point is not that we should abstain from all use of scientific technology and try to live a premodern life. He knows more than well that this would be not only undesirable but also impossible. His point is that the essence of technology has developed into a danger in becoming the *dominating* and, most often also taken for granted and therefore *barely visible*, worldview of the modern age. We must live within the "framework" of modern technology, since there is no other way to live today, but we can strive to make this meaning pattern of modern technology and science visible through a philosophical analysis, and take measures to prevent it from becoming the all-encompassing pattern of our being-in-the-world (Borgmann 2005).

Reflecting upon the meaning and significance of *medical* technology is a good way to save Heidegger's analysis from falling into traps of romantic anti-scientism. Heidegger could hardly deny that inventions such as X-ray, the medical laboratory, the artificial kidney, or antibiotics do more and better things to us than exposing us to a life in the *Gestell*. Therefore, it would be wrong, I think, to forge a necessary and immediate link between the use of modern technology and the domination of a technological worldview in Heidegger's writings. The essence of modern technology is not something technological, as Heidegger states several times in his essay, and this we can see even more clearly if we turn to a couple of lines from another text by Heidegger, published for the first time in 1958 but conceived as early as 1939, "On the Essence and Concept of *Physis*":

> Medical practice and technology (*techne*) can only cooperate with nature (*physis*), can more or less facilitate the health (of the patient), but as technology it can never replace nature and in its place become the principle of health as such. This could only happen if life in itself became a "technically" producible artifact, but if this were to become the case there would no more exist any health, as little as there would exist any being born or dying. (Heidegger 1978, 255, my translation)

To facilitate the health of a patient with the help of medical technology need not be identical to enforcing a "framework" of technology on him or her, a new way of defining, shaping, and producing health and life under the reign of medical science. But it is a constant *risk*. Hans-Georg Gadamer articulates this risk in his collection of essays *The Enigma of Health*, a philosophy of health and medicine which is deeply indebted to Heidegger's philosophy of technology:

> In medical science we encounter the dissolution of personhood when the patient is objectified in terms of a mere multiplicity of data. In a clinical investigation all the information about a person is treated as if it could be adequately collated on a card index. If this is done in a correct way, then the data (*Werte*) all belong to the person. But the question is nevertheless whether the unique value of the individual (*Eigenwert*) is properly recognized in this process. (Gadamer 1996, 81, translation modified)

The enframing of human being through medical science and technology takes place when the embodied complaints of the patient are taken out of the life-world context of human dialog and replaced by a medical-scientific analysis only. This, I think, is the core relevance of Heidegger's philosophy of medical technology for biomedical ethics that I will elaborate upon in what follows.

The contemporary debate about human enhancement in bioethics, discussing medical measures that go beyond the curing of diseases, has been very much focused on *genetic* interventions. Francis Crick and James Watson discovered the DNA molecule in the beginning of the 1950s, after Heidegger had conceived "The Question Concerning Technology," but we actually find some thoughts about how genetics may merge with information technology (cybernetics) in attempts to manipulate and control human being(s) in seminars that he conducted during the 1960s together with Eugen Fink and others (Heidegger 1986, 27–29, 313, 358). However, the richest source for Heidegger's approach to the nature and problems of medical practice is *The Zollikon Seminars* (Heidegger 2001a).

HEIDEGGER AMONG THE DOCTORS

During the 1960s Heidegger held several lectures for medical students in the little Swiss town of Zollikon at the invitation of the psychiatrist Medard Boss, who was trying to make use of Heidegger's philosophy in the version of psychotherapy he was developing: *Daseinsanalyse* (the "analytic of Dasein" is Heidegger's own name for the philosophy of being-in-the-world he had developed in *Being and Time*). Heidegger thinks that phenomenological philosophy is very important to doctors for the very reason that they should not fall under the spell of technology: "It is of utmost importance that we have *thinking* doctors, doctors who do not rest content with abandoning the field of medicine to scientific technicians" (Heidegger 2001a, 103). Heidegger approaches this importance (*Not*) in the seminars by focusing upon two themes: the problem of *method* and the problem of *embodiment*. He takes these themes, or problems, to be identical in medicine, since the problem of embodiment (*Leib*) is first and foremost a problem of method (2001a, 93). Heidegger characterizes the scientific method by going back to the scientific revolution in the seventeenth century—Galileo and Descartes—and the ways of thinking they inaugurated.

Heidegger claims that an essential split between the human subject and the objects of nature was put in place by the scientific revolution, and he also claims that this split robs human beings of their own nature, since the human subject itself becomes an object: "Engaged in such a modern science is a dictatorship of mind (*Diktatur des Geistes*), that degrades the mind itself to a handling of calculable operators" (Heidegger 2001a, 107). This reification of human being becomes a central part of modern scientific medicine when the body is viewed as a machine, a metaphor used by Descartes and since then dominating the medical field. But the human body is not only a biological object; it is also a way of being:

> Everything that we refer to as our lived body (*unsere Leiblichkeit*), including the most minute muscle fibre and the most imperceptible hormone molecule, belongs essentially to our mode of existence. This body is consequently *not* to be understood as lifeless matter, but is part of that domain that cannot be

objectified or seen, a being able to encounter significance, which our entire being-there (*Da-sein*) consists in. This lived body (*dieses Leibliche*) forms itself in a way appropriate for using the lifeless and living material objects that it encounters. In contrast to a tool, however, the living domains of existence cannot be released from the human being. They cannot be stored separately in a tool-box. Rather they remain pervaded by human being, kept in a human being, belonging to a human being, as long as he or she lives. (Heidegger 2001a, 232, translation modified)

The important thing here is not that Heidegger appears to be unaware of the medical technology of organ transplantation, rapidly developing at the same time he is speaking (with organs being carried around in tool-boxes) (Svenaeus 2010); the important thing is the fundamental difference he makes between the body as a biological object (*Körper*) and the body as a way of being-in-the-world (lived body: *Leib*). That "the body is pervaded (*durchwaltet*) by human being (*Mensch-sein*)," as Heidegger says, means that the body understands and inhabits the world. Heidegger expresses this in his late talks to Boss and to the latter's medical students through the neologism "Das Leiben des Leibes": human existence is a "bodying forth" in the meaning-structures of the world, and this is something that must not be missed by the doctor if he is going to be able to help his patients (2001a, 86–87). Psychosomatic medicine is the most obvious example of this, but Heidegger's remarks are not restricted to instants when the body displays physiological signs of stress and unresolved unconscious conflicts.

As a contrast to the scientific method, Heidegger articulates the phenomenological method as a way of philosophizing in which the ways of the lived body can be articulated and understood. Examples he gives are the understanding the meaning of a blush, the feeling of a pain, or the experience of sorrow, phenomena that cannot be measured and made intelligible by medical physiology, but which can nevertheless be essential for the doctor to understand in meeting with the patient (Heidegger 2001a, 81). These are bodily phenomena, but they are nevertheless pregnant with meaning that cannot be articulated by the scientific, but only by the phenomenological, method. The same goes for the effects that pharmaceuticals may have on persons in their intercourse:

From the fact that something can be brought about in bodily being through chemical interventions the conclusion is drawn that the origin and cause of the mental in human beings is physiological chemistry. This is wrong, for something that is a requirement for an existential relation between human beings is not its cause, not its yielding cause (*hervorbringende Ursache*), and consequently not its origin. The existential relation does not consist of molecules, does not come into being through molecules, but is also not without that which can be reinterpreted as a physiological-molecular happening. (Heidegger 2001a, 155, translation modified)

Doctors, according to Heidegger, should by no means be hostile to science, but they should learn to see the limitations and dangers of acting *only* as scientists in their profession when they are meeting patients with bodily problems, since this could, as Heidegger alarmingly puts it, "lead to the self annihilation (*Selbstzerstörung*) of human being" (2001a, 95). The annihilation of human being, not as a biological being, of course, but as a being-in-the-world, is therefore a problem and danger that stems from choosing the scientific method as the only one relevant in medicine. This is also the danger that Heidegger sees in using medical technology in attempting to help patients. The greatest danger is not that the pieces of modern technology would by themselves dominate or make the patient as a person disappear from the attention of the doctor; although this may happen in the individual case, the danger is that the scientific attitude finds a dominating *hold* by way of the technology that makes the attitude in question harder to critically scrutinize and complement with the phenomenological point of view.

The two brief examples Heidegger gives of medical technologies in *The Zollikon Seminars* confirm this interpretation, since they do not portray the technology in question as an installment of the *Gestell*, but rather as a danger of facilitating the domination of the scientific method (at the expense of the phenomenological method) in medicine. Both examples concern the brain, which is obviously central to Heidegger's concerns, not only because he is speaking with psychiatrists, but also because we are talking about the "organ of thinking." The first example is EEG:

> We do not have any possibilities to know how the brain bodies forth in thinking. What we see in an EEG picture has nothing to do with the bodying forth of the brain (*mit dem Leiben des Gehirns*), but with the fact that the brain can also be thought about and visualized as a chemical-physical piece of matter (*Körper*). (Heidegger 2001a, 197, translation modified)

The second example of a medical technology mentioned by Heidegger is even more interesting, since it concerns a form of treatment that was highly disputed, one might even say demonized, in the 1960s: electroconvulsive therapy (2001a, 196). But Heidegger does not make any comments about punishment and control being enacted through the therapy in question; his main concern is instead to show that the machine can only release (*auslösen*) moods, not produce them, since moods derive their meaning from human being as a being-in-the-world.

IMPLICATIONS FOR BIOMEDICAL ETHICS

The main lesson taught by Heidegger to the doctors in Zollikon seems to be that they should be wary of letting the scientific attitude dominate their encounters with patients. Medical science has to find its proper place in relation to the phenomenological method of interpreting the being-in-the-world of the patient in medical practice. Heidegger's main concern in the seminars is with pinpointing the origin and nature of the scientific method, in combination with introducing the phenomenological method as an alternative perspective in medicine. But medical science, as we all know, does not only represent the threat of reifying the suffering of patients; it has also led to major breakthroughs in helping patients with diseases that could not be treated by premodern doctors. These breakthroughs have come to the fore in the form of different medical technologies making diagnosis, prevention, and treatment of diseases possible (Reiser 2009). The technologies in question may well harbor the risk of "dissolving" the person, as Gadamer says in the quote earlier, "annihilating" her, as Heidegger puts it, but they can also save a person's life, a service I think no one would like to abstain from in situations of impending suffering.

Given the fact that Heidegger does not provide us with this analysis himself, do we have any ways of distinguishing between medical technologies that we could use without being swallowed up by the *Gestell* and the ones we should abstain from using because they will make us inhuman? Yet Heidegger's concern is not mainly with individual examples of technologies but rather with what he calls their essence. The *Gestell* is not more or less present in an individual piece of modern technology; it is the framework of meaning that puts the different pieces together, making us view nature as a product with utility value only. Acknowledging this clarification, I think it still makes sense to ask about the effect or risk an individual technological invention may harbor in putting us on a track to a form of life in which the essence of modern technology comes to dominate our worldview and actions. The individual instantiations of modern technology are not just like *any* part of the world. If they were, why would Heidegger concern himself with *technology* in the first place in spelling out the dangers of the *Gestell* in his writings?

In evaluating the risks a type of technology will harbor in making us see and think about things as resources only, we could pick up on Heidegger's analysis in *The Zollikon Seminars* of the importance of human embodiment for our being-in-the-world (Heidegger 2001a). We could argue that medical technologies that divorce us from our current embodied life form tend to rob us of our personhood and all the human values that go with it (Agar 2013; Hauskeller 2014). The *Leib* is our fundamental contact with nature, not only as something that we make use of, but as something that we *are* and must *respond* to rather than try to dominate and install new standards for. Heidegger's early emphasis on finitude ("being-towards-death") as the source of meaning for human existence, and his attempts to analyze this form of life through the significance of different forms of attunements that make us present with others in the world and for ourselves (as embodied), plotted already in *Being and Time*, would fit well with such attempts to find a human measure for medical technologies (Heidegger 1996).

Admittedly, the criterion would have to be developed and refined in different ways in order to solve the hard cases. It is easy to make an argument with the help of such a criterion that we should refrain from uploading our brains to computers in order to live forever, or from cloning babies to be grown in artificial wombs, but what about the borders of assisted reproduction and the limits of organ transplantation? In many cases the same technology will have "good" and "bad" uses—think of the current use of respirators or genetic diagnosis. And the impact of medical technologies should not be thought about only through the drastic examples of making human life radically different by "producing" human life, as Heidegger himself puts it in the quote from "On the Essence and Concept of *Physis*" earlier (1978, 255), but also through examples of technologies that tend to narrow the scope of health by inventing new diseases, or by expanding the borderlines of the diseases that we currently treat (Conrad 2007; Stempsey 2006).

PHENOMENOLOGY OF HEALTH

Indeed, the phenomenon of health itself could be looked upon as a particularly urgent theme to study and explicate from a phenomenological point of view for a contemporary medicine that tries to answer to the dangers of modern technology that Heidegger spells out in his writings. As Heidegger writes, if life were to become a technically producible artifact "there would no more exist any health, as little there would exist any being born or dying" (1978, 255). Heidegger himself never carried out such an analysis of the meaning of health and illness in his works, but I think it is obvious from what we find in *The Zollikon Seminars* that it would have to proceed from a position giving priority to the lived body and the life-world (being-in-the-world) of human being, rather than from a position giving priority to applied medical science.

I have myself in other books and papers tried to show with the aid of Heidegger's philosophy how the healthy versus the ill life can be explicated as *homelike* versus *unhomelike* being-in-the-world (Svenaeus 2000). Illness is an *alienating* mood overcoming a person and engaging him or her in a struggle to remain at home in face of the loss of meaning and purpose in life.

To be ill means to be not at home in one's being-in-the-world, to find oneself in a pattern of disorientedness, resistance, helplessness, and perhaps even despair, instead of in the familiar transparency of healthy life.

It is important to stress the fundamental difference between a phenomenological illness concept in a theory such as this and the concept of disease in its biomedical sense (Carel 2008). A disease is a disturbance of the biological functions of the body (or something that causes such a disturbance), which can be detected and understood only from the perspective of the doctor investigating the body with the aid of his or her hands or medical technologies. The patient can also adopt such a scientific perspective toward his or her own body and speculate about diseases responsible for suffering. But the suffering itself is an illness experience of the person who is in a world, embodied and connected to other people around him or her. Illness has meaning, or, perhaps, rather *disturbs* the meaning processes of being-in-the-world in which one is leading one's life on an everyday level.

Gadamer, in *The Enigma of Health*, points out, in the spirit of Heidegger, that health cannot be produced by the doctor using technical and scientific skills; rather, health must be *re-established*, as something that has been lost, by helping the patient to heal himself or herself. Health, according to Gadamer, is a kind of self-restoring balance, and the doctor provides the means by which a state of equilibrium can re-establish itself on its own power:

> Without doubt it is part of our nature as living beings that the conscious awareness of health conceals itself. Despite its hidden character, health nonetheless manifests itself in a kind of feeling of well-being. It shows itself above all where such a feeling of well-being means that we are open to new things, ready to embark on new enterprises and, forgetful of ourselves, scarcely notice the demands and strains which are put upon us. . . . Health is not a condition that one introspectively feels in oneself. Rather it is a condition of being there, of being in the world, of being together with other people, of being taken in by an active and rewarding engagement with the things that matter in life. . . . It is the rhythm of life, a permanent process in which equilibrium re-establishes itself. (Gadamer 1996, 112–114, translation modified)

The conceptual backdrop for Gadamer's analysis of health in the preceding quote is undoubtedly Heidegger's phenomenology of everyday human being-in-the-world, found in *Being and Time*, which is also the starting point for my own analysis of suffering and illness (Svenaeus 2000). Despite the fact that Heidegger did not address and develop any phenomenology of health himself in approaching technology and medicine, his philosophy offers a promising starting point in such endeavors.

Heidegger's and Gadamer's philosophies can help us to see how the scientific attitude in medicine must always be balanced by and integrated into a phenomenological way of understanding the life-world concerns of patients. The difference between the scientific and the phenomenological method in medicine is articulated by Heidegger in distinguishing two different ways of studying the human body: as biological organism and as lived body. Medicine needs to acknowledge the priority of the lived body in addressing health as a way of being-in-the-world, and not as the absence of diseases only. One important consequence of this explication of Heidegger's philosophy of technology is that the philosophy in question is by no means hostile to technology when it comes to medical practice. The old medical advice of helping nature to heal itself can sit well with modern technological inventions for the diagnosis, prevention, and cure of diseases, but the perspective of the lived body as a way of being-in-the-world will also make us wary of the technologies that tend to block life-world concerns in order to prolong or even produce life as a goal in itself.

ENHANCEMENT AND MEDICALIZATION

The main focus of the enhancement and post humanism debates in biomedical ethics so far have been future technologies that will make it possible to genetically design persons in vitro or radically transform them by way of prostheses that are surgically mended to the body and the brain in a cyborg manner (More and Vitra-More 2013). In contrast to science-fiction technologies, which may make it possible to develop creatures with an intelligence, moral capacity, physical strength, and life length beyond the human, cosmetic surgery and various pharmaceuticals currently prescribed show us what medical enhancement looks like already today. Cosmetic surgery is by definition in the business of changing our looks according to cultural norms, rather than repairing injuries or congenital defects, and it is often criticized for reinforcing sexist, ageist, and racist aesthetic ideals (Sullivan 2001). According to such a critique, the enforcement of these ideals by way of surgery not only prohibits rather than supports the flourishing of the persons that are operated on, but it also makes life worse for *other* individuals, who do not apply to the norms (who cannot afford or do not wish for surgery). In addition to cosmetic surgery, medication for sexual dysfunction, baldness, menopause, premenstrual syndrome, and a whole flora of steroids and anti-ageing pills are all examples of contemporary enhancement drugs. However, the most challenging cases of enhancement today are found within psychopharmacology.

Pharmaceuticals are clearly examples of biomedical technology, and in the case of psychopharmacology the targets of the chemicals are the functions of neurons of the brain, making the drugs into "neuro-technologies" (Rose and Abi-Rached 2013). The advent of Prozac in the late 1980s inaugurated a debate about what it meant to be put in a state that was "better than well" by way of psychiatric medication (Elliott and Chambers 2004; Kramer 1994; Healy 1999; Svenaeus 2007). The new antidepressants (SSRIs, SNRIs, and others) transformed the treatment of mood disorders—depression as well as anxiety disorders—in the 1990s and sold in numbers beyond imagination. The rapidly increased use of Ritalin and other drugs used to treat ADHD (attention-deficit/hyperactivity disorder) during the same period of time proved to be a parallel example of how psychopharmacological drugs have effects on mood and personality traits of millions of people (Conrad 2007; Saul 2014). What is striking in surveying these two examples, as well as many other pharmacological enhancement technologies of today, is the way the technologies are implemented: not by directly subscribing to enhancement but instead by expanding the domain of the diseased and disordered. In a way this is the inevitable consequence of how pharmaceuticals are tested, approved, and sold according to a system of clinical trials developed already in the 1960s (Healy 1999). In order to get a drug into the system the pharmaceutical company developing and eventually selling it needs to get the drug approved for the treatment of a diagnosed disease or mental disorder (the latter is the preferred term for diseased states of the brain and soul in psychiatry). Consequently, the enhancement of moods and personality of patients must always take place as a curing or relieving of an unhealthy state of being. Naturally, pharmaceutical companies are trying to push the inclusiveness of the diagnoses they are developing drugs to treat by way of marketing, sponsoring, and other interactions with doctors and patient groups (Elliott 2010).

As the French historian and philosopher of medicine Georges Canguilhem remarks, the meaning of the Latin and Greek roots of the word *normal* are to "make geometrically square" and "enforce grammatical order," respectively (Canguilhem 1991, 239, 244). Canguilhem was, indeed, Michel Foucault's teacher, and in these etymologies we already discern the latter philosopher's analysis of "biopolitics" as a dominating practice and discourse in modern Western societies (Foucault 1990). According to the theory of biopolitics, the successes of the new antidepressants and ADHD medications are both examples of *normalization* in the sense that the norms for feeling and behaving well in contemporary Western culture and societies are made tighter and less inclusive with the help of the drugs. In tandem with this narrowing tendency of the healthy, the cultural ideals influencing what we may term human *flourishing* in contrast to human suffering also change in our society. Antidepressants and ADHD medications foster the ideal of a positive, in-control energetic and socially competent personality that it is now possible to achieve by way of taking medication. There are no more excuses for staying melancholic and neurotic or disorganized and impulsive if this can be fixed with the help of a drug.

When the new pharmaceuticals have been introduced, the old ways of life are no longer viewed as cases of unhappiness or socially cumbersome behavior; they are viewed as states of mental disorder. Normalization by way of pharmaceuticals is consequently typically a process of *medicalization* that expands the domains of the unhealthy at the expense of parts of the previously healthy and/or socially deviant behavior, previously likewise considered abnormal, but in a moral sense relating to cultural ideals and not to theories of mental disorder. Medical enhancement, which in the standard bioethical definition is that which takes us *beyond* the curing of diseases, is currently argued for and propagated in terms of achieving health, not in terms of making people "better than well." This is clearly a medicalization process in the descriptive sense of the word; the numbers of diagnoses of ADHD, depression, and anxiety disorders *have* skyrocketed, and in all three cases involve 5–10 percent of the population each year in the United States and many other Western countries. The important question is whether the rise of diagnoses is also a process of medicalization in the *normative* sense, meaning that a large number of the newly diagnosed patients are actually healthy and not ill in spite of what the doctors claim.

Perhaps Prozac and Ritalin are neuro-technological examples of *producing* health rather than reinstating it—by way of producing newly diagnosed individuals that are treated with the drugs—in the way that Heidegger and Gadamer put it in their critique of modern technology (Heidegger 1978, 255; Gadamer 1996, 81)? Since some of the patients treated with antidepressants and ADHD medicines describe their experiences as having never before felt the way they now feel, and some of them even have the experience of "being themselves" for the first time on the drug (Kramer 1994), the answer to this question seems to be yes: Health is not brought back by helping the body to reinstate its lost norms, but it is produced as a novel state of being. Gadamer actually criticizes modern psychiatry for exactly this reason:

> I am thinking of the world of modern psychiatric drugs. I cannot separate this development entirely from the general instrumentalization of the living body that also occurs in the world of modern agriculture, in the economy and in industrial research. What does it signify that such developments now defines what we are and what we are capable of achieving? Does this not also open up a new threat to human life? Is there not a terrifying challenge involved in the fact that through psychiatric drugs doctors are able not only to eliminate and relieve various organic disturbances, but also to take away from a person her deepest distress and confusion? (Gadamer 1996, 77, translation modified)

The keyword to understanding the instrumentalization-medicalization process of psychopharmacology from a phenomenological point of view is, I think, the concept of *alienation*. Psychiatric drugs (when they are effective) relieve patients of their suffering as they become more at home in their life on the interconnected levels of embodiment, everyday engagement in the world with others and life narrative. The fear that Gadamer harbors is that the drugs by doing this—by relieving symptoms like feelings of hopelessness, anxiety, and restlessness—also may separate the person from his or her true self. When the pills flatten the life moods of the patient, he or she is no longer forced to challenge himself or herself on the true meaning of his or her life: what he or she wants to accomplish and who he or she wants to be. By producing health the drugs would therefore—at least in some cases—alienate the patient from his or her true self.

PSYCHIATRY AND THE *DSM*

Mental illness, like somatic illness, is usually connected to agonizing feelings and difficulties in carrying out everyday actions. These feelings and disabilities are experienced in a bodily manner by the person suffering from them. Anxiety disorders and depression are connected to having panic attacks and experiencing moods of sadness and boredom, which make themselves known in making the body painful, immobile, and paralyzed, the lived body being unable to make itself at home in the world (Svenaeus 2007). ADHD, is defined by patterns of inattention and hyperactivity visible from the actions of persons and surely also experienced as moods which "fill up" the body in struggling to concentrate or stay calm.

Similar cases could be made for other mental disorders manifesting themselves as alienating processes within the domains of the lived body and the everyday being-in-the-world of the patient (Fuchs 2000; Fulford 1989). But what about the existential domains of suffering that Gadamer fears will be eradicated by Prozac and Ritalin? The reason for his fear is that existential suffering in situations that are possible to endure and survive will often lead to a fuller life *in the long run*, because the suffering person will get to know himself or herself through the life crisis and change his or her life goals in this process (Madison 2013). Somatic illness typically involves existential suffering only in severe cases, whereas mental illness involves existential suffering in most cases, also in the cases referred to as mild and looked upon as bordering on unhappiness. Accordingly, somatic illness can (in severe cases) give rise to existential suffering, whereas in the case of mental illness it is usually present.

That existential suffering is typically involved in a different and more constitutive way in mental illness than in somatic illness—actually, from the phenomenological point of view, "mental" and "somatic" illness both involve the lived body—means that we should be even more cautious in subjecting the field of psychiatry to technologies that bring instrumentalization and medicalization in their footsteps. We have concentrated on the prescription of certain types of pharmaceuticals, but an even greater danger from the phenomenological viewpoint lies in the standardization brought by the increasing use of diagnostic manuals, like the *Diagnostic and Statistical Manual of Mental Disorders* or *DSM* (APA 2013a). These are surely pieces of technology that may subject us to the *Gestell*, the enframing worldview that Heidegger held to be at work in modern technology and science.

The risk with using diagnostic manuals in psychiatry is not only over diagnosis and medicalization of healthy behaviors and feelings, which are rather cases of political- or existential- than illness-suffering by the phenomenological characterizations I have given earlier. The risk is also that persons are stereotyped, made into their diagnoses instead of being approached and understood in an empathic manner addressing life-world concerns. Psychiatry carried out predominantly by way of the *DSM* clearly harbors precisely the instrumentalizing tendency that Heidegger saw at work in power plants and coalmines; what is being enframed in this case is not only (human) nature, but also personhood and ways of life. The use of Ritalin, then, may have a stereotyping outcome as it concerns moods and ways of being-in-the-world, but perhaps more problematically, the psychiatric diagnosis itself has the tendency to map and sort persons into ready-made categories like ADHD.

Chapter 10

Breathlessness: From Bodily Symptom to Existential Experience

Tina Williams and Havi Carel

> Existentially, breathlessness is a constant reminder of impending mortality. Most of us want to die in our sleep with no knowledge of the event. Not only do patients with chronic, progressive lung disease know of their impending death months, years or decades ahead of the day, they fear how they will die, with the fear of suffocation always somewhere in their minds.
>
> —Currow and Johnson, "Dyspnoea"

This chapter uses a phenomenological approach to investigate the philosophical significance of a common yet debilitating experience: the experience of severe and pathological breathlessness. Using two key examples of breathlessness in the case of respiratory disease (somatic) and in anxiety disorders (considered as mental disorder) we show why a phenomenological approach to the study of these experiences is needed and how the distinction between the somatic and the mental comes under pressure when considering a complex phenomenon like breathlessness.

We see the distinction between the somatic and the mental as emerging from a key problem in modern health care: a disproportionate commitment to a worldview that prioritizes the physiological over the holistic (Aho and Aho 2009). This worldview can be associated with problems in healthcare provision, communication between health professionals and ill persons, and in outcomes (see Carel 2013a; Toombs 1987; Department of Health 2011). This approach, we suggest, gives rise to a failure to adequately account for the alterations in the lifeworld of the respiratory patient. This approach also occludes the complex and shifting nature of breathlessness, which is a unique medical symptom, as we explain below.

As a result of the prioritization of the physiological, we suggest that patients are subject to unnecessary suffering, inappropriate treatments, increased failure rates in outcomes, and epistemic injustice (cf. Carel and Kidd 2014; Critchton et al. 2016). Moreover, we suggest that clinicians' knowledge, understanding, and treatment of comorbid mental health conditions in respiratory patients is lacking and further exacerbates an already complex and debilitating health concern.

Furthermore, research shows that the impact of patients' socioeconomic, cultural, and mental health status affects the development, treatment, and management of respiratory disorders, and so needs to be addressed in the context of respiratory medicine (Wilson 2006). For instance, studies show that patients with chronic obstructive pulmonary disorder (COPD) are often poor, working-class smokers (Pauwels and Rabe 2004). We thus argue that socioeconomic status is part of patients' life-world and therefore plays a constitutive role in their health and well-being (Department of Health 2008; Gysels and Higginson 2008; Marmot 2010).

In those with a mental health diagnosis, rates of respiratory disorders increase, as many patients with depression or anxiety (for example) also smoke to cope with their anxiety (Wilson 2006; van Manen et al. 2002). One study found anxiety and depression rates of 80 percent in COPD patients who smoke (Kunik et al. 2005). In prison populations, up to 90 percent are smokers, and many have smoking-related disorders as well as mental health conditions, both of which are underdiagnosed, alongside restricted access to pulmonary rehabilitation, an efficacious intervention for breathlessness discomfort (Turner and Jefford 2013). So it is also a health inequality issue (Department of Health 2010; Social Exclusion Task force 2010).

Focusing on phenomenological descriptions of the person as being-in-the-world can help us begin to address inadequate understandings of respiratory illness. This has been the focus of the Life of Breath, a Wellcome Trust–funded research project we are members of (www.lifeofbreath.org). Indeed, our work suggests that a phenomenological framework captures how the structures of experience and the possibilities of certain experiences are changed in patients with breathlessness and panic disorder (Carel, Dodd, and Macnaughton 2015). Moreover, this approach can help explicate the "problem of differentiation" whereby clinicians and patients alike struggle to distinguish breathlessness caused by respiratory illness from that caused by panic anxiety.

We argue that phenomenological description and explanation is indispensable to our understanding of the difficulties faced by patients. Attention to the life-world of the patient is essential to making their experience intelligible. It is also indispensable to medical understanding of the impact of breathlessness on conditions that challenge this dichotomous understanding, which, in turn, results in compartmentalized treatment of these illnesses. We hope that the reconceptualization of breathlessness disorders in phenomenological terms will contribute to improved patient care, reduced misunderstandings and epistemic injustice, and improved ability to address the interrelated issues which arise from these illnesses.

Many studies show significant barriers in place for those with physical illnesses comorbid with mental health conditions; in this context, many physical symptoms are at risk of being dismissed due to the mental health diagnosis, resulting in integrated care obstacles (Gysels and Higginson 2008). This is a further reason to study these disorders. Detailing the experiences of such patients is important in order to understand how and why this happens, and suggest ways to address these troubling problems (Rethink Mental Illness 2012; Department of Health 2011; Hegarty 2011).

BREATHLESSNESS: FROM SYMPTOM TO EXPERIENCE

The ability to breathe underpins human life; it is vital to all we do. Not only do we unconsciously alter our breathing when talking and moving; we can also control our breath to dive, avoid inhaling toxic fumes around cities, and calm ourselves. In people with respiratory disease, the struggle to breathe is often a mortal threat.

Imagine sprinting up several flights of stairs and getting out of breath. Now imagine feeling like that *all the time*. When you cannot catch your breath terror, panic and a sense of suffocation overcome you. Thus anxiety often accompanies pathological breathlessness, due to a constant sense of threat and bodily betrayal (Smoller et al. 1996; Carel 2016). Importantly, this experience is largely invisible and difficult to describe, despite being one of the leading causes of suffering in the UK, and a significant cause of death that is on the rise (World Health Organization 2016). This invisibility stems in part from stigma attached to breathlessness (associated with smoking) and pronouncedly to mental illness, due to perceptions of responsibility and weakness of will (Crichton et al. 2017). This invisibility also has an embodied dimension: When the breath is stifled, talk is silenced, communication cut off and in its extreme manifestation, both panic and oxygen deprivation can significantly impact thinking itself (O'Donnell et al. 2007; LeDoux 2015).

However, can we sharply distinguish the physiological from the mental in the experience of breathlessness? Can we separate somatic sensations from how they are experienced, interpreted, and expressed? In our view, the answer is no. Breathlessness is a unique medical symptom and experience that of its essence involves sensation, cognition, and reasoning, none of which are reducible to the other. To think of it purely in physiological terms is inadequate as the experience has significant emotional, cognitive, and interpretative dimensions. Thus we have a significant and common medical symptom that unsettles the distinction between somatic and mental symptoms and disorders.

How is breathlessness typically characterized in both medicine and lay knowledge? While the physiological components are bound to a wide variety of subjective and cultural ideas about breath, and thus may vary considerably, typical sensations include feeling short of breath, winded, difficulty in inhalation or exhalation, air hunger, chest tightness, and discomfort when breathing (Carel 2014). Not every experience of breathlessness includes every sensation, nor is it at the same intensity for different episodes and there is much felt variation between and within individuals (Abernathy and Wheeler 2008; Smoller et al. 1996; Lansing et al. 2009).

In terms of the etiology of pathological breathlessness, no two cases of underlying dysfunction will necessarily result in the same felt intensity or severity of the experience (Abernathy and Wheeler 2008; Haugdahl et al 2015). Apart from the varying subjective qualities of breathlessness, and a wide range of underlying causes, intensity can also be difficult to measure, rendering evaluation, treatment, and management difficult and sometimes ineffective (American Thoracic Society 1995). Diagnosing and assessing breathlessness typically follows the medical model, insofar as the pathophysiology is sought, via physical examination, patient history, and diagnostic tests. These include spirometry and lung function tests, as well as inventories such as the Chronic Respiratory Disease questionnaire (CRQ). If the condition is not traced to a cause, or if the breathlessness cannot be relieved, management of symptoms is sought to reduce intensity, distress, and any comorbid mental or physical conditions, but these do not necessarily address the shrinking world of the patient.

In many respiratory conditions, the dysfunctional breathlessness cannot be corrected and so the patient's abilities and lived experience are altered irrevocably (Gysels and Higginson 2008). In these cases, there will be varying levels of disability that are likely to worsen over time, but are often unlike other chronic disease progressions because of the impending and ever-present nature of episodic attacks (Eccleston 2016). For instance, acute exacerbations of respiratory infections can often result in death. As a patient put it, "If you can't breathe you don't live" (Nicholls 2003, 132). Understanding, managing, and attending to the patient experience—including their voice when they are not too breathless to talk—can be a matter of life and death. Without such study, high rates of suffering from the misdiagnosis, underdiagnosis, and undertreatment of breathlessness will continue (Currow and Johnson 2015).

The term *breathlessness* needs to be conceptually clarified to investigate whether it captures a common feature and so has corresponding clinical utility, or if the experiences differ widely and require us to modify our conceptualization of pathological breathlessness and correlating clinical understanding. For example, in the case of pernicious anemia, a breathlessness symptom previously classed as "shortness of breath" has now been changed to be described as "the sighs" to capture the difference between these experiences. Patients who experience air hunger feel that they struggle to get the air in and out. Those with pernicious anemia describe the feeling of needing to gulp in air at a slow, steady pace when exerted but, importantly, do not encounter difficulty in doing this. Thus the term *breathlessness* in these two cases does not refer to the same type of experience (Haugdahl et al. 2017). Hence understanding, defining, and labeling different types of breathlessness is important so that clinician and patient can differentiate between different types of breathlessness to get to the correct diagnosis. Careful attention to such differences can aid our understanding of the lived experience of specific types of breathlessness, alongside improving clinician knowledge, which may help prevent misdiagnosis or unnecessary treatment for asthma, a common misdiagnosis in cases of pernicious anemia (Chanarin 1992).[1]

ANXIETY AND BREATHLESSNESS

With the progressive and irreversible nature of COPD, differing rates of felt breathlessness, inflammation of the airways, sputum accumulation, and resultant cough, it is unsurprising that there is a higher prevalence of anxiety disorders in these patients compared to the general population. Studies suggest that anxiety disorders appear in approximately 50 percent of COPD patients (compared to about 6 percent in the general population). Other mental health conditions such as depression and agoraphobia are also more likely to appear in that population (Smoller et al. 1996). Effects such as restricted mobility, lower reported quality of life, worsening overall health, and functional disability are often consequences of anxiety, even in those without respiratory disorders. These issues are often underdiagnosed and undertreated in comorbid respiratory cases, worsening the impact of these disorders on the patient (McManus et al. 2016). Mental symptoms are often ignored or seen as an inevitable consequence of respiratory disease (Maurer et al. 2008).

Studying breathless and anxious experience can help us understand problems in the medical attitude to illness. One overarching problem is the reduction of the suffering person to biological processes; this ultimately separates the body from its subject (cf. Merleau-Ponty 1962; Aho and Aho 2009; Carel 2016; Ratcliffe 2015; Svenaeus 2000; Toombs 1987). Further, many mental disorders are not easy to differentiate from physical disorders (Ratcliffe 2015). Depression and anxiety disorders include physiological distress such as breathlessness, rapid heart rate, gastro-intestinal upset, and other flu-like somatic symptoms (Kirkengen 2010; Ratcliffe et al. 2013). So how can we capture and address these varied illness experiences included in comorbid respiratory and anxiety disorders? This is what we call the problem of differentiation.

The definition of anxiety disorders, found in the *Diagnostic and Statistical Manual of Mental Disorders* (American Psychiatric Association, *DSM-5* 2013a), relies on differentiating between fear and anxiety as an appropriate response to a real or impending threat, as opposed to an anticipatory state related to distressing distorted thoughts or irrational beliefs regarding certain situations, bodily feelings, and other perceived threats (cf. Esser et al. 2015). Anxiety often leads to avoidance behaviors that may temporarily reduce anxiety symptoms, yet increasingly result in hypervigilance, reduced activities, and maintaining the fight-or-flight response (*DSM-5* 2013a, 189).

As we are focusing on anxiety and its relationship to the lived world of the breathless person, an immediate difficulty arises because the anxiety response often arises from the fear of having an acute breathlessness episode, a potential threat to life experienced by the patient previously, and thus a realistic concern. Past events of acute breathlessness inform the present and arouse anxiety about the future. It is difficult for patients and clinicians to initially distinguish between the breathlessness caused by panic anxiety and the underlying respiratory illness. Moreover, anxiety is often experienced prior to breathing difficulties, as a warning that blood oxygen levels are low (see below). This, again, demonstrates that aspects of breathing disruption are nonreducible to discrete physiological, emotional, and psychological elements. Intense fearful thoughts, including thinking about death, fear of losing control, and feeling hopelessness and confusion, are also frequently reported (Willgoss et al. 2012).

We suggest, therefore, that three themes in the comorbidity of breathlessness and anxiety are revealed by a phenomenological analysis:

a   A problematic relationship with breathing: Anxiety is not only a cause of breathlessness, nor a separate symptom. On the one hand, anxiety can warn of low blood oxygen saturation prior to the experience of breathlessness, and thus predates the conscious somatic experience (Eccleston 2016). On the other, idiopathic anxiety episodes often occur in social situations such as visiting crowded spaces, and thus exacerbate physiologically caused breathlessness. This often results in a vicious cycle whereby anxiety and breathlessness trigger one another, and patterns of panic and fear of losing control lead one to reduced activities, social isolation, and resultant deconditioning that worsens health and increases the likelihood of depression (Willgoss et al. 2012; Eccleston 2016). As Willgoss notes:

"It's like a vicious circle. Your breathing gets bad so you get anxious, then you get afraid, and your breathing gets worse, which makes you more afraid" (Willgoss et al. 2012, 565).

Such vicious cycles reinforce the "big five": physiological, emotional, cognitive, behavioral, and situational binds that are triggered in anxiety and breathlessness, making it much harder for the patient to break free from the panic (Wells 1997; LeDoux 2015). Avoidant behavior and hypervigilance leave the patient exhausted and on constant high alert (LeDoux 2015, 17). Further, breathlessness conditions such as asthma are more common in those with comorbid anxiety and depressive symptoms, with a higher prevalence in women, pointing to gendered and social contributions to the development of these disorders (Kewalramani et al. 2008; Kirkengen 2010; cf. Hegarty 2011).

b Anxiety, like severe breathlessness, is often experienced as uncontrollable, with an almost constant fight to regain control, as panic and helplessness are felt while trying to control the anxiety. One could attempt to regain control by practicing "self-talk" (Willgoss et al. 2012), or by employing safety behaviors such as sitting by exits. This may alleviate some of the stress in the short term but also creates an association between these behaviors and prevention of anxiety, which becomes distorted so that elements of magical thinking and further avoidance behaviors come into play. This maintains the anxiety or panic disorder as the patient does not challenge his or her beliefs about anxiety and its relationship to his or her condition (Wells 1997).
c The life-changing and life-limiting nature of such experiences. Experiences of anxiety and severe breathlessness are often described as traumatic and isolating with some patients referring to them as "near-death experiences" (Willgoss et al. 2012). Feeling unable to breathe adequately, being smothered, or unable to escape often causes meta-worry (worry about worry) due to the fear of an uncontrollable panic attack. Furthermore, caregivers often underestimate the severity and intensity of breathing distress due to its terrifying yet subjective and silent nature (cf. Binks et al. 2016). Indeed, the persistent worry and sense of impending doom overlaps with another anxiety disorder, generalized anxiety disorder (GAD), and so multiple morbidities can interact and reinforce feelings of loss of control. Not even sleep can offer respite in some cases: Many respiratory patients suffer from nocturnal hypoxemia. A consequence of this is startled awakening and disturbed sleep, described as feeling suffocated, choking, and terrified of dying "making anxiety as a 24-hour ongoing disorder" (Alkhuja 2013, 82).

When the triggers to the occurrence of panic attacks and anxiety are vague and the episodes idiopathic, the patient does not know when the next attack will occur. This can be understood in terms of the world itself becoming an object of fear for the patient and explains why some anxiety patients become housebound even when their breathlessness is not caused by an underlying physiological pathology. Here, panic anxiety is not just due to bodily betrayal; the threat of breathlessness can be viewed as a threat with both an internal and external source. Internally, the body is experienced as a source of threat with breathlessness causing the fear of choking, suffocation, and loss of control. Panic attacks thereby alienate the patients from their usual being at home in the world, with the threat posed by one's own self felt as a bodily or brain betrayal as the fear and anxiety take over despite no discernible underlying pathology (Svenaeus 2000). Externally, the world can be viewed as a threat with cognitions of not feeling safe due to the world's hostility and potential source of the onset of another attack: for instance, when pollen sets off an asthma attack, or when a panic attack has previously occurred in a supermarket or other public place under the stigmatizing gaze of others in the world. Others, too, can be perceived as sources of danger to the anxious person, whether it is through worry of judgment when undergoing a breathless, panicked episode to medical stereotyping of a mental health diagnosis. Further avoidance and withdrawal from social, medical, and everyday situations can lead to agoraphobia and becoming housebound, restricting patients' lives and future experiences.

We suggest that psychiatric and psychological conceptualization and treatment for anxiety present difficulties related to separating symptoms into cognitive, affective, physiological, and temporal categorizations, which we contrast with the lived experience of these conditions as arising out of and affecting the life-world of the patient. These are experiences that, when studied, reveal the primordial, interrelated, and mutually impacting features of these disorders. Reducing anxiety to faulty information processing leading to false beliefs and negative thinking cuts off the potential revelatory power of these experiences (cf. Wells 1997; LeDoux 2015). We suggest that this is where phenomenology can supplement medical accounts.

Anxiety already has a complex history in philosophical thought; thinkers such as Kierkegaard and Heidegger argued for the power of anxiety in creatively shaping human existence. The focus on the productive role of anxious feelings in providing an opportunity for reflection, has, we argue, been stripped away from the perspective of clinical psychology and psychiatry, which view anxiety as a dysfunctional condition that must be treated rapidly with little consideration of its existential meanings and its impact on the patient's agency and self-understanding (cf. NICE 2011; Haugdahl et al. 2015). In other words, the potential revelatory power of anxious experience lies in the experience telling us that something is wrong in how we live; that only "I" can take responsibility for my facticity and use this opportunity to choose who I want to be (Heidegger 1962, 304).

O. van den Bergh (2016) argues that interpretation, subjective certainty, past experiences, fear of bodily sensations, and interoceptive bias have an important role in the perception of breathlessness. Developing disambiguation strategies for dealing with the fear of bodily sensations and ambiguity in decision making would help patients cope with their comorbid symptoms and increase feelings of agency; but this is possible only through exploring these experiences in terms of their lived world and subjective interpretation. This is a world that includes environmental and socioeconomic factors and how these affect autonomous agents, who understand how their illness alters their life. They can then reflect on the transformations to their experience and take a stance on their existence, instead of feeling powerless and isolated by the alienating, depersonalized, and controlling features of the illness and the healthcare setting. However, anxiety is often dismissed as an irrational experience to be treated by cognitive restructuring, pharmacological interventions, or behavioral therapies (Teachman et al. 2010). Again, the physiological focus means that the symptoms are to be treated while the existential meaning and social or environmental factors often remain unaddressed.

The potential meaning and intelligibility of these disorders in the context of individual human existence, discourse, and social structures impacting self-understanding and potential positive aspects of anxiety is therefore closed off. Perhaps attending to the anxious experience in relation to the insidious increase of respiratory disease in the current climate can tell us more about modern vulnerabilities and concerns in an era of environmental and political instability. At the very least more should be done to recognize the relationship between anxiety and respiratory illnesses, the consequences of undertreatment and underdiagnosis, and finally the lack of treatment options in integrating these areas of illness into the patient's healing (Department of Health 2008).

A PHENOMENOLOGY OF ANXIOUS BREATHLESSNESS

We now turn to phenomenology to reveal the experiential features of anxious and breathless experiences (Carel 2008, 42). Studying breathlessness via a phenomenological lens uncovers the normal, pre-reflective ways of existing in the world, providing opportunities for self-reflection and understanding. Carel's (2013b) analysis of illness as a limit case of embodied experience describes how illness pulls us out of our everyday taken-for-granted existence (the "natural attitude"). It can be philosophically productive in that it can show us how we normally exist in the world and provide us with deeper self-understanding (Carel 2013b, 346). Tacit areas of our existence such as bodily freedom, the habitual body, intentionality, and motility are uncovered and altered by attention to these breathless experiences (cf. Merleau-Ponty 1962). In fact, the phenomenological reduction and bracketing of the natural attitude is analogous to the distancing effect that illness creates (Carel 2013b). We step back from our everyday absorption in the world through breathless experiences and can reflect on the structures of embodied experience through this distancing. Like Heidegger's (1962) notion of angst, possibilities, projects, and our everyday living become radically inaccessible when meaningful existence collapses.

Disclosive affectivity thus implicates the central significance of the body in human experience despite the noted absence in Heidegger of an explicit analysis of the body. Mood, or attunement, is not a mental intentional state accessible only to the conscious subject. Moods color our interactions within the world and shape how things appear and matter to us (Heidegger 1962, 227; Ratcliffe 2008).

Can this phenomenological notion of the collapse of intelligibility in angst map onto anxiety as defined in psychiatric classification manuals such as the *DSM*? We suggest so. Certainly cases of specific phobias are more akin to the ontic descriptions of fleeing from owning up to one's own self and of misinterpreting the self in terms of *das Man* (Heidegger 1962, 164–165). However, the loss of significance and looming threat can cause momentary or enduring collapses into the angst that Heidegger described. Indeed, the anxiety and panic in these anxious experiences may arguably also be ontic versions of angst where the self is covered over and fear displaced onto an undefined threat. However, we believe that there is still a utility to exploring these experiences. This is because they shed light on human freedom and our reflexive natures which enable us to utilize anxious experience to reflect on who we are. In other words, while gripped by angst, the understanding of what it means to be, or existence as a whole, can come into view (Carel 2013a).

In both experiences (of breathlessness and of angst) what remains most vivid even after the collapse of intelligibility and the ensuing practical paralysis is the confrontation with our own death. Studying these experiences reveals that one day I will no longer exist. That nothingness can overwhelm me at any time. Once I face this, embracing the full awareness of my own death, I can reclaim my existence and stop it being governed by the demands and interpretations of others (Heidegger 1962, 308).

This account fits with the changes to body image, self-identity, and self-understanding frequently reported by patients with dyspnea and panic disorder (Carel 2013b; Carel 2016). As previously described, rather than the body being in the background while people are going about their daily activities, they now become aware of new limitations: Breathlessness and a tight chest bring their awareness back to the body and how they can no longer live carefree, but rather exist under the constant threat of mortality. Their body image is altered through changes to embodiment and existential threat via breathlessness (Carel 2016; Haugdahl et al. 2017). They may no longer understand themselves as healthy, or identify as an athlete, as illness progresses and restricts these possibilities.

Breathlessness and anxiety experiences thus cause a shift in the life-world and embodied experience of the patient. They must find new ways of coping with changes in their habitual repertoire, due to the closing down of certain possibilities (Carel 2016). Indeed, the initial crisis of symptom appearance or diagnosis often causes grief and so it is important that clinicians are aware of emotional needs the patients may have by considering their experiences as illuminated by phenomenology (cf. Merleau-Ponty 1962, 189). Evidence shows that phenomenological descriptions match qualitative research and patient descriptions of their disorders and so reflect the reality of the patient experience (Ratcliffe and Broome 2012).

We suggest that in cases of common but severe mental disorders such as panic disorder comorbid with respiratory illness, the pre-anxious, pre-breathless body is often hard to re-access. Knowledge of the habitual body performing certain roles and actions becomes so remote that the memory of them almost takes on a "dream-like quality" (Ratcliffe 2013). This can in part account for the insidious character of these disorders: Not only are these routines and possible ways of being closed off to me, I cannot remember taking them up and enacting them nor imagine doing so in the future. Their significance and meaning have been suspended and no longer show up as something that I could do, nor that I want to any longer (Carel 2011). In chronic illness, the habitual body often adapts to the losses in motor habits and previously enjoyed activities, but these lost abilities still hold significance and meaning for the sufferer that may begin to diminish as time passes. They must adapt to the new limitations by carefully attending to their new embodied situation:

> It may be said that the body is "the hidden form of being our self," or on the other hand, that personal existence is "the taking up and manifestation of a being in a given situation." (Merleau-Ponty 1962, 192)

However, there are potential positive aspects to these experiences. The loss of significance described here as caused by these comorbid illnesses can be recovered whence the body is opened once again

> to others or to the past, when it opens the way to co-existence and once more (in the active sense) acquires significance beyond itself. Moreover, even when cut off from the circuit of existence, the body never quite falls back onto itself.

Even if I become absorbed in the experience of my body and in the solitude of sensations, I do not succeed in abolishing all reference of my life to a world. (Merleau-Ponty 1962, 191)

The world is always calling to me to respond in addition to the intentionality directed toward the vista in front of me, or of consideration of my next task. Anxiety is thus a temporary experience, but still one with the power to disrupt this return. Healthcare practitioners can help aid an incorporation of these experiences into the life of the patient to return him or her to the world of concern, pointedly by the concepts of leaping ahead of the patient, rather than leaping in and removing his or her agency (Heidegger 1962, 159). Exploring the life-world of the patient and the impact of these complex syndromes on his or her ability-to-be is thus imperative.

This focus may also prevent hermeneutical injustice, a subtype of epistemic injustice, defined as "the injustice of having some significant area of one's social experience obscured from collective understanding owing to hermeneutical marginalization" (Fricker 2007, 158). The lack of shared hermeneutical resources specifically catering to anxious respiratory patients may be attributable to testimonial injustice, with patient knowledge of the severity of their breathlessness silenced or discounted by clinicians who instead focus on their prior mental health diagnosis, socioeconomic status, and prejudices stemming from smoking status (Crichton et al. 2017). The consequences of breathlessness, from struggling to talk to increasing rates of physical disability, possibly leading one to become housebound, contribute to these already-significant barriers in communicating suffering to clinicians due to being too breathless and exhausted to talk or access appropriate treatment for mental and somatic symptoms, for example, to be able to attend various clinics for treatment, and even to think.

The lack of appropriate contact between the patient and clinician is "insufficient to be able to truly understand the challenges that people face in the attempt to integrate a chronic illness into their lives" (Fraser, Kee, and Minick 2006, 550). Indeed, we suggest that phenomenological exploration reveals there should be a refocusing on their lived experience rather than on treating the symptoms in isolation from one another. For instance, addressing breathlessness symptoms or fatigue as discrete fails to capture the wider picture of the debilitating effects of chronic respiratory illnesses, aspects that include social isolation, difficulty in attending outpatient facilities due to fluctuating symptoms, reduced mobility, and so on. The picture can be disjointed, and knowledge and treatment lacking.

As phenomenology reveals, we are active agents in the world, skillfully coping with encountered entities; that skillful coping is disrupted in chronic illness. We can therefore see why medical treatment can be alienating:

Agency is handed over to those assumed to have the best knowledge and skills. A clinician may further alienate a patient when frustration with their failure to attend a pulmonary rehabilitation session or complete homework, for instance, shows their lack of understanding or appreciation of the impact the disorder has on the person and fails to appreciate how intrusive biomedicine can be to patients' personal lives.

CONCLUSION

Within biomedical practice, large differences exist between how practitioners think about disease and illness and how patients experience their illness (Toombs 1987, 1993; Carel 2013a). For example, medical practitioners often thematize illness in terms of patterns of symptoms that persist over time. The symptoms are measured, tested, and form part of the constitution of a functional abnormality, a disease. Yet for the patient, the illness is experienced as a way of being, to be lived through and coped with (Carel 2013a).

How these experiences affect patients' understanding of their disorders is often overlooked. The patients respond to their diagnosis and illness experience, reflecting on what these experiences mean to their current and future ways of living (Jutel 2011). With a diagnosis of a chronic illness, the patients may understandably respond with despair, or the realization of the transience of life and an opportunity to take control of their remaining health (ibid.). Other patients struggle to make sense of their experiences through medical narratives alone (Svenaeus 2000). Such a reductive view fails to capture human existence as an embodied, self-interpreting agency in a world with others, who can also take a stand on the patient's illness.[2] Although an objective medical focus on disease has its place in managing the disorder and alleviating suffering, this view is incomplete (Svenaeus 2000; Kirkengen 2010).

Biomedicine neither prioritizes nor fully utilizes patient experience of medical care despite medicine's stated commitment to patient-centered care (NICE 2011). The consequences of this range from failing to meet patient needs comprehensively to lacking a complete, adequate picture of the effects of illness and medical intervention on the patient. Indeed, the patients' experience of their disorder in the clinical encounter and management of their disorders often reveals injustices committed against them (Carel and Kidd 2014). We suggest that phenomenological description, for example, the patient toolkit developed by Carel (2012b, 2013a), can thematize patient experiences and provide deeper knowledge and understanding of these human ways of being and experiences of medical care.

Phenomenology is free of naturalistic or scientific commitment to ways of ordering experience and entities in the world. Diverse experiences of illness across episodes, individuals, and even cultures are not subsumed under preexisting categories or epistemological frameworks. Instead patient experiences are listened to and described, with shared themes and features of illness appearing without any dogmatic structuring from the listener. This allows the patients to be heard, and a study of alterations in their existence through their experiences to be attended to. Attending to illness phenomenologically discloses the shared world of meaning whereby features of illness experiences are described in order for the patient and those around him or her to understand the changes brought about through illness. Practically, this knowledge can be used in practitioner training to redress issues such as communication difficulties.

Ultimately, phenomenology provides a framework to describe the closing down of possibilities and human ways of existing. In contrast to phenomenological description, then, naturalistic or biomedical accounts continue to fail in accounting for these differences. Phenomenology hence provides a descriptive and interpretive framework to describe these transformations to lived experiences and personhood, which can complement medical understanding of illness experiences. It also offers freedom from certain metaphysical or epistemological commitments that underpin reductive accounts of human existence. For example, Nicholls argues that chronic breathlessness can be viewed as "a product of a person's life experience rather than as a patho-physiological entity" (Nicholls 2003, 124). In contrast to seeing illness as a manifestation of an underlying disease process, he argues for the importance of the personal meaning of illness in qualitative research, underscoring a move from biomedical traditional focus on symptom descriptions to an account that captures a fluid, complex set of experiences that evidence-based medicine (EBM) fails to appreciate (Nicholls 2003, 125).

As we have described here, breathlessness conditions often have subjective multidimensional phenomena at their heart: personal, interpersonal, social, cultural, emotional, and metaphysical. Indeed, sometimes only the patients can interpret these experiences and so a phenomenological analysis is indispensable (Nicholls 2003; Carel 2013b; Ratcliffe 2012).

Furthermore, the interaction between these varied elements is often underplayed in healthcare research (Nicholls 2003, 123). Rather than explaining illness responses as emerging rational narratives incorporated into the ill person's bodily schema or identity, "chronic illness is a more complex, fluid, dynamic phenomenon that current biomedicine would have us believe" (ibid.).

Analogously, depression and anxiety disorders are not easily predictable in this manner either: spontaneous remission, worsening, and "good days/bad days," for instance, show up the relational characteristics of illness experiences. In other words, embodied existence is not *partes extra partes*. It is unified and modified both by the body as constitutive for experience, and perception and the world shaping this experience, including the stance that the patient takes upon his or her illness.

Finally, we have seen how anxiety and breath are deeply related: The onset of anxiety can reveal oxygen deprivation. Episodes of breathlessness due to either "cause" are difficult to differentiate at first, and subjective variances that do not match objective measurements occur. Dualistic thinking underlies physical and mental clinical practice which causes many problems in understanding and treating certain illnesses. For instance, patients referred often struggled at first with their diagnosis of anxiety disorder; after many tests and referrals, they felt sure their symptoms (shortness of breath or heart palpitations) were due to a somatic disease. This demonstrates the implicit dualistic thinking that underlies conceptions of mental disorders being in the mind, and physical symptoms as caused by a somatic disease and this is what patients have inherited from our social and medical milieu.

A potential remedy to these problems has been suggested by attending to the lived experiences of the anxious respiratory patient to understand the meaning and significance of these complex conditions. Such attention can aid the development of truly patient-centered integrated health care that evidence demands in such complex cases.

ACKNOWLEDGMENTS

We thank the Wellcome Trust who generously funded the research for this chapter through the Life of Breath project (www.lifeofbreath.org, grant number 103340).

NOTES

1. Another example of how phenomenological description can help distinguish between two conditions is that of breathlessness in asthma and in COPD (Simon et al. 1990; cf. Lansing et al. 2009). It seems that the term *breathlessness* may not describe the same type of experience in every case. We claim that it is important to have conceptually clear accounts not only for clinical purposes, for example, to avoid misdiagnosis but also to understand what we mean by the term in order to understand the lived experiences of those who suffer from breathlessness and to reduce the alienation patient reportedly experience in the medical encounter (Toombs 1987). Unfortunately mental health practitioners are only just getting training on chronic illness integrated health care in the UK, so this was a tentative process.

2. The invitation to reflection and to philosophize, to reexamine and reinterpret one's life alongside modifying movements and goals uncovers edifying possibilities that illness presents (Carel 2011, 2016; Kidd 2012).

Chapter 11

Heideggerian Ethics and the Permissibility of Bio- and Nano-Medicine

Tara Kennedy

From a medical perspective, bio- and nanotechnologies are exciting due to their great potential to improve and even revolutionize the way we treat disease. At the same time, their proposed use often raises difficult and, in some cases, troubling ethical questions. It may seem strange to suggest that we turn to Martin Heidegger to resolve moral dilemmas of this sort, given his reputation among some philosophers as anti-technology. Yet far from advocating a one-dimensional rejection of technology as a whole, Heidegger offers us a fairly nuanced view, one that distinguishes between technologization and the various technological devices that increasingly populate our lives. Moreover, his later thought includes an implied ethics, which, when coupled with his views on technology, provides us with a means for evaluating individual technologies on a case-by-case basis, rather than simply accepting or rejecting technology outright. Some proposed uses of bio- and nanotechnologies have the potential to make such profound changes to human life that we might question whether or not their use is compatible with the survival of humanity as we know it. Heidegger's perfectionist ethics is ideally suited to deal with this topic because the virtues it calls for are drawn from his phenomenological examination of what it means to be human and to consciously embody that essence. In what follows, I will examine some uses of bio- and nanotechnologies in the medical field through the lens of Heidegger's thought to show how his normative phenomenology might be used to shape the practice of medicine.

Heideggerian ethics is borne of his struggle with the project of describing a fundamental ontology. Rather than uncovering the most basic ontological unit, Heidegger finds that the history of Western metaphysics comprises a series of different answers to the question, "What is an entity?" Concluding then that humankind's understanding of the being of entities is temporary and historically contingent, Heidegger identifies what he sees as the chief reigning paradigms, each of which secures the ontological intelligibility of the age for a time by telling humankind what things are in a bipartite way, that is, ontologically and theologically (Thomson 2005). These ontotheological epochs find their culmination in the metaphysics of Friedrich Nietzsche, who, Heidegger claims, leaves a legacy of nihilism in his wake by positing the whole of being to consist in eternally recurring will to power, despite the former's attempt to evade, through this very notion of will to power, what he saw as the ever-spreading nihilism of the Judeo-Christian tradition.[1] For Heidegger, Nietzsche's thought is fundamentally nihilistic in that the exploitation and overcoming that characterize the drama of the will to power has no purpose other than its own continuance and growth. Nietzsche (1966) tells us that "life simply *is* will to power," and, that, in turn, it is *"essentially* appropriation, injury, overpowering of what is alien and weaker; suppression, hardness, imposition of one's own forms, incorporation and at least, at its mildest, exploitation" (203). As participants in a constant battle of generation, domination, and degeneration, entities exist as meaningful only to the degree that they contribute to our own individual dominance and overcoming. Ontological meaning is therefore equivalent to instrumental value; in effect, Heidegger argues, according to Nietzschean metaphysics, existence is, at its core, nothing more than a collection of resources standing by to be optimized (*Bestand*), a mode of revealing he refers to as "enframing" (*Gestell*). In enframing, quality dissolves into nothing more than a matter of quantity.

In Heidegger's work, enframing comes to be associated with technology, and it is this fact that helps explain why he is frequently, though mistakenly, taken to be something of a Luddite. He teaches us that *technê* has its origins in, and is a form of, *poiêsis*, the disclosure of ontological possibility. "*Technê* belongs to bringing-forth, to *poiêsis;* it is something poetic" (1977, 13). Through *poiêsis* an entity is "brought forth" into the world from the ontological depths of being as such, Heidegger's name for that which is no thing and yet makes possible all things, that source from which any particular thing receives its existence. Being as such is paradoxically revealed through its concealment: It is the ontological condition for the possibility of ontic actualities, and so necessarily retreats when any one possibility for existence obtains. As *Dasein*, humankind is unique in its essential ability to testify to this retreat, to appreciate the infinite ways in which presencing can occur; Dasein is capable of a singular receptivity to being as such. That is, Dasein is, in her *essence*, that being sensitive to the ontological flowering of entities and the inexhaustibility of meaning and worth inherent in them.

Yet, as Nietzsche's metaphysical heirs, we find ourselves in a world in which enframing structures the way things show up for us. Modern technology breaks from its origins in *poiêsis* by imposing a quantifiable ontological meaning onto entities rather than allowing space for being as such to make the grant of disclosure. "The revealing that holds sway throughout modern technology does not unfold into a bringing-forth in the sense of *poiêsis*. The revealing that rules in modern technology is a challenging [*Herausfordern*], which puts to nature the unreasonable demand that it supply energy that can be extracted and stored as such" (Heidegger 1977, 14). For Heidegger, then, this nihilistic dystopia is particularly distressing in that it threatens the very essence of humanity. Under the spell of enframing, Dasein mistakenly believes he has determined the meaning of a thing's existence when he has determined its instrumental value. He becomes increasingly skilled at calculative thinking, that is, at measuring, counting, and quantifying, but at the cost of his vital capacity for meditative thinking, that form of being-with-things in which he is capable of testifying to *poiêtic* disclosure. The skilled enframer becomes a masterful economist, controlling, organizing, and ordering about the resources at his disposal.

Herein lurks the hints of a Heideggerian ethics. For Heidegger, thinking is comportment; he lays out a theory of action in which the highest form is meditative thinking. "The essence of action is accomplishment. To accomplish means to unfold something into the fullness of its essence, to lead it forth into this fullness—*producere*. Therefore only what already is can really be accomplished. But what 'is' above all is being. Thinking accomplishes the relation of being to the essence of the human being" (2006, 239). To act is to play some role in the ontological realization of entities. Dasein is that being who is characterized by her participation in *poiêsis*, a participation that comes about through her exercise of meditative thinking. Therefore action is, in its truest sense, thought. If this is the case, then the way we think determines the moral quality of our actions. The essence of action is to lead entities forth from ontological possibility to actuality, while the essence of Dasein is the kind of thinking that facilitates this. In effect, then, Dasein is, in an essential sense, called on to testify to *poiêtic* presencing and to look after the space in which it occurs. If we are meditative thinkers, our actions will tend toward the virtuous. If, however, we hone our skill at calculative thinking, and if we fail to safeguard the space of ontological disclosure and instead participate in imposure, our actions will be characterized by vice.

We receive some instruction as to the virtues required by this perfectionist form of ethics in Heidegger's discussions of the notion of dwelling. While we all dwell by residing in one place or another, Heidegger uses this term to refer to a specific kind of living, namely, the moral life. He (2006) says, "*Ethos* means abode, dwelling place. The word names the open region in which the human being dwells. The open region of his abode allows what pertains to the essence of the human being, and what in thus arriving resides in nearness to him, to appear. The abode of the human being contains and preserves the advent of what belongs to the human being in his essence" (269). This space in which we dwell, in which we can experience the good life, is one that affords us a clear view of the worth of the things that populate the world around us. It is a space in which things have the room to show themselves as inexhaustibly meaningful. If we excel ethically, then we set down roots in such a place, and we build our homes and lives there. And indeed, Heidegger's (2001b) penchant for etymology leads him to assert a connection between the words "dwelling," "building," and "to be." "*Bauen* [building] originally means to dwell . . . What then does *ich bin* mean? The old word *bauen*, to which the *bin* belongs, answers: *ich bin, du bist* mean: I dwell, you dwell. The way in which you are and I am, the manner in which we humans *are* on the earth, is *Buan*, dwelling. To be a human being means to be on the earth as a mortal. It means to dwell" (145). Building and dwelling then are not separate activities, nor are they superficial activities that occupy our time here and there. There is, of course, an ontic sense in which we build and in which we dwell, but in a more important sense building and dwelling pervade every facet of our lives when we seek to make them moral ones.

Heidegger (2001b) asserts that this dwelling calls on us to free things, and to preserve and safeguard them, concluding, "*The fundamental character of dwelling is this sparing and preserving*" (147). Because dwelling is essentially a comportment that reflects a deep commitment to meditative thinking, the "sparing and preserving" constitutive of it involves not only not hurting things, but letting them show themselves as they will and not, instead, as we will. Although this might then sound like an ethics of inactivity, we are fundamentally unable to step back from things entirely, to let all things come to presence without human interference. Being-in-the-world is at the same time being-inextricably-bound-up-with-the-world, and the ways in which we free things to show themselves involve a caring and nurturing attitude. Dwelling is both an attitude of receptivity to being as such and an active responsiveness to what it has to say. It requires that we actively protect and help hold open that clearing in which things can appear. Indeed, Heidegger further tells us that dwelling "*also* means at the same time to cherish and protect, to preserve and care for, specifically to till the soil, to cultivate the vine. Such building only takes care—it tends the growth that ripens into its fruit of its own accord" (145). The ripening of ontological fruit requires us to fight for the recognition of the worth of entities in the face of an ontotheology that would turn them into *Bestand*.

Fruit of the ordinary variety is often rather fragile, requiring a gentle hand from propagation through maturation and harvesting. Phenomenology teaches us that, in fact, all things are fundamentally vulnerable. Corporeal entities are not perfect islands; the others with whom we share the world, whether non-sentient entities or other Dasein or something somewhere in between, enter into the space of our sensory experience. Indeed, they sometimes enter into us at the porous borders between ourselves and the world. Maurice Merleau-Ponty (1968) argues that as we go out into the world, it simultaneously comes into us: "Because my eyes which see, my hands which touch, can also be seen and touched, because, therefore, in this sense they see and touch the visible, the tangible, from within, because our flesh lines and even envelops all the visible and tangible things with which nevertheless it is surrounded, the world and I are within one another.... Between my body looked at and my body looking, my body touched and my body touching, there is overlapping or encroachment, so that we must say that the things pass into us as well as we into the things" (123). From the benign to the most violent, this "overlapping or encroachment" that characterizes the world means that at all times the vulnerability of things is an issue. The good news is that if we remember this universal vulnerability, we can remember to be gentle in our being-with-others. When we begin to dwell, Iain Thomson (2011) argues, "we learn to approach the humble things, other animals, and human beings that constitute our worlds with care, humility, patience, thankfulness, and ... even awe, reverence, and love" (104). These virtues that we can embody in our dealings with others, then, arise from a phenomenological analysis of our being-in-the-world and are justified by our essence as the meditative thinker. We are called on to be humble enough to know we do not control *poiêtic* disclosure, patient enough to wait for its arrival, caring enough to protect the space of ontological arrival, grateful enough to play this role, reverent enough to find a joy in the ever-coming meaningfulness of things, and heedful enough to remain alert to the danger of enframing.

When this danger surfaces, how does the Heideggerian ethical account recommend we fight against it? Does taking up the fight mean revolting against technologization in the form of rejecting technology outright? Or is it possible to dwell with technology? To be sure, technologization, according to Heidegger, is devastating from a metaphysical, ontological, and ethical standpoint. But to escape the devastation, indeed to rebuild a new world, one populated by real entities rather than *Bestand*, Heidegger (1977) argues that we not simply revolt against technology. To do so is to remain enslaved by technology; he says that we are "unfree and chained to technology" whether we are happy Luddites or happy enframers (4). Rather, we need to see our way through and past the landscape created by enframing. In a well-known move, he quotes Friedrich Hölderlin: *"But where the danger is, grows/The saving power also"* (28). As a mode of revealing, technology can point us back to a more meaningful engagement with the things of this world if only we keep recognizing it for what it is. That is to say, to be conscious of technology as a mode of revealing is to remain conscious of the fact that there exist many modes of revealing. In turn, we become open to the infinite possibilities for worth in everything, we acknowledge that quantity does not equate to quality, and we free ourselves from the enslavement of technologization. Thus we have the virtue of releasement (*Gelassenheit*) by which we use technology but refuse to let it use us. "We can use technical devices, and yet with proper use also keep ourselves so free of them, that we may let go of them any time. . . . We can affirm the unavoidable use of technical devices, and also deny them the right to dominate us, and so to warp, confuse, and lay waste our nature. . . . I would call this comportment toward technology which expresses 'yes' and at the same time 'no,' by an old word, *releasement toward things* (*Die Gelassenheit zu den Dingen*)" (Heidegger 1966, 54). Given the ubiquity of technology in modern life, this virtue, perhaps to a greater degree than some of the others, may be best understood as an ideal to attain to. Nevertheless, with time and practice, the virtue of letting go, releasement, is a skill that Dasein can develop.

If we do not completely accept or reject technology outright but instead allow *Gelassenheit* to characterize our relationship with it, then it is in theory possible that any technological device is ethically permissible on this account. Yet, when we evaluate them on a case-by-case basis, we find that some are more likely to lend themselves to the services of enframing. In fact, as we will see, the use of some technologies will prove to be too inconsistent with our essence as meditative thinkers for Heidegger's ethics to find their use acceptable. For the purpose of examining these potential technologies, it may be helpful to set out some criteria according to which individual technologies can be evaluated. To that end, the following list may prove useful in making determinations of this sort.[2] To be ethical on this account, then, any particular technology must not:

1 prevent Dasein from embodying her essence, or constitute a grave threat to her ability to do so;
2 permanently close off, through the use of technological imposure, future possibilities for *poiêtic* disclosure;
3 be motivated by strictly calculative thinking, that is, be a manifestation of nothing but the desire to manage, control, and optimize;
4 treat other entities merely as resources (*Bestand*); and
5 decide the ethical issue only in terms of ontic harms, though it must be sensitive to ontic harms.

Armed with these criteria and some of the virtues that Heidegger's normative phenomenology calls for, we can now turn to bio- and nanotechnologies in order to evaluate their use in the practice of medicine. These technologies are especially concerning for many as they pose risks of a higher order than do previously used technologies due to their potential to make widespread, lasting, and radical changes to the world as we know it. In a well-known article, Bill Joy (2000) argues for the complete cessation of the development of such technologies on the basis that they could lead to the end of the human race. Others have been highly critical of this idea for a number of reasons, citing, for example, the potential benefits such technology offers and the danger that, despite a moratorium on its development, there would be some that would develop it anyway, leaving the more ethically minded defenseless against the unscrupulous (Kurzweil 2006; More 2006). We are obliged, then, to determine whether or not these technologies have a place in the art of healing. Their proposed medical uses are wide-ranging, and we will be able to examine only a few here. Perhaps these can serve as illustrations, however, of how Heidegger's ethics deals with issues of this sort.

Bio- and nanotechnologies have been touted as being superior drug delivery vehicles and contrast agents. For example, the chemotherapy drug paclitaxel has traditionally been delivered dissolved in strong organic solvents that, while making it possible for the drug to reach the target, have been associated with serious side effects and toxicities. If paclitaxel is instead encapsulated in a nano-delivery system, studies show that higher doses can reach the tumor with much less toxicity (Ma and Mumper 2013). Just as promising, a recent development using nanoparticles may help prevent a very rare but devastating side effect of current gadolinium-based contrast agents in medical imaging. In some patients, the use of these traditional contrast agents causes a condition known as nephrogenic systemic fibrosis, which can lead to death. The only known risk factor is significant kidney dysfunction, which can therefore preclude some patients from getting MRIs. Researchers have recently developed a contrast agent that works in a similar way but that avoids the use of gadolinium, relying instead on iron oxide nanoparticles with a charged coating, meaning those patients would not be prevented from receiving an MRI (Wei et al. 2017).

When considering uses such as these, the main concerns have to do with what we might call the generic objections that crop up around the use of these technologies. For example, predictability is a potential problem. Despite what we know about biology, genetics, and chemistry, it is not clear how well we can say what will come of new or unusual interactions of biological and genetic materials in complex systems. Nanomaterials are especially worrisome when it comes to predictability as their increased surface area to volume ratio means that they can behave in novel ways as compared to their bulk counterparts. Moreover, their small size could affect our ability to control them as they may easily travel beyond their target area, perhaps, for example, crossing the blood brain barrier when it is not intended that they do so. Furthermore, there is a risk that nanomaterials could accumulate in tissues and cause illness or even death. I do not find these objections to be so compelling as to rule out the use of such technologies in these capacities altogether. Although, for example, the risks of nanotoxicity due to bioaccumulation and the dangers having to do with their heightened reactivity should be taken seriously by the physician scientist, we can minimize their risks by subjecting them to the rigorous testing we expect from scientific studies. They do not appear to violate any of the criteria set out earlier, and they seem compatible with the notion of a physician who is deeply respectful of his or her patients, humble in his or her practice, and compassionate with the others who co-constitute his or her world. Therefore, I submit that, according to the phenomenological ethics defended here, such uses are ethically permissible.

More complicated ethical questions are raised by technologies that make changes to the genetic line, for instance, the gene-editing tool CRISPR-Cas. This relatively new technology makes possible the correction of diseases and disabilities caused by an abnormality in the DNA by slicing out the offending sequence of nucleotides in the gene and repairing it. While most researchers have so far refrained from using genetic engineering of this sort on viable human embryos, at least one lab claims to have used CRISPR-Cas9 in the fertilization of human eggs in order to repair the mutation that causes a form of hypertrophic cardiomyopathy, a disease that can lead to sudden cardiac death. Predictability, as mentioned earlier, is a concern here; the possibility for unintended adverse consequences makes some worry about this form of genetic manipulation. In this vein, some point to the link between sickle-cell anemia and resistance to malaria to show that unfavorable medical conditions can sometimes confer advantages that would also be eliminated if they were edited out of the genome. Moreover, the use of CRISPR-Cas9 carries the risk of off-target effects, in which additional sections of the genome, unrelated to the area of concern, are edited. Some of these mistakes are predictable, but others are not, nor are the consequences they may have. I would respond to concerns regarding predictability in much the same way here as I did when they arose in the use of nano-enhanced contrast agents and drug delivery systems. Should, for example, the possibility of off-target effects caution against the use of these technologies? They need not, though a great deal of work remains to be done before the dangers surrounding predictability can be minimized to a point at which they become an acceptable tradeoff for the benefits to be had. The technology holds such great promise that simply rejecting it outright would itself be irresponsible. Rather, researchers and physicians have an obligation to be innovative in developing these technologies, conscientious in subjecting them to rigorous testing, and attentive in their eventual use.

In addition to questions about predictability, some would argue that, should we get used to the idea of using genetic engineering to cure conditions that cause pain and suffering, we will inevitably relax the standard according to which such technology is deemed permissible. That is to say, today we edit out cardiomyopathy, and tomorrow we eliminate deafness or achondroplasia. Those with such conditions are frequently found to resist attempts to classify their conditions as regrettable and maintain that instead the "correction" of their condition at birth would have been unfortunate. For one father, misgivings accompanied the thought of repairing the genes responsible for his daughter's albinism, which in turn left her unable to see well: "He believes that if he had had the option to edit blindness out of Ruthie's genes before she was born, he and his wife would have jumped at the chance. But now he thinks that would have been a mistake: doing so might have erased some of the things that make Ruthie special" (Hayden 2016, 403). From a Heideggerian standpoint, the testimony of these individuals raises the ethically concerning possibility that the use of CRISPR-Cas to genetically engineer out seemingly undesirable diseases and disabilities may lead to the elimination of instances of *poiêtic* disclosure that we ought to instead retain, for both ontic and ontological reasons.

Does such genetic engineering then violate the second criterion identified earlier, that is, is it unethical on the grounds that it represents a case in which humans risk closing off *poiêtic* possibilities through technological imposure? Can we imagine instances in which, for example, selecting for a particular eye color or sex would be acceptable? To be sure, we can envision some cases in which genetic engineering would constitute *technê* as opposed to *poiêsis*. Parents who want to engineer their progeny to have physical or mental characteristics that would allow them an advantage in the marketplace years down the road would seem motivated by a desire to control and manipulate. It might be tempting to cast any and all uses of genetic engineering in such a light. That is, all genetic engineering is an instance in which Dasein helps some ontological possibility to obtain, and it may seem that this can always be described in terms of enframing. This would, however, be to misinterpret Dasein's role in *poiêsis*, which, while needing to avoid willful manipulation of how things reveal themselves, need not be a completely passive role. Rather, Dasein may actively help bring things from their ontological concealment into the clearing of the world. Indeed, for Heidegger, the artist does precisely this (Heidegger 2001b; Thomson 2011). And although the artist is the paradigm example, our ordinary lives abound with opportunities to help direct *poiêtic* disclosure, whether it be in the homemaker's cultivation of a sense of warmth in the living space, the child's creative play, or the horticulturist's shaping of the bonsai. I see no prima facie grounds for denying that the genetic engineer can also participate in *poiêsis*. Some types of technology lend themselves more readily to the service of enframing—and I would be sympathetic to those who would argue that nano- and biotechnologies fall into this category—but there is nothing to prohibit the health professionals who use them from remaining conscious of the saving power of technology, namely, its potential to remind us that enframing is only one way, among many, that things show themselves to us.

If this is the case, then an analogy might be made between the scientist and the artist. Both have the capacity to listen to being as such and the things themselves while practicing their craft. Thomson (2011) reports that Michelangelo supposedly saw "David" in the block of marble and carved it accordingly. The artist's way of listening to things by way of facilitating disclosure is in stark contrast to the way the happy enframer manipulates matter. "[A] skillful woodworker notices the inherent qualities of particular pieces of wood—attending to subtleties of shape and grain, different shades of color, weight, and hardness—while deciding what might be built from that wood. . . . Then contrast, on the other hand, a technological making that imposes a predetermined form on matter without paying heed to any intrinsic potentialities, the way an industrial factory indiscriminately grinds wood into woodchips in order to paste them back together into straight particle board, which can then be used flexibly and efficiently to construct a maximal variety of useful objects" (21).

It seems entirely possible, then, that, provided it is not motivated by the drive to order and manipulate, the use of CRISPR-Cas9 to select against a debilitating disease is ethical. Consider, for example, the genetic abnormality resulting in Trisomy 13 or 18. Both conditions involve significant pain and suffering, followed by an early childhood death. Some might argue that making the pain and suffering that can be avoided a significant factor in deciding the issue risks turning Heidegger's phenomenological ethics into consequentialism. The two ethical systems differ significantly, however, in their ontological assumptions. Moreover, the consequentialist is content to consider the matter decided provided the ontic harms involved are minimalized. The Heideggerian ethicist, on the other hand, attends primarily to the ontological harms to be avoided. This does not mean, though, that he remains insensitive to ontic pain, suffering, or happiness. Indeed, phenomenology teaches us that our basic experience is as a vulnerable being whose world is co-constituted by other vulnerable beings. Our being-with these others requires of us a sensitivity to their pain and suffering, and therefore the comportment of dwelling calls for care, love, respect, compassion, and sympathy. Thus, using genetic engineering to select against diseases like Trisomy 13 or 18 is ethical because, first, genetic engineering may be a form of *poiêsis* and, second, its use can be informed by the ontological concerns at hand while simultaneously tending to the ontic harms that these diseases engender.

What, then, of the argument made by the father of the girl with albinism? Couldn't one argue that, as his take on the issue indicated, some important form of *poiêsis* would have been excluded from the world had his child's condition, however debilitating, been eliminated? Might it not be argued that, in the long term, some *poiêtic* possibilities might be eliminated permanently? For example, potential parents who carry the genes for cystic fibrosis might be eager to genetically select against it. Over time, it seems possible the disease could be completely edited out of the species. But if this ethical account prohibits us from using technologies in a way that permanently eliminates some forms of *poiêsis*, then wouldn't that be wrong? Presumably at least some would argue yes, among them a historian quoted in the same article who, despite needing to spend up to forty hours a week treating her cystic fibrosis, claims she would not genetically cure her condition were a fix available. "'There are some great things that come from having a genetic illness,' she says" (Hayden 2016, 405). We should note first that deliberately selecting against some genetic possibility does not necessarily entail an unethical act of imposure since every instance of artistic creation involves a selecting against. Michelangelo created "David" rather than "Joan." My choice to grow bell peppers in the garden prevents me from cultivating tomatoes instead, since my space and time is limited. Being limited beings, our dealings with things in the world necessarily involve our seeing them in finite ways. This does not preclude our appreciation of them as having infinite worth, and provided we listen to what being as such has to say to us in guiding our attempts to shape ontological disclosure, then we embody the artist rather than the enframer.

What becomes explicit, in light of these testimonies, is the need, if and when the technologies become available, for discussion, informed by both medical professionals and patients, regarding the diseases we ought to genetically eliminate. Some conditions will be found to involve relatively little suffering, for example, color blindness. Should those with the condition profess that great advantages accompany it, then we would have to find it unethical to erase the condition from the genome since we have a responsibility to respect and safeguard *poiêtic* disclosure. At the other end of the spectrum we would find diseases like Trisomy 13 and 18 that contain great amounts of pain and suffering, with little to no benefit. These we have an ethical obligation to eliminate, since we are called on by Heidegger's ethics to show love and compassion. The tougher cases, of course, would be the many who fall between the two extremes and that complicate our ability to dwell comfortably with these technologies. As this phenomenological normativity arises in the world co-constituted by our fellow Dasein, we do well to engage in conversation with the community of meditative thinkers in order to decide the issue when it comes to any particular disease or defect.

The foregoing cases of genetic engineering focus on cases involving pain and suffering. How should we understand those cases where the consideration of ontic suffering cannot help decide the issue? Is it ethical, for instance, to genetically select for a particular eye color? So-called designer babies raise the ire of those who believe that genetically engineering a baby for any reason other than to correct a defect would necessarily be a display of hubris, shallowness, and manipulation. Michael J. Sandel (2007), for example, claims that genetic enhancement and genetic engineering "represent a kind of hyperagency, a Promethean aspiration to remake nature, including human nature, to serve our purposes and satisfy our desires. The problem is not the drift to mechanism but the drive to mastery" (26–27). Although this sounds rather Heideggerian, he fails to provide an ontological basis for his claims, while nevertheless concluding that genetic engineering and enhancement are unethical. I agree that from the perspective of the Heideggerian ethicist, attempts to control and manipulate procreation are what makes problematic the desire to have a hand in the genetic makeup of our children. That is, he is correct to point out that it is not the technology itself, "the drift to mechanism," that is questionable, but the "drive to mastery," the attitudes that accompany the use of such technology. I would argue, however, that although one engaging in genetic engineering might be more likely to be thinking calculatively rather than meditatively, thus violating the third criterion, this is not necessarily the case.

Let us imagine that the global human population experiences the catastrophic loss of 98 percent of the blue-eyed population due to some new virus. If left to chance, blue-eyed humans could, in this scenario, become a thing of the past. Would it be ethical to select for blue eyes in order to see to the continuation of this particular phenotype? This seems to me to be a case in which we ensure the disclosure of *poiêtic* possibilities in peril. In safeguarding the space in which they might arise, in ensuring that that space stays open in the future, Dasein as genetic engineer acts ethically. I think, however, that even less dramatic cases of genetic engineering, namely, engineering for aesthetic purposes, can be morally permissible on this account. Why couldn't, for example, selecting for the eye color of one's offspring resemble more the decisions that the artist makes rather than those the selfish enframer makes? Suppose a couple has several children who all strongly resemble each other, but can imagine a different combination of their features lurking somewhere behind this dominant phenotype. Could a deliberate selection for some of their recessive genes be akin to Michelangelo seeing "David" in the block of marble? While I acknowledge the concern that such genetic engineering would, more often than not, take the form of enframing rather than artistic facilitation of disclosure, there is no reason to rule out the latter possibility altogether.

To take things even a step farther, we might consider how a Heideggerian ethics might handle one more instance of the use of bio- and nanotechnologies in the practice of medicine. Specifically, let us examine the issue of genetic enhancement. This may seem to stray from our primary topic, that of the employment of a phenomenological ethics in the practice of medicine. Medicine is used to treat conditions that affect normal healthy functioning and to restore the patient to their usual, that is to say, ordinary level of ability. Enhancement, on the other hand, seeks to transcend the ordinary capacities of the human in some way. Should enhancement become a common practice, however, what counts as ordinary functioning now might one day be considered a debilitating condition in need of correction. That is, suppose the majority of the population undergoes treatments that extend their range of vision to several miles. The minority with ordinary vision may, in comparison, seem disabled. Therefore, at least some genetic enhancements raise the possibility of the medicalization of the human condition and, accordingly, the question of whether or not a phenomenologically ethical doctor would engage in practices that contribute to such a state of affairs.

While it would be instructive to examine any possible genetic enhancement, it might be most interesting to consider the ultimate enhancement, namely, immortality, no less because death and the physician are frequently at odds. While medical professionals do not always argue that a prolonged life is preferable to death, physicians are more often than not tasked with trying to delay its inevitability. Would an enhancement that eliminated mortality then be a triumphant win for the practice of medicine? Proposals along these lines include the use of innovative technologies to fight disease while simultaneously preventing or repairing tissue degeneration and other age-related bodily or mental deterioration. Should such maintenance be provided continuously, death could be prevented indefinitely, leading to a sort of default immortality. Others have suggested more radical ways of avoiding finality; some argue that in the future we might be able to download the individual consciousness onto a hard drive, make backup copies, and thereby live on for as long as we might wish in cyber form.

It seems to me that, according to the phenomenological ethics defended here, enhancements that proffer a cure for mortality would be unethical. In short, in eliminating death, they eliminate three aspects of the human experience that help to structure our world and what it means to be Dasein. First, the fact that they eliminate death is itself a problem. Among the few constants in human life is the knowledge that it is finite. Death sets a limit point beyond which any particular human being may not venture. Our mortality is one of the human limitations that ensure that we never have an omniscient, omnipotent, omnipresent encounter with the world. Heidegger (2001c) tells us, "The *world worlds*, and is more fully in being than the tangible and perceptible realm in which we believe ourselves to be at home. World is never an object that stands before us and can be seen. World is the ever-nonobjective to which we are subject as long as the paths of birth and death, blessing and curse keep us transported into being" (43, translation emended). The way in which we are tied to this world, the way in which it rises up to meet us, requires of us that we are finite creatures for whom time is an issue. To eliminate death as a reference point is to render one of the ways in which we ordinarily make sense of our lives meaningless. It is to interfere with the way the "world worlds" for us, to the point that, should it disappear, the world might no longer world for us or, what amounts to the same thing, we might no longer dwell in the world. Secondly, immortality would eliminate our vulnerability, the blessing and curse that helps ensure we are the faithful neighbors of being as such. Our own vulnerability makes possible our recognition of the others we encounter as fundamentally vulnerable too, essential for the cultivation of the virtues called for on this ethical account.

Finally, those proposed forms of immortality that would eliminate our experience as embodied beings likewise take away an essential part of what it means to be human. Hubert Dreyfus (2009) explains, "Our form of life is organized by and for beings embodied like us: creatures with bodies that have hands and feet, insides and outsides; that have to balance in a gravitational field; that move forward more easily than backwards; that get tired; that have to approach objects by traversing the intervening space, overcoming obstacles as they proceed, etc. Our embodied concerns so pervade our world that we don't notice the way our body enables us to make sense of it" (19–20). We are our bodies; just like death and vulnerability, embodiment helps to structure our world and affords us a certain understanding of it. Our embodied dwelling has so little in common with the experience of a cyber-bound data set, no matter how conscious, that this futuristic possibility amounts, paradoxically, not to a kind of human immortality, but instead the rise of the posthuman. This would make the physician who provides access to technologies that eliminate death the midwife of posthumanity. Whatever the physician's role is normally understood to be, it is not that.

The foregoing examination of some of the bio- and nanotechnologies that may impact the practice of medicine is admittedly brief. There are a great many more proposed uses, each of which raises interesting, important, and difficult questions. Those selected will hopefully have provided at least some idea of how Heidegger's phenomenological ethics might assist us in sorting out those technologies that are compatible with a comportment of dwelling. Because Heidegger distinguishes between enframing and individual technologies, he not only allows us to consider them individually but also requires of us that we do so. The time to engage in deliberations about bio- and nanotechnologies is now, before their widespread use brings about changes to Dasein's world and essence that cannot be undone.

NOTES

1. Briefly, the ontological aspect of ontotheology is that ontological unit that is most basic, while the theological piece is that which is highest and most complete, that which justifies the whole of existence. According to Heidegger, will to power is the ontological aspect because it represents the most fundamental element of existence. Eternal recurrence is the drama of will to power viewed from without; it is that which makes sense of the whole and is thus the theological piece. For a thorough explanation of Heidegger's work on ontotheology, see Thomson (2005).

2. I do not claim that this list is exhaustive; it may be possible to identify other criteria that would be relevant and informed by a Heideggerian ethics. It should also be recognized the criteria represent related and overlapping concerns and that, therefore, they are not meant to be understood as completely distinct areas of concern. Finally, these criteria may be relevant in more than just the area of medical ethics; indeed I have written elsewhere about how we might use these criteria to make determinations in, for example, animal ethics and environmental ethics.

Part IV

EXISTENTIAL HEALTH

Chapter 12

Losing the Measure of Health: Phenomenological Reflections on the Role of *Techne* in Health Care Today

Carolyn Culbertson

Health care today presents us with one of the great ironies of our time. On the one hand, modern health care is more effective than ever at preserving and prolonging human life and at treating symptoms of illness. During the nineteenth century, average life expectancy hovered around forty years in the United States—nearly half of what it is today. Infant survival rates have similarly skyrocketed. In the year 1900, 10 percent of infants in the United States died within their first year of life, and in many urban areas the infant mortality rate was closer to 30 percent (Klein 2004). The rate in the United States is now about 0.5 percent (Kochanek et al. 2016). Again, the gains are staggering. Examined this way, the success of modern health care is strikingly clear. Medical advancements have also significantly alleviated the physical pain that traditionally accompanies many forms of illness. Despite such clear successes, however, sharp criticisms of the healthcare system today are common. There are many reasons for this. For example, many people in the United States today are rightly concerned about the costliness of quality healthcare services and the inability of many people to afford these services. Yet even those who do have access to health care often find the service they receive to be less therapeutic than they expect and often even a source of some distress. Already feeling disrupted by illness, people can become even more unsettled as they are passed around to a series of providers with whom they have no established relationship and as their experience of illness becomes translated into the data that is useful for biomedical diagnosis and treatment. The technical character of the interaction between doctor and patient today also means that there tends to be little time or even reason for conversation. The patient speaks with the doctor only briefly, and it is almost always the doctor who guides the conversation. This then is the great irony. While health care today is more effective than ever at keeping human beings alive, it has never been more estranging.

To better understand this strange predicament, it is helpful to see it in historical context, that is, to see how approaches to health have changed over the centuries leading up to the modern day and to understand what other approaches have been or are currently in danger of becoming left behind. One particularly powerful analysis of this kind is offered by the twentieth-century German philosopher, Martin Heidegger. Within the discipline of philosophy, Heidegger is not generally considered to have made significant contributions to fields like philosophy of medicine or medical ethics, and indeed Heidegger himself voiced concerns about the stratification of philosophy into such subdisciplines (Heidegger 1993a); however, as I will explain here, his work on the history of science and the history of the concept of nature nevertheless offers highly relevant insights for those interested in better understanding the failures of our current biomedical model of health care. In his essay, "The Question Concerning Technology" (1993c), first published in 1954, Heidegger argues that the aim of modern science as a whole is the reduction of nature to what can be calculated, controlled, and manipulated by human technology. For Heidegger, the control and manipulation of nature is not only a new means employed by modern medicine. It is in many ways an end in itself. This analysis, I will argue, is already quite helpful in shedding light on the strange predicament of health care today. A few years after "The Question Concerning Technology," however, Heidegger makes even clearer how his critique of modern science bears upon contemporary medicine. In the *Zollikon Seminars* (2001a), a series of lectures given from 1959 to 1969 in collaboration with the psychiatrist, Medard Boss, Heidegger argues that medicine shares this same fate insofar as it is deeply informed by the worldview of modern science. It loses touch with any measure of health other than its own technological ordering. Heidegger's analysis is highly effective at contextualizing modern medical science, allowing us to better understand the limits of its competency. However, I will argue that, in order to fully understand the strange predicament of modern health care today, we need not only an account of its domination by modern science but also an account of what is being usurped, that is, that primordial praxis of understanding and tending to health that was once the domain of wise women and medicine men and that continues even today as a largely non-institutionalized lay practice. For just as nature even today has not been entirely reduced to what can be manipulated by human technology, health is—despite the encroachment of modern science into medical practice—still not reducible to mastery over the body. I will argue here that Heidegger's own account in the *Zollikon Seminars*, then, goes only so far in bringing to light this primordial praxis, and that it is Hans-Georg Gadamer, Heidegger's student, who offers a more robust phenomenology of health in his work, *The Enigma of Health*. Thus, I turn to Gadamer in this chapter to understand this primordial praxis of health care and the measure of health it continues to offer us even today, despite the encroachments of modern science.

One of the most profound philosophical and social contributions that Heidegger made during his lifetime was no doubt his analysis of how our lives and our way of thinking in the modern age have become thoroughly enmeshed with technology. Typically, we think about technologies as tools—tools that we use to accomplish ends that we already have and that we put to work in a world whose reality is independent of this technology. One makes such assumptions when one believes, for example, that massive investment into the construction of military weaponry is always a response to some real need for defense and not the setting forth of reality as a hostile, threatening territory, or, likewise, that implementing scientific strategies of organizational management across a university is a natural response to real organizational needs and not a fundamental change to the raison d'être of the university. In "The Question Concerning Technology," though, Heidegger explains that technology is not simply a means of accomplishing some end but also a way of revealing the world in a particular way. He insists: "What is decisive in *technē* does not at all lie in making and manipulating, nor in the using of means.... It is as revealing, and not as manufacturing that *technē* is a bringing-forth" (1993c, 319). On a certain view, then, the development of a massive military arsenal can be adequately understood as the production of material which, if it lies latent and unused, has no effect on the world that we live in. According to Heidegger's argument in "The Question Concerning Technology," though, even if their capacity for destruction is not put to use, the creation of these weapons has a definite effect. During a period of nuclear proliferation, for example, the world is transformed into a hostile territory, so hostile that it seems, in turn, to warrant the stockpiling of nuclear arms. The error, then, is that idea that the world we live in is, at its core, independent from and indifferent to technology. This misses the ontic function of technology. With every technological development, there is not just an intervention into being but an interpretation of being and, along with this, of our own proper activity as human beings.

This is nowhere clearer than in the case of cosmetic technology today. Ever since the mid-twentieth century when women in wealthy societies became consumers with disposable income, companies have marketed to them an endless stream of products for cosmetic enhancement (Wolf 2002). In recent decades, this array of products has come to include an assortment of more invasive surgical procedures aimed at reducing signs of aging and any other disobedient bodily elements—stubborn bulges, varicose veins, and so on. In the past two or three decades, men have increasingly been targeted with a similar line of products promising endless youth, fitness, and virility. The way that these products are marketed suggests that they have been developed simply in order to satisfy preexisting needs and desires. Botox is only an innovative way of supplying women's age-old demand for products that make them appear younger. So the story goes. If *technē* is not just a means to an end but a way of revealing though, then something different is going on. The development of these new cosmetic technologies has begun to reveal the human body as a malleable material whose appearance is to be managed and even reconstructed through the use of scientifically developed interventions—as many as one can possibly afford.

It is common for us today to see these developments as very recent phenomena with no real precursors in history and as relatively autonomous phenomena—unbound by any natural constraints. After all, we know that it was only recently in history that the female body came to be seen as a malleable material to be managed by an array of technological interventions sold on the market.[1] This suggests that this kind of development is quite new. Heidegger insists, though, that we consider the advent of modern science in the seventeenth century as an important precursor to modern technology, for it is at this time—long before the development of atomic energy or elective cosmetic surgery—that nature was first configured as "a calculable coherence of forces" (1993c, 326) knowable and quantifiable in advance. One finds this precise projection of nature already underway, Heidegger (1967) argues, in Isaac Newton's *Mathematical Principles of Natural Philosophy* and Rene Descartes's *Rules for the Direction of the Mind*, where it is presented as an essential part of general scientific method. For Heidegger, this development in modern science centuries ago paved the way for the technological configuration of nature we know today, where nature is set forth as "standing-reserve" (*Bestand*).

In "The Question Concerning Technology," Heidegger describes this process as entailing the transformation of natural beings into objects whose energy is to be extracted and stored (1993b, 322). Wind, water, soil—these are no longer just made use of by human beings who inhabit a limited enclave within nature. They are seen from the start as resources and are altered accordingly. They become, along with nature as a whole, the object of human control and manipulation. Heidegger illustrates the shift that takes place from premodern technology to modern technology as follows:

> The earth now reveals itself as a coal mining district, the soil as a mineral deposit. The field that the peasant formerly cultivated and set in order appears different from how it did when to set in order still meant to take care of and maintain. The work of the peasant does not challenge the soil of the field. In sowing grain it places seed in the keeping of the forces of growth and watches

over its increase. But meanwhile even the cultivation of the field has come under the grip of another kind of setting-in-order, which sets upon nature. It sets upon it in the sense of challenging it. Agriculture is now the mechanized food industry. Air is now set upon to yield nitrogen, the earth to yield ore, ore to yield uranium, for example; uranium is set upon to yield atomic energy, which can be released either for destruction or for peaceful use. (1993c, 296)

Here Heidegger clearly emphasizes a difference between premodern and modern technology and an important difference at that. Human interactions with nature have indeed clearly and drastically changed. Nature is now understood as nothing but what can yield abstract quantities of value, and the extraction of such value seems to have no other end than further and further accumulation in kind. In such a context, new technologies are regarded as "productive," while our larger and more enduring goals as a species or as a particular social enterprise (e.g., a university) become less and less clear. Writer and social critic, Paul Goodman, makes a similar observation when he describes the way that the functions of social enterprises today are quickly adapted to whatever new technologies are available, regardless of the long-term consequences. Goodman (1969) observes the absurdity of the situation in his own postwar America:

Technologists rush into production with neat solutions that swamp the environment. This applies to packaging products and disposing of garbage, to freeways that bulldoze neighborhoods, high-rises that destroy landscape, wiping out a species for a passing fashion, strip mining, scrapping an expensive machine rather than making a minor repair, draining a watershed for irrigation because (as in Southern California) the cultivable land has been covered by asphalt. Given this disposition, it is not surprising that we defoliate a forest in order to expose a guerrilla and spray teargas from a helicopter on a crowded campus.

As both Goodman and Heidegger make clear, this change in human society marks a seismic historical shift. The application of technology becomes an end in itself, even after it starts to diminish our quality of life by wreaking havoc on the earthly and social environments where we have long flourished. Yet, in the passage quoted earlier, however, Heidegger also points to something continuous between the premodern and modern situation. In both situations, one works on natural beings in order to bring about a desired end. In the traditional agricultural practice that Heidegger describes here, there is already a use of *technē*, a way of revealing "whatever does not bring itself forth and does not yet lie here before us" (1993c, 295). It is this basic human activity that precedes and enables modern science and technology. The peasant that Heidegger describes, however, cultivates the land in a way that cares for and maintains it. Her way of cultivation works with the natural forces of growth. As premodern *technē*, it is, as Harold Alderman (1978) puts it, not "domineering and challenging" like modern technology, but "responsive and contemplative" (44). This responsiveness requires as much good sense about how and when to hold back (e.g., how not to overwork the soil or overwater the crop) as it does knowledge of what one ought to do. Modern *technē*, on the other hand, seems to have left behind this kind of skill. Any decision to hold back and refrain from acting upon objects is today interpreted as a lack of skill. The assumption, after all, is that the most skillful of artisans would be those who can bring about whatever the prescribed outcome is and can do so at will.

It is this transformation in the history of *technē* that we must understand if we are to make sense of how we arrived at the strange predicament of health care today where costly technological innovations are constant despite their ambiguous returns.[2] In "The Question Concerning Technology," though, Heidegger does not yet make the link between this transformation and changes in health care. Five years after the publication of the essay, however, Heidegger began meeting with Boss and fellow psychiatrists in Zollikon and started to trace out the impact that this shift in technology has had on human society's approach to health. There he made clear that it is not only water and land that are reduced to what is calculable and manipulable; it is increasingly the human body itself.[3] He explains how, given their grounding in science, physicians today view the human body in terms of abstractions, that is, as a collection of abstract quantitative data whose calculability is guaranteed by the *technē* of medical science itself. They view the body, that is, as the modern scientist views nature. Heidegger explains, "The basic characteristic of nature represented by the natural sciences is conformity to law. Calculability is a consequence of this conformity to law. Of all that is, only that which is measurable and quantifiable is taken into account. All other characteristics are disregarded" (2001a, 25). To understand Heidegger's point, one need only consider the number of medical instruments developed over the past two centuries that are designed to translate our bodily functions into quantitative data. From the thermometer to the electrocardiogram to the algorithms used in computer-assisted diagnosis, such instruments play a central role in contemporary medicine.[4] Indeed, the health of the body becomes increasingly understood according to various biostatistical readings. Any sense of health other than one that can be calculated and manipulated directly by medical technology, Heidegger explains, has begun to appear as unreal.

In the *Zollikon Seminars*, Heidegger attempts to highlight this historical shift to his audience of psychiatrists in order to shed light on the limits of modern science as a foundation for medical practice. Heidegger is, therefore, primarily focused on laying bare the particular history out of which contemporary medical practice emerges. One might wonder, then, what, if anything, Heidegger's account can contribute to a critical evaluation of this state of affairs or to a better understanding of health and health care. Can a project aimed only at revealing the limits of contemporary medical practice contribute to either? Certainly there are moments in the seminars where Heidegger highlights the palpable failure of medicine today to understand and effectively treat sickness through an entirely biomedical approach. At one point, for example, he exclaims: "That which can be calculated in advance and that which is measurable—only that is real. How far can we get with a sick person [with this approach]? *We fail totally*!" (my emphasis) (Heidegger 2001a, 19). Heidegger's language here is clearly evaluative and not just descriptive in character. He does not just accept the encroachment of modern technology into medicine without voicing any criticism. He recognizes that this development has led modern health care to fail at its primary endeavor of healing. He is attuned, in other words, to that problem of health care that I spoke about at the beginning of this chapter. He sees that, when the human body is reduced to what can be calculated and manipulated, we end up with a very limited *technē* of the body.

The fate of the human body at the hands of medical science, then, is not unlike that of the land at the hands of modern agricultural science as Heidegger had earlier described in "The Question Concerning Technology." Whereas agriculture in the premodern world worked with the natural forces of growth, modern agriculture attempts to supplant those natural forces with its own measure. Likewise, the trajectory of modern medicine is no longer to work with the natural forces of health in the body but to bring the body entirely under the control of medical technology. In "The Question Concerning Technology," however, Heidegger had highlighted the fact that, although threatened by the spread of modern technology, there are older, more primordial forms of *technē* still in operation today. In the passage quoted earlier from the chapter, Heidegger finds this skill manifest in the peasant who still cultivates land in the twentieth century as it had traditionally been cultivated. Her practice, still to this day, requires her to care for and to be attentive to the changing needs of the land as she benefits from it. In the *Zollikon Seminars*, however, Heidegger is largely silent about what primordial practices of healing operate today and stand in tension with biomedical science. Indeed, he compares modern medicine to its premodern counterpart only in order to highlight a relationship to nature that seems today virtually lost and unthinkable to modern habits of mind. Unfortunately, one does not find, then, a thorough phenomenological reconstruction of health or healing in Heidegger's seminars. This is undertaken not by Heidegger but by his student, Hans-Georg Gadamer, starting in 1965 with the publication of "Apologia for the Art of Healing," published while Heidegger was giving his lectures in Zollikon.

Like Heidegger, Gadamer also recognizes the drastic changes that have taken place in medical practice during the modern era. He discusses, for example, the increasing degree to which doctor–patient and nurse–patient meetings are mediated through technology. Like Heidegger, Gadamer identifies this development as part of a wider trend of rapid automatization with which social consciousness has not kept pace. That "the progress of technology encounters an unprepared humanity" (1996, 24) is nowhere clearer than in today's doctor's office. The effect of all of this, Gadamer makes clear, is that human beings are increasingly alienated by the healthcare experience. The experience is no longer one of human beings helping other human beings restore the kind of balance that is valuable to them and that is traditionally valued by their community. With increased automatization and quantification, the measure of health is taken out of human hands. Gadamer points out that this is inevitably alienating, not only for those subjected to the analysis and treatment as patients, but also for those practitioners of medicine—doctors, nurses, and so on, who must interact with patients in this way. He writes, "Modern science and the ideal of objectification demands of all of us a violent estrangement from ourselves, irrespective of whether we are doctors, patients or simply responsible and concerned citizens" (Gadamer 1996, 70).

Like Heidegger, Gadamer recognizes that training in health professions today is entirely focused on becoming familiar with the physical body as understood in anatomy, physiology, and biology and on knowing how to use the tools and technologies developed by modern science to diagnose and treat physical symptoms. Unlike Heidegger, however, Gadamer reminds us time and again that actually working in the field of health care today calls for much more than this. It calls not just for the application of scientific methods but for judgment, which draws its power from the practical experience of listening and responding to patients. To communicate effectively with a patient about an illness and a treatment plan, for example, it helps to be aware of the conscious goals and unconscious habits in the person's life that are likely to be disrupted by the illness and the treatment and how hard these disruptions are likely to be for them. It is important to be aware, for example, that, if a person suffers from the loss of speech (aphasia) as the result of a stroke, this will probably disrupt life for him or her even more drastically than effects like joint pain, given the vital role that speech plays in virtually all human communities. Such a comparison cannot be made, however, as important as it is, by the scientist who aims to see the patient disinterestedly as a physical object among others. It requires that one attempt to transport oneself into the patient's particular form of life and to consider the effects from this vantage point. Similarly, when doctors must decide whether or not to counsel a family about palliative care options or whether to offer a medication to alleviate pain, they must inevitably take into account—and even, temporarily at least, take on—the norms of the patient and the society the patient lives in. To make these judgments wisely, they must take to heart, for example, what makes a life worth living for this person and his or her community or, in the case of pain medication, what quality and quantity of pain the patient and his or her community would likely find acceptable, tolerable, or even valuable. While their scientific training does not prepare doctors or nurses to make such judgment calls, they are nevertheless making them on a daily basis.

These examples help to make clear what Gadamer means when he points out that, despite the purely technical training that they receive, practicing medicine today comes with great social and political responsibility (1996, 23). As Gadamer puts it, "Once science has provided doctors with the general laws, causal mechanisms and principles, they must still discover what is the right thing to do in each particular case, and this is something which hardly seems to be predictable or knowable in advance" (1996, 95). Medical researchers do not need to make such judgments except when there are practical consequences to their research (which there often are). On the other hand, medical *practitioners* need to make these judgments all of the time. In fact, as soon as they withdraw such judgment from the process, as soon as medical technology is applied independently of such judgment, we find ourselves in that predicament with which I began—with an approach to healing that appears ambiguously productive and destructive. In this situation, as Goodman (1969) explains, "Incommensurable factors, individual differences, the local context, the weighting of evidence are quietly overlooked though they may be of the essence. The system, with its subtly transformed purposes, seems to run very smoothly; it is productive, and it is more and more out of line with the nature of things and the real problems."

For Gadamer, then, despite the encroachment of science into medical practice in the modern age and the danger this presents, modern medicine remains enmeshed with a *praxis* of healing that has much deeper roots. This is, as we just saw, apparent in medical practitioners' continued and constant need for practical judgment. It is also apparent, Gadamer argues, in the need to know, as medical practitioners, how and when to *hold back*. Recall that in "The Question Concerning Technology," Heidegger had described what differentiates the peasant's agricultural art from modern agricultural technology today: Modern agriculture, as an imprint of modern science, sees the land as a means of accumulation and as an object to be controlled and manipulated for this purpose. The peasant, however, as discussed earlier, works with the natural forces of growth and the possibilities and constraints of the land itself. As part of her practice, she must care for and maintain the land itself, and this requires her to know when and where not to plant. She may even practice, as the ancient Israelites did, a Shemittah year every seven growing seasons

(Leviticus 25: 3–6) to let the land repair itself. Likewise, medical practitioners must also know how and when to hold back in different ways.

There are times, for example, when a physical therapist must hold back and let his patient get to her feet by herself, just as a family doctor will at times advise letting a cold run its course rather than administering antibiotics and a cardiac specialist will avoid any further invasive procedures after surgery in order to let the patient's body heal. In each of these cases, the doctor is holding back in order to allow the body's own forces of homeostasis to work. This effort, returning the body to the point of its own equilibrium, is central to the practice of medicine. Quoting Gadamer on this point, Fred Dallmayr (2000) explains:

> In its self-balancing capacity nature discloses itself as something which, "as it were, holds to its own course and does so in and of itself." Although amenable to some corrective measures, this course itself is not the outcome of construction or production. In regard to human illness and health, the genuine work of medical practice can consist not in Promethean "making," but only in the attempt "to restore an equilibrium that has been disturbed." (159)

As part of this respect for natural equilibrium, though, doctors today must also know when and how to hold back when it comes to diagnosis. In the course of diagnosis, doctors today work with a nosological system of classification that automatically subsumes a patient's situation under general categories. These classifications are certainly a necessary feature of medical science, but practitioners in the field need to watch for when these general schemata cover over particular complexities of the patient's situation that require attention. What's more, as I have argued elsewhere (Culbertson 2016), they must also know when to hold back from interpreting a patient's condition for him or her—to allow that patient to negotiate for himself or herself the meaning of his or her condition. When treating human beings, after all, this is part of what it means to respect their own natural forces of growth.[5]

Despite the influence of modern science on the art of healing, then, doctors and nurses today must still exhibit a sort of modesty as part of their practice. Thus, Gadamer (1996) argues: "Among all the sciences concerned with nature the science of medicine is the one which can never be understood entirely as a technology, precisely because it invariably experiences its own abilities and skills simply as a restoration of what belongs to nature" (39). As much as we tend to think about the skilled artisan today as the one who can immediately bring about whatever desired effect is willed, it is still the case that the doctor does not *produce* health. Instead, she tries to work with the body's natural forces of growth, and, if she wants to genuinely heal, she must also be attentive to the precarious equilibrium of the patient's life while doing so. It is this equilibrium, Gadamer argues, that is the basic phenomenon of health—a phenomenon that is perfectly familiar and everyday yet, as inherently incalculable, goes entirely ignored by biomedical science.

In his "Apologia for the Art of Healing," Gadamer likens this incalculable practice of finding equilibrium to the body's own way of finding its balance. Balance, like health, is something we generally give no mind to unless we lose it. Just as I do not think about health until I fall ill, I do not think about the fact that I must keep balance as I walk or stand until I suddenly trip and fall or an infection leaves me dizzy and unsteady on my feet. "What a remarkable thing it is," Gadamer exclaims, "that a slight pitch in balance counts as nothing, that we can tilt almost until falling and then swing back into equilibrium. Yet, on the other hand, whenever we go beyond this point of balance, we fall into irreversible misfortune" (1996, 78). Only when this reversal occurs and I suddenly find myself off balance, do I realize the complex and delicate process of stabilization that is taking place right under my nose every second of the day. Moreover, when my balance is thrown off, what is required to restore it is different each time. Once lost, I must keep myself loose so that I can *find* my balance again. I have to heighten my responsivity to my environment. Indeed, if I fail to regain my balance, Gadamer explains (1996), it will not be because I did not exert enough force but "because there was too much force in play" (37).

These peculiar and unique features apply, for Gadamer, not only to the experience of finding physical balance when one is trying to keep oneself upright but to the task of healing as well. Medical practice too also seeks to restore the equilibrium of a person's life. Moreover, it too is a practice that, at one level, defies articulation as a technical science, because it requires the practitioner to pay attention to the particular equilibrium of each individual's life. This is the primordial practice of health care that, although increasingly endangered, is nevertheless still part of the everyday experience of today's practitioners, just as it is part of the lived experience of health and illness.

Heidegger was right, then, that medical practitioners today who treat patients as objects of scientific knowledge would do well to reflect on the limits of the biomedical approach to healing. After all, as I have argued here, this approach has led to the deep alienation that many people today regularly experience in the healthcare system. This alienation is not only a matter of individual suffering. What is at stake, as Heidegger makes quite clear, is the relationship of the human being to nature and to itself as a natural being. At the same time, as I hope to have shown here through Gadamer's work, medical practitioners are well positioned to intervene against technocratic discourse today, because they do not simply encounter their patients as their scientific training has prepared them to encounter them. In the actual practice of medicine, the health of the patient is never altogether reducible to the data produced from an electrocardiogram, and the patient himself of herself is never just the image on an MRI. Likewise, even as scientific discourse encroaches more and more on our experiences of health and illness today, if Gadamer is right, then we will continue to put stock in a standard of health that is irreducible to such biostatistical measures. For despite the biomedical determination of sickness, it is still the case that even the chronically ill individual will strive to restore as much equilibrium as possible in their lives, and we will, I imagine, still want to call those gifted at helping them to restore this equilibrium "healers."

NOTES

1. For a description and an analysis of this development, see Bartky (1990, 63–82).

2. Notably, such technological innovations today often come with the cost of alienating patients. Paul Goodman (1969) identifies this as the hidden cost of over-technologizing health care. He explains: "Our contemporary practice makes little sense. We have expensive technology stored in specialists' offices and big hospitals, really unavailable for mass use in the neighborhoods; yet every individual, even if he is quite rich, finds it almost impossible to get attention to himself as an individual whole organism in his setting. He is sent from specialist to specialist and exists as a bag of symptoms and a file of test scores."

3. Already in "The Question Concerning Technology," Heidegger makes clear that, as modern technology develops, humans become not just the agents of technological manipulation and control but the objects of these forms of ordering as well (1993c, 323). Francoise Dastur (2012) makes a similar point when she writes that, in the age of genetic manipulation, the human being "has itself become an object of technology, and not merely the subject of technical action" (14).

4. As Fredrik Svenaeus (2000) explains, the introduction of such scientific instruments into medical practice during the nineteenth and early twentieth centuries gave medical practice a new air of objectivity and a new credibility that it had not previously enjoyed. With this new air of objectivity, however, also came a new distance and disconnect between patient and physician. Svenaeus explains: "Instead of watching, feeling and listening to the patient, the latter can be projected on to a screen by way of medical technology. On this screen the patient's variables can be studied and discussed by a team of physicians. Perhaps the patient is also permitted some comments or at least questions in this conversation, but the attention is not primarily upon him anymore, but upon the variables given by medical technology" (33).

5. My argument here is not an argument for valuing patient autonomy, although this ideal has been the standard in the field of medical ethics for some time. The primary issue with modern health care today, I argue, is not that it deprives the patient of individual autonomy but that it alienates patients. This alienation is rooted in the automatization of medical practice discussed earlier, which, among the other worrisome outcomes explored here, renders meaningless any effort on the part of the patient to interpret her condition for herself.

Chapter 13

Existential Medicine and the Intersubjective Body

John Russon and Kirsten Jacobson

Traditionally, medicine has been based on an organic interpretation of the human body. In this way, health and disease in the human being are understood in the same way that we understand the normal or abnormal functioning of other organisms—plants and animals—that make up our natural environment. While there is something unquestionably right about this model of medicine, in that it clearly does speak to the functioning of our organic bodies, it falls short of grasping the true character of the human body, namely, that it is an *existential* reality, and it also therefore stands as an insufficient model for human medicine. Most importantly, grasping the existential character of the human body is recognizing it as an intersubjective and hence expressive body. Correspondingly, an existential conception of medicine requires treating the body first and foremost as a reality situated within and participating in relationships of recognition and communication.

This notion of an existential conception of medicine is not new: It was given an extraordinarily rich and insightful treatment in 1966 by J. H. van den Berg in *The Psychology of the Sickbed*, and more recently Fredrik Svenaeus (2011) has done an excellent job of articulating the basic relevance of Heidegger's notion of being-in-the-world for the philosophy of medicine. We understand our approach to be of a piece with these earlier analyses, but we take a unique slant by emphasizing the distinctive character of the body within the existential perspective opened up by Heidegger, a theme powerfully articulated in Heidegger's *Zollikon Seminars* (2001), but especially developed in the French existentialists Sartre and Merleau-Ponty.[1]

We will lay out our conception of existential medicine in three sections. First, we will outline the distinctive way that the body is understood within the context of existential phenomenology. Second, using the examples of inflammatory bowel disease and infection with HIV, we will explore how this existential conception of the body leads us to recognize a different "essence" to these experiences of illness than does organic medicine. Third and finally, we will consider how our reconceptualization of illness leads as well to a reconceptualization of health; this last reflection will also motivate a critique of contemporary, institutionalized health care.

THE EXISTENTIAL CONCEPTION OF THE BODY

An existential conception of medicine depends on an existential conception of the body. To grasp the existential conception of the body, one must grasp the interrelation of three phenomenological aspects of our experience: First, the body is one's "I can"; second, the "I" is always implicated in relationships of mutual recognition, always a participant member of a "we"; and, third, our reality as a participant in a "we" is always experienced in and through a *world*—in other words, we experience our relations with others not just as one discrete aspect of experience but in and as the very fabric of our being-in-the-world. Let us consider each of these three notions in turn.

What does it mean to refer to the body as the "I can"? The body can, of course, be understood as a thing in the world—it *is* a thing in the world. *My* body, however, is not just one among many things in the world, but is the very medium and means of my existence, of my existence *as* an experiencing subject, of my "I." My body is distinguished from all other things in the world by the way that I *experience* it. And how, fundamentally, do I *experience* my body? I experience it *as my ability to act*. In a typical situation, I am absorbed with my surroundings, grabbing the cup, answering the telephone, running to the bus, and so on. In such situations, my attention is "occupied," so to speak, by the cup, the telephone, or the bus, which I experience *as* graspable, *as* answerable, *as* accessible by running. In each case, my attention is occupied by the thing that is the explicit object of my intention and action, but, though my body as such is not the focal object of my attention, I experience that focal thing *in terms of* the capacities for interaction with things that my body affords. My fundamental experience of my body is not the detached recognition of it as a thing in the world, but is rather the non-thematized experience of it as the very condition of my *having* things—my *having* a world—at all.

Just as my primary experience of my body is *as* my ability to interact with the things of my world, so do things at root exist for me first as calls to action, as invitations, solicitations, or demands that elicit from me—from my body—a behavioral response. Prior to being the objects of intellectual reflection, things are, so to speak, "under my skin" as prods and provocations summoning up my action, as, for example, the stairs that call forth my raised step or the handrail that draws my hand to it before I have even noticed them explicitly. My body and the things of my world thus form an interlocking system, my body's powers illuminating for me the meaning of things and things illuminating for me the resources that are my body. As Merleau-Ponty (1963) writes in "The Philosopher and His Shadow,"

> The relation between my body's movements and the thing's "properties" which they reveal is that of the "I am able to" to the marvels it is within its power to give rise to. And yet my body must itself be meshed into the visible world; its power depends precisely on the fact that it has a place *from which* it sees. Thus it is a thing, but a thing I dwell in. . . . We can just as well say that the entire functioning of the body proper hangs upon the perceived thing the circuit of behavior closes upon. (166, 173)

My body and things form an interlocking system such that I experience myself as *in* a world that calls for my action. To conceive the body existentially is thus to recognize that, first and foremost, my body exists for me as *my capacity to have a world*, and the specific powers of my body determine the specific parameters in which the world can present itself to me as meaningful.

This interlocking system of body and world means that it is as true that things reveal to me the nature of my body as it is true that my body reveals to me the nature of things. This point is especially pertinent for grasping the second essential feature of the existential conception of the body, namely, its essentially intersubjective nature. The world that we live in is a human world: We experience ourselves as persons in the midst of other persons. Now, just as we noted about our own bodies, we can note about another person that she is a thing in the world. A person is a very special sort of thing, though, and understanding what kind of thing the other person is allows us to understand the distinctive way that person impinges upon and reveals the existential nature of the body.

A person is there, present before one as that animate body grasping a cup or answering a telephone, but to experience that presence *as* a person is precisely to experience that bodily presence as the *annunciation* of a human reality—a person—that can never itself be present before one: A person, *as a person*, is always *inherently* absent from one's experience inasmuch as that person, (like oneself), is a center of meaning and initiative: That person is a *subject*, and hence never adequately presented in any object.[2] And, furthermore, inasmuch as that person is an experiencing subject, one thus necessarily exists for that subject as an object in *her* world. This recognition of the other as a subject has the further implication that to experience that body over there as the presentation of a subject is to experience *oneself* as an object of that person's experience: I experience the other *as* a person in and as experiencing myself as an object *for* her.

Now, we noted earlier, that the body is the "I can," it is our capacity for engaging with objects. But how is it, then, that my body is my capacity for experiencing that object that is another subject? On the one hand, as we have just seen, it is in and as experiencing my body as an object that I experience myself in the presence of another subject. Our experience of other persons, though, does not stop at the simple fact of an encounter between aliens; on the contrary, we experience other persons—just as we experience other things—as realities *with which we can interact*. The most relevant sense of our bodily "I can" in relation to the experience of other people is this, its capacity for interaction with them. The interaction with other persons, though, unlike the material interaction of physical bodies, takes a fundamentally different form from bodily contact as such and the bodily changes that thus result; interactions with other persons take the form of *communication*; that is, it takes the form of the *intersubjective* contact and the *intersubjective* changes that can result *through* bodily interaction. It is thus in its capacity for *expression* that the body exists for us as the "I can" by virtue of which we are able to interact with other persons.[3]

In expression, my body becomes a sign: I use my hand to wave "hello" to you, I shake my head to say "no," I hug you to express my compassion for you in your suffering, or, most fully, I expel breath from my mouth to make the sounds that you and I recognize as language. In each case, the present bodily action—waving, head-shaking, hugging, or making a sound—is not itself the proper content or object of your experience or of mine; instead, at least in the case of successful communication, each of us is occupied with *what is expressed in and through* that present action, that *gesture*. The waving, head-shaking, hugging, and sound-making and their bodily effects upon you can all be studied and understood physiologically, but your *understanding* of my expression of sympathy, enthusiasm, or disagreement is not the same as the simple feeling of objective pressure against your skin, the excitation of receptors within your retina, the transduction of sound waves in your inner ear, and so on; on the contrary, it is your *recognition* of what I *as a subject* am expressing to you *as a subject*. The realities of expression are enacted within the materiality of our bodily interaction, but they exist only insofar as they are matters of our intersubjective recognition. The bodily, existentially speaking, is our means of participating in the unique space of shared experience.

Though our sharing of experience with others can take the form of an explicitly thematized action, such as asking a stranger for permission to sit at the table she is using or trying to get the attention of one's friend who is otherwise occupied, our sharing of experience is not always or even, indeed, typically such a thematic matter. More commonly and more fundamentally, our sharing of experience is the already, mutually accomplished medium for our engagement with the things of our world: Our sharing of experience with others is primarily the way in which we inhabit a world *together*, a cohabitation that is thus the implicit meaning of our explicit, thematic interactions with other things. Indeed, because our very sense of self is rooted in the dialog of "recognition" that we enact with others, it is this basic meaning that is the pivot for the meaning of our world and, hence, of the things that make up that world.[4] When, with the support of their parents, infants learn to walk, for example, new spaces, new things, and new activities become available and thus alive to them, and these spaces, things, and activities, as well as being an enrichment to the material contents of their world are also new and richer means for their enjoyment of inhabiting the reality of their shared life with their parents. Similarly, when adolescents are given permission to walk somewhere on their own, new sites for exploration appear for them in the neighborhood they have "seen" so many times before and, again, just as this is a material expansion of the material possibilities of their world, so is their engagement with them an engagement with their parental "permission" (just as any previous "illegitimate" entry into these places would have been experienced by them as exciting precisely because it was transgressive of that permission). And, of course, the inhabitation of these new worlds by the child or the adolescent—the world made available through walking or the world made available through solitary travel—is not just an inhabitation shared with parents and familiar others, but is also a world shared with strangers. A female adolescent, for example, may be given permission to walk a certain distance away from her family home during the day, but not at night, owing to her guardian's perceived sense that there may be people out at night that she should not encounter. And, indeed, as she herself experiences her adolescent body changing, she may, with fear or excitement, pointedly find her inhabitation of public spaces to be an engagement with strange others inasmuch as she experiences her body as an object of their sexualized gaze. Walking through the grocery store may no longer feel like the simple and innocent thing it formerly was—a solely instrumental activity, or a fun part of family life—but may become a threatening or exhilarating challenge as she experiences others who previously would not tend to notice her now inspecting and evaluating her. In all these cases, we can see both how our bodily engagement with the world is implicitly an engagement with other people and, reciprocally, how our engagement with other people is enacted as our bodily engagement with the world.

Existentially conceived, then, the body is not understood as an organism (though, to be sure, it *is* an organism). First, the body, existentially conceived, is my capacity to be *in the world*: It is my "I can," by which I participate with things in constituting the tissue and fabric—the very "flesh"—of the world.

More specifically, the body, existentially conceived, is my lived capacity to participate in a world with other people. In this sense, my body, existentially conceived, is (a) *how I* am on display to others and (b) my capacity to express myself to others. It is this conception of the existential body that must underlie truly human medicine. Let us now consider this conception of the body as our capacity to participate in the intersubjective world can inform medical practice.

ILLNESS IN THE CONTEXT OF INTERSUBJECTIVE RECOGNITION

Because I live my body as my being an object for others, I experience my body as the site for their approbation and desire or, alternatively, their disapprobation and disgust. While a so-called medical model of medicine need only construe an illness as a disease—as a dysfunctional state of an organic system—an existential medicine must recognize the illness as a malady of the body-as-site-of-intersubjective-recognition as much as a malady of the body as an organism. Any medical problem raises these themes: One can experience the black eye one has from being punched in the face as a horrible embarrassment, in the case, for example, of an abused wife who finds it a challenge both to reveal to others that she was involved in such a bad situation and to reveal to herself that she has failed to live up to her husband's expectations, no matter how unjust his assessment and subsequent reaction may have been; one can also equally experience the black eye as a "medal" of which one is proud, in the case, for example, of a pre-teen boy who is eager to display to his peers that he has entered the world of fist-fighting.[5] These *existential* realities of the black eye cannot be analyzed or understood in biological terms; they are, however, the *lived reality* of the black eye: they are *what it is* as a property of the body of this person. Furthermore, as the preceding example shows, there is no way to deduce from the organic situation—the bruised tissue around the eye—what that existential reality is: The existential reality of this and any such illness *cannot be grasped in separation from the lived experience of the person who suffers it*. At the same time, the need to go beyond the objective terms of the bodily condition to the subjective terms of the human situation does not make the meaning of the illness something mysterious, nor does it make it a matter of private stipulation; on the contrary, as our examples also make clear, it is quite possible to understand the significance of the illness through grasping the situation of that person.[6] The limitations of the "objective" analysis are thus not a matter for "throwing up one's hands." They indicate, rather, that medicine cannot honestly claim to care for the health of people—that is, to be *healthcare*—if it restricts its diagnoses and treatments to impersonal and generic interpretations: an authentic, human medicine—an existential medicine—must *in principle* include the personal interaction between healthcare providers and patient, oriented to the understanding of the *meaning*—the *necessarily personal* meaning—of the illness.[7] *Any* medical situation is a phenomenon of the existential body and, thus, like our example of the black eye, engages the reality of that body as the way the person is on display before others. Some medical conditions, at least in our contemporary culture, thematize this dimension very dramatically, and we will briefly consider two such condition: IBD (inflammatory bowel disease) and HIV-AIDS (human immunodeficiency virus-acquired immune disorder).

"Inflammatory bowel disease" is a name that covers two distinct conditions, Crohn's disease and ulcerative colitis, that are characterized by a chronic inflammation of the digestive tract; both are autoimmune disorders, and there is no known cure for either. Symptoms associated with these conditions include bloody diarrhea, painful bowel movements, fecal incontinence, and, consequently, weight loss and fatigue. These symptoms can be more or less severe, and they can manifest themselves at unpredictable times over the course of an entire life. These conditions are normally treated with a mixture of drug therapies or surgery; in some cases, surgery may include the creation of a stoma—an opening in the abdomen—to which is attached an ostomy bag for the collection of stool.

IBD is a medical condition that is powerfully correlated with issues of stigma.[8] Because IBD involves feces, it engages with issues that are socially taboo; coupled with the fact that the disease can, unpredictably, involve incontinence and extensive use of the toilet, this condition can produce reactions of disgust, certainly in the one suffering from it but especially from others who are confronted with it. As a consequence, people suffering from IBD can feel stigmatized because of their condition. Furthermore, because these issues of taboo and disgust are closely integrated with our most intimate sense of what is proper and improper—what is "clean" and what is "dirty"—such reactions typically carry with them an implicit moral weight. As a result, the stigmatized person can feel that he or she is morally criticized and held responsible for having the "disgusting condition" and bringing it into the world.[9]

Reaction to the stigma associated with IBD can manifest itself in various different arenas. Because stigma is primarily a social matter—a matter of how one stands in the perception of others—the issues associated with it especially show up in sites where the engagement with others is thematized. Those who experience the symptoms of IBD may, for example, be unwilling to seek medical help in the first place out of a sense of the embarrassment or shame they anticipate feeling in talking with the clinician. Again, they may be reluctant to reveal their condition to their intimate companions—whether family members or romantic partners—out of fear of the reaction they might receive. (In fact, online support groups have proved especially valuable for sufferers from IBD, presumably because the relative anonymity of online interaction offers individuals a buffer from the direct experience of the encounter with another person.) And, in general, social activity in general—whether at work, at school, or for recreation—may seem intimidating, and the individual with IBD may well fear or retreat from such situations.[10]

Let us reflect briefly on these issues of the stigma of IBD and the various forms reaction to it can take in terms of the toll they take on the life of the individual with IBD. The stigma associated with IBD can result in the person with IBD being subjected to unfair treatment from employers or fellow employees, from teacher or fellow students, from medical practitioners, or, indeed, from family members and friends. In this sense, IBD brings with it the possibility of substantial practical problems in the most substantial and the most intimate sectors of life in addition to the severe problems of self-esteem and, in general, in happiness and a sense of joyful existence. Fear of such consequences can fuel an attitude of withdrawal and secrecy, which, in the very act of trying to ward off these crippling life problems, may produce comparably troubling results of social alienation and personal unhappiness as well as practical problems caused by reluctance to seek medical help or to solicit the care of potentially supportive individuals.

What is particularly noteworthy here, and the reason we have chosen to emphasize this particular condition, is that in IBD a problem of the body precisely intervenes in our participation in intersubjective life—that is, *for* the one suffering from IBD *and for* most others with whom that person deals, the condition is precisely a malady *of the existential body*: It is one's "I can" with respect to other people that is damaged through the inflammation of the bowel. In other words, *as a lived experience*, IBD is an *existential* problem rather than simply a physiological phenomenon. Said otherwise, the problem a person with IBD faces is not primarily a problem with the bowels: It is primarily a problem with living a happy and healthy *life*, with how one has and navigates an interhuman world.

Something quite similar can be seen in the case of persons suffering from HIV-AIDS. HIV is a virus that attacks the immune system, destroying the CD4 ("T") cells that fight infection; AIDS—acquired immune deficiency syndrome—is the condition that results from prolonged damage to the immune system by HIV, a condition in which the infected individual is subject to any number of opportunistic infections with which the compromised immune system can no longer cope. Currently, there is no cure for HIV infection, though antiretoviral therapy (ART), introduced in the 1990s, can significantly mitigate the effects of infection if taken correctly, every day. Because HIV is typically contracted through sexual activity or through sharing a needle used for injection with a person infected with HIV, this infection, like IBD, draws our attention to matters that are generally taboo or considered "dirty," with the result that HIV-AIDS, like IBD, is a condition marked by stigma; indeed, it has not been uncommon to hear AIDS interpreted as divine punishment for immoral behavior.[11]

The stigma associated with HIV-AIDS can result in the infected individual being subjected to many forms of disabling discrimination, including such substantial matters as loss of employment, refusal of housing or, indeed, refusal of medical treatment; at a more intimate, personal level, these individuals may suffer from being shunned by family, by friends, or by the wider community; and, of course, these forms of discriminatory treatment, as well as the condition itself, may have crippling effects on the infected individual's sense of self-worth. And, as in the case of IBD, the way infected individuals react to the stigma can itself magnify their problems. Phil Hutchinson and Rageshri Dhairyawan (2017a) have systematically articulated five ways in which the shame experienced in response to the stigma of HIV-AIDS can produce severe problems for the infected individual. The experience of shame can prevent the infected individual from going for testing, when early diagnosis is one of the most important factors in controlling the infection; it can encourage the infected individual not to disclose the condition to medical practitioners, which can affect the timely diagnosis of problems; it can inhibit the infected individual from rigorously maintaining antiretroviral therapy (ART), which dramatically reduces the effectiveness of the therapy; it can lead the infected individual not to disclose his or her condition to partners in situations where that would otherwise be desirable; it can trap the individual in a "psychological hell."[12]

As a *lived experience* of illness, then, rather than as an *organic condition* of disease, HIV-AIDS is prominently characterized by the problematic negotiation of intersubjective and psychological life experienced by the infected individual.[13] As Hutchinson and Dhairyawan (2017b) write,

> The bio-chemical and the psycho-social are fully intertwined in the pathology of HIV, and to make this claim is uncontroversial. We know that poverty, culturally-bestowed attitudes to sex and sexuality, laws on sex work, drug use, immigration, and poor mental health, to name but a few items from a long list, are significant drivers of infection rates, take-up of testing, and development of clinical AIDS. Believing we can achieve good clinical treatment and public health policy without taking full account of the psycho-social aspects of HIV pathology is folly. (6–7)

With the destruction of the T-cells, the *intersubjective life-world* of the infected individual is compromised—it is the *existential* body that is ill—and successful management of the illness requires careful attention to the nature and dynamics of these existential problems.

We have chosen to discuss the examples of IBD and HIV-AIDS because these are two conditions that dramatically thematize the intersubjective dimensions of illness. The point, however, is that *all* medical problems are such existential problems, because all medical problems are problems *of a person*. Through the organism, a *person* is injured, and it is a *person* who must be treated, and the treatment ought, therefore, to address the injury as belonging to a way of being-the-world.

EXISTENTIAL MEDICINE AND AUTHENTICITY

The existential conception of the body requires us to reconceive illness, and it similarly requires us to reconceive "recovery." On the "medical" model, recovery is a matter of recuperating the normal state of organic functioning. An existential conception of health, however, is not articulated in terms of the organism, but in terms of the existential needs of the human being. Most strikingly, this entails that existential health and illness do not vary directly with organic health and disease.

Existential health is ultimately a matter of what Heidegger called "authenticity" (*Eigentlichkeit*): It is a matter of living in a way that is true to our existential reality. Fundamentally, our reality is the fact that we are *free*, and this fact of freedom entails that the terms of our life are not—*cannot be*—given to us in advance; instead, we are ourselves ultimately responsible for establishing the terms in which our lives are meaningful. In short, the fact of our freedom means that it is incumbent upon us to *recognize* our freedom—to recognize about ourselves that we must find for ourselves the answers to our questions about life rather than looking for someone or something else in the world to supply those answers for us. Our existential health, then, fundamentally depends upon whether we have made this recognition or whether we are living in denial of our freedom. The crucial thing to note here is that this recognition is possible in situations of organic disease just as much as it is possible in situations of organic health and, equally, living in denial of our freedom is just as easy in conditions of organic health as it is in conditions of organic disease.

This recognition of the dissymmetry between existential and organic forms of health and illness is, in fact, quite pertinent to our analyses of IBD and HIV-AIDS as existential problems. This is because individuals suffering from each of these conditions sometimes strikingly report that their organic maladies are actually a *blessing*. Frohlich (2014), for example, reports that many individuals with IBD who turned to their romantic partners for support actually felt that their IBD strengthened their relationship. Indeed, he writes that,

> The stigma people experienced, however, was far overshadowed by the support they received from those around them. Those in committed romantic

> relationships often believed that the disease strengthened that relationship, not harmed it. (132; cf. 130)

and

> This dichotomy [of good and bad] was also expressed by many of the participants in this study: there is much bad that comes with this disease, but there is also much good, and the good outweighs any temporary stigma—perceived or realized. (134)

Whether or not the results of Frohlich's study are representative of the population of people with IBD as a whole, they indicate the important reality that *how* we live our situations is not inflexibly determined by the objective features of that situation, and situations of organic disease can in fact be provocative occasions for recognizing what it is that truly matters to us in life. This point is even more powerfully made by Renée Gilhousen (2017) in her study of individuals suffering from HIV-AIDS in rural Appalachia. Through her interviews with individuals with HIV-AIDS, Gilhousen discovered a characteristic narrative arc that developed in their self-interpretation as persons with HIV-AIDS. Specifically, after initial forms of self-interpretation that reflected low self-esteem and considerable pessimism about life, the individuals in her study typically eventually developed the view that it was the difficulties forced upon them by their illness that required them to own up to the realities of their own lives, and they subsequently credited their illness with being their occasion for positive self-transformation.[14] With IBD and HIV-AIDS, then—both of which are lifelong conditions—a situation of existential health understood as authenticity is both compatible with and perhaps even encouraged by the situation of organic disease.

This conclusion points to a final observation about the problems of an organic model of human health and illness. We have so far been arguing that the organic model of medicine fails to recognize the distinctly *human* dimensions of illness and thus fails to address the real problems people face. Beyond this "sin of omission," though, we can also recognize a "sin of commission" in contemporary organic medicine. Specifically, contemporary medicine, as an institution, actually often *works against* existential health in that, as a *rhetorical* system, it precisely encourages the denial of our existential reality.

Hutchinson and Dhairyawan (2017a), in their study of shame and stigma in HIV-AIDS, make the important point that the attitudes involved in shame and stigma are not deliberately formed propositional beliefs of the form "I think that . . ." On the contrary, the attitudes intrinsic to experiences of stigma and shame are more deeply held, "framing" perspectives that belong to one at an unreflective, affective level. Consequently, these attitudes are not changed by argument; if they are changed, they are changed by a fundamental reorientation in "how one sees things" (4, 7–8). Furthermore, these "framing" views are culturally rooted, which is to say they are not so much a matter of how an individual has come to interpret things as they are the correct assimilation by that individual of the values expressed to him or her behaviorally, materially, and structurally by the persons and institutions that define his or her life-world.[15] Whereas we can identify organic causes for organic diseases, when we seek the etiology of *existential* illnesses, we must look for the forces in the life-world that have shaped how those experiences have come to have the *meaning* they have. What the analysis of Hutchinson and Dhairyawan draws our attention to is that the values embedded within our formal and informal social institutions—including our institutions of healthcare—are significantly responsible for how we define our experiences and hence how we interpret our illnesses. The very fact of the stigmatization of IBD and HIV-AIDS—and hence the cause of much of the suffering of individuals in these situations—is the system of values embedded in our social practices and institutions; consequently it is by changing these values rather than by discovering new forms of biochemical therapy that much of the suffering associated with IBD and HIV-AIDS will be alleviated.

In light of this analysis, we can note the *existential* force of the massive system of institutionalized health care and all its attendant institutions, such as pharmaceutical companies, insurance companies, and medical schools. Inasmuch as these institutions are premised on the "medical" model of health and disease, which treats human illness as an organic matter, these institutions powerfully *work against* existential health insofar as they precisely encourage in us a false self-interpretation in which we deny *our own* responsibility for establishing the terms in which our lives are meaningful, and instead treat our bodies as mere things in the world rather than as the very medium of our existence, of our way of being-in-the-world. The institutional model of medicine is based on values of instrumentality, security, and impersonality, all of which are fundamentally impoverished models of human meaning.[16] For instance, in her study of the narrative surrounding birth that pregnant women heard and adopted, Lesley Kay (2015) notes that it was virtually universal for the women of this generation to think of childbirth as a painful situation to be managed, and one that would be justified by the fact of a healthy baby. Such a narrative, first of all, is a bulwark in defense of the standard operating procedures of contemporary hospitals, which is to say, it is, effectively, the voice of the hospital speaking through the voice of the expectant mother, rather like a ventriloquist. Second, and perhaps more strikingly, though, such a narrative does not treat the experience of childbirth as something of intrinsic worth. Indeed, there is no sense in it at all that it is an experience that one might find "meaningful"; instead, it is construed as an instrumental state to be managed instrumentally. The power of implicit, cultural narrative to shape our experience shows up strongly here insofar as an experience so rich in human significance has become interpretively shaped as a simple biological issue (even veering on a problem), and its existential significance erased. Just as these values have been put in the mouths of expectant mothers by the immersion of these women in a social and cultural world shaped and structured by the rhetoric of the institutions of contemporary healthcare, so have these values in general become our unquestioned presumption—our "frame," in the language of Hutchinson and Dhairyawan (2017a, 2017b)—in interpreting our own conditions of health and illness more broadly.

We have tried here to outline the basic meaning of an existential conception of the body, illness, and medicine. On the one hand, this is a model for interpreting the situations of individuals living with specific illnesses. On the other hand, though, it is a model for the very system of healthcare: a model that stands in critical opposition to the prevailing rhetoric embodied in contemporary, institutional practices of healthcare and, indeed, a model that cannot be realized without fundamental changes in the current institutional system.

NOTES

1. Our approach throughout is rooted in Heidegger's analysis of "being-in-the-world" in *Being and Time* (1962), relying especially on his discussions of "world," "being with," "discourse," and "authenticity." Our interpretation of the philosophical import of these notions especially draws on Merleau-Ponty's analysis in "The Body as Object and Mechanistic Physiology" and "The Body as Expression and Speech," Part I, chapters 1 and 6, respectively, of *Phenomenology of Perception* (2012).

2. This theme is studied in detail in chapter 1 of Russon (2017).

3. For the fuller articulation of this notion, see Russon (2016b). For the existential import of this notion, see Jacobson (2016).

4. For a fuller development of the themes in this paragraph, see Russon (2014) and Jacobson (2011).

5. On the existential dimensions of bruises and other forms of visible wounds or scars, see Buchbinder and Eisikovits (2003), Phillips (2003), and Anderson (1999, especially p. 239).

6. See Hutchinson and Dhairyawan (2017a): "Understanding an emotional expression will therefore be arrived at through reconstructing the (internal) relationship that holds between a person's conceptualisation of a situation (including their conceptualisation of self) and the concept of the emotion" (4).

7. Such an approach is, therefore, necessarily qualitative and interpretive, and involves the role of the doctor as participant, rather than a quantitative and procedural method in which the doctor is merely an observer. Such an approach brings problems that cannot be avoided: because the interaction is personal rather than impersonal, there are unavoidable problems of bias and trespass. See Maxwell (2013) and van Manen (1997) for rich discussions of qualitative method.

8. For discussion of stigma in relation to IBD and related conditions, see Smith, Loewenstein, Rozin, Sherriff, and Ubel (2007), Frohlich (2014), Jones, Keefer, Bratten, Taft, Crowell, Levy, and Palsson (2009), Norton, Dibley, and Bassett (2013), and Dibley, Coggrave, McClurg, Woodward, and Norton (2017). Also, the authors wish to thank Lesley Dibley for extensive insights into stigma and disease that she shared with us during the August 2017 workshop "The Body as We Live It: Phenomenological Approaches to Embodiment and Illness" held by the Institute for Hermeneutic Phenomenology at the University of Colorado College of Nursing.

9. On this theme of disgust and moral disapprobation, see Hutchinson and Dhairyawan (2017a, especially p. 7). For further discussion of stigma, see also the classic work on shame by Goffman (1974) and also Falk (2001).

10. For an overview of all of these issues, see Frohlich (2014, especially 126–128).

11. On the theme of stigma and HIV-AIDS, Parker and Aggleton (2003), Hutchinson and Dhairyawan (2017a, 2017b), and Fowler (2014).

12. See especially Hutchinson and Dhairyawan (2017b) for an extended discussion of these five problems.

13. For the distinction between illness and disease, see Engelhardt (1982).

14. See also Carel (2007, 2008) and Jacobson (2016) on the topic of positive transformations that can come with a chronic and/or life-threatening illness.

15. See Hutchinson and Dhairyawan (2017a, 3–4) and Hutchinson and Dhairyawan (2017b, 3–4).

16. For a fuller development of this theme, see Russon (2016a). These characteristics of contemporary, institutional health care reflect the "enframing" that Heidegger (1993c) identifies with the technological worldview.

Chapter 14

Health Like a Broken Hammer or the Strange Wish to Make Health Disappear

Nicole Piemonte and Ramsey Eric Ramsey

> Now on to the totally different "cares." Since I have never stayed in such a hotel, and since I am not familiar with the customs as far as my "suit" is concerned, I must indeed go along with how they do it there. Therefore, I request some very brief instruction from you. I thought this: a suit for travel, a lighter one for the stay, and a "black" one for evenings. Surely, one does not have to drag an uncomfortable hat along. The Basque beret is enough.
>
> —Martin Heidegger to Medard Boss before his trip to Sicily

Even Martin Heidegger—the philosopher who showed us how much of our living is shaped not by our genuine intentions but rather by what "they" say is right or good or fashionable—cannot escape the clutches of "the they," at least not when it comes to choosing the proper attire for his trip to Sicily. The "they" (*Das Man*) it seems, is inescapable. While a cursory reading of Heidegger's masterwork *Being and Time* might leave one with the impression that an authentic confrontation with death or anxiety encourages a total untethering from the "they" and a more genuine way of living, such a reading fails to account for the moments when Heidegger makes the philosophical argument for the impossibility of such untethering. And perhaps nowhere is this point set into relief more than during a critical illness.

Illness has the strange consequence of manifesting health: We see health most clearly when it disappears. When friends or family tell us they are ill, we ask of one another, "What's the matter?" It may seem as though we are asking—and believe we are asking—only about the (dys)function of someone's biological body. Yet, such a question is much more complex than it seems. If we are listening well, we hear that this question solicits an account of how possibilities show (or no longer show) themselves to the one who is ill; it asks whether and how she has "fallen out of things" and why "something is not right because it is not as it was." And in response to our question, we might hear how one has grown unaccustomed to oneself, how on has lost the way things were before one was ill or injured. Like Heidegger's famous example of the hammer that could not be seen until the hammering went awry, so health comes to the fore most forcefully when it is absent. "The sick person," says Hans-Georg Gadamer, "is no longer simply identical with the person he or she was before. For the sick individual 'falls out' of things, has already fallen out of their normal place in life" (1996, 42).

In what follows, we will show how common responses to this falling out of a "normal" place in life incited by critical illness often take two distinct and seemingly contradictory forms that dwell strangely alongside one another: (a) to *evade* illness and quickly restore the physical body to its previous state and (b) to respond to the ethical or social imperative to *intentionally confront* illness, so as to allow for personal transformation that leads to a life lived with more purpose, immediacy, and authenticity. The tension between these two responses suggests that falling out of the "they" is not always an unequivocal good, at least not when it comes to health and illness, for belonging to the "they-self" is something of a privilege, reserved only for those "healthy" enough to take *being* for granted. Although it is true that serious illness—when the appropriate discursive context is created—has the potential to loosen the hold of the inauthenticity of the "they" and toward more intentional living (and dying) (Aho 2016), it is important to consider how and why this falling out can feel isolating, burdensome, and even intolerable. When illness presents itself and the apparent seamlessness of everyone else's life becomes conspicuous, being wrenched from the "they" can be more fearsome than freeing.

A restoration of health is, in some senses, a return to the "they" or "a they"—and this return might not be as damning as some Heidegger interpreters make it sound. As such, in what follows, we explore the tensions and contradictions that both constrain and broaden our response to serious illness, arguing ultimately for a nuanced understanding of "restoration" so that patients and clinicians may find their way toward a shared meaning rich enough to make health disappear again.

HEALTH AS AN ENIGMA

> But what is well-being if it is not precisely this condition of not noticing, of being unhindered, of being ready for and open to everything?
>
> —Hans-Georg Gadamer, *The Enigma of Health*

In good health when all feels as it should, the corporeal body usually disappears or becomes inconspicuous.[1] Gadamer refers to this as a tacit or "natural equilibrium" of the body (1996). In good health, the lived-body, which cannot be measured or studied like the corporeal body, is always already spatially attuned and engaged in the unobtrusive everydayness of life. However, when one becomes ill or injured, the lived-body and the corporeal body intrude on one another, and the body presents itself as object, even as one remains in one's lived embodiment in the world. In other words, the taken-for-granted interrelation or synergy of body and world begins to break down, and a "disturbance" is created in something that previously escaped one's attention almost entirely. Suddenly, the corporeal body—which usually fades into the background of everyday life—forces itself into awareness.

It is precisely the change in the average everydayness of one's life wrought by illness or injury that matters most to patients. Someone with rheumatoid arthritis, for example, does not understand her illness only as chronic inflammatory disorder, but as something that interrupts her everyday way of being in the world. Her body becomes noticeable and draws attention to its taken-for-granted functioning, and habitual tasks that were once given little thought force themselves into view: Stairs become unclimbable, preparing dinner impossible, or holding one's child unbearable. The lived experience of illness reveals that it is not simply the case that the body becomes a conspicuous problem when one becomes sick or injured, but that this causes one's entire way of being to change, including the way one makes (or can no longer make) sense of the world around her. Serious illness can dissolve any semblance of a coherent life trajectory, intensifying experiences of the present and alienating the sick person from her future (Svenaeus 2011). The future, especially during a terminal illness, becomes uncertain and is no longer guaranteed. In this way, a person who is ill or injured cannot be understood as a self-contained corporeal body separate from the context in which he or she dwells (Aho 2008).

Philosopher Fredrik Svenaeus uses the work of Heidegger to offer an explication of such life breakdowns that can occur during illness, describing them as experiences of "unhomelike being-in-the-world" (2011, 35). According to Heidegger, we always already understand the world into which we are thrown (1962, 174). Most of the time, our ability to dwell in the world understandingly is seamless and unbroken, and the world seems homelike, relatively stable, and comfortable. Health, for Svenaeus, represents a homelike being-in-the-world, where the lived-body comports itself with ease, with little intrusion of corporeal dysfunction and bodily breakdown. The connection between body and world is harmonious, and one feels at home in the world around her. Serious illness or injury, however, "break[s] in on us," and such serious intrusions resist meaning and can threaten our homelike being-in-the-world (335). Because illness disturbs our meaning-making capacity, it is not only the body that becomes alien or uncanny, but one's entire way of being. What is more, this disruption of meaning—as well as the plans, expectations, and relationships that change or fall away—can occasion feelings of fear, isolation, and anxiety. In his moving and insightful illness narrative about his experiences of having a heart attack at age thirty-nine and a serious cancer diagnosis the following year, sociologist Arthur Frank (1991) speaks to the way illness can alter aspects of one's entire life, leading to the experience of unhomelikeness. Though he points out that different illnesses "set in place different possibilities" for everyone and that each individual's interpretation of his or her illness will vary, Frank maintains that there appears to be a "common core of what critical illness does to a life" (6). As he describes it: "Critical illness leaves no aspect of life untouched. . . . Your relationships, your work, your sense of who you are and who you might become, your sense of what life is and ought not to be—these all change, and the change is terrifying" (6). Illness, then, is an alteration of our possibilities, which is especially true for terminal illness, as it touches our possibility for being anything at all.

Health, though invisible to us most of the time, grants us both corporeal and interpretive capability, allowing material possibilities to be realized (Ramsey 1998). In other words, I am what I am able to do; possibilities are the understanding of the interplay among what I am able to see (i.e., interpret), what I am bodily capable of undertaking, and what is materially present in this situation before me. When illness breaks in, however, our health (or un-health) suddenly becomes noticeable, disrupting our lived body and altering our interpretation of the world around us, thereby modifying—or perhaps even dissolving—our possibilities. As Frank puts it, "What happens when my body breaks down happens not just to that body but also to my life, which is lived in that body. When the body breaks down, so does the life" (Frank 1991, 8).

HEALTH, ILLNESS, AND THE "THEY"

> Illness is the night-side of life, a more onerous citizenship. Everyone who is born holds dual citizenship, in the kingdom of the well and in the kingdom of the sick. Although we all prefer to use only the good passport, sooner or later each of us is obliged, at least for a spell, to identify ourselves as citizens of that other place.
>
> —Susan Sontag, *Illness as Metaphor*

Although illness involves much more than bodily dysfunction, it is often the case that mainstream Western medicine too narrowly interprets what it means to be ill, and therefore, what it means to be restored. In medicine, the "kingdom of the sick" is seen not as an inevitable destination, but rather as a dreadful and pitiable place that ought to be avoided. In discussing such taken-for-granted assumptions of medical practice, Frank employs the trope of "narrative plotlines" to describe the dominant discourse of contemporary Western medicine (Frank 1997). According to Frank, the prevailing narrative of medicine is one of "restitution," which highlights medicine's capacity to identify biological dysfunction, intervene appropriately, and ultimately restore health. In other words, this oversimplified plotline communicates the modernist expectation that there exists a remedy for every ailment, and because this narrative requires a mechanistic understanding of the body, it is quite palatable to modern medicine. According to Frank, "Restitution requires fixing, and fixing requires such a mechanistic view" (88). Perhaps the ultimate limitation of the restitution narrative and its "single-minded *telos* of cure" is that chronic or incurable illnesses—because there is no hope for cure or physical restitution—cannot be a part of the plot.

This is, of course, a generalization, and there are certainly exceptions to such trends. There are many—especially those who work in palliative and hospice care—who remain critical of the dominant curative ethos of mainstream medicine. Perhaps this is because when dying patients become "untreatable," medicine's implicit assumptions about cure and restoration become rather obvious. When restoration is impossible and physicians who see themselves as "curers" thus retreat from patients, the existential suffering of the terminal patient is left largely unaccounted for. In his most recent book, *Being Mortal: Medicine and What Matters in the End*, physician Atul Gawande (2014) recounts some of his final encounters with a dying patient that speak to this point. "We had no difficulty explaining the specific dangers of various treatment options," he says, "but we never really touched on the reality of his disease.... We could never bring ourselves to discuss the larger truth about his condition or the ultimate limits of our capabilities, let alone what might matter most to him as he neared the end of his life" (7). When treating biological disease is no longer an option for patients, medicine's narrow focus comes into view, and we begin to see the rather limited ways medicine addresses the various and complex ways people experience illness.

However, this narrow response to illness—to ameliorate disease and "cure" the body—is often welcomed by patients, and understandably so. Serious diagnoses, and the existential anxiety that often accompanies them, are terrifying. Both clinicians and patients often desire to disburden themselves—to use Heidegger's term—of this anxiety (*Angst*). The goal of cure serves an important, though usually unconscious, function in the face of illness, for focusing on the pathophysiology that can be treated is much easier to manage than existential suffering or impending demise. This is one way to make sense of the decisions made by patients who very near the end of their lives may choose to continue curative interventions, despite these interventions having little or no benefit or even intensifying suffering.[2]

The "They" and Inauthentic Understandings of Illness and Death

Though it is possible to respond to anxiety *authentically* by recognizing the precariousness of our being and releasing ourselves from attempts to control this precariousness, the most common response to such anxiety is an *inauthentic* turning away from this anxiety and turning toward what Heidegger calls the "they"—in other words, turning toward an understanding of things (like death) after they have been "levelled down" through public interpretation (1962, 165). Often, our response to anxiety involves, as Aho (2003) puts it, "a 'flight' back into the illusory stability of our daily routines as a 'they-self'" (8). Perhaps the most dangerous interpretation offered by the "they" surrounds the issue of existential death and anxiety. Because, as Heidegger says, we desire to "cover up" our "ownmost Being-towards-death [by] fleeing *in the face of it*," one can easily run toward the tranquilizing interpretations of death that "they" offer (1962, 295; emphasis in original). So, even when anxiety reveals to someone that her existence is tenuous and not guaranteed, the "they" cover-over the reality of her *own* death. Although "they" might agree that everyone dies, death is treated as a remote possibility, something that happens to other people in the world but not to me (Inwood 1997). Heidegger says it best:

> The "they" has already stowed away an interpretation for [death] . . . as if to say, "One of these days one will die too, in the end; but right now it has nothing to do with us." . . . In such a way of talking, death is understood as an indefinite something which, above all, must duly arrive from somewhere or other, but which is proximally *not yet present-at-hand* for oneself, and is therefore no threat. . . . The "they" gives its approval, and aggravates the *temptation* to cover up from oneself one's ownmost Being-towards-death. (1962, 297; emphasis in original)

In talking about death as an "event" or "thing" that is always yet-to-happen, the "they" covers over one's ever-present possibility for death or for the kind of suffering that collapses one's meaningful world. In so doing, the "they" transmutes ontological anxiety "into fear in the face of an oncoming event" (1962, 298).

Distilling anxiety into "fear of something" and death into a thing or event that is "not yet" makes these world-shattering phenomena appear as though they might be controlled. And because the "they" is entrenched in a distinctively modern epistemological framework that views "beings" as various subjects and objects that are most fully known through calculative investigation, such a view of death as a self-contained event—as an observable, measurable, and perhaps controllable "thing" that occurs to us later on in life—seems natural and perhaps even progressive and enlightened. As Heidegger points out, our "plunge" into the "they" remains hidden to us "by the way things have been publicly interpreted, so much so, indeed, that it gets interpreted as a way of 'ascending' and 'living concretely'" (1962, 223). Verifiable, scientific understandings of death and suffering, though they cover up so much of the lived experience of such phenomena, present themselves as the best way to think through and "manage" such issues. The attempt to restore the body, then, is akin to the attempt to restore one to her previous "they-self"; if her corporeal body can be physically restored, then perhaps she can return to that time when her body was not a problem and life could be lived without interruption, fear, and uncertainty.

Approaching illness and death in this way might feel safer and might even be lauded by the "they" as the best way to manage them; yet, such an approach conceals the *meaning* behind these phenomena. Our existential anxiety discloses the fact that our existence as we know it is tenuous. We desire to flee from the anxiety that both comes from and reveals this structural instability—that is, we usually want to turn away from the reality that we are a being whose being inescapably projects itself toward death. However, for Heidegger, a recognition of our being-towards-death can, in fact, free us for "authenticity" because facing our existential anxiety snatches us out of the clutches of the "they" (1962, 307). Confronting our anxiety—rather than disburdening ourselves of it—frees us from the grip of death anxiety, allowing us to see and choose among our finite and everyday possibilities *for ourselves*. In authentically confronting our death, we no longer desperately need the "they" in order to distract or disburden us from our anxiety, and we are free to be true to ourselves and decide for ourselves how we want to live. In this way, the anxiety that comes with the recognition of our ever-present potential for suffering and world collapse can be both limiting and generative. Although such anxiety can be frightening and can cause us to lead diminished lives in our futile attempts to flee from it, it can also call us toward authenticity—if we are willing to respond to its call.

The call to authenticity comes from myself in my anxiety showing me that my death or world collapse is something I face alone. A recognition of this "non-relational character of death" lays a claim on me and "individualizes [me] down to [my]self," pulling me out of the anonymous mode of the "they-self" (1962, 308). I begin to see that the "they's" attempts to avoid or control suffering, death, and world collapse are unavailing, and I am, therefore, made "*free for* the freedom of choosing [my]self and taking hold of [my]self" (232). It might be said that Frank, who experiences the total breakdown of his world during his illness, responds to this call to authenticity. Frank's narrative reveals a willingness to confront both the existential anxiety brought upon by his being ill and his potential for a total world collapse, and this confrontation changes him: "The ultimate value of illness," Frank says, "is that it teaches us the value of being alive" (Frank 1991, 120). Death no longer appears to him as something from which to flee, and Frank is free to develop his own interpretation of death: "Death is no enemy of life; it restores our sense of the value of living.... To learn about value and proportion we need to honor illness, and ultimately to honor death" (120).

In his article that appeared in the *New York Times* in 2015 not long before his death, Oliver Sacks expressed a similar sentiment as he faced and reflected upon his recent terminal diagnosis:

> I feel intensely alive, and I want and hope in the time that remains to deepen my friendships, to say farewell to those I love, to write more, to travel if I have the strength, to achieve new levels of understanding and insight ... I feel a sudden clear focus and perspective. There is no time for anything inessential. I must focus on myself, my work, and my friends. I shall no longer look at "News-Hour" every night. I shall no longer pay any attention to politics or arguments about global warming. (2015)

In confronting suffering and death, things become clearer and priorities change. For Frank (1991), this meant that his reentry into the "healthy" mainstream after his recovery was rather difficult, as he "now knew that the way [he] and others lived was a choice, and often not the best one" (132). This authentic awareness of our finitude—of our inevitable projection toward no-longer-being-able-to-be—is not a macabre obsession with death and mortality. Rather, it is a genuine acknowledgment of the finite nature of our identity or existence that "pervades and shapes [our] whole life," freeing us *for* death, and thus freeing us for authentic living (Inwood 1997, 61). In recognizing (and then anticipating and reminding ourselves) that our world as we know it has the potential to shatter at any moment, we might begin to appreciate and deepen our present being-in-the-world. In being resolute—which comes with facing one's vulnerability and then anticipating the possibility of world collapse—"one becomes," as Heidegger (1962) says, "free *for* one's own death, one is liberated from one's lostness in those possibilities which may accidentally thrust themselves upon one" (308; emphasis in original). As such, life can be lived with more immediacy and care.

Authenticity and Illness
When the Imperative Is too Much to Bear

Though the idea of living life more fully in the midst of illness sounds admirable, we might wonder when this imperative for authentic resoluteness in the face of extraordinary suffering becomes burdensome itself. Cannot "authentic" living be just as isolating and unbearable as inauthentic living and dying? Is not a desire for physical restoration—a returning to one's former self—understandable? Gadamer (1996) reminds us, simply enough, that a longing to flee back into the comfort of who we were before, even if we were dwelling in the anonymous mode of the "they," is more than reasonable: "The individual who now lacks and misses something previously enjoyed still remains oriented towards returning to that former life" (42). To be bodily restored, to return to who I was, to be once again a person for whom living was seamless and possibilities were endless are sensible—and perhaps even "good"—desires. And even if there are "better" or more authentic ways to respond to the uncertainty and anxiety that usually accompany serious illness, it may be the case that one is simply "not up for it." Illness—and the fatigue, nausea, pain, and weakness that can accompany it—is onerous, and adding to that the expectation that one ought to honestly confront my finitude and allow it to transform me can simply be too much. In her work *Cancer Made Me a Shallower Person: A Memoir in Comics* (2006) finished shortly before she died of breast cancer, Miriam Engelberg writes in her introduction,

> They say hardship reveals one's true character, and it was clear right away that I wouldn't be the heroic type of cancer patient portrayed in so many television shows and movies. My immediate response was to spend a lot of time in front of the television. I didn't go inward, I looked for pop culture distraction. . . . When I was first diagnosed, I felt pressure to become someone different—someone nobler and more courageous than I was. But maybe nobility and courage aren't the only approaches to life with an illness; maybe the path of shallowness deserves more attention! (xiii)

Engelberg's use of "They" here is important, as it points to the expectation or imperative alluded to above that one ought to confront her illness with bravery and intentionality. In some ways, it suggests that the expectation to become authentic can be just as *in*authentic as fleeing from the reality of death by seeking curative treatment alone. Unflinching acceptance of and commitment to the transformative power of illness may be yet another instantiation of what "they" believe one ought to do in the face of tragedy.[3]

Is it possible that Engelberg's "shallow" response to her illness is more genuine than a somber confrontation of her impending demise, that it is something that she chooses *freely*, despite what "they" say? Undoubtedly, one could argue that Engelberg, in the act of creating a comic memoir about her illness experience, is actually more reflective than most during critical illness. Nevertheless, Engelberg's emphasis on the need for the shallow made through both image and text throughout her book helps us understand the constant pull between recognizing that life is finite and fragile and longing for a return to the way things once were. Her witty reflections on her desire to be unreflective blur the lines between intentionality and distraction, pointing not only to Heidegger's reminder that moments of authenticity are fleeting and must be uncovered "again and again" (1962, 265), but also to the fact that the two common responses to critical illness outlined earlier are not mutually exclusive: One can desire physical restoration while also remaining open to the new possibilities illness reveals to her. As such, the longing to return to who one was before she was sick should not always, or only, be interpreted as a desire to disburden herself of the constant possibility of being nothing at all.

When someone like Engelberg finds herself in the kingdom of the sick, it is not as if she has suddenly been made free to recognize the banality of her former life and subsequently grasp this new life by the proverbial horns. Even during critical illness, expectations abound that can serve as their own "they-self" notions of how to respond, whether it is stoic acceptance and subsequent transformation or a myopic focus on physical restoration. It is true that illness can reveal the possibilities and relationships that we once took for granted, but serious illness also reveals those things that are no longer within our reach. In the kingdom of the sick, especially during terminal illness, so many things are no longer possible for me: attending children's future graduations and weddings, planning for retirement, taking that once-in-a-lifetime trip across the globe. Even the seemingly trivial and mundane serve as painful reminders that I have fallen out of things; television advertisements, ten-year vehicle warranties, and magazine articles on "aging gracefully" all presuppose that I am able—or will live long enough—to benefit. Because the "they" of illness can be profoundly lonely, a return to the "they" of health is desirable—even if "they" are all deluded and naïve when it comes to recognizing life's frailty and precariousness. The trouble is that a return to my former "they-self" is impossible. For better or worse, one can never return to who she once was or how she once saw the world around her, even if her body is fully restored.

The Impossibility of Returning to or Untethering from the "They"

Just as health becomes visible during illness, so too does the recognition of the kingdom or "they-self" in which we currently dwell or that which we no longer inhabit. When we say that the ill person falls out of things, we are not implying that he or she falls out of the "they" and into his or her authentic, individualized self. For Heidegger, being *in*authentic is simply our everyday way of being; we cannot help but be inauthentic, since our world is public and shared, and we come to know such a world in relation to those around us. An indispensable part of being human is being-with-others-in-the-world, and as such, our lives, identities, and understandings are shaped by those with whom we share our world (Aho 2003, 7). As Heidegger points out, to exist means to be "thrown" into a world that already has meaning, and, as a result, one is already "fallen to"—or absorbed in—the way "they" interpret the world (1962, 223). Without the "they," it would be impossible to interpret phenomena, make decisions, or understand things at all (Inwood 1997).[4] If we did not have shared language and interpretations, for example, it would be quite difficult to get on in the world. For Heidegger, then, we most often dwell as a "they-self," and being authentic is a rare and fleeting derivative mode of our more common, inauthentic, everyday selves (1962, 168).

The relation any of us has to the "they," although variable, is one from which we can never be untethered completely. Because our being-in-the-world is always meaningful, and always meaningful because it is always already entwined in a complex web of relations (the web of signification) with other things and with other persons, our having-to-be-in-the-world is always a having-to-be-in-relations. Although Heidegger makes it clear he is not doing some version of sociology, his explication of the "they" helps us understand why we must first be socialized into a way of being "like everyone else" before we are able to undertake any attempts to twist free from it. Thus, in becoming authentic, we are always in some manner attempting not to *break from* the "they," but rather to re/appropriate our relation to it in some particular way. Heidegger calls successful attempts of twisting away "a modification of the 'they.'" Consequently, "modification" describes the only way one is able to alter one's being inescapably tethered to the "they." Indeed, Heidegger ends his initial discussion of the "they" in *Being and Time* by saying: "Authentic being-one's-Self does not rest upon an exceptional condition of the subject, a condition that has been detached from the 'they;' it is rather an existentiell modification of the 'they'" (168; emphasis in original).[5] Heidegger uses this word "modification" in numerous places in *Being and Time* and always to remind us that changes are, as the etymology of the word suggests, alterations and appropriations of that which is already being lived. Each time Heidegger describes an ontological structure of our being, any change to the structure can only be seen as a modification and never the complete overcoming or eradication of it.

If we pursue this etymology further, we see modifications are linked to a "bringing things up to date." Illness, as the falling out of health, creates the new time of our understanding; it is this new date or time—that is, the changes in our way of being in the world currently—that reveals the need for a modification of the accustomed understanding we have of ourselves. The incongruity between our understanding of who we are now and who we once were, along with the incongruity between the "they" in which we find ourselves and the one from which we have fallen, can feel impossible to reconcile. More than this, the understanding that we can never return to who we were, even if we are bodily restored, can be frightening. As McQuellon and Cowan (2000) put it, "No one returns unchanged from such a confrontation with death" (313). The "they" of health will never quite understand what it is like to confront the facticity of their mortality or their no-longer-being-able-to-be, and this fact can feel isolating for those who are sick, injured, or dying. For better or worse, in illness, our interpretation of the world around us is fundamentally and irrevocably different, and a return to who we once were before we are sick or injured is unlikely.

Although one cannot untether from the "they" but only enter into a modified version of it, we wonder if one would even choose to untether if one could. Those who are ill, it seems, still *want* a "they." This is how we understand support groups and survivor communities. To be sure, one never falls ill alone. Because one's being-in-the-world is always a being-with-others, each modification is in the last instance a modification of our care, and thus a new way of disclosing possibilities for oneself and others. Thinking along with Heidegger, we see that illness is suffered by everyone connected to the one whom we say is ill; the illness alters every single relation. As we are nothing but our relations, and a significant change to one of them alters all the others, illness (though not illness alone) sets into relief the structure of the interrelated nature of self. But even if it were possible to do so, it is unlikely that one would want to suffer illness alone. What one wants, rather, is to not feel so acutely that one has fallen out of the kingdom of the well, to not feel that the world as one knew it is no longer one's.

We might say that what one wants is to be restored, though not in the narrow sense of the word. Restoration requires qualification, for it is possible to be physically restored and never uncover authentic living, just as it is possible to be restored through illness while never physically recovering anything at all. Getting back to health, then, is getting back to living well. It may well be the case that getting back to genuine health so understood does not require what is called in everyday talk "making a full recovery." We might recover more life even as our body never quite gets back to what it was before illness, just as we might get all the way back bodily (or indeed, in some cases, even better than before) and yet not better our flourishing in the least. Of course, there are any number of mixed conditions to be obtained between these extremes, but each of them comes as one's relation and understanding of the "they-self" is modified. Illness, while it does not disclose the future for the first time, does often disclose the future in a new way, in this acute manner, for the first time.

WORKING TOWARD RESTORATION TOGETHER

> If Sigmund Freud in a famous challenge put forward the sentence: Where it (id) was, ego should become, Heidegger would say: Where Anyone (Das Man) was, authenticity should become. . . . Authentically living persons are those who understand themselves as survivors, as those whom death has passed over and who conceive of the time it will take for a renewed, definitive encounter with death as a postponement.
>
> —Peter Sloterdijk, *The Critique of Cynical Reason*

We could say, then, in light of these Heideggerian insights (and we see this is the ancient Stoics as well) when one receives a serious or terminal diagnosis it should always be for the second time. Awareness of our finitude, which is the heart of what we "are," is always the first encounter with a terminal diagnosis, yet one we often do not "get." This is the force of the concluding words from the preceding Sloterdijk epigraph: Living is always a postponement of an encounter with death. To be sure, being-towards-death ought not be an anxious waiting, a passing of time until the inevitable, nor a morose nihilism. It needs to be a part of flourishing. Being in a good state of health might really mean understanding the complexity of being-in-the-world. And, ironically, it may be those who currently confront or have confronted a critical illness who are the "healthiest," in that they are positioned particularly well to embrace this understanding.

While those who are or have been seriously ill are precisely those who have the capacity to live most authentically (if, of course, it is not forced upon them), there is rarely space for such authenticity to flourish. Especially in the world of medicine, being ill is not seen as a "dangerous opportunity" for living more genuinely as Frank calls it, but rather as a state of vulnerability, abnormality, and otherness. For those of us who work in hospitals and clinics, there is a strange and unspoken incongruity between the monotony of our daily routine and the presence of those who might be experiencing the crisis of their lives. Rather than feeling homelike for patients, the hallways of the hospital are suffuse with feelings of impotence and shame—feelings that one ought not be there, that honest expression of suffering is to be kept to oneself. As Frank explains, "'Objective' talk about disease is always medical talk. Patients quickly learn to express themselves in these terms, but in using medical expressions, ill persons lose themselves" (1991, 12). Even if one were to come to see oneself, one's body, and one's world differently through illness, few of those engaged in contemporary medical practice are interested in listening. Narrow conceptions of restoration limit what is spoken and heard in the clinical encounter and intensify the estrangement between doctors and patients.

What is needed, then, is a different, broader understanding of restoration. Could it be that restoration has less to do with repairing the body (as important as it is) and more to do with returning those who are ill to a more homelike way of being-in-the-world? In other words, ought the practice of medicine attempt to make our falling out of health less acute and less lonely? If so, it might mean that in addition to treating the biological body, an effort is made to make patients feel acknowledged and heard, to make the "they" of illness less alienating, to create a space where the articulation of a person's *illness experience* can be expressed and heard alongside conversations about the objectified body and disease processes.

Then again, maybe drawing a line between the "they" of health and the "they" of illness and attempting to make one seem just as homelike as the other is misguided. Though it is true that the "theyself" can be modified, it is not the case that those who are ill no longer share a "they" with those who are not. Rather, the difference between the two is that those who are ill are often more attuned to the facticity of the "theyself"—that is, they can see that the border between the kingdoms of the well and the sick has been left wide open. As a result, most of those who are ill recognize genuine living and dying as possibilities and can more readily choose such possibilities for themselves. So, rather than making the "they" of illness more homelike, perhaps we should work toward blurring the line between the healthy and the ill, toward traveling to the borderlands. What would it be like if all of us, especially clinicians, allowed ourselves to see that becoming a citizen of the kingdom of the ill or injured can happen at any moment? And what if we began to see that it is those who are ill who disclose this truth to us? According to Heidegger, such "co-disclosure" might be possible, as those who have responded to the call to authenticity can "let the Others who are with [one] 'be' in their ownmost potentiality-for-Being" (Heidegger 1962, 344).[6] If Heidegger is right, this has quite interesting implications for health care and healthcare practice. It might be the case, for example, that a patient's confrontation with suffering and death can personally affect the doctor who is caring for the patient, even revealing to the doctor her ownmost potential for world collapse and thus her own potential for authenticity. As McQuellon and Cowan (2000) see it, when a patient faces the end of life, it is true that only one person is dying; however, the doctor who enters into the patient's experience is facing death as well (312). In this way, the doctor "vicariously" experiences her own potential for world collapse through her patient.[7] With this in mind, clinicians might begin to see encounters with patients as life-giving, as moments that bring deeper meaning and purpose to their lives. Indeed, more than patients are in need of restoration; our clinicians and trainees also suffer within a system that places such little value on vulnerability and human connection. Perhaps recognizing that we are all at home in a world together—that we all share the potential for suffering, love, and death—can draw the healthy and the ill toward one another and toward genuine restoration.

None of this is easy, however. It takes great effort to be in a constant mode of modification, to be one who is fully aware and awake to the decision to modify, to be one who is responsible for deciding that this is how one's having-to-be is being accomplished, especially when doing so is contrary to how "they" seem to do things. That said, seen from a grander point of view, social progress is in fact conserved by a type of institutionalization of certain modifications that have, as it were (and in a very un-Heideggerian phrase), become the norm. Heidegger, in fact, puts it this way:

> *The "they" is an existentiale; and as a primordial phenomenon, it belongs to Dasein's positive constitution.* It itself has, in turn, various possibilities of becoming concrete as something characteristic of Dasein [*seiner daseinsmässigen Konkretion*]. The extent to which its dominion becomes compelling and explicit may change in the course of history. (1962, 167; emphasis in original)

Social progress in any area of our social life—and here, health and healthcare practice are among them—is the institutionalization of freedom, a freedom that offers more possibilities for more people. Due to social and political struggle, modifications of the "they" that offer these greater possibilities for greater numbers often become in time "what everyone knows." For example, "they" used to say women could not vote in the United States; they used to say separate but equal is an ethical education policy; "they" currently say capitalism is compatible with democracy and justice. In these first two instances, we have institutionalized new understandings that have brought progress to these social relations. Many believe we are called to bring a radical modification to the last of these, and the dream of the progressive left is that someday soon they will no longer say such a thing. Maybe we can hope for the same within the institution of medicine; we can hope that patients no longer say that they do not feel heard by their doctors, that they feel alone and invisible (or perhaps too conspicuous) in their illness. Maybe Heidegger is right that the "they" does have various possibilities that can come to characterize who we are and can, indeed, change the course of history. The question we are left with is, "how"? How are institutional spaces created in health care for connection and openness, for a new understanding of restoration?

As with most things, the answer begins with education. The failure of medicine to address the complex realities of illness and the kinds of suffering that extend beyond the workings of the biological body are long-lived and persistent problems, and often they are traced back to the ways doctors are trained. In the 1960s, philosophers, theologians, and practitioners began to draw attention to the fact that a kind of medical care that privileges fixing the physical body fails to address the lived experiences of patients, and these early medical humanists (though they did not yet refer to themselves as such) expressed concerns about medical education, "for the way medical students of the rising generation were being trained and, in particular, for what was lacking in their education" (Carson et al. 2003, n.p.). Over the years, educational interventions centered on developmental approaches to professionalism that value ideas about the journey of becoming a doctor—rather than simply "acting" like a professional—have been and are continuing to make strides in medical education. Yet, taken together, these approaches are limited by the fact that they do not take seriously the idea that medical education significantly contributes to the personal and moral formation of the whole self—a self that is formed, in part, by the existential anxiety produced in the face of our shared vulnerability and finitude. As such, we need to draw attention to the formative process of medical training and work toward creating a pedagogical culture that fosters more expansive notions of care, awakens students to the reality of shared human suffering, and encourages self-reflection and authentic engagement with others.[8]

Because true healing requires authentic engagement, one of the goals of medical education, along with teaching requisite scientific and clinical knowledge, should be to cultivate an authentic understanding of care, which requires students to break free from narrow, but pervasive, narratives of fixing, curing, and restoring. Although, from a Heideggerian perspective, authentic being comes only after a resolute return to the world following a total collapse, this, of course, does not mean that medical educators should seek to provoke a word collapse among their students (this happens often enough on its own). It does mean, however, that students must slow down and recognize the human elements of medicine, reflect on who they are becoming and want to be, and question the assumptions and values of the systems in which they participate.

Undoubtedly, asking for a culture change in academic medicine is asking quite a lot. Society, however, has asked even more of our doctors. In many ways, the world of medicine is a concentration of the all-to-human elements of being alive: birth, death, illness, suffering, isolation, fear, love, uncertainty. Nearly every person who cares for the sick crosses the threshold into the space where human mortality and finitude—and the feelings of helplessness associated with them—come to the fore. And unfortunately, we often fail to prepare them well for such an undertaking. We must, then, encourage other ways of knowing, thinking, and relating in medical education, and a space should be created for physicians and physicians-in-training to learn about and reflect upon the distress and pain that can arise when caring for sick patients and their families. If this were to happen, future clinicians might begin to see the inherent contradictions people face when they fall ill. They might come to see that a promise to return someone to exactly who she was before she was seriously ill may be just as nearsighted as expecting a patient to stoically embrace her suffering in order to be transformed by a critical illness. And they might come to see that those who practice medicine ought to remain open and attuned—allowing patients to choose for themselves how they will respond to illness—and commit to do the best by their patients as they join alongside them for the journey toward modification and mutual flourishing.

NOTES

1. For an extended look at the body's role in shaping experience, see Leder, D. 1990. *The absent body*. Chicago, IL: University of Chicago Press.

2. For example, research has shown that chemotherapy may have an anxiety-reducing effect for patients, as they feel that they are "actively fighting" the cancer. See Edwards, B., Clarke, V. 2004. The psychological impact of a cancer diagnosis on families: The influence of family functioning and patients' illness characteristics on depression and anxiety. *Psycho-oncology* 13(8): 562–576; see also Lannaman, J.W., Harris, L.M. 2008. Ending the end-of-life communication impasse: A dialogic intervention. In L. Sparks, D. O' Hair, and G. Kreps (eds.), *Cancer, communication, and aging* (293–320). Cresskill, NJ: Hampton.

3. For more on the problem of pervasive positivity and optimism surrounding cancer in American culture, see chapter 1 of Barbara Ehrenreich's *Bright-sided: How positive thinking is undermining America*. New York: Picador, 2010.

4. As Heidegger says, "Dasein is for the sake of the 'they' in an everyday manner and the 'they' itself articulates the referential context of significance" (1962, 167).

5. It should be noted that Heidegger later appears to contradict this idea, stating, "It has been shown proximally and the for the most part [that] Dasein is not itself but is lost in the they-self, which is an existentiell modification of the authentic self" (1962, 365). Whether the "they-self" is an existentiell modification of the authentic self or vice versa, the two, it seems, are inextricably bound up with one another.

6. Heidegger goes on to say that Dasein can "co-disclose this potentiality in the solicitude which leaps forth and liberates. When Dasein is resolute, it can become the 'conscience' of Others."

7. It should be noted that the inverse of this also can be true; it is possible that a doctor, who is resolute herself and does not turn away from the frightening reality of finitude, might co-disclose her authenticity to her patient, helping a patient (who is ready) to confront his own potential for death or world collapse: "Professionals [and others who care for the patient] can help someone who is dying to wrest life-enhancing meaning and value from a situation in which many can find only despair. They do so primarily by their willingness to engage in authentic conversation with the one who is dying" (McQuellon and Cowan 2000, 316).

8. For an extended look at the limits of current medical training and potential changes to medical pedagogy, see Piemonte, N. (ed.). 2017. Medical humanities. Special issue, *Review of Communication* 17 (3).

Chapter 15

What is it to "Age Well"? Re-visioning Later Life

Drew Leder

THE PROBLEMS WITH "SUCCESSFUL AGING"

We live in an ageist culture. The "we" to whom I refer is the United States as well as many other Western industrialized countries. Elders are marginalized within capitalist systems that prefer to hire young "more vigorous," "up-to-date" and cheaper, employees. Seniors serve as the butt of jokes in popular media—or have gone missing. Watching many TV shows, or scanning social media, one might almost forget that they exist—everyone featured has a lithe young body, or aspires to it, using the latest cosmetics, weight-loss and fitness plans, or "rejuvenating" surgeries. We seem to live in fear and denial of our aging, and of the aged, just as we do of the dead and dying—and of course these fears are not unrelated. Even Happy Birthday cards available for purchase become increasingly insulting the older one gets: "Wrinkles, wrinkles in your skin . . . feel them flutter in the wind. Peeing every time you sneeze, climbing stairs can make you wheeze . . ." and so on.

This ageism goes hand-in-hand with an unprecedented surge in the numbers of people living to an older age. Since 1900 the average life span has increased from forty-seven years to seventy-nine in the United States, with those age sixty-five and above forming the fastest-growing age-group. A good half of those who, in the history of humankind, have ever reached this senior age are currently alive. These added years, or decades, suggest an important shift in the trajectory of a human life (Roszak 2009).

Our notion of what this means for us as individuals, and societies, has not kept pace. Setting aside for a moment the fear and mockery associated with ageism I will examine our visions of what it means to *age successfully*. I will briefly characterize four models of successful aging evident in our social practices and discourse, and the deficiencies associated with each.

First is what I will term the *preventive* vision: This focuses on the medical prevention of disease, disability, and death. One has aged well when one has successfully defeated, or at least delayed, many of the bodily and mental modes of deterioration associated with later life, for example, the "peeing" and "wheezing" referred to in the previous birthday card, or worse, the dark pains and disabilities associated with chronic illness. The prolongation of healthy life to its possible limits constitutes the model of successful aging medically construed.

Then, too, there is widespread emphasis on a second model: that of *prosperity*. No one wishes to outlive one's money, aging into destitution and neglect. We keep careful watch over our personal retirement funds, worrying whether there will be enough, or hope that Social Security will remain solvent and sufficient into the future. Perhaps this fear is alleviated in cultures with a better safety-net for its vulnerable citizens, but many in the United States judge successful aging as involving prosperity—at least to the degree of having financial security. For some this takes the form of true wealth accumulation in order to gratify late-life personal wishes, and/or pass on a sizeable inheritance.

Then, too, there is the model of *productive* aging. In later life one still wants to feel useful, vigorous, contributory, respected. Within our society this is often demonstrated by one's continued capacity for productive work, whether this takes the form of corporate employment, "blue-collar" labor, house and family maintenance, and/or volunteerism. One may delay retirement as long as possible or is urged to fill those retirement years with productive activity. Then, too, we are told by direct-to-consumer TV advertisements that we can attain late-life sexual productivity by the treatment of conditions like "erectile dysfunction." The natural lessening of libido is medicalized as a preventable disease: This shows how the "preventive," "productive," and "prosperity" models of successful aging can all synergize.

This also relates to the last version of successful aging which, in keeping with my alliterative bent, I will label the *pleasure* model. We are familiar with the vision of the "golden years" accorded a senior, a time to rest and enjoy the fruits of lifelong labors. For some this might be fulfilled by reading a novel in front of a crackling fireplace. More often, media advertisements idealize and monetize late-life pleasures, in the form of cruise-ship travel, high-end retirement properties or communities, and other seductions for those with the requisite funds. Rather than remaining *productive* members of the capitalist economy, here seniors play the role of *pleasure-seeking* consumers.

I will suggest that such images of "successful aging," involving prevention, prosperity, productivity, and/or the pursuit of pleasures, are all deficient. Moreover, *they are deficient in similar ways* though their foci seem to differ and sometimes even stand in opposition.

First, they fail to define what is unique and meaningful about later life. Many cultures and religions, as we shall soon see, revered elderhood as a special time of life, offering distinctive opportunities and benefits to both individual and community (Schachter-Shalomi and Miller 1995). On the contrary, the visions of "successful aging" we have been exploring focus on prolonging midlife goods, often beyond their natural ken. While the prevention of illness and poverty, the maintenance of productivity, the pursuit of pleasures are worthy goals, they tell us little about the unique value of old age.

Furthermore, though positive on the surface, they continue to associate later life with a series of potential diminishments to be defeated: sickness, destitution, disability, and the loss of enjoyment. As such, ideals of "successful aging" still embody the cultural fear of and resistance to old age spoken of earlier. "Successful aging" becomes a kind of negative of a negative, rather than envisioned as a creative and significant life stage in itself.

Moreover, these modes of successful aging necessarily create a class of individuals who, by definition, have aged poorly or wrongly. One well-done, but typical in this regard, book by Rowe and Kahn entitled *Successful Aging* (1998) summarizes more than a decade of research supported by the MacArthur Foundation. Successful aging was there characterized as (a) involving a low-risk of disease and related disabilities; (b) a high level of functioning, both physical and mental; and (c) a continued active engagement with life. "In sum, we were trying to pinpoint the many factors that put one octogenarian on cross-country skis and another in a wheelchair" (Rowe and Kahn 1998, xii). But necessarily many of us will end up wheelchair-bound. As we age we may unavoidably struggle with illness and disability. Many will also live with financial stress through no fault of their own; be without the funds or inclination to pay for consumerist pleasures; and perhaps be unwilling or unable to maintain midlife productivity. Does this mean such people have aged "unsuccessfully"? We need to know far more about that person in the wheelchair, his or her dreams, prayers, friendships, and character (Hillman 2000), before using that person as a cautionary tale.

For these models of "successful aging" finally do not explore in a holistic and deep way the existential meaning of a human life (Leder 1998; Crowther et al. 2002). Physical health, financial prosperity, productivity, and pleasure do capture surface modes of well-being which, admittedly, are of great importance. Who would not want these, when attainable? But a person can be lacking in one or more of these, and despite such deficits, or even on occasion *because of* such deficits, he or she can build a rich and meaningful life. For such a person, elderhood may be a time to reap the wisdom accumulated over decades of experience; explore new territories; meet and surmount extreme challenges; become more vulnerable, and thereby more compassionate; turn to matters of the spirit with an urgency or maturity that was lacking in youth;

and so on. Clearly we will have to expand our sense of successful aging, or as I will hereafter call it, "aging well"—that is, exemplifying "weal"—true well-being—in later life.

Just as we don't need to reinvent the wheel, we don't need to reinvent the weal associated with elderhood. Surveying cultural, historical, and religious traditions, we find many positive archetypal images associated with the elder that can inspire our cultural re-visioning. In my book, *Spiritual Passages* (1997), I take up twelve such images. Here I will speak briefly of four. In keeping with my alliterative flourish (for good or ill) I will here call these, respectively, the elder as "Contemplative," "Contributor," "Compassionate Companion," and "Creative." Playing with language, we could think of these four "Cs" as like four *seas* upon which one embarks in discovery of one's late-life self, or four ways to *see* the elder anew while avoiding ageist presumptions.

THE CONTEMPLATIVE

> When a householder sees his skin wrinkled, and his hair white, and the sons of his sons, then he may resort to the forest. . . . Let him always be industrious in reciting the Veda; let him be patient of hardships . . . and compassionate toward all living creatures. . . . In summer, let him expose himself to the heat of five fires, during the rainy season live under the open sky, and in winter be dressed in wet clothes, thus gradually increasing the rigour of his austerities. . . .
>
> Let him always wander alone, without any companion, in order to attain final liberation. . . . All that has been declared above depends on meditation.
>
> —*Laws of Manu* (200 BCE to 200 CE)

To a twenty-first-century Western reader the preceding ancient Hindu text presents quite a forbidding vision of "aging well." It is starkly opposed to all models of "successful aging" hitherto discussed. This forest elder is not manifesting financial prosperity nor customary forms of social productivity. He or she is not in pursuit of pleasure or illness prevention—quite the contrary, as indicated by the challenging austerities voluntarily undertaken.

To make sense of this we need to place it back in context. In the Hindu tradition, spiritual realization is commonly viewed as the ultimate goal of life. Elderhood provides unique opportunities to move toward, or even attain, enlightenment. In midlife, social *dharmic* duties weigh heavily; one is busy raising a family, making a living, caring for elders, contributing to the community. Later life is seen as a time to turn these responsibilities over to the next generation. One is now freer to focus with a single-minded energy on the aim of spiritual liberation.

Furthermore, the aging process presents a challenging, but ultimately helpful, curriculum in this regard (Dass 2001). It presses one to move beyond identification with the body, now deteriorating; to transcend all the social roles (parent, worker, community member) that had previously defined one; to face the fact of death, and therefore the question of eternal life. We are thus pushed beyond the shell of the "ego-self." Concurrently, later life provides the time and solitude needed for the study, prayer, and meditation that assists one to realize connection with a transpersonal Source.

Given our society's emphasis on business (busy-ness) and productivity, the elder-as-contemplative is a somewhat counter-cultural ideal. Yet it has much to teach us. Instead of resisting the "losses" associated with aging, the Indian model suggests how we might lean into them, uncovering graces and opportunities. True, we are not going to dash off alone into the forest. (Even in India, the solitary elder-retreatant is rare, though elders may join an *ashram*, a spiritual community.) Yet contemporary applications can easily be imagined. For example, clearing out the clutter in our attic, or downsizing to a smaller living quarters, has an element of the forest-retreat: It can be a time to simplify and refocus our life. So too, can we embrace retiring from a job, or becoming an "empty-nester" when children move out. These are losses, but also opportunities to expand contemplative space and time. As Thoreau wrote, "I love a broad margin to my life. . . . I realized what the Orientals mean by contemplation and the forsaking of works" (1983, 156–157). For many of us this "broad margin" proves most realizable in later life, even though, or because, we are marginalized by the larger society.

Yet much depends on our response to the aging process. The loss of midlife health and vigor; of job, status, income, and social engagements; of children who move away, and loved ones who die; all this can be depressing, even devastating. The Hindu model reminds us of a transcendent dimension that nonetheless abides, and may be found through spiritual practices like scriptural study and meditation. Of course, contemplation can take many forms: the enjoyment and creation of art; wanders in nature (there are reasons the ascetic pursues his or her quest *in the forest*, as did Thoreau); taking periodic retreats for self-exploration; ritualizing important transitions like retirement; keeping a Sabbath rhythm to one's daily and weekly life; and so on.

In our rush-rush multitasking culture, elders are often mocked for driving slowly, sitting around without getting much done, and being technologically "out of it." Sometimes diminished activity can be a sign of deterioration and disability. But, paradoxically, it can also be a sign of existential health: The contemplative elder reminds us all to slow down, to be more quiet and present.

THE CONTRIBUTOR

> I am an Eagle Clan Mother of the Onondaga nation. . . . People choose a clan mother by watching how she has lived her life and cared for her family. . . . because that's evidence that she will take care of all the people as if they were her children. . . . She must be someone who is able to give advice on how to handle difficult situations.
>
> Clan mothers also have the duty of selecting a candidate for leadership chief in the clan. . . . If we see him going in a way that is not acceptable, we must approach him and remind him of his responsibilities. . . .
>
> One of my deepest concerns right now is about our youth. . . . I tell them, if you find yourself in a position where you have to make a major decision, think about the things that are taught in the [Onondaga] Longhouse, and ask yourself, "Is this going to bring harm to myself, or to any other living thing?" Basically, that's what we call respect—respect for yourself, respect for people around you, and respect for the earth.
>
> —Audrey Shenandoah, interview *The Book of Elders*

We move on to another example of ways to "age well." At first glance this archetype looks quite opposed to the first. Rather than departing on contemplative retreat, the elder, in this case represented by an Eagle Clan Mother of the Onondagas (one of the six Iroquois nations in Northeastern United States), remains present, active, and of great service within the tribe. I thus call such a person the "Contributor." (Johnson 1994, 194).

Is this, then, similar to what I earlier called the "productive" model of successful aging? Not exactly. The Eagle Clan Mother is not focused on "producing" anything in the usual economic or technological sense. Rather she serves as a mentor, caregiver, and wisdom-keeper.

From whence comes the *wisdom* often associated with elderhood—at least in traditional cultures? One source is long life experience. The elder not only is a living record of tribal history, but has hopefully learned from a personal history filled with mistakes and false starts as well as achievements. He or she is able to share these lessons, gracefully mentoring the youth who are willing to receive.

If "she has lived her life well" the elder has experienced and demonstrated responsibility. She may herself have parented a child, and been deepened by that journey. Yet the fact that one's own children are now likely grown and independent allows an expansion of the sphere of concern such "that she will take care of all the people as if they were her children." Elderhood frees one up to offer gifts in an open-handed way that may not have been present in youth and midlife when the focus was on establishing an identity and minding one's interests.

Concern can even expand to future generations and the Earth. Having lived a long time one can see how far-reaching consequences slowly unfold and must be considered before rushing into action. In the words of Oren Lyons, Faith Keeper of the Turtle Clan of the Onondaga Nation, "We are looking ahead, as is one of the first mandates given to us as chiefs . . . to make every decision that we make relate to the welfare and well-being of the seventh generation to come. . . . We consider: will this be to the benefit of the seventh generation?" (Lyons 1980, 203–204).

Of course, this kind of far-sighted elder wisdom is not simply an automatic result of having lived a long time. We find it exemplified in certain public figures—Nelson Mandela, the Dalai Lama, Mother Theresa, come to mind—but it is sadly lacking in other older leaders. This pattern may be reduplicated within our family. One grandfather may be wise and loving, another a bull-headed curmudgeon. Why the difference?

Part of the answer might lie in the individual's realization, or lack thereof, of the previous archetype of the Contemplative. While at first glance this seemed the opposite of the Contributor, they can play a synergistic role throughout life. Those who have contemplated the nature of self and Spirit, the wishes and feelings of others, the consequences of one's actions, and the state of one's character are far more likely to manifest contributory wisdom in later years.

If individuals often fail to realize this archetype, our culture has also failed to honor it. Older workers are laid off, decades of valuable experience discarded, in favor of younger employees presumed to be more productive and tech-savvy. Older relatives may be pushed out of the family structure and into nursing homes or retirement communities. Sometimes this is necessary and beneficial, but it can also diminish intergenerational links. Reverence for "elders" is all too often replaced by pity, scorn, or neglect of "the elderly."

Yet as we look at the world around us, filled as it is with superficiality and short-sightedness, threatened by racism, xenophobia, and warfare, along with global dangers like nuclear weapons and climate change, we have never been more in need of elder-wisdom. Schachter-Shalomi has proposed establishing a council of elders who, like the Eagle Clan Mother, could remind our world leaders of their responsibilities (1997, 67). Some more modest programs exemplify this archetype in action. For example, the AARP's Experience Corps matches thousands of older adults with young children at risk, in a mentoring/tutoring process that enriches all participants. AARP also offers annual prizes honoring individuals over fifty who tackle major social problems in a creative way. In the words of CEO Jo Ann Jenkins, "The AARP Purpose Prize is all about a new story of aging—focusing on experience and innovation and the idea that our aging population is an untapped resource full of possibilities" (AARP 2017). As our population ages, the historically unprecedented number of elders is usually cast as a social burden. But what if it were also seen as a social asset, a vast potential reservoir of contributory wisdom?

THE COMPASSIONATE COMPANION

From an account by a Maryknoll Sister, serving as principal of a Peruvian school, until crippling progressive rheumatoid arthritis forced her back to the United States for surgery:

> I remember thinking that even though my hands were going to be broken and crooked, they would still be sacred to me. I'd use them to bring something to somebody, I didn't know what. My hands could be the compassionate hands of Christ as much as the hands of the doctors and nurses.
> So I sought to be able to enter into the world of the sick, and to live with the mystery of suffering. I saw that I had to enter into my own experience of pain, and to face up to it, and to allow myself to be changed by it. Without that nothing could be done. I saw that healing comes from owning our own wounds in the first step to moving beyond them.
> I returned to Peru at a lower altitude. Almost everything had changed, especially my attitude toward the people I was working with. I could feel their terrible poverty and pain in a whole new way. In fact it seemed as if I was seeing it for the first time. How often I'd rushed around trying to solve people's problems without really seeing them. . . . And so my ministry changed. It became the ministry of walking together. . . . Our pain and weakness and deformity proved to be teachers of a great mystery, a small introduction into the kind of dying from which new spirit is born. (Dass and Gorman 1985, 90–91)

The process of getting older often brings a series of physical and social insults. We no longer have our youthful vigor. Aches and pains accumulate. We may suffer from one or more debilitating or life-threatening conditions. The medical world offers some relief from our suffering, but can increase it in other ways as we are swallowed up into depersonalized environments, and perhaps subjected to painful, frightening, humiliating, and expensive procedures. All in all, aging is no picnic.

It would be a mistake if the preceding accounts of "aging well" minimize this truth. To do so would be to label as "failures" those who find getting old a tough haul. Better, as the Maryknoll Sister says, to enter into "the experience of pain, and to face up to it, and to allow [one]self to be changed by it." This too is the work of the elder, and worthy of being dignified with its own archetype.

I call this the "Compassionate Companion," and the previous story illustrates why. Faced with suffering any of us could become resentful and self-pitying, yet the Maryknoll Sister journeys in the opposite direction. Inspired by Christ—not as a far-off theological concept, but as an embodied being capable both of experiencing and of relieving suffering—her pain transmutes into compassion. This word etymologically derives from the Latin for "to feel or suffer" (*passio*), "with" (*com*) another. Suffering breaks open the Sister's heart, and gives her new insight into the suffering of those she has long labored to help.

While introduced through a Christian-inflected tale, this archetype hardly belongs to any one tradition. Buddhism, for example, is equally attuned to the centrality of suffering in human existence—that was the First Noble Truth Buddha pronounced after Awakening. According to legend he started life as a sheltered, cosseted prince until the day he witnessed in the streets a sick person, an old person, and a corpse, along with a spiritual aspirant. He came to realize the impermanence and suffering that haunts human life. No matter how strong our resistance and denial, how meticulous our exercise and vitamin regimens, as we age we too are likely to encounter—and become—that sick person, old person, and corpse. Yet this journey can awaken us not only in mind but in heart; along with wisdom, *compassion* is viewed as the greatest of Buddhist virtues.

I speak of the "compassionate *companion*" to stress that true compassion is nonhierarchical. Before developing rheumatoid arthritis the Sister had "rushed around trying to solve people's problems without really seeing them." There is an overtone of unconscious superiority, of doing good on behalf of those in need. Then an encounter with age and illness exposes her own vulnerability. She is no longer above, yet neither is she below, others. Her hands, "as much of the hands of doctors and nurses," can offer help. In "the ministry of walking together" she is a Compassionate Companion, accompanying all others in the human journey, which includes the necessity of pain and the opportunity to love.

I referred earlier to the cautionary contrast presented in *Successful Aging* between "one octogenarian on cross-country skis and another in a wheelchair." Yet the latter may too have "aged well," especially if this disability has fostered an open-hearted sensitivity to the well-being of others. If so, even while confined to a wheelchair, he or she may be an active giver of care.

The Compassionate Companion is also actualized when one learns how to *receive* gracefully. In fact, this can be the greater challenge for the elder who does not want to be a burden, and feels guilty and humiliated by the efforts of others. Yet we are all vulnerable and needy; the offices of giving and receiving will be exchanged many times over the course of a life, or even a single day. Learning to accept help with gratitude is itself a kind of gift offered to the one assisting. Finally, the very categories of "helper" and "helped" mingle or drop away (Dass and Gorman 1985, 18–49). We are all interdependent, companionate. Someone who embodies, and therefore teaches this truth, has indeed "aged well," even if lying on one's death-bed.

THE CREATIVE

> And God said to Abraham, "As for your wife Sarai, you shall not call her Sarai, but her name shall be Sarah. I will bless her; indeed I will give you a son by her." . . . Now Abraham and Sarah were old, advanced in years; Sarah had stopped having the periods of women. And Sarah laughed to herself, saying, "Now that I am withered, am I to have enjoyment—with my husband so old?". . . .
> Now Abraham was a hundred years old when his son Isaac was born to him. Sarah said, "God has brought me laughter; everyone who hears will laugh with me."
>
> —Genesis 17:15; 18:11–12; 21:5–6. *The Torah: A Modern Commentary* (Plaut 1981)

This biblical passage involves a linguistic joke: The name "Isaac" comes from the Hebrew word *yitzchak*, meaning "to laugh." His very existence involves a kind of cosmic joke that provokes Sarah's laughter—God bringing forth a child from such elderly parents! Moreover Sarah and Abraham undergo their own rebirth, symbolized by a name-change and a journey to a new land, as well as by Isaac's miraculous inception.

This story serves to introduce the archetype of elder as Creative. New lands, new identities, new births, can happen even in late life. This goes against the stereotype of the elderly as static and stodgy. "You can't teach an old dog new tricks." Yet there are many elders who blatantly contradict this saying. Through teaching this material I have met people who, in later life, have become involved in environmental activism; taken up new careers; explored spiritual practices far afield from their earlier religious training; become a teacher after years of learning, or a learner after years of teaching; separated after decades of marriage to explore an independent selfhood; pulled up stakes to move to a new city, coast, or intentional community; or learned to face death head-on without fear. It turns out you can teach an old dog new tricks. But much depends on whether he or she is still exploratory, creative, and receptive to the call of spirit, as were Sarah and Abraham. In the words of Carl Jung:

> A human being would certainly not grow to be seventy or eighty if this longevity had no meaning for the species. The afternoon of human life must certainly have a significance of its own and cannot be merely a pitiful appendage to life's morning. . . . Whoever carries over to this afternoon the law of the morning, or the natural aim, must pay for it with damage to his soul. (1933, 109)

The elder as Creative does not simply think back to the past, or repeat "the law of the morning." He or she is open to discovering new aims and identities. The work of youth and midlife is often that of establishing a firm ego-self in pursuit of worldly success. Yet this necessarily involves tamping down or failing to develop other parts of the self. There are wishes suppressed, relationships abandoned, paths not taken. We are often left with a burden of "unlived life." Yet the "diminishments" of later life—retirement, the empty nest syndrome, loss of youthful appearance and appetites—can also create zones of freedom, allowing new forms of expression and exploration. This is well captured by Jenny Joseph's much-beloved poem, "Warning" (1992):

> When I am an old woman I shall wear purple
> With a red hat which doesn't go, and doesn't suit me,
> And I shall spend my pension on brandy and summer gloves
> And satin sandals, and say we've no money for butter.
> I shall sit down on the pavement when I am tired,
> And gobble up samples in shops and press alarm bells,
> And run my stick along the public railings,
> And make up for the sobriety of my youth.
> I shall go out in my slippers in the rain
> And pick flowers in other people's gardens
> And learn to spit.
>
> You can wear terrible shirts and grow more fat
> And eat three pounds of sausages at a go
> Or only bread and pickle for a week
> And hoard pens and pencils and beermats and things in boxes.
>
> But now we must have clothes that keep us dry
> And pay our rent and not swear in the street
> And set a good example for the children.
> We must have friends to dinner and read the papers.
>
> But maybe I ought to practice a little now?
> So people who know me are not too shocked and surprised
> When suddenly I am old, and start to wear purple.

This is a reflection on the many ways aging can liberate us: from the demand for gender conformism in dress and body-type; from midlife practicalities; from pressures to obey social norms. After all, the elderly are often marginalized, de-sexualized, laughed off as foolish. Yes, this is ageist, but it can also open up space for free expression, just as Shakespeare's fools are emancipated to speak their minds in a way a courtier never could.

Of course, the fool gets away with it because he makes the king laugh. So, too, we laugh at Joseph's poem. And Sarah laughed when she heard the word of God. Humor is associated with this archetype of the Creative, for the ability to laugh and provoke laughter indicates resilience, joy, irreverence, and imagination are all still at play despite the losses associated with later life.

CONCLUSION

This chapter has asked "what is it to age well"? After criticizing some of the models of successful aging prevalent in our society involving (medical) prevention, (financial) prosperity, productivity, and pleasure, I have turned instead to traditional, often transcultural, archetypes, still applicable in the twenty-first century. Though there are many others, I have focused on four in particular: that of the elder as Contemplative, Contributor, Compassionate Companion, and Creative.

One might ask how they relate to one another, and to one's own life journey. There is of course no univocal answer. To a degree I have chosen these archetypes for their complementarity. An element of introspective withdrawal, as found in the Contemplative, is balanced by the social involvements that mark the Contributor. The Compassionate Companion lives with and learns from suffering and mortality. The Creative, on the contrary, is associated with humor and rebirth. As such, one might expect a full experience of later life to incorporate elements of all four archetypes, perhaps held in a yin-yang balance.

Yet one or another archetype might appropriately predominate for a given character type or situation. For example, someone might take a Contemplative bent in later life either because this was a lifelong disposition, or for the opposite reason—that earlier decades were so busy that now having a "broad margin on life" is a welcome switch. Another person may find it more natural and satisfying to fill his or her time with contributory activities, whether this takes the form of caring for grandchildren, mentoring younger colleagues, or political activism. Such predilections can also change from year to year as we age, depending on alterations in our social, financial, and physical condition, or simply shifts of the spirit as we respond to inward promptings.

There is then no one way to "age well." Withdrawal and contribution; sadness and humor; confronting death and experiencing rebirth; there are many forms "aging well" can take, whether—to use Rowe and Kahn's example—we do so on cross-country skis or in a wheelchair.

References

AARP. 2017. About the AARP Purpose Prize Award. http://www.aarp.org/about-aarp/purpose-prize/. Accessed on July 11, 2017.

Abecassis, M., Adams, M., Adams, P., Arnold, R. M., Atkins, C. R., Barr, M. L., Bennett, W. M. et al., Live Organ Donor Consensus Group. 2000. Consensus statement on the live organ donor. *JAMA* 284(22): 2919–2926.

Abernathy, A., Wheeler, J. 2008. Total dyspnoea. *Current Opinion in Supportive and Palliative Care* 2: 110–113.

Agar, N. 2013. *Truly human enhancement: A philosophical defense of limits*. Cambridge, MA: MIT Press.

Ahmed, S. 2004. Collective feelings, or the impression left by others. *Theory, Culture & Society* 21(2): 25–42.

———. 2006. *Queer phenomenology: Orientations, objects, others*. Durham and London: Duke University Press.

Aho, J., Aho, K. 2009. *Body matters: A phenomenology of sickness, disease, and illness*. Lanham, MD: Lexington Books.

Aho, K. 2003. Why Heidegger is not an existentialist: Interpreting authenticity and historicity in *Being and Time*. *Florida Philosophical Review* 3(2): 5–22.

———. 2008. Medicalizing mental health: A phenomenological alternative. *Journal of Medical Humanities* 29(4): 243–259.

———. 2016. Heidegger, ontological death, and the healing professions. *Medicine, Health Care and Philosophy* 19(1): 55–63.

Aho, K., Guignon, C. 2011. Medicalized psychiatry and the talking cure: A hermeneutic intervention. *Human Studies* 34(3): 293–308.

Alderman, H. 1978. Heidegger's critique of science and technology. In M. Murray (ed.), *Heidegger and modern philosophy* (35–50). New Haven, CT: Yale University Press.

Alkhuja, S. 2013. Anxiety Disorders in Patients with COPD. *Respiratory Care*. 58(10) e131; DOI: https://doi.org/10.4187/respcare.02716

Ambagtsheer, F., Zaitch, D., Weimar, W. 2013. The battle for human organs: Trafficking and transplant tourism in a global context. *Global Crime* 14(1): 1–14.

American Psychiatric Association (APA). 1994. *Diagnostic and statistical manual of mental disorders: DSM-4*. 4th edition. Washington, DC: American Psychiatric Press.

———. 2013a. *Diagnostic and statistical manual of mental disorders: DSM-5*. 5th edition. Washington, DC: American Psychiatric Press.

———. 2013b. Major depressive disorder and the "bereavement exclusion." https://www.psychiatry.org%2FFile%2520Library%2FPsychiatrists%2FPractice%2FDSM%2FAPA_DSM-5-Depression-Bereavement-Exclusion.pdf

American Thoracic Society. 1995. Standards for the diagnosis and care of patients with chronic obstructive pulmonary disease. *American Journal of Respiratory Critical Care Medicine* 152: S77–S121.

Améry, J. 1999. *At the mind's limits: Contemplations by a survivor on Auschwitz and its realities*. S. Rosenfeld and S.P. Rosenfeld (trans.) London: Granta Books.

Anderson, E. 1999. *The code of the street: Decency, violence, and the moral life of the inner city*. New York: Norton.

Aouizerate, B., Cuny, E., Martin-Guehl, C., Guehl, D., Amieva, H., Benazzouz, A. et al. 2004. Deep brain stimulation of the ventral caudate nucleus in the treatment of obsessive-compulsive disorder and major depression: Case report. *Journal of Neurosurgery* 101(4): 682–686.

Atwood, G. E. 2011. *The abyss of madness*. New York: Routledge.

Atwood, G. E., Stolorow, R. D. 2014. *Structures of subjectivity: Explorations in psychoanalytic phenomenology and contextualism*, Second edition. London and New York: Routledge.

Averill, J. 1968. Grief: Its nature and significance. *Psychological Bulletin* 70(6): 721–748.

Aydede, M. (ed.). 2005. *Pain: New essays on its nature and the methodology of its study*. Cambridge, MA: MIT Press.

Bachelard, Gaston. 1987. *The psychoanalysis of fire*. A. C. M. Ross (trans.) Boston: Beacon Press.

———. 2014. *The poetics of space*. M. Jolas (trans.) Harmondsworth: Penguin.

Bain, D. 2013. What makes pains unpleasant? *Philosophical Studies* 166: S69–S89.

Bartky, S. 1990. Foucault, femininity, and the modernization of patriarchal power. In *Femininity and domination: Studies in the phenomenology of oppression* (63–82). New York: Routledge.

Beauchamp, T. L., Childress, J. F. 2001. *Principles of biomedical ethics*, 5th edition. Oxford: Oxford University Press.

Biller-Andorno, N. 2011. Voluntariness in living-related organ donation. *Transplantation* 92(6): 617–619.

Binks, A., Desjardin, S., Riker, R. 2016. A preliminary study shows ICU clinicians under-estimate breathing discomfort in ventilated patients. *Respiratory Care*. 62(2): 150–155. DOI: https://doi.org/10.4187/respcare.04927

Binswanger, L. 1958a. The case of Ellen West: An anthropological-clinical study. In R. May, E. Angel, and H. F. Ellenberger (eds.), *Existence: A new dimension in psychology and psychiatry*. W. M. Mendel and J. Lyons (trans.) (237–364). New York: Basic Books.

———. 1958b. The existential analysis school of thought. In R. May, E. Angel, and H.F. Ellenberger (eds.), *Existence: A new dimension in psychology and psychiatry*. E. Angel (trans.) (191–213). New York: Basic Books.

———. 1962. *Grundformen und Erkenntnis menschlichen Daseins*. Munich, Germany: Ernst Reinhardt Verlag.

Borgmann, A. 2005. Technology. In H. Dreyfus and M. Wrathall (eds.), *A companion to Heidegger* (420–432). Oxford: Blackwell Publishing.

Boyar, J. I. 1964. The construction and partial validation of a scale for the measurement of the fear of death. *Dissertation Abstracts International* 25: 20–21.

Boym, Svetlana. 2001. *The future of nostalgia*. New York: Basic Books.

Bremer, S. 2011. *Kroppslinjer: kön, transsexualism och kropp i berättelser om könskorrigering*. Göteborg: Makadam.

Buber, M. 1972. *I and thou*. R. G. Smith (trans.) New York: Scribners.

Buchbinder, E., Eisikovits, Z. 2003. Battered women's entrapment in shame: A phenomenological study. *American Journal of Orthopsychiatry* 73: 355–366.

Bullington, J. 2013. *The expression of the psychosomatic body from a phenomenological perspective*. Berlin and Heidelberg: Springer.

Burnell, P., Hulton, S.-A., Draper, H. 2015. Coercion and choice in parent–child live kidney donation. *Journal of Medical Ethics* 41: 304–309.

Call, L. 2013. *BDSM in American science fiction and fantasy*. Basingstoke: Palgrave Macmillan.

Camus, A. 1989. *The stranger*. M. Ward (trans.) New York: Vintage International.

Canguilhem, G. 1991. *The normal and the pathological*. C. R. Fawcett and R. S. Cohen (trans.) New York: Zone Books.

Carel, H. 2007. Can I be ill and happy? *Philosophia* 35(2): 95–110.

———. 2008. *Illness. The cry of the flesh*. Durham: Acumen.

———. 2011. Phenomenology and its application in medicine. *Theoretical Medicine and Bioethics* 32(1): 33–46.

———. 2012a. Nursing and medicine. In S. Luft and S. Overgaard (eds.), *The Routledge companion to phenomenology* (623–632). London: Routledge.

———. 2012b. Phenomenology as a resource for patients. *Journal of Medicine and Philosophy* 37(2): 96–113.

———. 2013a. Illness, phenomenology, and the philosophical method. *Theoretical Medicine and Bioethics* 34(4): 345–357.

———. 2013b. Bodily doubt. *Journal of Consciousness Studies* 20(7–8): 178–197.

———. 2014. Ill, but well: A phenomenology of well-being in chronic illness. In J. Bickenbach, F. Felder, and B. Schmitz (eds.) *Disability and the good life* (243–270) Cambridge: Cambridge University Press.

———. 2016. *Phenomenology of illness*. Oxford: Oxford University Press.

Carel, H., Dodd, J., Macnaughton, J. 2015. Invisible suffering: Breathlessness in and beyond the clinic. *The Lancet Respiratory Medicine* 3(4): 278–279.

Carel, H. H., Kidd, I. J. 2014. Epistemic injustice in healthcare: A philosophical analysis. *Medicine, Health Care and Philosophy* 17(4): 529–540. DOI: 10.1007/s11019-014-9560-2

Carson, R. A., Burns, C. R., Cole, T. R. (eds.). 2003. Introduction. In *Practicing the medical humanities: Engaging physicians and patients*. Hagerstown, MD: University Publishing Group.

Casey, Edward. 1987. The world of nostalgia. *Man and World* 20(4): 361–384.

Chanarin, I. 1992. Pernicious anaemia. Diagnosis should be certain before treatment is begun. *British Medical Journal* 304: 1584–1585.

Chappell, T. 2007. Infinity goes up on trial: Must immortality be meaningless? *European Journal of Philosophy* 17(1): 30–44.

Christman, J. 2004. Relational autonomy, liberal individualism and the social constitution of the selves. *Philosophical Studies* 117: 143–164.

Cole, J. 2004. *Still lives: Narratives of spinal cord injury*. Cambridge, MA: MIT Press.

Conrad, P. 2007. *The medicalization of society: On the transformation of human conditions into treatable disorders*. Baltimore, MD: The Johns Hopkins University Press.

Corns, J. 2014a. The inadequacy of unitary characterizations of pain. *Philosophical Studies* 169: 355–378.

———. 2014b. Unpleasantness, motivational oomph, and painfulness. *Mind & Language* 29: 238–254.

———. 2015. The social pain posit. *Australasian Journal of Philosophy* 93: 561–582.

Crichton, P., H. Carel and I. J. Kidd. 2016. Epistemic Injustice in Psychiatry. *British Journal of Psych Bulletin* 41(2): 65–70. http://pb.rcpsych.org/content/pbrcpsych/early/2016/08/18/pb.bp.115.050682.full.pdf. DOI: 10.1192/pb.bp.115.050682

Crichton, P., Carel, H., Kidd, I. J. 2017. Epistemic injustice in psychiatry. *British Journal of Psychiatry* 41(2): 65–70.

Crossley, N. 2001. The phenomenological habitus and its construction. *Theory and Society* 30(1): 81–120.

Crouch, R. A., Elliot, C. 1999. Moral agency and the family: The case of living related organ transplantation. *Cambridge Quarterly of Healthcare Ethics* 8: 275–287.

Crowther, M. R., Parker, M. W., Achenbaum, W. A., Larimore, W. L., Koenig, H. G. 2002. Rowe and Kahn's model of successful aging revisited: Positive spirituality—the forgotten factor. *Gerontologist* 42: 613–620.

Culbertson, C. 2016. The omnipotent word of medical diagnosis and the silence of depression. *IJFAB: International Journal of Feminist Approaches to Bioethics* 9 (1): 1–26.

Currow, D. C., Johnson, M. J. 2015. Dyspnoea. Distilling the essence of breathlessness: The first vital symptom. *European Respiratory Journal* 45: 1526–1528.

Dallmayr, F. 2000. The enigma of health: Gadamer at century's end. In L. K. Schmidt (ed.), *Language and linguisticality in Gadamer's hermeneutics* (155–169). Lanham, MD: Lexington.

Dass, R. 2001. *Still here: Embracing aging, changing, and dying*. New York: Riverhead Books.

Dass, R., Gorman, P. 1985. *How can I help?: Stories and reflections on service*. New York: Alfred A. Knopf.

Dastur, F. 2012. *How are we to confront death?: An introduction to philosophy*. R. Vallier (trans.) New York: Fordham University Press.

Del Carmen, M. G., Joffe, S. 2005. Informed consent for medical treatment and research: A review. *The Oncologist* 10(8): 636–641.

Department of Health. 2008. *Commissioning IAPT for the whole community: Improving access to psychological therapies.* DH Publications: London.
Department of Health. 2010. *Inclusion health: Improving primary care for socially excluded people.* DH Publications: London.
———. 2011. *No health without mental health.* UK: Department of Health.
Social Exclusion Task Force. (2010). Inclusion health: Improving the way we meet the primary health care needs of the socially excluded. London.
Descartes, R. 1989. *Meditations on first philosophy.* J. Veitch (trans.) Buffalo, NY: Prometheus Books.
Deutsch, H. 1937. Absence of grief. *The Psychoanalytic Quarterly* 6: 12–22.
Devisch, I. 2010. Oughtonomy in healthcare. A deconstructive reading of Kantian autonomy. *Medicine, Health Care and Philosophy* 13(4): 303–312.
———. 2012. Co-responsibility: A new horizon for today's health care? *Health Care Analysis* 20(2): 139–151.
Devisch, I., Vanheule, S. 2014. Singularity and medicine: Is there a place for heteronomy in medical ethics? *Journal of Evaluation in Clinical Practice* 20(6): 965–969.
Dibley, L., Coggrave, M., McClurg, D., Woodward, S., Norton, C. 2017. "It's just horrible": A qualitative study of patients' and carers' experiences of bowel dysfunction in Multiple Sclerosis. *Journal of Neurology* 264(7): 1354–1361.
Donchin, A. 2001. Understanding autonomy relationally: Toward a reconfiguration of bioethical principles. *Journal of Philosophy and Medicine* 26: 365–386.
Dreyfus, H. L. 1991. *Being-in-the-world.* Cambridge, MA: MIT Press.
———. 2005. Foreword. In C. J. White (ed.), *Time and death.* Aldershot: Ashgate.
———. 2009. *On the internet.* New York: Routledge.
Eccleston, C. 2016. *Embodied: The psychology of physical sensation.* Oxford: Oxford University Press.
Ekstrom, M. P., Abernethy, A., Currow, D. C. 2015. The management of chronic breathlessness in patients with advanced and terminal illness. *British Medical Journal* 349: 1–7. DOI: http://dx.doi.org/10.1136/bmj.g7617
Elliott, C., Chambers, T. (eds.). 2004. *Prozac as a way of life.* Chapel Hill: University of North Carolina Press.
Engel, G. L. 1961. Is grief a disease? *Psychosomatic Medicine* 23: 18–22.
Engelberg, M. 2006. *Cancer made me a shallower person: A memoir in comics.* New York: Harper Perennial.
Engelhardt, H. T. 1982. Illnesses, diseases, and sicknesses. In V. Kestenbaum (ed.), *The humanity of the ill: Phenomenological perspectives* (142–156). Knoxville: University of Tennessee Press.
Epicurus. 1994. Letter to Menoeceus. In B. Inwood and L. P. Gerson (trans. and eds.), *The Epicurus reader.* Indianapolis, IN: Hackett.
Esser, R.W., Stoeckel, M.C., Kirsten, A., Watz, H., Lehmann, K., Taube, K., Büchel, C., Magnussen, H., Von Leupoldt, A. 2015. Neural correlates of dyspnea in COPD. *European Respiratory Journal.* 46. DOI: 10.1183/13993003.congress-2015. OA4954
Fairfield, P. 2014. *Death: A philosophical inquiry.* London: Routledge.
Falk, G. 2001. *Stigma: How we treat outsiders.* Amherst, NY: Prometheus Books.

Fernandez, A. V. 2014a. Depression as existential feeling or de-situatedness? Distinguishing structure from mode in psychopathology. *Phenomenology and the Cognitive Sciences* 13(4): 595–612.

Fernandez, A. V. 2014b. Reconsidering the affective dimension of depression and mania: Towards a phenomenological dissolution of the paradox of mixed states. *Journal of Psychopathology* 20(4): 414–420.

Fernandez, A. V. 2017. The subject matter of phenomenological research: Existentials, modes, and prejudices. *Synthese* 194(9): 3543–3562. https://doi.org/10.1007/s11229-016-1106-0

Fischer, J. M. 2009. *Our stories: Essays on life, death, and free will*. Oxford: Oxford University Press.

———. 2013. Immortality. In B. Bradley, F. Feldman, and J. Johansson (eds.), *The Oxford handbook of philosophy of death* (336–354). Oxford: Oxford University Press.

Fisher, H., Aron, A., Brown, L. L. 2005. Romantic love: An fMRI study of a neural mechanism for mate choice. *Journal of Comparative Neurology* 493: 58–62.

Fisher, T. 2010. Heidegger and the narrativity debate. *Continental Philosophy Review* 43: 241–265.

Forsberg, A., Nilsson, M., Krantz, M., Olausson, M. 2004. The essence of living parental liver donation—donors' lived experience of donation to their children. *Pediatric Transplantation* 8: 372–380.

Foucault, M. 1984. Dream, imagination, and existence: An introduction to Ludwig Binswanger's "Dream and Existence." *Review of Existential Psychology & Psychiatry* 19(1): 31–78.

———. 1990. *A history of sexuality. Volume 1: An introduction*. R. Hurley (trans.) New York: Random House.

Fowler, N. 2014. *AIDS: Don't die of prejudice*. London: Biteback Publishing.

Frances, A. 2013. The new crisis of confidence in psychiatric diagnosis. *Annals of Internal Medicine* 159(3): 221–222.

Frank, A.W. 1991. *At the will of the body*. Boston: Houghton Mifflin.

Frank, A.W. 1997. *The wounded storyteller: Body, Illness, and Ethics*. Chicago: University of Chicago Press.

Frankfurt, H. 1998. *The importance of what we care about*. Cambridge: Cambridge University Press.

Fraser, D; Kee, C., Minik, P. 2006. Living with Chronic Obstructive pulmonary Disease: Insiders' Perspectives. *Journal of Advanced Nursing* 55: 550–558.

Freeman, L. 2011. Reconsidering relational autonomy: A feminist approach to selfhood and the other in the thinking of Martin Heidegger. *Inquiry* 54: 361–383.

Fricker, M. 2007. *Epistemic injustice. Power and the ethics of knowing*. Oxford: Oxford University Press.

Frie, R. 1997. *Subjectivity and intersubjectivity in modern philosophy and psychoanalysis*. New York: Rowman & Littlefield.

———. 1999. Interpreting a misinterpretation: Ludwig Binswanger and Martin Heidegger. *Journal of the British Society for Phenomenology* 30(3): 244–257.

Friedman, M. 1997. Autonomy and social relationships: Rethinking the feminist critique. In D. Meyers (ed.), *Feminists rethink the self* (40–61). Boulder and Oxford: Westview Press.

Frohlich, D. O. 2014. Support often outweighs stigma for people with inflammatory bowel disease. *Gastroenterology Nursing* 37: 126–136.

Fuchs, T. 2000. *Psychopathologie von Leib und Raum: Phänomenologisch-empirische Untersuchungen zu depressiven und paranoiden Erkrankungen.* Darmstadt: Steinkopff.

———. 2013. Depression, intercorporeality, and interaffectivity. *Journal of Consciousness Studies* 20(7–8): 219–238.

———. 2016. Intercorporeality and interaffectivity. *Phenomenology and Mind* 11:194–209.

Fujita, M., Slingsby, B. T., Akabayashi, A. 2004. Three patterns of voluntary consent in the case of adult-to-adult living related liver transplantation in Japan. *Transplant Proceedings* 36(5): 1425–1428.

Fulford, K. W. M. 1989. *Moral theory and medical practice.* Cambridge: Cambridge University Press.

Gabara, S., Schön, S., Stendahl, S. 2015. Epidemiologi. *Svenskt Njurregister, Årsrapport*. http://www.medscinet.net/snr/rapporterdocs/Svenskt%20Njurregister%20 %C3%85rsrapport%202015.pdf. Accessed June 3, 2017.

Gadamer, H. -G. 1996. *The enigma of health.* J. Gaiger and N. Walker (trans.) Stanford, CT: Stanford University Press.

———. 2004. *A century in philosophy: Hans-Georg Gadamer in conversation with Riccardo Dottori.* New York: Continuum.

Gallagher, S., Jacobson, R. 2012. Heidegger and social cognition. In J. Kiverstein and M. Wheeler (eds.), *Heidegger and cognitive science* (213–245). London: Palgrave-Macmillan.

Gallagher, S., Morgan, B., Rokotnitz, N. 2017. Relational authenticity. In O. Flanagan and G. Caruso (eds.), *Neuroexistentialism: Meaning, morals, and purpose in the age of neuroscience.* New York: Oxford University Press.

Gawande, A. 2014. *Being mortal: Medicine and what matters in the end.* New York: Metropolitan Books.

Geniušas, S. 2015. The pathos of time: Chronic pain and temporality. *Dialogue and Universalism* 3: 25–38.

Gilhousen, R. 2017. *The lived experience of individuals living with human immunodeficiency virus (HIV) and acquired immune deficiency (AIDS) while residing in a rural region of Northern Appalachia*, Doctoral Dissertation, Duquesne University School of Nursing.

Goffman, E. 1974. *Stigma: Notes on the management of spoiled identity.* New York: Jason Aronson.

Goldie, P. 2011. Grief: A narrative account. *Ratio* 24(2): 119–137.

Goodman, P. 1969. Can technology be humane? *New York Review of Books* 13(9). http://www.nybooks.com/issues/1969/11/20/

Grahek, N. 2007. *Feeling pain and being in pain,* 2nd edition. Cambridge, MA: MIT Press.

Guignon, C. 1983. *Heidegger and the problem of knowledge*. Indianapolis, IN: Hackett.

———. 2011. Heidegger and Kierkegaard on death: The existentiell and the Existential. In P. Stokes and A. Buben (eds.), *Kierkegaard and death* (184–203). Bloomington: Indiana University Press.

Gunnarson, M. 2016. *Please be patient. A cultural phenomenological study of haaemodialysis and kidney transplantation care*. Lund: Lund University Press.

Gysels, M. Higginson, I.J. 2008. Access to services for patients with chronic obstructive pulmonary disease: The invisibility of breathlessness. *Journal of Pain and Symptom Management* 36(5): 451–460.

Hart, J. 1973. Toward a phenomenology of nostalgia. *Man and World* 6(4): 397–420.

Haugdahl, H. S., Dahlberg, H., Klepstad, P., Storli, S. L. 2017. The breath of life. Patients' experiences of breathing during and after mechanical ventilation. *Intensive Critical Care Nursing* 40: 85–93.

Haugdahl, H. S., Storli, S. L., Meland, B., Dybwik, K., Romild, U., Klepstad, P. 2015. Underestimation of patient breathlessness by nurses and physicians during a spontaneous breathing trial. *American Journal of Respiratory and Critical Care Medicine* 192(12): 1440–1448.

Hauskeller, M. 2014. *Better humans? Understanding the enhancement project*. London: Routledge.

Hawley, K. 2015. Trust and distrust between patient and doctor. *Journal of Evaluation in Clinical Practice* 21: 798–801.

Hayden, E. C. 2016. Tomorrow's children: What would genome editing really mean for future generations? *Nature* 530: 402–405.

Healy, D. 1999. *The antidepressant era*. Cambridge: Cambridge University Press.

Hegarty, K. 2011. Domestic violence: The hidden epidemic associated with mental illness. *The British Journal of Psychiatry* 198: 169–170. http://bjp.rcpsych.org/content/198/3/169.full. Accessed May 19, 2014.

———. 1962. *Being and time*. J. Macquarrie and E. Robinson (trans.) New York: Harper and Row.

———. 1966. Memorial address. *Discourse on thinking*. J. Anderson and H. Freund (trans.) New York: Harper and Row.

———. 1967. *What is a thing?* W. B. Barton, Jr., and V. Deutsch (trans.) Chicago: Henry Regnery.

———. 1977. *The question concerning technology and other essays*. W. Lovitt (trans.) New York: Harper and Row.

———. 1978. Das Ding. In *Vorträge und Aufsätze*. Pfullingen: Neske.

———. 1985. *History of the concept of time: Prolegomena*. T. Kisiel (trans.) Bloomington: Indiana University Press.

———. 1986. *Seminare*. Gesamtausgabe Band 15. Frankfurt am Main: Vittorio Klostermann.

———. 1993a. Letter on humanism. In D. F. Krell (ed.), *Basic writings*. New York: HarperCollins.

———. 1993b. The origin of a work of art. In D. F. Krell (ed.), *Basic writings*. New York: HarperCollins.

———. 1993c. The question concerning technology. In D. F. Krell (ed.), *Basic writings*. New York: HarperCollins.

———. 1993d. *Sein und Zeit*. Tübingen: Max Niemeyer.
———. 1996. *Being and time*. J. Stambaugh (trans.) Albany: State University of New York Press.
———. 2001a. *Zollikon seminars: Protocols-conversations-letters*. F. Mayr and R. Askay (trans.) Evanston, IL: Northwestern University Press.
———. 2001b. Building dwelling thinking. In A. Hofstadter (ed.), *Poetry, language, thought*. New York: Harper and Row.
———. 2001c. The origin of the work of art. In A. Hofstadter (ed.), *Poetry, language, thought*. New York: Harper and Row.
———. 2005. *Introduction to phenomenological research*. D. Dahlstrom (trans.) Bloomington: Indiana University Press.
———. 2006. Letter on humanism. In W. McNeill (ed.), *Pathmarks*. New York: Cambridge University Press.
———. 2008. *Phenomenological interpretations of Aristotle: Initiation into phenomenological research*. R. Rojcewicz (trans.) Bloomington: Indiana University Press.
Hillman, James. 2000. *The force of character and the lasting life*. New York: Ballantine Books.
Hofer, Johannes. 1934. Medical dissertation on nostalgia or homesickness. *Bulletin of the Institute of the History of Medicine* 2: 376–391.
Hoffman, P. 1983. *The human self and the life and death struggle*. Gainesville: University Press of Florida.
Hutchinson, P., Dhairyawan, R. 2017a. Shame and HIV: Strategies for addressing the negative impact shame has on public health and diagnosis and treatment of HIV. *Bioethics* 32(1): 68–76.
Hutchinson, P., Dhairyawan, R. 2017b. Shame, stigma, HIV: Philosophical reflections. *Medical Humanities* 43(4): 225–230.
Ihde, D. 1979. *Technics and praxis*. Dordrecht: Riedel.
Illbruck, Helmut. 2012. *Nostalgia: Origins and ends of an unenlightened disease*. Evanston, IL: Northwestern University Press.
Inwood, M. J. 1997. *Heidegger*. New York: Oxford University Press.
Jacobson, K. 2011. Embodied domestics, embodied politics: Women, home, and agoraphobia. *Human Studies* 34(1): 1–21.
———. 2016. Waiting to speak: A phenomenological perspective on our silence around dying. In S. K. George and P. G. Jung (eds.), *Cultural ontology: The self in pain* (75–92). New Delhi: Springer India.
James, I. 2006. *The fragmentary demand: An introduction to the philosophy of Jean-Luc Nancy*. Stanford, CA: Stanford University Press.
Jaspers, K. 1963. *General psychopathology*. Chicago: University of Chicago Press, 1963.
Johnson, Sandy. 1994. *The book of elders: The life stories and wisdom of great American Indians*. San Francisco, CA: HarperSanFrancisco.
Jones, M. P., Keefer, L., Bratten, J., Taft, T. H., Crowell, M. D., Levy, R., Palsson, O. 2009. Development and initial validation of a measure of perceived stigma in irritable bowel syndrome. *Psychology, Health and Medicine* 14: 367–374.
Joseph, Jenny. 1992. *Selected poems*. London: Bloodaxe.
Joy, B. 2000. Why the future doesn't need us. *Wired*. https://www.wired.com/2000/04/joy-2/

Jung, C. G. 1933. *Modern man in search of a soul*. New York: Harcourt, Brace.
Jutel, A. M. 2011. *Putting a name to it: Diagnosis in contemporary society*. Baltimore, MD: Johns Hopkins University Press.
Kay, L. 2015. Stories are difficult like that (unpublished doctoral research), University of Central Lancashire, UK.
Kewalramani, A., Bollinger, M.E., Postolache, T.T. 2008. Asthma and Mood Disorders. *International Journal of Child Health and Human Development*. 1(2): 115–123.
Kidd, I. J. 2012. Can illness be edifying? *Inquiry*: 55(5), 496–520.
Kim, Y., Wininger, K. M., Tye, S. J. 2016. Deep brain stimulation for treatment-resistant depression. In K. H. Lee, P. S. Duffy, and A. J. Bieber (eds.), *Deep brain stimulation: Indications and applications* (197–214). Oxford and New York: Pan Stanford Publishing.
Kirkengen, A. L. 2010. *The lived experience of violation. How abused children become unhealthy adults*. Bucharest, Romania: Zeta Books.
Klein, H. S. 2004. *A population history of the United States*. Cambridge: Cambridge University Press.
Kochanek, K. D., Murphy, S. L., Xu, J. Q., Tejada-Vera, B. 2016. Deaths: Final data for 2014. *National Vital Statistics Reports* 65(4). Hyattsville, MD: National Center for Health Statistics.
Kolodny, N. 2013. That I should die and others live. In S. Scheffler (ed.), *Death and the afterlife* (159–173) Oxford: Oxford University Press.
Konnopka, A., Schaefert, R., Heinrich, S., Kaufmann, C., Luppa, M., Herzog, W., König, H.-H. 2012. Economics of medically unexplained symptoms: A systematic review of the literature. *Psychotherapy and Psychosomatics* 81(5): 265–275.
Kouba, P. 2015. *The phenomenon of mental disorder: Perspectives of Heidegger's thought in psychopathology*. Dordrecht: Springer.
Knibbe, M. E., Maeckelberghe, E. L. M., Verkerk, M. A. 2007. Confounders in voluntary consent about living parental liver donation: No choice and emotions. *Medicine, Health Care and Philosophy* 10(4): 433–440.
Kraemer, F. 2013. Me, myself and my brain implant: Deep brain stimulation raises questions of personal authenticity and alienation. *Neuroethics* 6: 483–497.
Kramer, P. 1994. *Listening to Prozac*. London: Fourth Estate.
Kraus, A. 2003. How can the phenomenological-anthropological approach contribute to diagnosis and classification in psychiatry? In B. Fulford, K. Morris, J. Z. Sadler, and G. Stanghellini (eds.), *Nature and narrative* (199–216). Oxford: Oxford University Press.
Kunik, M. E., Roundy, K., Veazey, C., et al. 2005. Surprisingly high prevalence of anxiety and depression in chronic breathing disorders. *Chest* 127: 1205–1211.
Kusch, M. 2017. Analysing Holocaust survivor testimony: Certainties, scepticism, relativism. In S. Krämer and S. Weigel (eds.), *Testimony/bearing witness: Epistemology, ethics, history and culture*. London: Rowman and Littlefield International.
Kurzweil, R. 2001. Promise and peril. http://www.kurzweilai.net/promise-and-peril
Käll, L. F. 2009. Expression between self and other. *Idealistic Studies* 39: 71–86.
———. 2013. Intercorporeality and the shareability of pain. In L. F. Käll (ed.), *Dimensions of pain* (27–40). New York: Routledge.

———. 2014. Intercorporeality and the constitution of the body schemata. In R. F. Fox and N. M. Monteiro (eds.), *Pain without boundaries: Inquiries across cultures* (51–62). Oxford: Inter-Disciplinary Press.

Käll, L. F., Zeiler, K. 2014. Bodily relational autonomy. *Journal of Consciousness Studies* 21(9–10): 100–120.

Kärrfelt, H. M. E., Berg, U. B., Lindblad, F. I. E. 2000. Renal transplantation in children: Psychological and donation-related aspects from the parental perspective. *Pediatric Transplantation* 4: 305–312.

Lansing, R. W., Gracely, R. H., and Banzett, R. B. 2009. The multiple dimensions of dyspnea: Review and hypothesis. *Respiratory Physiology and Neurobiology* 167(1): 53–60.

Leder, D. 1990. *The absent body*. Chicago, IL: University of Chicago Press.

———. 1992. A tale of two bodies: The Cartesian corpse and the lived body. In D. Leder (ed.), *The body in medical thought and practice* (17–35). Dordrecht: Kluwer Academic Publishers.

———. 1997. *Spiritual passages: Embracing life's sacred journey*. New York: Tarcher/Putnam.

———. 1998. The trouble with successful aging. *The Park Ridge Center Bulletin* October/November: 10–11.

LeDoux, J. 2015. *Anxious: The modern mind in the age of anxiety*. London: Oneworld Publications.

Lennerling, A., Forsberg, A., Nyberg, G. 2003. Becoming a living kidney donor. *Transplantation* 76(8): 1243–1247.

Loeser, J. D., Melzack, R. 1999. Pain: An overview. *The Lancet* 353: 1607–1609.

Löwith, K. 1928. *Das Individuum in der Rolle des Mitmenschen*. In K. Stichweh (ed.), *Sämtliche Schriften* 1: 9–197. Stuttgart: J. B. Metzler.

Lyons, O. 1980. An Iroquois perspective. In C. Vescey and R. Venables (eds.), *American Indian environments: Ecological issues in Native American history* (202–205). Syracuse, NY: Syracuse University Press.

Ma, P., Mumper, R. J. 2013. Paclitaxel nano-delivery systems: A comprehensive review. *Journal of Nanomedicine and Nanotechnology* 4(2): 1000164.

Mackenzie, C., Stoljar, N. (eds.). 2000. *Relational autonomy: Feminist perspectives on autonomy, agency, and the social self*. Oxford: Oxford University Press.

Madison, G. B. 2013. *On suffering: Philosophical reflections on what it means to be human*. Hamilton: McMaster Innovation Press.

Malmqvist, E., Zeiler, K. 2010. Cultural norms, the phenomenology of incorporation and the experience of having a child born with ambiguous sex. *Social Theory and Practice* 36(1): 157–164.

Malpas, J. 1998. Death and the unity of a life. In J. Malpas and R. C. Solomon (eds.), *Death and philosophy* (120–134). London: Routledge.

Marmot, M. 2010. Fair society, healthy lives. The Marmot Review: Strategic review of health inequalities in England post-2010. Available at https://www.local.gov.uk/marmot-review-report-fair-society-healthy-lives

Marrato, S. L. 2012. *The intercorporeal self: Merleau-Ponty on subjectivity*. Albany: State University of New York Press.

Marx, W. 1987. *Is there a measure on Earth? Foundations for a nonmetaphysical ethics.* T. J. Nenon and R. Lilly (trans.) Chicago, IL: University of Chicago Press.

Matas, A. J. 2004. The case for living kidney sales: Rationale, objections and concerns. *American Journal of Transplantation* 4(12): 2007–2017.

Maurer, J., Rebbapragada, V., Borson, S., Goldstein, R., Kunik, M. E., Yohannes, A. M., Hanania, N. A. 2008. Anxiety and depression in COPD: Current understanding, unanswered questions, and research needs. *Chest* 134 (4 Suppl.): 43S–56S.

Maxwell, J. A. 2013. *Qualitative research design: An interactive approach*, 3rd edition. Los Angeles, CA: Sage.

May, T. 2009. *Death*. Stocksfield: Acumen.

McManus, S., Bebbington, P., Jenkins, R., Brugha, T. (eds.). 2016. *Mental health and wellbeing in England: Adult Psychiatric Morbidity Survey 2014*. Leeds: NHS Digital.

McQuellon, R. P., Cowan, M. A. 2000. Turning toward death together: Conversation in mortal time. *The American Journal of Hospice & Palliative Care* 17(5): 312–318.

Merleau-Ponty, M. 1962. *The phenomenology of perception*. C. Smith (trans.) London: Routledge.

———. 1963. The philosopher and his shadow. *Signs*. R. McCleary (trans.) Evanston, IL: Northwestern University Press.

———. 1964. *The primacy of perception*. Evanston, IL: Northwestern University Press.

———. 1968. *The visible and the invisible*. Evanston, IL: Northwestern University Press.

———. 2006. *The phenomenology of perception*. C. Smith (trans.) London: Routledge.

———. 2012. *The phenomenology of perception*. D. Landes (trans.) London: Routledge.

Minkowski, E. 1958. Findings in a case of schizophrenic depression. B. Blis (trans.) In R. May, E. Angel, and H. Ellenberger (eds.), *Existence* (127–138). New York: Simon and Schuster.

———. 1970. *Lived time: Phenomenological and psychopathological studies*. N. Metzel (trans.) Evanston, IL: Northwestern University Press.

Monaco, A. 2007. Is there a rationale for the kidney shortage? *Medicine and Health, Rhode Island* 90(3): 89–90.

Moore, A. W. 2006. Williams, Nietzsche, and the meaninglessness of immortality. *Mind* 115: 311–330.

More, M. 2001. Embrace, don't relinquish, the future. Available at http://www.kurz weilai.net/embrace-dont-relinquish-the-future

More, M., Vitra-More, N. (eds.). 2013. *The transhumanist reader*. Malden, MA: Wiley-Blackwell.

Morin, M. -E. 2016. Corps propre or corpus corporum: Unity and dislocation in the theories of embodiment of Merleau-Ponty and Jean-Luc Nancy. *Chiasmi* 18: 333–351.

Morris, K. J. 2013. Chronic pain in phenomenological /anthropological perspective. In R. T. Jensen and D. Moran (eds.), *The phenomenology of embodied subjectivity* (167–184). Dordrecht: Springer.

Nancy, J. -L. 1993. *The sense of the world.* J. S. Librett (trans.) Minneapolis: University of Minnesota Press.

———. 2000. *Being singular plural.* R. Richardson and A. O'Byrne (trans.) Stanford, CA: Stanford University Press.

Nancy, J. -L. 2008a. Corpus. R. E. Rand (trans.) New York: Fordham University Press

———. 2008b. *Dis-enclosure: The deconstruction of Christianity.* New York: Fordham University Press.

———. 2016. *Ego sum: Corpus, anima, fabula.* M.-E. Morin (trans.) New York: Fordham University Press.

National Institute for Health and Clinical Excellence. 2011. *Common mental health disorders: Identification and pathways to care.* London: Nice.

Nicholls, D. A. 2003. The experience of breathlessness. *Physiotherapy Theory and Practice* 19: 123–136.

Nietzsche, F. 1966. *Beyond good and evil: Prelude to a philosophy of the future.* W. Kauffman (trans.) New York: Random House.

Norton, C., Dibley, L. B., Bassett, P. 2013. Faecal incontinence in inflammatory bowel disease: Associations and effect on quality of life. *Journal of Crohn's and Colitis* 7: e302–e31.

Nussbaum, M. 1994. *The therapy of desire.* Princeton, NJ: Princeton University Press.

O'Donnell, D. E, Banzett, R. B., Carrieri-Kohlman V., Casaburi R., Davenport P.W, Gandevia S.C., Gelb A.F., Mahler D.A., Webb K.A. 2007. Pathophysiology of dyspnea in chronic obstructive pulmonary disease: A roundtable. *Proceedings of the American Thoracic Society* 4: 145–168.

Olde Hartman, T., Blankenstein, N., Molenaar, B., van den Berg, D. B., van der Horst, H., Arnold, I. et al. 2013. NHG guideline on medically unexplained symptoms (MUS). *Huisarts & Wefenschap* 56(5): 222–230.

Omar, F., Tufveson, G., Welin, S. 2010. Compensated living kidney donation: A plea for pragmatism. *Health Care Analysis* 18(1): 85–101.

Packard, M. G., McGaugh, J. L. 1992. Double dissociation of fornix and caudate nucleus lesions on acquisition of two water maze tasks: Further evidence for multiple memory systems. *Behavioral Neuroscience* 106: 439–446.

Parens, E. 2015. *Shaping our selves: On technology, flourishing, and a habit of thinking.* Oxford: Oxford University Press.

Parker, R., Aggleton, P. 2003. HIV and AIDS-related stigma and discrimination: A conceptual framework and implications for action. *Social Science and Medicine* 57: 13–24.

Pauwels, R. A., Rabe, K. F. 2004. Burden and clinical features of chronic obstructive pulmonary disease (COPD). *Lancet* 364: 613–620.

Perper, R. 2013. Grief, depression and the *DSM-5*. *San Diego Psychologist* 28(4): 5–8.

Phillips, C. 2003. Who's who in the pecking order: Aggression and "normal violence" in the lives of girls and boys. *The British Journal of Criminology* 43(4): 710–728.

Pies, R. 2014. The bereavement exclusion and DSM-5: An update and commentary. *Innovations in Clinical Neuroscience* 11(7–8): 19–22.

Plaut, W. G. (ed.). 1981. *The Torah: A modern commentary.* New York: Union of American Hebrew Congregations.

Pöggeler, O. 1989. *Martin Heidegger's path of being*. D. Magurshak and S. Barber (trans.) Atlantic Highlands, NJ: Humanities Press.

Price, D. M. 2000. Psychological and neural mechanisms of the affective dimension of pain. *Science* 288: 1769–1772.

Proust, Marcel. 1970. *The past recaptured*. A. Mayor (trans.) New York: Vintage Books.

Quirin, M., Loktyushin, A., Arndt, J., Küstermann, E., Lo, Y. Y., Kuhl, J., Eggert, L. 2011. Existential neuroscience: A functional magnetic resonance imaging investigation of neural responses to reminders of one's mortality. *Social Cognitive and Affective Neuroscience* 7(2): 193–198.

Radcliff-Richards, J. A. S., Daar, R. D., Guttman, R., Hoffenberg, R., Kennedy, U., Lock, M., Sells, R. A., Tilney, N. 1998. The case for allowing kidney sales. *The Lancet* 351(9120): 1950–1952.

Radden, J. 2009. *Moody minds distempered: Essays on melancholy and depression*. Oxford: Oxford University Press.

Ramsey, R. E. 1998. *The long path to nearness: A contribution to a corporeal philosophy of communication*. Atlantic Highlands, NJ: Humanity Books.

Ratcliffe, M. 2008. *Feelings of being*. Oxford: Oxford University Press.

———. 2013. Why mood matters. In M. Wrathall (ed.), *Cambridge companion to Being and time* (157–176). Cambridge: Cambridge University Press.

———. 2015. *Experiences of depression: A study in phenomenology*. Oxford: Oxford University Press.

———. 2017. Grief and the unity of emotion. *Midwest Studies in Philosophy* 41: 154–174.

Ratcliffe, M., Broome, M. 2012. Existential phenomenology, psychiatric illness and the death of possibilities. In S. Crowell (ed.), *Cambridge companion to existentialism* (361–382). Cambridge: Cambridge University Press.

Ratcliffe, M., Broome, M., Smith, B., Bowden, H. 2013. A bad case of the flu? The comparative phenomenology of depression and somatic illness. *Journal of Consciousness Studies* 20(7–8): 198–218.

Reiser, S. J. 2009. *Technological medicine: The changing world of doctors and patients*. Cambridge: Cambridge University Press.

Rethink Mental Illness. 2012. 20 years too soon. *Physical health: The experiences of people affected by mental illness*. https://www.rethink.org/media/511826/20_Years_Too_Soon_FINAL.pdf

Ricoeur, P. 1992. *Oneself as another*. Chicago, IL: University of Chicago Press.

Rosati, C. S. 2013. The Makropulos case revisited: Reflections on immortality and agency. In B. Bradley, F. Feldman, and J. Johansson (eds.), *The Oxford handbook of philosophy of death* (335–390). Oxford: Oxford University Press.

Rose, N., Abi-Rached, J. M. 2013. *Neuro: The new brain sciences and the management of the mind*. Princeton, NJ: Princeton University Press.

Roszak, Theodore. 2009. *The making of an elder culture: Reflections on the future of America's most audacious generation*. Gabriola Island, BC, Canada: New Society Publishers.

Routledge, Clay. 2015. *Nostalgia: A psychological resource*. London: Routledge.

Routledge, Clay, et al., 2010. A blast from the past: The terror management function of nostalgia. *Journal of Experimental Social Psychology* 44: 132–140.
Rowe, J. W., Kahn, R. L. 1998. *Successful aging*. New York: Pantheon/Random House.
Rowling, J. K. 2000. *Harry Potter and the goblet of fire*. New York: Scholastic Press.
Russ, A. J., Shim, J. K., Kaufman, S. R. 2005. "Is there life on dialysis?": Time and aging in clinically sustained existence. *Medical Anthropology* 24(4): 297–324.
Russon, J. 2014. Between two intimacies: The formative contexts of adult individuality. *Emotion, Space, and Society* 13: 64–70.
———. 2016a. Self and suffering in Buddhism and phenomenology: Existential pain, compassion and the problems of institutional healthcare. In S. K. George and P. G. Jung (eds.), *Cultural ontology of the self in pain* (181–195). New Delhi: Springer India.
———. 2016b. The body as site of action and intersubjectivity in Fichte's *Foundations of Natural Right*. In G. Gottlieb (ed.), *Fichte's foundations of natural right* (138–156). Cambridge: Cambridge University Press.
———. 2017. *Sites of exposure: Art, politics, and the nature of experience*. Bloomington and Indianapolis: Indiana University Press.
Ryder, J. G., Holtzheimer, P. E. 2016. Deep brain stimulation for depression: An update. *Current Behavioral Neuroscience Reports* 3(2): 102–108.
Ryle, G. 1949. *The concept of mind*. Hammondsworth: Penguin.
Sacks, O. 2015. Oliver Sacks on learning he has terminal cancer. *The New York Times*. http://www.nytimes.com/2015/02/19/opinion/oliver-sacks-on-learning-he-has-terminal-cancer.html
Salmon, P. 2007. Conflict, collusion or collaboration in consultations about medically unexplained symptoms: The need for a curriculum of medical explanation. *Patient Education and Counseling* 67(3): 246–254.
Sandel, M. J. 2007. *The case against perfection: Ethics in the age of genetic engineering*. Cambridge, MA: Harvard University Press.
Sartre, J.-P. 1956. *Being and nothingness*. H. E. Barnes (trans.) New York: Washington Square Press.
———. 1998. *Being and nothingness*. H. E. Barnes (trans.) New York: Routledge.
Sass, L. A., Parnas, J. 2003. Schizophrenia, consciousness, and the self. *Schizophrenia Bulletin* 29(3): 427–444.
Saul, R. 2014. *ADHD does not exist: The truth about attention deficit and hyperactivity disorder*. New York: HarperCollins.
Savulescu, J., ter Meulen, R., Kahane, G. 2011. *Enhancing human capacities*. Malden, MA: Wiley-Blackwell.
Scarry, E. 1985. *The body in pain: The making and unmaking of the world*. Oxford: Oxford University Press.
Schalow, F. 1994. The Kantian schema of Heidegger's late Marburg period. In T. Kisiel and J. van Buren (eds.), *Reading Heidegger from the start* (309–323). Albany, NY: SUNY Press.
Schachter-Shalomi, Z., Miller, R. 1995. *From age-ing to sage-ing: A revolutionary approach to growing older*. New York: Time Warner Books.

Scheffler, S. 2013. *Death and the afterlife*. Oxford: Oxford University Press.
Schüpbach, M., Gargiulo, M., Welter, M. L., Mallet, C., Béhar, C., Houeto, J. L. 2006. Neurosurgery in Parkinson disease: A distressed mind in a repaired body? *Neurology* 66: 1811–1816.
SFS 1995:831. Lag (1995:831) om transplantation m.m.
Shildrick, M. 2002. *Embodying the monster: Encounters with the vulnerable self*. London, Thousand Oaks, New Delhi: Sage Publications.
———. 2008. Contesting normative embodiment: Some reflections on the psycho-social. *Perspectives: International Postgraduate Journal of Philosophy* 1: 12–22.
Shusterman, R. 2005. The silent, limping body of philosophy. In T. Carman and M. Hansen (eds.), *The Cambridge companion to Merleau-Ponty* (151–180). New York: Cambridge University Press.
Simon, P. M., Schwartstein, R. M., Weiss, J. W., Fencl, V., Teghtsoonian, M., Weinberger, S. E. 1990. Distinguishable types of dyspnea in patients with shortness of breath. *American Review of Respiratory Disease* 142: 1009–1014.
Singer, L. 1981. Merleau-Ponty on the concept of style. *Man and World* 14(2): 153–163.
Slatman, J. 2014. *Our strange body. Philosophical reflections on identity and medical interventions*. Amsterdam: Amsterdam University Press.
Slatman, J., Zeiler, K., DeVisch, I. 2016. Can you restore your "own" body? A phenomenological analysis of relational autonomy. *American Journal of Bioethics* 16(8): 18–20.
Sloterdijk, P., Huyssen, A. 1988. *Critique of cynical reason*. Minneapolis: University of Minnesota Press.
Smith, D. M., Loewenstein, G., Rozin, P., Sherriff, R. L., Ubel, P. A. 2007. Sensitivity to disgust, stigma, and adjustment to life with a colostomy. *Journal of Research in Personality* 41: 787–803.
Smoller, J. W., Pollack, M. H., Otto, M. W., Rosenbaum, J. F., Kradin, R. L. 1996. Panic, anxiety and dyspnoea. *American Journal of Respiratory and Critical Care Medicine* 154: 6–17.
Smuts, A. 2011. Immortality and significance. *Philosophy and Literature* 35(1): 134–149.
Smyth, B. 2011. Foucault and Binswanger: Beyond the dream. *Philosophy Today* 55(Supplement): 92–101.
Snethen, J. A., Broome, M. E., Bartels, J., Warady, B. A. 2001. Adolescents' perception of living with end stage renal disease. *Pediatric Nursing* 27(2): 159–167.
Socialstyrelsen. 2017. Antal transplanterade organ 2000–2016. http://www.livsviktigt.se/SiteCollectionDocuments/Antal%20transplanterade%20organ%202000-2016%20%28f%c3%b6r%20webben%29.pdf. Accessed March 5 2017.
Solomon, A. 2001. *The noonday demon*. London: Vintage.
Sontag, S. 1978. *Illness as metaphor*. New York: Farrar, Straus and Giroux.
SOU 2015:84. *Organdonation. En livsviktig verksamhet*. Fritzes: Stockholm.
Spital, A. 2001. Ethical issues in living organ donation: Donor autonomy and beyond. *American Journal of Kidney Diseases* 38(1): 189–195.

———. 2005. More on parental living liver donation for children with fulminant hepatic failure: Addressing concerns about competing interests, coercion, consent and balancing acts. *American Journal of Transplantation* 5(11): 2619–2622.

Steinbrecher, N., Koerber, S., Frieser, D., Hiller, W. 2011. The prevalence of medically unexplained symptoms in primary care. *Psychosomatics* 52(3): 263–271.

Stempsey, W. E. 2006. Emerging medical technologies and emerging conceptions of health. *Theoretical Medicine and Bioethics* 27: 227–243.

Stolorow, R. D. 2007. *Trauma and human existence: Autobiographical, psychoanalytic, and philosophical reflections*. New York: Routledge.

———. 2011. *World, affectivity, trauma: Heidegger and post-Cartesian psychoanalysis*. New York: Routledge.

Stolorow, R. D., Atwood, G. E. 2017. The phenomenology of language and the metaphysicalizing of the real. *Language and Psychoanalysis* 6(1): 4–9.

Stanghellini, G., Aragona, M. (eds.). 2016. *An experiential approach to psychopathology: What is it like to suffer from mental disorders?* Switzerland: Springer.

Sullivan, D. 2001. *Cosmetic surgery: The cutting edge of medicine in America*. New York: Rutgers University Press.

Svenaeus, F. 2000. *The hermeneutics of medicine and the phenomenology of health: Steps towards a philosophy of medical practice*. Dordrecht: Kluwer.

———. 2007. Do antidepressants affect the self? A phenomenological approach. *Medicine, Health Care and Philosophy* 10: 153–166.

———. 2009. The phenomenology of falling ill. An explication, critique and improvement of Sartre's theory of embodiment and alienation. *Human Studies* 32(1): 53–66.

———. 2010. The body as gift, resource, or commodity: Heidegger and the ethics of organ transplantation. *Journal of Bioethical Inquiry* 7(2): 163–172.

——— 2011. Illness as unhomelike being-in-the-world: Heidegger and the phenomenology of medicine. *Medicine, Healthcare and Philosophy* 14: 333–343.

———. 2013. The relevance of Heidegger's philosophy of technology for biomedical ethics. *Theoretical Medicine and Bioethics* 34(1): 1–16.

———. 2015. The phenomenology of chronic pain: Embodiment and alienation. *Continental Philosophy Review* 48: 107–122.

Talero, M. 2005. Perception, normativity, and selfhood in Merleau-Ponty: The spatial "level" and existential space. *The Southern Journal of Philosophy* 43(3): 443–461.

Teachman, B. A., Make, C. D., Clerkin, E. M. 2010. Catastrophic misinterpretations as a predictor of symptom change during treatment for panic disorder. *Journal of Consulting and Clinical Psychology* 78(6): 964–973.

Theunissen, M. 1984. *The other*. C. Macann (trans.) Cambridge, MA: MIT Press.

Thomson, I. 2005. *Heidegger on ontotheology: Technology and the politics of education*. New York: Cambridge University Press.

———. 2011. *Heidegger, art, and postmodernity*. New York: Cambridge University Press.

Thoreau, H. D. 1983. *Walden and civil disobedience*. New York: Penguin Books.

Tong, T., Morton, R., Howard, K., Craig, J. C. 2009. Adolescent experiences following organ transplantation: A systematic review of qualitative studies. *The Journal of Pediatrics* 155(4): 542–549.

Toombs, S. K. 1987. The meaning of illness: A phenomenological approach to the patient-physician relationship. *The Journal of Medicine and Philosophy* 12: 219–240.

Toombs, S. K. 1993. *The meaning of illness: A phenomenological account of the different perspectives of physician and patient*. Dordrecht: Kluwer.

———. 1995. The lived experience of disability. *Human Studies* 18(1): 9–23.

———. 2001. Reflections of bodily change. The lived experience of disability. In S. K. Toombs (ed.), *Handbook of phenomenology and medicine* (247–261). Dordrecht: Kluwer Academic Publishers.

Trevarthen, C. 1979. Communication and cooperation in early infancy: A description of primary intersubjectivity. In M. Bullowa (ed.), *Before speech* (321–347). Cambridge: Cambridge University Press.

Trigg, Dylan. 2006. *The aesthetics of decay: Nothingness, nostalgia, and the absence of reason*. New York: Peter Lang.

———. 2012. *The memory of place: A phenomenology of the uncanny*. Athens: Ohio University Press.

———. 2016. *Topophobia: A phenomenology of anxiety*. London: Bloomsbury.

———. 2017. Chronophobe. *Etc Media* 110: 74–77.

Tugendhat, E. 1986. *Self-consciousness and self-determination*. P. Stern (trans.) Cambridge, MA: MIT Press.

Turner, N., Jefford, H. 2013. *Pulmonary rehabilitation in prisons*. Oxleas NHS Foundation. http://oxleas.nhs.uk/site-media/cms-downloads/Oxleas_COPD_GUIDE_for_web.pdf. Accessed August 2016.

Twichell, C. 2001. Toys in the attic: An Ars Poetica under the influence. In N. Casey (ed.), *Unholy ghost: Writers on depression* (21–28). New York: Perennial.

van den Bergh, O. 2016. The benefit of doubt: The role of subjective certainty in the perception of dyspnea and pain. *International Dyspnea Society*. http://www.dyspnea2016inparis.fr/program/poster-sessions/

van Manen, J. G., Bindels, P. J., Dekker, F. W. 2002. Risk of depression in patients with chronic obstructive pulmonary disease and its determinants. *Thorax* 57: 412–416.

van Manen, M. 1997. *Researching lived experience: Human science for an action sensitive pedagogy*, 2nd edition. London and Ontario: Althouse Press.

Varga S. 2012. *Authenticity as an ethical ideal*. New York: Routledge.

Villablanca, J. 2010. Why do we have a caudate nucleus? *Acta Neurobiologiae Experimentalis* 70(1): 95–105.

Vogel, L. 1994. *The fragile "we": Ethical implications of Heidegger's* Being and Time. Evanston, IL: Northwestern University Press.

Waldenfels, B. 1989. Körper—Leib. In J. Leenhardt and R. Picht (eds.), *Esprit/Geist. 100 Schlüsselbegriffe für Deutsche und Franzosen* (342–345). München: Piper.

Watts, M. 2011. *The philosophy of Heidegger*. Stocksfield: Acumen.

Wei, H., Bruns, O. T., Kaul, M. G., Hansen, E. C., Barch, M., Wisniowska, A., et al. 2017. Exceedingly small iron oxide nanoparticles as positive MRI contrast agents. *Proceedings of the National Academy of Sciences of the United States of America (PNAS)* 14(9): 2325–2330.

Weiss, G. 1999. *Body images: Embodiment as intercorporeality.* New York: Routledge.
Wells, A. 1997. *Cognitive therapy of anxiety disorders.* Wiley: Chichester.
Wikström, B., Fored, M., Eichleay, M. A., Jacobson, S. A. 2007 The financing and organization of medical care for patients with end-stage renal disease in Sweden. *International Journal of Health Economics and Management* 7: 269–281.
Wileman, L., May, C., Chew-Graham, C. A. 2002. Medically unexplained symptoms and the problem of power in the primary care consultation: A qualitative study. *Family Practice* 19(2): 178–182.
Willgoss, T. G., Yohannes, A. M., Goldbart, J., Fatoye, F. 2012. "Everything was spiraling out of control": Experiences of anxiety in people with chronic obstructive pulmonary disease. *Heart Lung* 41: 562–571.
Williams, B. 1973. *Problems of the self.* Cambridge: Cambridge University Press.
Wilson, E. A. 2004. *Psychosomatic. Feminism and the neurological body.* Durham and London: Duke University Press.
Wilson, I. 2006. Depression in the patient with COPD. *International Journal of Chronic Obstructive Pulmonary Disease* 1(1): 61–64.
Wittgenstein, L. 1953. *Philosophical investigations.* Malden, MA: Blackwell Publishing.
———. 1975. *On certainty.* D. Paul and G. E. M. Anscombe (trans.) Oxford: Blackwell.
Wolf, N. 2002. *The beauty myth: How images of beauty are used against women.* New York: HarperCollins.
World Health Organization. 2016. *Chronic Obstructive Pulmonary Disease* (COPD). Available at http://www.who.int/mediacentre/factsheets/fs315/en/. Accessed January 2017.
Zahavi, D. 2001. Beyond empathy: Phenomenological approaches to intersubjectivity. *Journal of Consciousness Studies* 8:151–167.
Zeiler, K. 2010. A phenomenological analysis of bodily self-awareness in the experience of pain and pleasure: On bodily dys-appearance and eu-appearance. *Medicine, Health Care and Philosophy* 13(4): 333–342.
———. 2013. A phenomenology of excorporation, bodily alienation, and resistance: Rethinking sexed and racialized embodiment. *Hypatia. A Journal of Feminist Philosophy* 28(1): 69–84.
———. 2014a. A philosophical defense of the idea that we can hold each other in personhood: Intercorporeal personhood in dementia care. *Medicine, Health Care and Philosophy* 17: 131–141.
———. 2014b. A phenomenological approach to the ethics of transplantation medicine: Sociality and sharing when living-with and dying-with-others. *Theoretical Medicine and Bioethics* 35: 369–388.
Zeiler, K., and Guntram, L. 2014. Sexed embodiment in atypical pubertal development: Intersubjectivity, excorporation, and the importance of making space for difference. In K. Zeiler, and L. Folkmarson Käll. (141–160) *Feminist Phenomenology and Medicine.* Albany, NY: State University of New York Press.
Zeiler, K., Guntram, L., Lennerling, A. 2010. Moral tales of parental living kidney donation: A parenthood moral imperative and its relevance for decision-making. *Medicine, Health Care and Philosophy* 13(3): 225–236.

Zeiler, K., Lennerling, A. 2014. Organdonation från förälder till barn: Starka känslor behöver inte vara hinder för autonomt beslut. *Läkartidningen* 55–56: 109–110.

Zeiler, K., Wickström, A. 2009. Why do "we" perform surgery on newborn intersexed children? The phenomenology of the parental experience of having a child with intersex anatomies. *Feminist Theory* 10(3): 355–374.

Ziegert, K., Fridlund, B., Linell, E. 2009. "Time for dialysis as time to live." Experiences of time in everyday life of the Swedish next of kin of hemodialysis patients. *Nursing and Health Sciences* 11: 45–50.

Zygon, J. 2007. Moral breakdown and the ethical demand: A theoretical framework for an anthropology of moralities. *Anthropological Theory* 7(2): 131–150.

Index

AARP's Experience Corps, 229
abode of human beings, 163–64.
 See also dwelling
acute exacerbations of respiratory
 infections, 148
ADHD. *See* attention deficit
 hyperactivity disorder
aeonic time, 56
affective situatedness, 42n8; mode of,
 29, 30
affectivity, xix–xx
ageist culture, 223
aging, 223–33; as challenging
 curriculum, 227; pleasure model,
 224; preventive model, 224;
 productive model, 224; prosperity
 model, 224; successful, 223–26;
 wisdom and, 228. *See also* elders
agriculture: modern, 185, 187;
 premodern, 185
Ahmed, Sarah, 84, 85
AIDS. *See* HIV-AIDS
Alderman, Harold, 184
American Psychiatric Association
 (APA), 5, 6
Améry, Jean, 73–74
anthropology: ontology *vs.,* 34
antidepressants, 141

anxiety, 149–50; breathlessness and,
 149–57; definition of, 150; as
 dysfunctional condition, 152; fear
 vs., 47, 48–49; Heidegger's analysis,
 46–49; as a mood, 46; negativity,
 47; nostalgia and, 43–56; panic,
 152; power and productive role of,
 152–53; as primordial, 49; taking
 flight, 49; temporality, 43–44;
 threat of, 53–55; uncanniness, 48;
 vertiginous, 47; world and, 48
APA. *See* American Psychiatric
 Association
"Apologia for the Art of Healing"
 (Gadamer), 185, 189
Arendt, Hannah, 24n2
attention deficit hyperactivity disorder
 (ADHD), 38, 143; medications for,
 141, 142
attunement, 76
Atwood, G. E., 20
authenticity, 6–9; illness and,
 212–14
automatization, 186
autonomous decision making, 82–83.
 See also bioethics; transplantation
average life span, 223
Averill, James, 4

Bachelor, Gaston, 51–52
Bain, D., 69
Ballard, J. G., 43
Being and Nothingness (Sartre), 8
Being and Time (Heidegger), xi, xiii, xvi, 29, 118, 132, 134, 138, 139; anxiety in, 45–46; at-homeness, 54; care in, 31; Dasein, xvii; hammer as an object, xvi; Heidegger's main goal in, 119; modification in, 215; mood, 75–76; "they" in, 205, 215
Being as a whole, 46–47
being-at-home, 45, 57; anxiety threatening, 54–55; concept of, 54; refamiliarization, 55, 56; spatial-temporal continuity, 55–56
being-for-others, 8
Being-in-the-world, 19–20
Being Mortal: Medicine and What Matters in the End (Gawande), 209
being-with-others, 6–9
being-with-others-in-the-world, 214
bereavement exclusion, 4; *DSM-4,* 4, 5; *DSM-5,* 4, 5
Bestand, 162, 164, 165, 182
Bichat, Marie François Xavier, 111–12
Binswanger, Ludwig, 7; "The Existential Analysis School of Thought," 33; on love, 31, 32; on temporality, 33–34
bio- and nanotechnologies, 166–74; contrast agents, 167; medical uses, 167; predictability concern of, 167–68; reasons for being critical of, 167; risks of higher order, 166–67; as superior drug delivery vehicles, 167
bioethics, 97–99
biomedical ethics, 137–38
blue-eyed population, 172
bodily certainty, 72
bodily doubt, 72
bodily expressions: language of, 85; in shared space, 84–86
body: engagement with the world, 195; existential conception of, 192–96; as "I can," 192, 194; interaction with other persons, 193; interlocking system, 193; in intersubjective world, 196–200; Merleau-Ponty on, 193; person, 193–94; as *res extensa,* 110; sharing of experience, 194–95; as sign, 194
Boss, Medard, xi, 134, 180
botox, 182
breathlessness, 145–57; anxiety and, 149–57; conceptualization of, 149; diagnosing and assessing, 148; dysfunctional, 148; overview, 145–47; pathological etiology, 148; pernicious anemia, 149
Buan, 164
Buber, Martin, 31
Buddha, 231
Buddhism, 231
Building, Dwelling, Thinking (Heidegger), 54
building and dwelling, 164
Bullington, J., 103, 104–7, 110
Burghölzli, xi

Camus, A., 3
Cancer Made Me a Shallower Person: A Memoir in Comics (Engelberg), 213
Canguilhem, Georges, 141
care: Binswanger on Heidegger's notion of, 31, 32; Heidegger's notion of, 31
Carel, Havi, 72
Cartesian isolated mind, 20
Casey, Edward, 51
categorial structure, 29
caudate nucleus (CN), 10; deep brain stimulation (DBS), 13
CD4 ("T") cells, 198, 199. *See also* HIV-AIDS
certainties, 73
Chappell, Timothy, 118
childbirth, 202
chronic obstructive pulmonary disorder (COPD), 146; anxiety disorders and, 149; mental health conditions and, 149. *See also* breathlessness

cogito ergo sum, 110–11
Cole, Jonathan, 77
comorbidity of breathlessness and anxiety, 150–51
compassion, 231
compassionate companion, elders as, 230–32
comportment: dwelling as, 164; thinking as, 163
contemplative elders, 226–27
contrast agents, 167
contributor, elders as, 228–30
conversion disorder, 102
COPD. *See* chronic obstructive pulmonary disorder
Corns, J., 69
corporeal body, 207
cosmetic surgery, 140
cosmetic technology, 181–82
Cowan, M. A., 215–16, 218
creative elders, 232–33
Crick, Francis, 133
CRISPR-Cas, 168
CRISPR-Cas9, 168, 170
Crohn's disease, 197. *See also* inflammatory bowel disease (IBD)
cultural worldview defense, 10
curmudgeons, 115, 116–18

Dasein, 7
Daseinsanalyse, 134
death: elimination of, 173–74; Heidegger's view of, 118–23; inauthentic understanding of, 210–12; non-relational character of, 211; premature, 117; Sartre on, 120; as a self-contained event, 211. *See also* immortality
Death and the Afterlife (Scheffler), 115
deep brain stimulation (DBS), 13–14
defamiliarization, 54, 55, 56
depersonalization, 40
depression, 4, 149–50; antidepressants, 141; characteristics, 38; grief *vs.,* 13–14; loss of feelings, 38–39; melancholic, 39–40; as modal disorder, 38
Descartes, Rene: *Meditations,* 110; metaphysical dualism, 18–19; *partes extra partes,* 108, 110; *Regulae ad directionem ingenii,* 182
Deutsch, H., 3–4
Dhairyawan, Rageshri, 199, 201–2, 203
Diagnostic and Statistical Manual of Mental Disorders (DSM), 18, 102; anxiety disorders, 150; as pseudo-scientific manual, 20; psychiatry and, 143–44
diagnostic manuals, 144. *See also Diagnostic and Statistical Manual of Mental Disorders (DSM)*
doctors: Heidegger and, 134–36; medical practice and, 188
Dreyfus, Hubert, 122, 174
drugs. *See* pharmaceuticals
DSM-4, 4
DSM-5, 4
dwelling, 54, 163–64; building and, 164; as comportment, 164. *See also* being-at-home

Eagle Clan Mother, 228, 229
Ego Sum (Nancy), 110
Eigentlichkeit, 6
elders: capitalist systems and, 223; as compassionate companion, 230–32; as contemplative, 226–27; as contributor, 228–30; as creative, 232–33; learning to receive gracefully, 231. *See also* aging
embodiment, xvi–xvii
emotional distress, 77; social pain, 69
emotional disturbances, 20
emotional dwelling, 23
emotional intentionality, two-sidedness of, 75–79
emotional trauma, 20–24; authenticity, 21–22; dissociation, 22; recurrence, 22; relational home, 21–22; therapeutic implications, 23–24

end-stage renal disease (ESRD), 81; bodily expressions, 88–90; living with, 86–87; symptoms of, 86
enframing, 162
Engel, G. L., 4
Engelberg, Miriam, 213–14
enhancement drugs, 140–43. *See also* pharmaceuticals
The Enigma of Health (Gadamer), 133, 139, 181
ESRD. *See* end-stage renal disease
estrangement, feelings of, 13
ethics of finitude, 24
excription, 113–14
existence as hermeneutic, xx–xii, xx–xxii
existential analysis, of Binswanger, 30–37; Foucault on, 34–36; Heidegger on, 32; Merleau-Ponty on, 36–37
existential authenticity. *See* authenticity
existential feelings, 17
existential hopelessness: phenomenological account, 20; Ratcliffe's analysis, 17–18, 20, 21
existential kinship-in-finitude, 24
"Existential Neuroscience: A Functional Magnetic Resonance Imaging Investigation of Neural Responses to Reminders of One's Mortality" (Quirin), 10

factical Dasein, 29
fear: anxiety *vs.,* 47, 48–49; intentional attitude of, 78; mood of, 77–78
fearfulness, 78
fearing, 78
feelings: of estrangement, 13; of helplessness, 13; of meaning in life, 13
fibromyalgia, 101
finitude, 22; ethics of, 24
Fink, Eugen, 134
Fischer, John Martin, 115, 126
Foucault, Michel, 28, 34–36, 37, 40, 41n1, 141

framing perspectives, 201–2
Frank, Arthur, 208, 209, 211–12, 217
Freud, S.: psychanalysis of hysteria, 102
Frohlich, D. O., 200–201
Fuchs, Thomas, 39

Gadamer, Hans-Georg: "Apologia for the Art of Healing," 185, 189; *The Enigma of Health,* 133, 139, 181; on health and illness, xvii, xx, 207; modern medical practice, 186–90; modern psychiatry, 142; natural equilibrium of body, 207; science of medicine, 188–89; training in health professions, 186
gadolinium-based contrast agents, 167
Gawande, Atul, 209
Gelassenheit, 166
gene-editing tool, 168
genetic engineering, 168–74; for aesthetic purposes, 172
genetic enhancements, 173–74
genetic line, technologies and, 168
Gilhousen, Renée, 201
giving-through-sharing, 84
Goldie, Peter, 15n3
Goodman, Paul, 183
Grahek, N., 69
grief, 3–4; Averill on, 4; depression *vs.,* 13–14; Engel on, 4; MDD *vs.,* 5, 5–6; relational authenticity and, 11–13
Gunnarson, Martin, 90

Harry Potter (Rowling), 22
Hart, James, 56
health: as an enigma, 206–8; existential conception of, 200; organic model of, 201; phenomenology of, 138–40; restoration of, 206, 216–21
health care, xi, 179–90; criticisms of, 179–80; institutionalized, 202–3; nineteenth century, 179
Heidegger, Martin, xi; on death, 118–23; factical Dasein, 29;

Nazism and, xi; technologization, 165; *Zollikon Seminars,* xi–xxiv, 180, 191. *See also* anxiety; death; health; illness; phenomenology; technologies; *specific work*
Heideggerian ethics, 161–74. *See also* bio- and nanotechnologies
helplessness: chronic pain and, 70; existential, 17–18, 20, 21; feelings of, 13
hermeneutic, existence as, xx–xxii
Hitchcock, Alfred, 56
HIV-AIDS, 198–200; antiretroviral therapy (ART), 198–99; description, 198; framing perspectives, 201–2; Gilhousen's study on, 201; shame, 199, 201; stigma, 199, 201; as taboo, 199
Hofer, Johannes, 50
Hölderlin, Friedrich, 165
home, 45, 52–53; as an atmosphere, 53; as a physical site/region, 52–53; refamiliarization, 55, 56; spatial-temporal continuity, 55–56. *See also* being-at-home; nostalgia
homelessness, 49
homeliness, 56
homesickness, 49, 52
Homo, 124
human/human beings, 28–29; abode of, 163–64; existentials, 29–30; modes, 29, 30; pre-ontological, 29
human lives/values, 116–18; in risk and urgency, 124–25; risk argument, 117; stages argument, 116–17; urgency argument, 117–18
Husserl, E., 54, 56, 103–4, 107, 111
Hutchinson, Phil, 199, 201–2, 203
hysteria: Freud's psychanalysis of, 102; symptoms, 102

"I and thou" relation, 31
Ideas II (Husserl), 103–4
illness: authenticity and, 212–14; in the context of intersubjective recognition, 196–200; cure, 209–10; Engelberg's response to, 213–14; Frank on, 208; inauthentic understanding of, 210–12; interpretation of the world in, 216; life breakdowns during, 207; lived experience of, 207; meaning-making capacity and, 208; new time of understanding created by, 215–16; organic model of, 201; Sontag on, 208; Svenaeus on, 207–8; Western medicine on, 208–9
illusion of perceptible essences, 19
imagination, nostalgia and, 51
immortality: genetic enhancement and, 173–74; and inhumanity, 123–25; risk and urgency posed by, 124–25. *See also* death
inauthenticity, 6–9
incarnation, 113
inconspicuous mood, 78–79
infant survival rates, 179
inflammatory bowel disease (IBD), 197–98; as an existential problem, 198; conditions, 197; Frohlich's study on, 200–201; intersubjective life, 198; stigma, 197–98; symptoms, 197; taboo, 197; unfair treatment to persons with, 198
informed consent, 97
inhumanity: immortality and, 123–25
institutionalized health care, 202–3
intentional feelings, 17
intercorporeality, 84, 89
interlocking system, of body and world, 193
Internet, 101
intimacy, 112
"Isaac," 232

Jaspers, Karl, 17
Jenkins, Jo Ann, 229
Johnson, Sandy, 228
Joseph, Jenny, 233
Joy, Bill, 167

Judeo-Christian tradition, 162
Jung, Carl, 232–33

Käll, Lisa Folkmarson, 85
Kay, Lesley, 202
kidney donations in Sweden, 81–82
Knibbe, M. E., 87
Körper, xvi, 103, 107, 111
Kraemer, F., 14
Kraus, Alfred, 39

later life. *See* aging; elders
learning to receive gracefully, 231
Leib, 103–4, 107, 111, 137–38
life expectancy: nineteenth century, 179
lived body, 83–84, 105–8; corporeal body and, 207; mental illness, 143–44
loss of feeling, 38–39; as feeling of not feeling, 39
loss of ipseity, 40
love: Binswanger on, 31, 32; Heidegger on Binswanger's account of, 32
Löwith, Karl, 7
Lynch, David, 56
Lyons, Oren, 229

MacArthur Foundation, 225
major depressive disorder (MDD): grief vs., 5, 5
Marx, Werner, 6; on shared mortality, 12
Maryknoll Sister, 230
May, Todd, 117–18
McQuellon, R. P., 215–16, 218
MDD. *See* major depressive disorder
meaning in life, feelings of, 13
medicalization, 140–43
medically unexplained physical symptoms (MUPS), 101–14; Bullington's approach to, 103, 104–7, 110; as economic burden, 101; examples of, 101; making sense of, 112–14; overview, 102–3; phenomenology and, 103–5; prevalence of, 101; social media and, 102; unexplained in, 101, 102, 106–7
medical practice: doctors, 188; Gadamer on, 186–90; modesty, 188; patients as objects of scientific knowledge, 189; restoring equilibrium of life, 189; science and, 186–87. *See also* technologies
medicine, 191–203; authenticity, 200–203; body, 192–200; Heidegger's philosophy of, 132–34; interaction between healthcare providers and patient, 197; medical model of, 196; overview, 191–92
Meditations (Descartes), 110
meditative thinking, 163; dwelling and, 164
melancholic depression, 39–40
memory: affective content, 51; volitional, 51. *See also* nostalgia
mental illness, 143–44
Merleau-Ponty, Maurice, xvi; on existential analysis, 36–37; on lived body, 106, 107, 108; *partes extra partes,* 108; *Phenomenology of Perception,* 36, 104, 108; "The Philosopher and His Shadow," 193
metaphysical dualism, 18–19
Michelangelo, 170, 171, 172
mind and world, 18–19
Minkowski, Eugène, 70–71
Mitsein, 6–7, 12
modes, 29
mood: anxiety as a, 46; enhancement of, 141; of fear, 77–78; Heidegger's idea of, 46; inconspicuous, 78–79; of profound despair, 76
mood disorders: antidepressants for, 141
Moore, A. W., 118
mortality, 173–74
multitasking culture, elders in, 227
MUPS. *See* medically unexplained physical symptoms

Nancy, Jean-Luc, 103, 107–13; on Descartes, 110; *Ego Sum,* 110; on Husserl, 111; on incarnation, 113; on *partes extra partes,* 108–9, 110
nanomaterials, 167–68. *See also* bio- and nanotechnologies
nature: human interactions with, 183
neuroscience, 9–11
"News from the Sun" (Ballard), 43
Newton, Isaac, 182
New York Times, 212
Nietzsche, Friedrich, 162
Nietzschean metaphysics, 162
nihilism, 162
nihilistic dystopia, 163
Nostalghia, 56
nostalgia: affective content of, 50–51; anxiety and, 43–56; bittersweet tonality of, 56; cinematic and literary treatments of, 56; etymology of, 50; home and, 45, 52–53; hypothesis, 49; intentionality of, 51, 55, 56; phenomenology of, 50–52; refamiliarization, 55, 56; reverie, 51–52; spatial-temporal continuity, 55–56; temporality of, 44–45
not-being-at-home, 48, 54
nothingness, 47
Nussbaum, Martha, 117

obsessive compulsive disorder (OCD), 13. *See also* depression
OCD. *See* obsessive compulsive disorder
On Certainty (Wittgenstein), 73
"On the Essence and Concept of *Physis*" (Heidegger), 133
ontic investigations, 28
ontological difference: Binswanger's misinterpretation, 30–34; concept, 27, 28; overview, 27–28
ontology, 28; anthropology *vs.,* 34
ontotheology, 164
organic model, of health and illness, 201
the Other, 8–9

paclitaxel, 167
pain: components, 77; mood, 75–76; as nonlocalized, 74; overview, 61–62; Scarry on, 76; as shape of our world, 78; in shared space, 84–86; social, 69; sociality of, 85; spatiotemporal constriction, 85; style of anticipation, 70–71, 72; trust, doubt and helplessness, 72–75; unpleasantness of, 68–71
pain asymbolia, 68, 69
panic anxiety, 152
"the Parade of the Immortality Curmudgeons," 115
parental live kidney donation, 89, 93–97. *See also* transplantation
Parnas, Josef, 40
partes extra partes, 108–10, 113; Descartes, 108, 110; Merleau-Ponty using, 108; Nancy using, 108–9, 110
pernicious anemia, 149
Perper, R., 5
person, 193–94
personality disorders, 38
pharmaceuticals, 140–43; for ADHD, 141, 142; antidepressants, 141; normalization, 141, 142; psychiatric drugs, 141, 142–43
phenomenology, xiv–xv; anxious breathlessness, 153–57; French, 34–37; of health, 138–40; MUPS, 103–5; of nostalgia, 50–52
"The Philosopher and His Shadow" (Merleau-Ponty), 193
Philosophiae Naturalis Principia Mathematica (Newton), 182
Pies, Ronald, 5
pleasure model, 224
pleasures: repeatable, 126
poiêsis, 162–63
portkeys, 22
power of anxiety, 152–53
prefrontal lobotomy, 71
premature death, 117
preventive model of aging, 224

primary intersubjectivity, 12
prosperity model of aging, 224
Proust, Marcel, 51, 56
Prozac, 140–41, 142, 143
psychiatric drugs, 142–43
psychiatry, and *DSM,* 143–44
psychoanalytic phenomenological contextualism, 20
The Psychology of the Sickbed (van den Berg, J. H.), 191
psychopathological conditions, 38
psychosomatics, 104–5. *See also* medically unexplained physical symptoms (MUPS)

"The Question Concerning Technology" (Heidegger), 132, 133–34, 180, 181, 182, 184, 185
Quirin, M., 10, 13

Radden, J., 69, 70
Ratcliffe, Matthew, 17–18, 78
Regulae ad directionem ingenii (Descartes), 182
relational home, 21–22
repeatable pleasures, 126
res extensa, 110
restitution, 209
restoration of health, 206, 216–21
reverie, 51–52
rheumatoid arthritis, 207
Ricoeur, P., 15n2
risk and urgency, 124–25
risk argument, 117
Ritalin, 141, 142, 144
Rosati, Connie S., 116–17

Sacks, Oliver, 212
Sandel, Michael J., 172
Sartre, Jean-Paul, xvii, 6, 44; on authenticity/inauthenticity, 8–9; *Being and Nothingness,* 8; on death, 120
Sass, Louis, 40
Scarry, Elaine, 76
Schachter-Shalomi, Z., 229

Schalow, Frank, 120–21
Scheffler, Samuel, 115–16, 117, 118, 123, 124, 126
schizophrenia: phenomenological literature on, 40; positive symptoms of, 40
Schüpbach, M., 13
Schwartz, Julia, 24n3
Sein und Zeit (Löwith), 7
self-infantilization, 74–75
sensation: pain and, 69
shared mortality, 12
shared space: pain and other bodily expression in, 84–86
Shenandoah, Audrey, 228
Shusterman, R., 103, 106, 107
Singer, Linda, 88
Sloterdijk, Peter, 217
smoking, 146
Smuts, A., 125–26
social pain, 69
Solomon, Andrew, 38–39
somatic illness, 143
Sontag, Susan, 208
space and time, xviii–xix
"*Sprachnot,*" 73
stages argument, 116–17
Stambaugh, Joan, 76
stigma: HIV-AIDS, 199; inflammatory bowel disease (IBD), 197–98
The Stranger (Camus), 3
subjectivity, 83–84; as intersubjectively, 84
successful aging: pleasure model, 224; preventive model, 224; problems with, 223–26; productive model, 224; prosperity model, 224
Successful Aging (Rowe and Kahn), 225
Svenaeus, Frederik, 191, 207
Sweden, 81–82; dialysis in, 81; kidney donations in, 81–82

taboo: HIV-AIDS as, 199; inflammatory bowel disease (IBD) as, 197
taking flight, 49
Talero, Maria, 87

Tarkovsky, Andrei, 56
T-cells. *See* CD4 ("T") cells
technê, 162, 169, 181, 182–85. *See also* medical practice; technologies
technologies: automatization, 186; being ethical, 166; bio- and nanotechnologies, 166–74; biomedical ethics, 137–38; enframing, 132, 162; fight against, 165–66; Heidegger's philosophy of, 131–44; as a mode of revealing, 165–66; as productive, 183; as tools, 181; transformation from premodern to modern, 182–84; ubiquity in modern life, 166. *See also* medical practice
technologization, 165
temporality: ontological meaning and structure of, 33–34
theory of action, 163
"they," 210–12; in *Being and Time* (Heidegger), 215; dangerous interpretation by, 210; Engelberg's use of, 213; modifications of, 215; relation to, 215; untethering from, 214–16; without, 215
"they-self," 214
thinking: as comportment, 163
Thomson, Iain, 165
time and space, xviii–xix
training in health professions, 186–87
transplantation: bioethics, 97–99; orientation toward, 92–93; overview, 81–83; parental choice, 93–97

trauma recovery, 22
trust: loss of, 73–75; self-infantilization, 74–75
tunnel vision, 22
Twichell, Chase, 38

ulcerative colitis, 197. *See also* inflammatory bowel disease (IBD)
uncanniness, 48
unheimlich, 48
unpleasantness of pain, 68–71
urgency argument, 117–18

van den Berg, J. H., 191
van den Bergh, O., 153
vertiginous anxiety, 47
Vertigo, 56
Vogel, L., 24
volitional memory, 51

"Warning" (poem by Joseph), 233
Watson, James, 133
Weiss, Gail, 84
West, Ellen, 33
Western medicine, 208–9
Williams, Bernard, 115
wisdom, aging and, 228
Wittgenstein, L., 19, 73
world: giving-through-sharing, 84; as a home-world, 48; and mind, 18–19
world as a home-world, 48

yitzchak, 232

Zollikon Seminars, xi–xxiv, 180, 191

About the Contributors

Kevin Aho is professor of philosophy and chair of the Department of Communication and Philosophy at Florida Gulf Coast University. He has published widely in the areas of existentialism, phenomenology, hermeneutics, and the philosophy of medicine. He is the author of *Existentialism: An Introduction* (2014), *Heidegger's Neglect of the Body* (2009), and *Body Matters: A Phenomenology of Sickness, Disease, and Illness*, with James Aho (2008).

Adam Buben is assistant professor of comparative philosophy at Leiden University in the Netherlands. His work has appeared in a variety of journals and edited collections, including the *British Journal for the History of Philosophy*, *Journal of the American Philosophical Association*, *Philosophical Papers*, and *Philosophy East and West*. He is also the coeditor of *Kierkegaard and Death* (2011) and the author of *Meaning and Mortality in Kierkegaard and Heidegger: Origins of the Existential Philosophy of Death* (2016).

Havi Carel is professor of philosophy at the University of Bristol. Her research examines the experience of illness and of receiving health care. She has published on the embodied experience of illness, epistemic injustice, and well-being within illness and on the experience of respiratory illness in particular in the *Lancet*, *BMJ*, *Journal of Medicine and Philosophy*, *Theoretical Medicine and Bioethics*, *Medicine, Healthcare and Philosophy*. She is the author of a number of books, including *Phenomenology of Illness* (2016), *Illness: The Cry of the Flesh* (2008, 2nd edition 2013), and *Life and Death in Freud and Heidegger* (2006). She is also coeditor of *Health, Illness, and Disease* (2012).

Carolyn Culbertson earned her PhD in philosophy at the University of Oregon and is currently assistant professor of philosophy at Florida Gulf Coast University. Her research focuses on twentieth-century Continental philosophy, especially the work of Martin Heidegger, and on theories of language within the Continental tradition. Her articles have appeared in journals such as *Continental Philosophy Review*, *Southwest Philosophy Review*, *Comparative and Continental Philosophy*, and *Philosophy Today*.

Anthony Vincent Fernandez is assistant professor of philosophy at Kent State University in Ohio. He works on classical and contemporary phenomenology, focusing especially on metaphysical and methodological issues in the application of phenomenology to the study of psychopathology. He has recently published in journals such as *Phenomenology and the Cognitive Sciences*, *Synthese*, and *Philosophy, Psychiatry, & Psychology*.

Shaun Gallagher is the Lillian and Morrie Moss Professor of Excellence in Philosophy at the University of Memphis and professorial fellow at the Faculty of Law, Humanities, and the Arts, University of Wollongong (AU). He is also honorary professor of health sciences at the University of Tromsø (Norway). His publications include *Enactivist Interventions* (2017), *A Neurophenomenology of Awe and Wonder* (2015), *Phenomenology* (2012), *The Phenomenological Mind*, with Dan Zahavi (2008, 2nd edition 2012), *Brainstorming* (2008), *How the Body Shapes the Mind* (2005).

Kirsten Jacobson is associate professor of philosophy at the University of Maine. She specializes in nineteenth- and twentieth-century Continental philosophy, and her research interests include the phenomenology of spatiality, the nature of home and dwelling, and more generally, the philosophical significance and status of the phenomenological method. Her published work has focused significantly on using Merleau-Ponty's phenomenology to conduct novel analyses of psychological and physiological illnesses and more generally to consider issues of "existential health."

Tara Kennedy received her PhD in philosophy from the University of New Mexico in 2014. Her research interests include Heidegger, phenomenology, environmental philosophy, and existentialism. In 2016 she published "The Ethics of Treating Animals as Resources: A Post-Heideggerian Approach," in *Frontiers of Philosophy in China*.

Martin Kusch is professor for applied philosophy of science and epistemology at the University of Vienna, Austria. He is the author of *Language as Calculus versus Language as Universal Medium* (1989), *Foucault's Strata* *and Fields* (1991), *Psychologism* (1995), *Psychological Knowledge* (1998), *The Shape of Action*, with H.M. Collins (1999), *Knowledge by Agreement* (2002), and *A Skeptical Guide to Meaning and Rules* (2006). Since 2014 he has been a PI of an ERC Advanced Grant Project on "The Emergence of Relativism."

Drew Leder is a professor of Eastern and Western philosophy at Loyola University Maryland. He has an MD from Yale University and a PhD from SUNY Stony Brook. His newest book is *The Distressed Body: Rethinking Illness, Incarceration and Healing* (2016), a follow-up to *The Absent Body* (1990), a phenomenological examination of the mind-body split. He writes in a scholarly vein on contemporary issues such as illness and our medical system, incarceration, and the ways we see and treat animals. He has also done groundbreaking work on aging as viewed within different traditions in *Spiritual Passages* (1997), as well as other books on cross-cultural spirituality and everyday life. He speaks and leads workshops around the country, and has had his work featured in leading newspapers and magazines.

Nicole Piemonte is assistant professor in the Department of Medical Education at Creighton University School of Medicine and an academic consultant at St. Joseph's Hospital and Medical Center in Phoenix, Arizona. She received a PhD in medical humanities from the University of Texas medical branch where she studied existential philosophy, literature and medicine, and medical epistemology. She recently published the book *Afflicted: How Vulnerability Can Heal Medical Education and Practice* (2017).

Ramsey Eric Ramsey is associate dean and professor with a joint appointment in Barrett, the Honors College and the New College of Interdisciplinary Arts and Sciences at Arizona State University West campus. He is a senior associate fellow of the International Institute of Hermeneutics. He has written three books and numerous articles and book chapters in philosophical hermeneutics and has lectured internationally in Europe and Latin America.

Matthew Ratcliffe is professor for theoretical philosophy at the University of Vienna, Austria. Most of his recent work addresses issues in phenomenology, philosophy of mind, and philosophy of psychiatry. He is author of *Rethinking Commonsense Psychology: A Critique of Folk Psychology, Theory of Mind and Simulation* (2007), *Feelings of Being: Phenomenology, Psychiatry and the Sense of Reality* (2008), *Experiences of Depression: A Study in Phenomenology* (2015), and *Real Hallucinations: Psychiatric Illness, Intentionality, and the Interpersonal World* (2017).

John Russon is professor of philosophy at the University of Guelph and the director of the Toronto Summer Seminar in Philosophy. He is the author of six books, including *Human Experience: Philosophy, Neurosis, and the Elements of Everyday Life* (2003), which develops an existential approach to mental health; *Bearing Witness to Epiphany: Persons, Things, and the Nature of Erotic Life* (2009), which develops an existential interpretation of sexuality, ethics and politics; and *Sites of Exposure: Art, Politics, and the Nature of Experience* (2017), which draws on the artistic and religious traditions of different cultures to explore the fundamental tensions and values that shape our personal and political lives. He is also the author of many scholarly studies in phenomenology and other aspects of the history of philosophy.

Jenny Slatman is professor of medical humanities in the Department of Culture Studies at Tilburg University, the Netherlands. She has published widely on issues of embodiment in art, expression, and contemporary medical practices. Her publications include a book-length philosophical study on the meaning of expression in the work of the French philosopher Merleau-Ponty: *L'expression au-delà de la représentation. Sur l'aisthêsis et l'esthétique chez Merleau-Ponty* (2003), and the monograph *Our Strange Body: Philosophical Reflections on Identity and Medical Interventions* (2014). In 2017 Slatman was awarded a 1.5 million euro grant from the Netherlands Organization for Scientific Research (NWO) for her research project *Mind the Body: Rethinking Embodiment in Healthcare*. This project will focus on the meaning of embodiment in health practices pertaining to MUPS (medically unexplained physical symptoms), obesity, and depression, while exploring how health professionals, patients, and the wide audience talk about and deal with body-mind issues.

Robert D. Stolorow, PhD is a founding faculty member and training and supervising analyst at the Institute of Contemporary Psychoanalysis, Los Angeles; founding faculty member at the Institute for the Psychoanalytic Study of Subjectivity, New York City; and a clinical professor of psychiatry at the UCLA School of Medicine. He is the author of *World, Affectivity, Trauma: Heidegger and Post-Cartesian Psychoanalysis* (2011) and *Trauma and Human Existence: Autobiographical, Psychoanalytic, and Philosophical Reflections* (2007), and coauthor of *Worlds of Experience: Interweaving Philosophical and Clinical Dimensions in Psychoanalysis* (2002), *Working Intersubjectively: Contextualism in Psychoanalytic Practice* (1997), *Contexts of Being: The Intersubjective Foundations of Psychological Life* (1992), *Psychoanalytic Treatment: An Intersubjective Approach* (1987), *Structures of Subjectivity: Explorations in Psychoanalytic Phenomenology and Contextualism* (1984, 2nd edition 2014), *Psychoanalysis of Developmental Arrests:*

Theory and Treatment (1980), and *Faces in a Cloud: Intersubjectivity in Personality Theory* (1979, 2nd edition 1993). He is also coeditor of *The Intersubjective Perspective* (1994).

Fredrik Svenaeus is professor of philosophy at the Centre for Studies in Practical Knowledge, Södertörn University, Sweden. His main research areas are philosophy of medicine, bioethics, medical humanities, and philosophical anthropology. He is the author of five books, the most recent one being *Phenomenological Bioethics: Medical Technologies, Human Suffering, and the Meaning of Being Alive* (2017).

Dylan Trigg is Lise Meitner Fellow at the University of Vienna, Department of Philosophy. His research focuses on the phenomenology of embodiment, issues in aesthetics, and twentieth-century French philosophy. He is the author of several books, including *Topophobia* (2016), *The Thing* (2014), *The Memory of Place* (2012), and *The Aesthetics of Decay* (2006).

Tina Williams is a philosophy of medicine PhD student on the Wellcome Trust–funded "Life of Breath" project at the University of Bristol. Her research focuses on the philosophy of breathing and breathlessness in physical illnesses, mental disorders, and everyday life. With a background in philosophy, she is also qualified in cognitive behavior therapy managing depression and anxiety disorders in both primary care and a holistic charitable setting, and works as a mental health advocate with people sectioned under the Mental Health Act. Within philosophy, she is currently interested in philosophy of medicine, particularly phenomenology, pneuma, illness, and mental health.

Kristin Zeiler is professor (*biträdande*) at the Department of Thematic Studies: Technology and Social Change, Linköping University, Sweden. Zeiler's research examines issues of embodiment, subjectivity, and expressed and enacted normativities within medicine, and how experiences of pain, illness, or bodily variation can help shape our self-understandings and ways of engaging with others and the world. Her research also engages with ethical questions that arise in medicine, from phenomenological and hermeneutical perspectives, and contributes to areas such as philosophy of medicine, feminist theory, empirical philosophy, and bioethics. Among her publications are the edited volumes *Feminist Phenomenology and Medicine,* with L.F. Käll (2014) and *Bodily Exchanges, Bioethics and Border Crossing*, with E. Malmqvist (2015). Her articles have appeared in journals such as *Hypatia: A Journal of Feminist Philosophy, Feminist Theory, Bioethics, and Medicine, Health Care and Philosophy.*

Made in United States
Troutdale, OR
01/15/2024